Anonymous

The book of Joshua:

With notes, maps, and introduction

Anonymous

The book of Joshua:
With notes, maps, and introduction

ISBN/EAN: 9783337732875

Printed in Europe, USA, Canada, Australia, Japan

Cover: Foto ©ninafisch / pixelio.de

More available books at **www.hansebooks.com**

The Cambridge Bible for Schools
GENERAL EDITOR :—J. J. S. PEROWNE, D.D.,
DEAN OF PETERBOROUGH

THE BOOK OF
JOSHUA,

WITH NOTES, MAPS, AND INTRODUCTION

BY

THE REV. G. F. MACLEAR, D.D.,
HEAD MASTER OF KING'S COLLEGE SCHOOL, LONDON.

EDITED FOR THE SYNDICS OF THE UNIVERSITY PRESS.

Cambridge:
AT THE UNIVERSITY PRESS.

London: CAMBRIDGE WAREHOUSE, 17, PATERNOSTER ROW
Cambridge: DEIGHTON, BELL, AND CO.

1880

[*All Rights reserved.*]

Cambridge:
PRINTED BY C. J. CLAY, M.A.
AT THE UNIVERSITY PRESS.

CONTENTS.

		PAGE
I.	INTRODUCTION.	
	Chapter I. The Book of Joshua	5—8
	Chapter II. The Life of Joshua	9—15
	Chapter III. The Work of Joshua	15—22
	Chapter IV. Joshua as a type of Christ	22—26
	Chapter V. Analysis of the Book	26—30
II.	Text and Notes	31—215
III.	General Index	216—227
IV.	Index of Words and Phrases explained	228

※ The Text adopted in this Edition is that of Dr Scrivener's *Cambridge Paragraph Bible*, which will account for a few variations, chiefly in the spelling of certain words, and in the use of italics. For the principles adopted by Dr Scrivener as regards the printing of the Text see his Introduction to the *Paragraph Bible*, printed at the Cambridge University Press.

"As I was with Moses, so I will be with thee: I will not fail thee, nor forsake thee." Josh. i. 5.

> "The voice that from the glory came
>   To tell how Moses died unseen,
> And waken Joshua's spear of flame
>   To victory on the mountains green,
> Its trumpet tones are sounding still,
>   When Kings or Parents pass away,
> They greet us with a cheering thrill
>   Of power and comfort in decay."
>
> Keble's Christian Year.

INTRODUCTION.

CHAPTER I.

THE BOOK OF JOSHUA.

1. THE Pentateuch is followed in the Jewish Canon by a series which bears the name of *Neviim Rishonim*, "the earlier Prophets[1]", and comprises Joshua, Judges, the first and second Books of Samuel, and the two Books of Kings. This series contains the history of the Israelites,
   (*a*) As governed by the successor of Moses and the elders who outlived him;
   (*b*) As governed by native kings;
   (*c*) As subject to foreign invaders.
2. The first of these Books, *the Book of Joshua*, derives its name, not from its Author, but from the great hero, whose exploits are therein related, and who succeeded to the command of the people after the death of the great Hebrew Lawgiver, and led the nation into the Promised Land.
3. The claims of the Book to a place in the Canon of the Old Testament have never been disputed, and its authority is confirmed by allusions to the events recorded in it, which are found in other Books of Holy Scripture.
4. These allusions are found in (*a*) *the Psalms,* (*b*) *the Prophets,* (*c*) *the New Testament;*
   Thus (*a*) in Pss. xliv. 2, 3, lxviii. 12—14, lxxviii. 54, 55, we find reference made to the events which succeeded the Exodus from Egypt, the expulsion of the Canaanites, the

---

[1] The Jewish division of the Old Testament into (*a*) *the Law,* (*b*) *the Prophets,* (*c*) *the Hagiographa,* is at least as old as the time of our Lord.

division of the land among the tribes of Israel, and the subsequent apostasy of the people.

Again (*b*) in Is. xxviii. 21, reference is made to the victory in the valley of Gibeon, and, *in Hab.* iii. 11—13, to the miracle which attested that victory, the Divine march "through the land in indignation," and the "threshing of the heathen" in the Divine anger.

Again (*c*) in Acts vii. 45, St Stephen alludes to the bringing of the Ark into the land of Canaan, and the driving out of the nations by Joshua; while *the writer of the Epistle to the Hebrews* (iv. 8) speaks of "the rest" which Joshua gave, in part and in part only, to the people; (xi. 30—31) of the fall of Jericho; the faith of Rahab; and her shelter of the spies; and lastly St James (ii. 25) mentions the same Canaanitess as "justified by her works, when she had received the messengers and sent them out another way."

5. *By whom was it written?* Nothing can be said to be really known as to the authorship of the Book[1]. Jewish writers and the Christian Fathers ascribe it to Joshua himself[2]. Others conjecture that it was composed by Eleazar, or Phinehas, or one of the elders who outlived Joshua, or Samuel, or Jeremiah; while others have not hesitated to ascribe it to one who lived after the Babylonish captivity.

6. Many arguments may be alleged which point to Joshua, in preference to any other person, as the *compiler*, at any rate, of the greater portion of its contents. For

(*a*) The example of his predecessor Moses could not but

---

[1] "It should be observed," it has been said, "that in accepting the written chronicles of any nation as substantially true, we are not accustomed to depend on the personal character of each particular annalist. The trustworthiness of the pictured narratives which cover the temples and tombs of Thebes, or of those equally wondrous inscriptions discovered in the record chambers of Nineveh and Babylon, is not disputed because we do not know by what particular scribes or priests they were originally composed; nor would the attestation be of much value if we did. And many ancient MSS., which throw light on the history of our own country, are the work of men of whom nothing has come down to us but the faded relics of their earnest toil."

[2] This view has been embraced in recent times by König and, as regards the first half of the book, by Hävernick.

have suggested to him the composition of a record of the fulfilment of the Divine Promises through his leadership;

(*b*) No one was better qualified by his position to describe events, in which he had taken so distinguished a part, and to collect the documents contained in the Book;

(*c*) No one would have been more anxious to treasure up in writing his own last addresses and solemn warnings to the people[1];

(*d*) No one else could have recorded with such accuracy the account of the commands he received from the Most High, and of his own interviews with his Mysterious Visitor, "the Prince of the Host of Jehovah[2]."

7. But while the Book appears to have been compiled by one, who lived in the time of the events recorded, and was, indeed, an eye-witness of them, there are scattered up and down it a number of historical allusions, which clearly point to a date beyond the death of Joshua. Amongst these may be enumerated,

(*a*) The capture of Hebron by Caleb and of Debir by Othniel[3];

(*b*) The remark that "the Jebusites dwelt with the children of Judah at Jerusalem[4];"

(*c*) The capture of Laish by the warriors of the tribe of Dan[5].

(*d*) The account of Joshua's death[6].

8. While, then, there is evidence that much of the materials may have been *collected and furnished* by Joshua himself, we

---

[1] Josh. xxiii., xxiv.
[2] Josh. i. 1, iii. 7, iv. 1, 2, v. 2, 9, 13, vi. 2, vii. 10, viii. 1, x. 8, xi. 6, xiii. 1, 2, xx. 1, xxiv. 2.
[3] Comp. Josh. xv. 13—20 with Judg. i. 10—15.
[4] Comp. Josh. xv. 63 with Judg. i. 8.
[5] Comp. Josh. xix. 47 with Judg. xviii. 7. It is true that, if we consulted only the Book of Joshua, we might suppose these conquests to have been completed before Joshua's death, as he lived for several years after he had dismissed the people to their possessions, but when we refer to the parallel passages, it is clear they were not completed till after his death. See Keil's *Commentary*, Introd. p. 46.
[6] Josh. xxiv. 29—33. All these incidents, it will be noticed, may very well have taken place within twenty or twenty-five years after Joshua's death.

shall not in all probability be far wrong in conjecturing that the Book was composed partly from personal observation and inquiry, partly out of authentic documents already in existence, by one of "the elders who overlived Joshua[1]," and within a few years after his death.

9. *For what object was it written?* Resuming, as it does, the history of the Chosen People at the death of Moses, it was not intended to be a mere biography or a mere collection of authentic documents. It serves as a link between what precedes and what follows[2], and is designed to shew the faithfulness of Jehovah to His Word of Promise, and to illustrate the operations of His grace and mercy, whereby He placed the people in possession of the land, which He had promised as an inheritance to Abraham, Isaac, and Jacob[3].

10. In respect to style, the Book of Joshua is less archaic than the Pentateuch, but more so than the Books of Kings and Chronicles. In reading it, it is well to bear in mind the extreme antiquity of the documents on which it rests. We need not, therefore, expect to find in it marks of the finished composition which belong to a later age. The style is plain and inartificial. The narrative follows the course of thought and feeling on the part of the writer, rather than any formal method of arrangement, and sometimes, when the conclusion of any record is deemed of special importance, it is apparently anticipated by the writer, and afterwards restated, though not always in the same identical terms.

---

[1] Josh. xxiv. 31.
[2] Just as the Acts of the Apostles is the link between the Gospels and the Epistles of the New Testament.
[3] "The design of the writer," observes Keil, "was not merely to display the great deeds of Joshua, nor even to trace the history of the theocracy under him, and thus continue the narrative contained in the Pentateuch from the death of Moses to that of Joshua; but to furnish historical evidence that Joshua, by the help of God, faithfully performed the work to which the Lord had called him; and by the side of that to shew how, in fulfilling the promises which He gave to the patriarchs, God drove out the Canaanites before Israel, and gave their land to the twelve tribes of Jacob for a permanent inheritance."—Keil's *Commentary*, Introd. p. 2.

CHAPTER II.

THE LIFE OF JOSHUA.

1. It is a natural transition from the Book of Joshua to the life and career of the great hero from whom it derives its name. His life falls into three divisions:—
(*a*) His life in Egypt;
(*b*) His life in the desert of Sinai;
(*c*) His life in Canaan.

2. (*a*) *The life of Joshua in Egypt.* He, who first bore the name which is now "*above every name*[1]," was born during the weary years of the bondage of his nation in Egypt. His father was Nun[2], of the powerful tribe of Ephraim. Of his mother we know nothing.

3. His original name was Oshea or Hoshea[3], "*salvation.*" This, as we shall see, was afterwards changed to Jehoshua or Joshua, "*the salvation of Jehovah*[4]." Modified, like many other Hebrew names in their passage through the Greek language, "Joshua" took the form sometimes of "Jason," but more frequently of ΙΗΣΟΥΣ, JESUS, "which has now become indelibly impressed on history as the greatest of all names."

4. Growing up a slave in the brickfields of Egypt he must have witnessed at once the idolatries of that mystic land, and the moral and social degradation of his countrymen. He must

---

[1] Phil. ii. 9.
[2] The descent of Nun from Ephraim is given in 1 Chron. vii. 20—27.
[3] "The same with the name of the *son of Azaziah*, ruler of Ephraim (1 Chron. xxvii. 20); of *the son of Elah*, king of Israel (2 Kings xvii. 1); of *the son of Beeri*, the prophet (Hos. i. 1)." Pearson *On the Creed*, Art. 11.
[4] "If unto the name Hoseah we add one of the titles of God, which is *Jah*, there will result from both, by the custom of the Hebrew tongue, *Jehoshua*; and so not only the instrumental, but also the original cause of the Jews' deliverance will be found expressed in one word: as if Moses had said, This is the person by whom God will save this people from their enemies." *Ibid.*

have beheld, as he could scarcely have beheld it anywhere else, the adoration of *the creature rather than the Creator*[1] carried to its furthest point, and divine honours paid not only to the sacred black calf Mnevis, to his rival the bull Apis, to the mighty Pharaoh, the Child, the Representative of the Sun-God, but to almost everything in the heaven above, and the earth beneath, and the water under the earth. His early experience thus made him acquainted with the fascination, which the idolatries around exercised upon his countrymen, and give special force to his declaration afterwards to the heads of the ransomed nation, when located in the Land of Promise, " *Your fathers worshipped other gods in Egypt*[2]."

5. Here too he experienced the bitterness of cruel bondage, while beneath a burning rainless sky, the sons of Jacob toiled naked and in gangs under the lash in the quarries or the brickfield, or followed the oxen over the shadeless furrows, or in long rows monotonously threshed out the corn, while the gay barges of their masters sailed up and down the canals and rivers, and the royal chariots with their outriders, and the priests and officers of state, passed unheeding along the streets[3].

6. (*b*) *Life of Joshua in the Sinaitic desert.* Nearly forty years must thus have passed away. At length the hour of deliverance came. Moses returned from Midian, and Joshua witnessed the judgments of the Most High on *the land of Ham*[4], and shared in the hurried triumph of the Exodus. It is in the Sinaitic desert that he first comes before us with any prominence. Moses, who had doubtless already noticed signs of his fitness as a military leader, selected him to take the command of the people in the engagement with Amalek at Rephidim[5], and "he discomfited Amalek and his people with the edge of the sword." From this day forward he takes the position of "minister," or attendant on the great Lawgiver. With him he ascends the mountain-range of Sinai at the first giving of the Tables of the Law[6], and is the first after the forty days of waiting

[1] Rom. i. 25.
[2] Josh. xxiv. 14.
[3] Drew's *Scripture Lands*, p. 30.
[4] Ps. lxxviii. 51, cv. 23, 27.
[5] Exod. xvii. 9—14.
[6] Exod. xxiv. 13.

INTRODUCTION. 11

for his return to accost him on his descent[1]. His younger ears first catch the confused sounds which roll up the mountain side from the tented plain below, and with the interpretation of the uncertain noise most natural to a soldier[2], he says at once to Moses, *There is a noise of war in the camp*[3]. He learns from the mouth of the Lawgiver the true explanation of the sounds, and witnesses his righteous anger, as he casts out of his hands the precious Tables, and breaks them before the eyes of the offending people[4].

7. When we next hear of him it is on the occasion of the prophesying of Eldad and Medad, when he would have his master rebuke them, and received the well-known reply, "Would God that all the Lord's people were prophets, and that the Lord would put His Spirit upon them[5]." From this point we seem to lose sight of him altogether till the people were at the very gates of the Promised Land, and Moses resolved to send from Kadesh-Barnea twelve spies to search out the length and breadth of the territory, and ascertain its character, its products, and its inhabitants[6]. Of the Twelve Joshua was now one, and considering the important part he was himself destined to take in the actual conquest of the country, and the service he had already rendered to the great Lawgiver, it is easy to understand why the latter now changed his name from *Hoshea* to *Jehoshua*, an alteration which was a *God speed!* to the spies on their departure[7].

8. As the attendant of Moses and the most distinguished of the Twelve, Joshua undoubtedly stood at the head of those thus sent forth on their arduous mission. With them he traversed the land as far north as Rehob[8] on the way to Hamath in the

---

[1] Exod. xxxii. 17.
[2] See Professor Blunt's *Undesigned Coincidences*, p. 66; Bp Wilberforce's *Heroes of Hebrew History*, p. 133.
[3] Exod. xxxii. 17. [4] Exod. xxxii. 19.
[5] Num. xi. 26—29.
[6] Num. xiii. 1—20; Deut. i. 23.
[7] Kurtz *On the Old Covenant*, III. 284. The occurrence of the new name in Exod. xvii. 9, xxiv. 13, and Num. xi. 28, may be accounted for on the supposition of a *prolepsis*, of which there are many examples in the Pentateuch.
[8] Num. xiii. 21.

valley of the Orontes. Then, ascending by the south, they approached Hebron, and in a valley opening on the city plucked pomegranates, and figs, and the famous cluster of grapes, and from "the valley of the Cluster" returned to the camp and their brethren after an absence of forty days[1]. As might be expected from all that had gone before, Joshua did not now fail to display proofs of the same courageous faith, which had procured for him the command against Amalek. He and Caleb alone of all the spies did not discourage the hearts of their brethren, but entreated them to go up and possess the land[2]. Their words, however, fell on unheeding ears, and in just retribution for their rebellious faithlessness the fiat went forth that none of that generation should enter the Promised Land[3].

9. We hear nothing of Joshua during the weary years of wandering that now commenced in the Sinaitic peninsula. We know, however, that he must have witnessed the rebellion of Korah, Dathan, and Abiram, and the terrible penalty which it entailed[4]; the death of Miriam, and her burial in her desert-grave at Kadesh[5]; the one failure of his own trusted leader, when *he spake unadvisedly with his lips*[6]; the death of Aaron and his entombment on Mount Hor[7]; the battles of Jahaz[8] and Edrei[9], and the conquest of Eastern Canaan, and the frustration of the fell designs of Balaam by the righteous zeal of Phinehas[10]. None of the varied lessons, we may be sure, which these events were designed to teach, would be lost on one like Joshua, and when the hour came for Moses to "go the way of all the earth," his constant "attendant" had already justified the confidence, with which, acting on the Divine command[11], the great Prophet solemnly and publicly invested him as his successor with definite authority over his brethren, and gave him his last charge[12].

---

[1] Num. xiii. 22—25.
[2] Num. xiv. 6—9.
[3] Num. xiv. 22, 23.
[4] Num. xvi., xvii.
[5] Num. xx. 1.
[6] Num. xx. 7—14; Deut. xxxii. 51; Ps. cvi. 32, 33.
[7] Num. xx. 23—29.
[8] Num. xxi. 23, 24.
[9] Num. xxi. 33—35.
[10] Num. xxv. 1—18.
[11] Num. xxvii. 18.
[12] Num. xxvii. 22, 23; Deut. xxxi. 14, 23.

10. (c) *The career of Joshua in Canaan.* This parting charge to Joshua brings us to the threshold of the Book, which bears his name, to the day when having reached, according to Josephus, his 85th year[1], he assumed the command of the people at Shittim[2], and commenced those victorious campaigns, which in seven years laid six nations and thirty-one kings prostrate at his feet.

11. These campaigns form the subject of the first part of this Book, and need not be detailed here. In the conduct of them Joshua displayed throughout the same high qualities which first won for him the confidence of Moses. He was the soldier, "the first soldier," it has been said, "consecrated by the sacred history," blameless, fearless, straightforward. He was "strong, and of a good courage." He was "not afraid nor dismayed[3]." "He turned neither to the right hand nor to the left; but at the head of the hosts of Israel he went right forward from Jordan to Jericho, from Jericho to Ai, from Ai to Gibeon, to Bethhoron, to Merom. He wavered not for a moment, he was here, he was there, he was everywhere, as the emergency called for him[4]." The carrying out of the charge he received from God with a remarkable simplicity of unquestioning faith was the key-note of his whole career. While, moreover, he was the brave, undaunted, leader, the terrible exactor of the judgment of Jehovah in reference to a people sunk in idolatry and sensuality, he was ever gentle and merciful towards the sinner. In the presence of Achan the armed warrior is transformed into the loving father, pleading, remonstrating, sympathizing, pronouncing upon the transgressor, not in passion, but with calm dignity, the doom he had brought upon himself, as being under the ban of God.

12. But besides his work of war, there was also his work of peace. When strengthened from on high, "he had passed through those scenes of blood which were appointed for him," he proceeded to divide the conquered territory amongst the victorious tribes. This he carried out not with the self-seeking

---
[1] *Ant.* V. 1. 29.
[2] Josh. I. 1, 2.
[3] Josh. i. 7, 9, 18.
[4] Stanley's *Lectures*, I. p. 229.

of an Oriental despot, but on principles, "which place the conquest of Palestine even in that remote and barbarous age, in favourable contrast with the arbitrary caprice by which the lands of England were granted away to the Norman chiefs[1]." With order and method, with appeals to the sacred lot before the Tabernacle at Shiloh, and in the presence of the Highpriest and the elders of the nation, the conquered territory was distributed. When provision had been made for all the rest, then, not till then, did he claim any provision for himself. Modest and disinterested, he asked only for a small inheritance in the rugged mountains of his native tribe of Ephraim, and there he built the city of Timnath-serah.

13. Hither, when his commissions had been fully enacted, the land divided, the Tabernacle set up at Shiloh, the Cities of Refuge appointed, the priestly and Levitical cities arranged—he retired, and there dwelt in peace for some eighteen years of rest. At length he became aware that he too, like Aaron on Mount Hor, like Moses on the top of Pisgah, must be gathered to his fathers, and go the way of all the earth. Summoning, therefore, the tribes of Israel, with the elders, and judges, and officers, to Shechem, he gave them his last charge. He reviewed their past history as a family, a tribe, a nation. He recounted all the merciful acts of their invisible King, and then he bound them with his parting words to an everlasting covenant of faithfulness to the God, Who had done such great things for them, and set up a stone pillar under the sacred oak of Abraham and Jacob, writing out the words of the covenant in *"the Book of the law of God"* (Josh. xxiv. 26).

14. And now all was over. His work of war and his work of peace alike were ended. All that human agency could effect for the well-being of his people had been done. He bade every man depart after the solemn scene at Shechem to his inheritance, and shortly *"after these things Joshua, the servant of the Lord, died, being an hundred and ten years old, and they buried*

---

[1] Arnold's *History of Rome*, I. p. 266, quoted in Stanley's *Lectures*, I. p. 265.

INTRODUCTION. 15

him in the border of his inheritance in Timnath-serah" (Josh. xxiv. 29, 30),

> "Great in council and great in war,
> Foremost captain of his time,
> Rich in saving common sense,
> And, as the greatest only are,
> In his simplicity sublime[1]."

CHAPTER III.

THE WORK OF JOSHUA.

1. It is impossible to disconnect the life and character of Joshua from the work, which the Divine Command called upon him to accomplish.

2. This work was undoubtedly of terrible severity. The command of Moses respecting the nations of Canaan required their complete extermination. *"Thou shalt save nothing that breatheth,"* said the Lawgiver, and Joshua strictly fulfilled this order. He passed from Jericho to Ai, from Ai to Makkedah, from Makkedah to Libnah, from Libnah to Lachish, from Lachish to Eglon, from Eglon to Hebron, from Hebron to Debir, and "smote them with the edge of the sword, and utterly destroyed all the souls that were therein; he left none remaining[2]."

3. Such acts, done in obedience to the Divine Command, have often[3] been strongly urged as objections against the Old Testament morality, and have been placed "among the many cruel things which Moses did and commanded." Hence, some of the older Rabbinical writers have endeavoured to soften

---

[1] Tennyson's *Ode on the Death of the Duke of Wellington*.
[2] Josh. x. 39.
[3] The adversaries of Judaism and Christianity in the second and third centuries urged them. Comp. Josephus *c. Apion.* I. 28; Origen *c. Celsum*, III. 5; S. Cyril *cont. Jul.* VI.

down the more rugged features of the narrative, by affirming that Joshua sent three letters to the land of the Canaanites before the Israelites invaded it; or rather, that he proposed three things to them by letters; that those who preferred flight, might escape; that those who wished for peace, might enter into covenant; and that such as were for war, might take up arms[1].

4. The instructions[2] however to which this view appeals, prescribe this course of action only in reference to *foreign enemies, not Canaanites*. "Thus shalt thou do," said the Lawgiver, "unto all the cities *which are very far off from thee, which are not of the cities of these nations*[3]." The Canaanite cities and their inhabitants are thus expressly exempted from the operation of such merciful alternatives. "Of the cities of these people, which the Lord thy God doth give thee for an inheritance, *thou shalt save alive nothing that breatheth; but thou shalt utterly destroy them*[4].

5. But as the possession of Canaan is uniformly represented as the free gift of God to the Israelites[5], so the conquest of Canaan is uniformly represented as an act of righteous judgment against its inhabitants. Their moral degeneracy had reached a point to which no other people presented a parallel. The abominations they practised[6] are represented to have been of a kind which might be said to call to heaven for vengeance. The idolatrous rites, to which they were addicted, tended to defile their very consciences, and the pollutions they habitually practised were a disgrace to humanity. Their land is repre-

---

[1] See Selden *de Jure Nat.* I. VI. 13; Dean Graves *on the Pentateuch*, Part III.; Lect. I.

[2] Deut. xx. 10—14.

[3] Deut. xx. 15.

[4] Deut. xx. 16, 17. Comp. Num. xxi. 2, 3, 35, xxxiii. 52—54.

[5] Comp. (*a*) Exod. xxiii. 32, xxxiv. 12 sqq.; (*b*) Num. xxxiii. 52 sqq.; (*c*) Deut. vii. 1 sq. The idea that in conquering Canaan the Israelites were but recovering the property of their ancestors is inconsistent with the language of Gen. xvii. 8, xxvi. 3, and such transactions as those recorded in Gen. xxiii. 4, xxxiii. 19.

[6] Their false religion cannot be regarded as a mere error of judgment. Cruelty the most revolting, and unnatural crimes the most defiling, were inseparably connected with its celebration.

INTRODUCTION. 17

sented as unable to endure them any longer, as "vomiting out its inhabitants," and therefore, it is added, "the Lord visited their iniquity upon them[1]."

6. This judgment, however, it is to be remembered, was not inflicted upon them summarily, or without warning. God waited patiently for five hundred years, and during this period addressed to them many calls to repentance. So early as the time of Abraham He had warned them of His wrath against sin, and especially the sins to which they were addicted, by the awful destruction of the cities of Sodom and Gomorrah[2]. He had given them the blessing of the presence and example of eminent men, as Melchizedek and Abraham, and He had forborne to punish them for many ages because the cup of their *iniquity was not yet full*[3], and in order that a season for repentance might still be granted them. But they *knew not the day of their visitation*[4], and still persisted in their iniquity.

7. But even when their cup was well-nigh full, the Divine judgment did not descend without giving repeated indications of its approach. The Canaanites heard of the punishments inflicted by the God of Israel upon the inhabitants of Egypt, and of the wonders which He wrought at the passage of the Red Sea[5]. When again the Israelites stood at the very threshold of the Promised Land, and it might have been supposed that the Sword of Vengeance, which had so long hung in suspense, would have at once descended, it was again held back, and during the wandering in the wilderness, a further space of forty years was granted for repentance and amendment[6].

---

[1] Lev. xviii. 24, 25, 30; Deut. xii. 30, 31. "It is an eternal necessity," even Ewald remarks, "that a nation such as the majority of the Canaanites then were, sinking deeper and deeper into a slough of discord and moral perversity, must fall before a people roused to a higher life by the newly awakened energy of unanimous trust in Divine Power." Ewald's *History of Israel*, II. 237, E. T.
[2] Gen. xix. 1—24.   [3] Gen. xv. 16.
[4] Luke xix. 44.   [5] Josh. ii. 10, 11.
[6] See the argument well stated in Fairbairn's *Typology of Scripture*, II. pp. 432—436.

JOSHUA 2

8. Nay, when all had proved in vain, and mercy at length gave place to judgment, the overthrow of the nations on the East of Jordan, of *great kings, famous kings, mighty kings*[1], with their *fenced cities, high walls, gates and bars*[2], warned them of the mighty Invisible Power that fought on the side of the strange People, so lately freed from Egyptian bondage. And as though this was not enough, as though no proof should be wanting that the campaign to be waged was not the victory of one nation over another, but God's controversy with degrading idolatry, and unnatural and unbridled licentiousness, the invaders themselves, when they suffered themselves to be enticed into the orgies of Baal-peor, experienced a fearful punishment for their apostasy. The Promise made to Abraham, Isaac, and Jacob, did not exempt them from the penalty of their misdoings. A plague broke out amongst them, which swept off upwards of twenty-four thousand, while the princes of the tribes at the command of Moses slew the guilty with unsparing vigour, and hanged them up before the Lord[3].

9. But even at the eleventh hour, when at last the fiat went forth, and instead of cutting off the guilty nations, as He had done in the case of the cities of Sodom and Gomorrah, by an earthquake, or a famine, or a pestilence, God entrusted the sword of vengeance to Joshua, was ever campaign waged in such an unearthly manner as that now inaugurated by the leader of the armies of Israel?

10. At the passage of the Jordan, in the capture of Jericho, the Israelites were allowed to do literally nothing but look on and obey the commands of Him Who fought for them. Every impulse of nature to attack the city, to try upon its towers and battlements the skill of military science, as then known, was checked and restrained. The power of faith was tried to the uttermost in consenting to play what must have seemed a useless, almost a ridiculous part, in the face of a disciplined host, watching from their ramparts the strange evolutions of warriors, who had lately triumphed over Sihon at Jahaz, and Og in his

---

[1] Ps. cxxxv. 10—12.   [2] Deut. iii. 5, 6.
[3] Num. xxv. 1—15.

basaltic Thermopylæ at Edrei, but who were now constrained to submit to an inexplicable edict of complete inactivity.

11. Nor was the same supernatural check upon the ordinary impulses of humanity maintained only during the mysterious preparations for the fall of Jericho. It was enforced as rigidly when the city had been captured. The excesses, which were the rule of the age on the reduction of a conquered city, which stand out in such painful relief in the inscriptions of Assyrian kings[1], and which have too often disgraced even Christian armies, were absolutely unknown. The city, indeed, was devoted to destruction, and all that were in it, but the conquerors were forbidden under the severest penalties to appropriate to themselves the least benefit from the spoils.

12. But when Jericho had fallen, observe the strange halt at Gilgal. What was its object? Not to divide the spoil, for everything had been devoted to Jehovah. Not to celebrate a

---

[1] Comp. *The Annals of Assur-Nasir-Pal*, sometimes called Sardanapalus:

74   while in Commagene
75 I was stationed, they brought me intelligence that the city Suri in Bit-Khalupe had revolted
*   *   *   *   *
77 chariots and army I collected   *   and the rebellious nobles
90 who had revolted against me and whose skins I had stripped off, I made into a trophy: some in the middle of the pile I left to decay; some on the top
91 of the pile on stakes I impaled; some by the side of the pile I placed in order on stakes; many within view of my land
92 I flayed; their skins on the walls I arranged.
93 I brought AHIYABABA to Nineveh; I flayed him and fastened his skin to the wall
*   *   *   *   *
113 from Kinabu I withdrew; to Tila I drew near;
115 with onset and attack I besieged the city; many soldiers I captured alive;
117 of some I chopped off the hands and feet; of others the noses and ears I cut off; of many soldiers I destroyed the eyes;
118 one pile of bodies while yet alive, and one of heads I reared up on the heights within their town; their heads in the midst I hoisted; their boys
and their maidens I dishonoured.

See *Records of the Past*, Vol. III. 39—50; *Cuneiform Inscriptions of Western Asia*, I. 17—27, and comp. it with other passages in the Assyrian records.

triumph, for in the capture the people had been little more than spectators. What, then, was its purport? *To renew the rite of circumcision; to celebrate the Passover; to remind the people of their solemn moral and religious obligations.*

13. Again when Ai had been reduced, after a delay and a discomfiture caused by a single act of disobedience, why was the strange march undertaken to Shechem with the priests, and the ark, and a deputation from all the tribes? *To build an altar; to offer sacrifices; to set up stones, and plaster them with plaster; to inscribe upon them the words of the law; to proclaim from the slopes of Ebal and Gerizim its blessings upon purity, justice, order, truthfulness between man and man, and its curses upon impurity, injustice, sensuality, and wrongdoing*[1]. Was ever an invading army, before or since, made to feel more completely that it was no work of their own in which they were engaged; that they were simply the instruments in the accomplishment of Divine retribution upon a guilty race; that even as regards themselves, their tenure of the land thus conquered must depend upon the preservation of pure morality?

14. And was the lesson taught with such scrupulous care taught in vain? Did Joshua shew himself like other "scourges of God," simply an incarnation of brute force and resistless might? His gentleness towards Achan, his faithfulness towards the Gibeonites, the mode in which he carried out the division of the land, the solemnity of his last charge, prove the exact contrary. He could not have preserved untarnished that simplicity and gentleness, that piety and humility which distinguished him to the end, had he not kept clear before his eyes the unique and unearthly character of the commission entrusted to him, had not every other feeling given place to the conviction that he was simply the instrument in carrying out a sentence not his own upon a long-tried but reprobate people.

15. And what is true of him is in a great measure true also of the Israelites themselves. If in their subsequent history they had shewn themselves brutalized by the scenes through which they now passed, if they had proved afterwards violent,

---

[1] Josh. viii. 33, 34.

tyrannical, cruel, unscrupulous, utterly indifferent to human feelings, and addicted to massacre and bloodshed, these results might have been traced to the campaign in which they were now engaged. But this, without doubt, was not the case. We nowhere find any traces of that terrible exultation in the infliction of pain as pain, of that horrible gloating over the miseries and sufferings of conquered peoples which disfigure the records of other nations. They passed through all the stages of their chequered history with the warning repeated in their ears again and again, that they held the land by no other tenure than that which the Canaanites were destroyed for infringing; that if they failed to maintain purity of worship or purity of life they would subject themselves to the same doom, which would be inflicted by penalties as tremendous, and very often as indiscriminating as those which they were commissioned to inflict on the nation they cast out before them.

16. "The Israelites' sword," says an eminent writer[1], "in its bloodiest executions, wrought a work of mercy for all the countries of the earth to the very end of the world. They seem of very small importance to us now, those perpetual contests with the Canaanites, and the Midianites, and the Ammonites, and the Philistines, with which the Books of Joshua and Judges and Samuel are almost filled. We may half wonder that God should have interfered in such quarrels, or have changed the course of nature, in order to give one of these nations of Palestine the victory over another. But in these contests, on the fate of one of these nations of Palestine, the happiness of the human race depended. The Israelites fought not for themselves only, but for us. It might follow that they should thus be accounted the enemies of all mankind; it might be that they were tempted by their very distinctness to despise other nations. Still they did God's work; still they preserved unhurt the seed of eternal life, and were the ministers of blessing to all other nations, even though they themselves failed to enjoy it." "If Israel," says another writer, "had been subdued by the Canaanites, if the separated seed had been mingled with the heathen,

[1] Arnold's *Sermons*, VI. 35—37.

if it had learned their ways, if the worship of Chemosh and Molech and Astarte had superseded the worship of Jehovah, how had all the grand designs of redemption been frustrated in their development! The cry of Joshua after the flight at Ai would have been the despairing utterance of the race of men, 'And what wilt Thou do unto Thy great name?' More also in Joshua's history than anywhere else besides, may the troubled soul—perplexed and harassed by the sight on this sin-defiled earth of wars, battles, slaughters, pestilences, earthquakes, miseries, and treasons—rest itself, though it be with a deep sob of a present broken-heartedness, in the conviction that God has a plan for this world; that in the end it does prevail; that the Baalim of heathen powers must fall before Him; and that His kingdom shall stand for ever and ever in its truth and righteousness and love[1]."

CHAPTER IV.

JOSHUA AS A TYPE OF CHRIST.

1. An Introduction to the Book of Joshua would be incomplete without a notice of the typical character of his life and his work. Holy Scripture itself suggests the consideration of the successor of Moses as a type of our Lord and Saviour[2], and the more we reflect upon the subject, the more striking does this feature of his career appear.

2. "It is not often," it has been remarked, "either in sacred or common history, that we are justified in pausing on anything so outward and usually so accidental as a name[3]." But, if ever there be an exception, it is in the present instance. The original name of the leader of the hosts of Israel, *Hoshea*, Salvation,

---

[1] Bp Wilberforce's *Heroes of Hebrew History*, pp. 145, 146.
[2] Acts vii. 45; Heb. iv. 8.
[3] Dean Stanley's *Lectures on the Jewish Church*, I. 229.

was changed, as we have already seen[1], to *Jehoshua*, or *Joshua*, "*God's Salvation*," or "*Jehovah the Saviour*" (Num. xiii. 16, xiv. 6, 30). In the Greek translation of the Bible this name is always rendered by the word ΙΗΣΟΥΣ, JESUS, whence its use in the New Testament.

3. And as with the name, so with its purport. The first Joshua was but a man, and by the power of Jehovah enabled the Israelites to vanquish the nations of Canaan, and saved them from the innumerable dangers that beset them. "*Thou shalt call His Name JESUS*," said the angel Gabriel to Joseph, at the time of the first Advent of our Lord, "*for He shall save His people from their sins*[2]." "Joshua saved Israel not by his own power, not of himself, but God by him; neither saved he his own people, but the people of God; whereas Jesus Himself by His own power, the power of God, shall save His own people, the people of God. Well therefore may we understand the interpretation of His Name to be *God the Saviour*[3]."

4. The career of a Conqueror thus marked out for the first Joshua, "the first soldier consecrated by the sacred history," prepares us for and receives its complete fulfilment in the career of Him, Who came into the world that He might fight against and *destroy the works of the Devil*[4]. He bade His disciples "be of good cheer," for He had "*overcome* the world[5]," and as the Conqueror and the Rewarder of them that conquer, He is frequently revealed in the Apocalypse[6].

5. Again, where was the first part of Joshua's life spent? Was it not in Egypt? There he was the companion of the rest of his nation in their sorrows; he was one with them in their afflictions; he shared their labours in the brick-kilns of Egypt; in all their afflictions he was afflicted. And even so our Lord, remaining the Son of God most High, became JESUS, the Son of Mary, and condescending *to be made in the likeness of men*[7], was in all points like unto His brethren, and

[1] See above, p. 9.
[2] Matt. i. 21.
[3] Pearson *On the Creed*, Art. II.
[4] 1 John iii. 8.
[5] John xvi. 33.
[6] See Rev. ii. 7, iii. 5, 12, vi. 2, xi. 15, xii. 11, xvii. 14, xxi. 7.
[7] Phil. ii. 7; Heb. ii. 14.

whereas *He Himself hath suffered being tempted, He is able to succour them that are tempted*[1].

6. Joshua, moreover, succeeded Moses and completed his work. The hand of the great Lawgiver brought the people out of Egypt, "but left them in the wilderness, and could not seat them in Canaan[2]." This was reserved for Joshua his successor. Now Moses is often taken for the doctrine delivered, or the books written by him, that is, the Law[3]. And *the Law was given by Moses, but grace and truth came by Jesus Christ*[4], by Whom *all that believe are justified from all things, from which they could not be justified by the Law of Moses*[5].

7. With this typical name, and in this order of succession, Joshua entered on his leadership, and at the banks of Jordan God began to "magnify him," and to make manifest to Israel his credentials as their appointed chief. Even so his great Antitype begins His office at the banks of Jordan. His feet are dipped in the selfsame rushing stream, and no sooner has He come up therefrom, and "sanctified water to the mystical washing away of sin," than the Spirit descends upon Him, and the Voice is heard, "Thou art My beloved Son, in Thee I am well-pleased[6]."

8. At the Jordan, again, Joshua directed that from its bed twelve stones should be taken by twelve men chosen out of the people, to be for evermore a witness to the nation of their deliverance. So after His baptism in Jordan the second Joshua began to choose His twelve Apostles, those foundation-stones in the Church of God, whose names are in the *twelve foundations* of the wall of *the holy city, the new Jerusalem*[7]. "Twelve stones, Joshua buried under the returning waters of Jordan; and over the first twelve Apostles, Jesus let the stream of death flow as over others; whilst they were repeated in their office of

---

[1] Heb. ii. 18.
[2] Pearson *On the Creed*, Art. II.
[3] Comp. Luke xvi. 29, 31, xxiv. 27; John v. 45, 46; Acts vi. 11, 13, 14, xv. 21, xxi. 21; 2 Cor. iii. 15.
[4] John i. 17.   [5] Acts xiii. 39.
[6] Matt. iii. 17; Mark i. 11; Luke iii. 22.
[7] Rev. xxi. 14.

witnesses to Him by all the enduring succession of His earthly ministers with whom He is, even unto the end of the world[1]."

9. Having led the people through the Jordan, and renewed the Covenant of Circumcision[2], and conquered for them their foes, Joshua assigns to them their inheritance, but directs that they must fight for their possessions against the remnants of their enemies, if they would maintain their conquest. And even so Jesus, though He brings His people into the spiritual Canaan of His Church, calls upon them to fight manfully under His banner against the foes, whom He hath not driven out all at once[3], but left to try and prove them, whether they will turn to account the fair inheritance He hath bestowed upon them.

10. When Joshua's great work is over, his work of war and his work of peace, he ascends the hill of Ephraim and dwells in his own possession. But this has fallen to him, not as to others of his brethren by the casting of the sacred lot. Rather has it been yielded to him as his own right in respect to the work of conquest which he has achieved. And thus too, when His work was over—the work which the Father had given Him to do[4]—our Lord ascended up on high to the heaven in which He was before, His own by right, His own by conquest, and there *for ever sat down on the right hand of God; from henceforth expecting till His enemies be made His footstool*[5].

11. Once more. Before Joshua departed and was gathered unto his fathers, he summoned to him all the heads of the tribes, and described to them in solemn words, the work that lay before them, and set forth the mighty Future destined to be theirs if they would be loyal to their Invisible King, and cleave earnestly to the God, Who had done such great things for them. And so did the great "Captain of our Salvation," before He ascended up on high, summon to meet Him on a mountain in Galilee, the heads and representatives of His Church, and proclaim to them the greatness of the work, to which they had

---

[1] Bp Wilberforce's *Heroes of Hebrew History*, p. 156.
[2] Comp. Josh. v. 2; Rom. ii. 29; Col. ii. 11.
[3] See Josh. xiii. 7—32.
[4] John xvii. 4.   [5] Heb. x. 12, 13.

been called, and the true source of the strength, in which it should be accomplished, saying, "*All power is given unto Me in heaven and in earth; go ye, therefore, evangelise all nations, and lo I am with you alway, even unto the end of the world*[1]."

12. Lastly, Joshua smote the Amalekites and subdued the Canaanites; by the first, making way to enter the land, by the second, giving possession of it[2]. And even so, Jesus our Lord in a spiritual manner goeth in and out before us against our spiritual foes, opening and clearing our way to heaven. For every one, who follows Him, He divides the cold waters of death, "setting against their utmost flood the Ark of the Body which He took of us, and in which God dwelleth evermore; so making a way for His ransomed to pass over to the mansions, which He has prepared for them, from the foundation of the world."

CHAPTER V.

ANALYSIS OF THE BOOK.

1. The following Analysis will give an idea of the contents of the Book of Joshua.
2. It may be regarded as consisting of three parts;
   (i) The Conquest of Canaan;
   (ii) The Division of Canaan;
   (iii) Joshua's Farewell.

PART I.

THE CONQUEST OF CANAAN. i.—xii.

Section I. **The Preparation.**
 (a) *The Summons to the War.*
  (α) The Command of God to Joshua ....i. 1—9.
  (β) The Command of Joshua to the people...i. 10—18.

---

[1] Matt. xxviii. 18, 19, 20.   [2] Pearson *On the Creed*, Art. II.

INTRODUCTION.

(b) *The Mission of the spies to Jericho.*

   (α) The sending of the spies .... ii. 1—7.
   (β) Their reception by Rahab .... ii. 8—21.
   (γ) Their return to Joshua .... ii. 22—24.

Section II. The Passage of the Jordan.

(a) *The Divine Guidance.*

   (α) The Preparations of Joshua .... iii. 1—13.
   (β) Jordan turned backwards .... iii. 14—17.
   (γ) Completion of the Passage .... iv. 1—18.
   (δ) The Memorial at Gilgal .... iv. 19—24.

(b) *The Consecration to the Holy War.*

   (α) Renewal of the Rite of Circumcision .... v. 1—9.
   (β) Celebration of the Passover .... v. 10—12.
   (γ) Appearance of the Prince of Jehovah's host .... v. 13—15.
   (δ) Instructions as to the capture of Jericho vi. 1—5.

Section III. The Conquest of Southern and Central Canaan.

(a) *The Capture of Jericho.*

   (α) The Preparations .... vi. 6—14.
   (β) Capture and Destruction of the City ...... vi. 15—27.

(b) *First Advance against Ai.*

   (α) The sin of Achan .... vii. 1.
   (β) The repulse from Ai .... vii. 2—5.
   (γ) Joshua's Prayer .... vii. 6—15.
   (δ) Detection and Punishment of Achan ...... vii. 16—26.

(c) *Second Advance against Ai.*

   (α) Stratagem of Joshua .... viii. 1—13.
   (β) Capture and destruction of the city ...... viii. 14—29.
   (γ) Renewal of the Covenant at Ebal .... viii. 30—35.

(d) *The Battle of Bethhoron.*

   (α) League of the Canaanite kings against Israel .... ix. 1, 2.
   (β) The Fraud of the Gibeonites .... ix. 3—15.
   (γ) The League with Gibeon .... ix. 16—27.
   (δ) Investment of Gibeon by the Five Kings x. 1—5.
   (ε) Relief of the city by Joshua .... x. 6—15.
   (ζ) Flight and destruction of the Five Kings x. 16—43.

Section IV. **The Conquest of Northern Canaan.**
  (a) *The Northern League.*
    (α) The Gathering of the Kings ....xi. 1—6.
    (β) The Battle of the Waters of Merom ......xi. 7—9.
    (γ) The Defeat of Jabin..........................xi. 10.
    (δ) Subjugation of the North.................xi. 11—23.
  (b) *Review of the Conquest.*
       Catalogue of the conquered kings
    (α) Of Eastern Palestine ....xii. 1—6.
    (β) Of Western Palestine ....xii. 7—24.

PART II.

THE DIVISION OF CANAAN. xiii.—xxi.

Section I. **The Partition of Eastern Canaan.**
  (a) *The Mosaic Settlement.*
    (α) The Divine Command to divide the land xiii. 1—7.
    (β) Provision for the tribe of Levi ....xiii. 8—14.
    (γ) Possessions of the tribe of Reuben.........xiii. 15—23.
    (δ) Possessions of the tribe of Gad ....xiii. 24—28.
    (ε) Possessions of the half tribe of Manasseh xiii. 29—33.
  (b) *Commencement of the Distribution* ....xiv. 1—5.
  (c) *The Possession of Caleb..* ....xiv. 6—15.

Section II. **Division of Western Palestine.**
  (a) *Territory of the tribe of Judah.*
    (α) Its boundaries ....xv. 1—12.
    (β) Petition of Achsah ....xv. 13—20.
    (γ) Cities in the South ....xv. 21—32.
    (δ) Cities in the *Lowlands*.....................xv. 33—47.
    (ε) Cities in the *Mountains* ....xv. 48—60.
    (ζ) Cities in the *Wilderness* ....xv. 61—63.
  (b) *Territory of the tribes of Ephraim and Manasseh.*
    (α) Boundaries of the Territory.................xvi. 1—4.
    (β) Territory of the tribe of Ephraim ....xvi. 5—10.
    (γ) Territory of the tribe of Manasseh.......xvii. 1—13.
    (δ) Complaint of the sons of Joseph...........xvii. 14—16.
    (ε) Reply of Joshua ....xvii. 17, 18.

INTRODUCTION. 29

(*c*)   *Territory of the seven remaining tribes.*

   (α)   The Tabernacle set up at Shiloh ....xviii. 1—10.
   (β)   Territory of Benjamin ....xviii. 11—28
   (γ)   Territory of Simeon ....xix. 1—9.
   (δ)   Territory of the tribe of Zebulun... . ...xix. 10—16.
   (ε)   Territory of the tribe of Issachar ....xix. 17—23.
   (ϛ)   Territory of the tribe of Asher ....xix. 24—31.
   (η)   Territory of the tribe of Naphtali ....xix. 32—39.
   (θ)   Territory of the tribe of Dan ....xix. 40—48.
   (ι)   Joshua's possession ....xix. 49—51.

Section III.   **Appointment of the Cities of Refuge.**

The Divine Command ....xx. 1—3.

   (α)   Choice of the Cities...........................xx. 4—6.
   (β)   Three east of the Jordan ....xx. 7.
   (γ)   Three west of the Jordan...................xx. 8, 9.

Section IV.   **Appointment of the priestly and Levitical cities.**

The Demand of the Levites ....xxi. 1—3.

   (α)   The compliance ....xxi. 4—8.
   (β)   Cities of the Kohathites
      (1)   The sons of Aaron ....xxi. 9—19.
      (2)   The other Kohathites ....xxi. 20—26.
   (γ)   Cities of the Gershonites....................xxi. 27—33.
   (δ)   Cities of the Merarites.....................xxi. 34—42.
   (ε)   Conclusion ....xxi. 43—45.

PART III.

Joshua's Farewell.   **xxii.—xxiv.**

Section I.   **Release of the Two Tribes and a half.**

(*a*)   *The Departure.*

   (α)   Exhortation of Joshua ....xxii. 1—8.
   (β)   Return of the Tribes ....xxii. 9.

(*b*)   *The Disagreement.*

   (α)   Erection of the Altar ....xxii. 10.
   (β)   Embassy of Israel..............................xxii. 11—20.
   (γ)   The Explanation ....xxii. 21—31.
   (δ)   Return of the Embassy ....xxii. 32—34.

Section II. **The Parting of Joshua.**

  (a) *The First Address.*
- (α) Exhortations to fidelity .... xxiii. 1—11.
- (β) Warnings against apostasy .... xxiii. 12—16.

  (b) *The Second Address.*
- (α) Last counsels............................... xxiv. 1—15.
- (β) Renewal of the Covenant .... xxiv. 16—28.
- (γ) Death of Joshua .... xxiv. 29—31.
- (δ) Burial of the bones of Joseph .... xxiv. 32.
- (ε) Death of Eleazar .... xxiv. 33.

THE BOOK OF
JOSHUA.

1—9. *The Command of God to Joshua.*

Now after the death of Moses the servant of the LORD 1 it came to pass, that the LORD spake unto Joshua the son of Nun, Moses' minister, saying, Moses my servant 2 is dead; now therefore arise, go over this Jordan, thou, and

CH. I. 1—9. THE COMMAND OF GOD TO JOSHUA.

1. *Now*] Rather, **And**. The usual connective particle. It implies that something has gone before, of which it is the continuation. Compare the opening words of the Books of Exodus, Leviticus, Numbers, and Judges. Here, as often afterwards, the Book of Joshua presupposes that of Deuteronomy.

after the death of Moses] in the land of Moab on the eastern side of the Jordan, where he was buried over against the idol sanctuary of Beth-Peor (Deut. xxxiv. 6). Through thirty days of stillness, the camp had been full of weeping and mourning for the great Lawgiver.

Joshua the son of Nun] For an outline of his life see Introduction.

Moses' minister] Joshua is not spoken of as Moses' "*servant*," but as his "*minister*." Comp. Ex. xxiv. 13; Deut. i. 38. For his formal appointment to the office see Num. xxvii. 15 ff.

2. *Moses my servant*] Comp. Deut. xxxiv. 5. The highest possible title under the theocracy. Joshua as yet is but the "attendant" of Moses. The higher title is given him in Josh. xxiv. 29.

this Jordan] one of the most singular rivers in the world, which "has never been navigable, and flows into a sea that has never known a port." Observe

(*a*) *Its name.* It is never called "the river" or "brook," or by any other name than its own, "the Jordan"="*the Descender.*"

(*b*) *Its sources.* Far up in northern Palestine, the fork of the two ranges of Anti-Libanus "is alive with bursting fountains and gushing streams," every one of which sooner or later finds its way into a swamp between *Bâniâs* and Lake *Hûleh*. Two of these streams deserve special attention, (i) one at *Bâniâs*, (ii) the other

all this people, unto the land which I do give to them, *even
3 to the children of Israel.* Every place that the sole of your
foot shall tread upon, that have I given unto you, as I said
4 unto Moses. From the wilderness and this Lebanon even
unto the great river, the river Euphrates, all the land of the

> at *Tel-el-Kâdy*. The former is the *upper*, the latter the *lower* source
> of the "River of Palestine."
> (*c*) *Its course*, which is marked by three distinct stages:
>   (i) Enclosed within the ranges of Lebanon and Anti-Lebanon,
>   which run parallel to the Mediterranean from north to south, its
>   streams—for as yet it can hardly be called a single river—fall
>   into the lake called of old Merom, then Samaelon (= "*the High
>   Lake*"), now *Hûleh*. "Half morass, half tarn, this lake is...
>   surrounded by an almost impenetrable jungle of reeds abounding
>   in wild fowl."
>   (ii) Here it might seem destined to end,—like the Barada "the
>   river of Damascus" in the wide marshy lake, a day's journey
>   beyond that city,—but "the Descender" is not thus absorbed.
>   Fed, like the lake itself, by innumerable springs in the slopes of
>   Lebanon, and met by a deep depression for its bed, it rushes
>   with increased rapidity three hundred feet downwards into the
>   Lake of Gennesaret, which is about the same length as our own
>   Windermere, but of much greater breadth.
>   (iii) At the mouth of the Lake it is about 70 feet wide,—"a lazy
>   turbid stream, flowing between low alluvial banks"—and here
>   again it might seem to have closed its course. But it issues forth
>   once more, now a foaming torrent, and plunges through twenty-
>   seven rapids, with a fall of a thousand feet, on its lowest and
>   final stage, into the Dead Sea.
> (*d*) *Its windings*. The distance from the Lake *el-Hûleh* to the Sea of
> Tiberias is nearly 9 miles, that from the Lake to the Dead Sea about
> 60 miles. But within this latter space the river traverses a distance
> of at least 200 miles. Darting first to the right, then to the left,
> then to the right again, "as if sensible of his sad fate," to use the
> quaint words of Fuller, "and desirous to deferre what he cannot
> avoid, he fetcheth many turnings and windings, but all will not avail
> him from falling into the Dead Sea." See Stanley's *Sinai and
> Palestine*, pp. 282, 283; Thomson's *Land and the Book;* Ritter's
> *Geography of Palestine;* Macgregor's *Rob Roy on the Jordan*.
> **3.** *as I said unto Moses*] Comp. Deut. xi. 24; Josh. xiv. 9.
> **4.** *From the wilderness*] For the boundaries of the Land of Promise
> compare (*a*) Gen. xv. 18—21; (*b*) Exod. xxiii. 31; (*c*) Num. xxxiv. 1—
> 12; (*d*) Deut. xi. 24. They were to be, *on the South*, the desert of
> *El-Tîh; on the North*, Mount Lebanon; *on the East*, the Euphrates; *on
> the West*, the Mediterranean Sea.
> *this Lebanon*] Compare also *v.* 2, "*this* Jordan," and Deut. iii. 25.
> The river was visible and lay close at hand; the Lebanon range (= "*the
> white Mountain*") could be discerned, though at a great distance.

Hittites, and unto the great sea *toward* the going down of the sun, shall be your coast. There shall not any man be 5 able *to* stand before thee all the days of thy life: as I was with Moses, *so* I will be with thee: I will not fail thee, nor forsake thee. Be strong and of a good courage: for 6 unto this people shalt thou divide for an inheritance the land, which I sware unto their fathers to give them. Only 7 be thou strong and very courageous, that *thou* mayest observe to do according to all the law, which Moses my servant commanded thee: turn not from it *to* the right hand or *to* the left, that thou mayest prosper whithersoever thou goest. This book of the law shall not depart out of thy mouth; but 8 thou shalt meditate therein day and night, that thou mayest observe to do according to all that is written therein: for then thou shalt make thy way prosperous, and then thou shalt have good success. Have not I commanded thee? 9 Be strong and of a good courage; be not afraid, neither be thou dismayed: for the LORD thy God *is* with thee whithersoever thou goest.

the great river] "The great flood Eufrates," Wyclif. This is the term (comp. Gen. ii. 14, xv. 18) most frequently used in the Bible for the Euphrates, a word of Aryan origin, denoting "*the good and abounding river*," the largest, the longest, and by far the most important of the rivers of Western Asia.

the land of the Hittites] This nation was descended from Cheth (A.V. "Heth"), the second son of Canaan. We first meet with them in Gen. xxiii. 3—5, when Abraham bought from "the children of Heth" the field and the cave of Machpelah. On their relation to the other nations of Canaan see below. They are here put for the Canaanites generally.

5. *as I was with Moses*] "The narrative labours to impress upon us the sense that the continuity of the nation and of its high purpose was not broken by the choice of person and situation."

I will not fail thee] Comp. Deut. xxxi. 6, 8; 1 Chron. xxviii. 20. The words are cited in Heb. xiii. 5, "Let your conversation be without covetousness; and be content with such things as ye have: for he hath said, *I will never leave thee, nor forsake thee.*"

8. *This book of the law*] Joshua is admonished that the Law must be strictly and carefully observed, if the great work, to which he had been called, was to be successfully accomplished. He was "to read, mark, and inwardly digest it," and carry out its provisions to the letter.

9. *Have not I commanded thee?*] Observe the repetition of the words of exhortation. The Hebrew leader is reminded again and again that it was not his work but God's work, which he had been raised up to carry out. Comp. Deut. xxxi. 7, 8, 23.

10—18. *The Command of Joshua to the People.*

10,11 Then Joshua commanded the officers of the people, saying, Pass through the host, and command the people, saying, Prepare you victuals; for within three days ye shall pass over this Jordan, to go in to possess the land, which 12 the LORD your God giveth you to possess it. And to the Reubenites, and to the Gadites, and to half the tribe of

10—18. THE COMMAND OF JOSHUA TO THE PEOPLE.

10. *the officers*] Or, *Shoterim*. The word denotes (1) literally a "writer," or "scribe;" then (2) an overseer, in whose office were combined various duties, including enrolments, orders &c., also genealogies; (3) a magistrate, prefect, leader of the people, especially, as here, the leaders, officers, of the Israelites in Egypt and in the desert. Comp. Num. xi. 16, xxxi. 14, 48; Deut. i. 15, xvi. 18, xx. 5, 8, 9, xxxi. 28. Their duties were at once civil and military.

11. *Prepare you victuals*] The word denotes (a) *food got in hunting;* (b) *food of any kind*, especially *provisions for a journey*. Comp. Exod. xii. 39, "neither had they prepared for themselves any *victual ;"* Josh. ix. 11, 14; Judg. vii. 8, "So the people took *victuals* in their hands, and their trumpets;" 1 Sam. xxii. 10, "And he inquired of the Lord for him, and gave him *victuals."* The need of the provision on this occasion is explained by the cessation of the Manna. See below, ch. v. 12.

within three days] Comp. ch. iii. 1, 2. The order appears to have been given on the 7th day of the month Nisan, for the people crossed the Jordan on the 10th. The expedition, therefore, of the spies occupied from the 5th to the 8th of the month, and the message to the eastern tribes was sent during the same interval.

12. *the Reubenites*] Gadites, and the Half-Tribe of Manasseh, on account of their wealth in flocks and herds (Num. xxxii. 16, 24), had received already their possessions in "the forest-land," "the pasture-land" of the country beyond the Jordan, the territory of the conquered kings Sihon and Og. The remote downs of this portion of Palestine received a special name, "Mishor," expressive of their contrast with the rough and rocky soil of the west. "The vast herds of wild cattle which then wandered through the woods, as those of Scotland through its ancient forests, were in like manner, at once the terror and pride of the Israelite,—"the fat bulls of Bashan." The king of Moab was but a "great sheep-master," and "rendered" for tribute a "hundred thousand lambs, and an hundred thousand rams, with the wool" (2 Kings iii. 4). And still the countless herds and flocks may be seen, droves of cattle moving on like troops of soldiers, descending at sunset to drink of the springs—literally, in the language of the Prophet, "rams and lambs, and goats, and bullocks, all of them fatlings of Bashan" (Ezek. xxxix. 18). See Dean Stanley's *Lectures on the Jewish Church*, I. 217, 218; *Sinai and Palestine*, App. § VI.

Manasseh, spake Joshua, saying, Remember the word which 13
Moses the servant of the LORD commanded you, saying,
The LORD your God hath given you rest, and hath given
you this land. Your wives, your little ones, and your cattle, 14
shall remain in the land which Moses gave you on *this* side
Jordan; but ye shall pass before your brethren armed, all
the mighty *men* of valour, and help them; until the LORD 15
have given your brethren rest, as *he hath given* you, and they
also have possessed the land which the LORD your God
giveth them: then ye shall return unto the land of your
possession, and enjoy it, which Moses the LORD's servant
gave you on *this* side Jordan *toward* the sunrising. And 16
they answered Joshua, saying, All that thou commandest us
we will do, and whithersoever thou sendest us, we will go.
According as we hearkened unto Moses in all *things*, so will 17
we hearken unto thee: only the LORD thy God be with thee,
as he was with Moses. Whosoever *he be* that doth rebel 18
against thy commandment, and will not hearken unto thy
words in all that thou commandest him, he shall be put to
death: only be strong and of a good courage.

13. *Remember the word*] Num. xxxii. 20—24 is quoted, not literally, but freely according to the sense.
hath given you rest] Comp. Deut. xxv. 19, "It shall be, when the Lord thy God hath *given thee rest from all thine enemies* round about, in the land which the Lord thy God giveth thee for an inheritance to possess it." Into this "rest" the disobedient did not enter (Num. xiv. 28—30; Ps. xcv. 7—11; Heb. iii. 11—18), but the true "Rest," the complete "Sabbath-keeping," still remaineth for "the people of God" (Heb. iv. 9).
this land] Compare verse 2 and Deut. iii. 18, the land in which the whole people as yet and the speaker also were, the land east of the Jordan.
14. *ye shall pass over*] According to the promise solemnly given, Num. xxxii. 17, 27, 32.
all the mighty men of valour] Not the whole of the adults who were fit for war, and who numbered, according to Num. xxvi. 7, 18, 34, upwards of 136,930 men, but 40,000 "prepared for" war, Josh. iv. 13.
16. *All that thou commandest us*] A joyful answer instinct with a spirit of true fraternal love and resolute obedience.
17. *only the Lord thy God*] The promise of the Two Tribes and a Half closes with the same call to trust and confidence in the Most High, which God Himself had already addressed to Joshua.

3—2

1—7. *The Mission of the Spies to Jericho.*

2   And Joshua the son of Nun sent out of Shittim two men to spy secretly, saying, Go view the land, even Jericho. And

CH. II. 1—7. THE MISSION OF THE SPIES TO JERICHO.

1. *sent out*] Or, *had sent*. Comp. ch. i. 11, iii. 2. This was probably on the same day that Joshua received the Divine command to cross the Jordan.

out of Shittim] Comp. Num. xxxiii. 49, xxv. 1; Jos. iii. 1; Mic. vi. 5. The full name of the place is given in the first of these passages, "*Abel Shittim*" = "the Meadow" or "Moist Place of the Acacias." It was in the "Arabah" or Jordan valley opposite Jericho, at the outlet of the *Wâdy Heshbon*, about 60 stadia = 3 hours from the place of crossing the river. "We were in the plain of Shittim, and on climbing a little eminence near, we could see the rich wilderness of garden, extending in unbroken verdure right into the corner at the north-east end of the Dead Sea, under the angle formed by the projection of the mountains of Moab, where the *Wady Suiweimeh* enters the lake. It is now called the *Ghor es Seisaban*.... Among the tangled wilderness, chiefly near its western edge, still grow many of the acacia trees, 'Shittim' (*Acacia sayal*), from which the district derived its appropriate name of Abel-ha-Shittim, 'the meadow or moist place of the acacias;'" Tristram's *Land of Israel*, p. 524.

two men] "Young men" according to the LXX. and ch. vi. 23. Brave, doubtless, and prudent, such as Joshua, who had himself been one of the twelve spies (Num. xiii. 16), would be likely to select, knowing, as he knew, all the dangers to which they would be exposed.

Jericho] "The first stage of Joshua's conquest was the occupation of the vast trench, so to speak, which parted the Israelites from the mass of the Promised Land," and which was dominated by the city of Jericho, a place of great antiquity and importance. It derived its name, = "the City of Palm Trees," from a vast grove of noble palm-trees, nearly three miles broad, and eight miles long, which must have recalled to the few survivors of the old generation of the Israelites the magnificent palm-groves of Egypt. The capture of Jericho was essential for two reasons:

(*a*)   Standing at the entrance of the main passes from the valley into the interior of Palestine,—the one branching off S. W. towards Olivet, and commanding the approach to Jerusalem, the other, to the N. E., towards Michmash, which defends the approach to Ai and Bethel—it was the key of the country to any invader coming as Joshua did from the East.

(*b*)   It was for that age a strongly walled town and "enjoyed the benefit of one, if not two, of those copious streams which form the chief sources of such fertility as the valley of the Jordan contains." Its reduction, therefore, must have been the first object of the operations of Joshua on entering the land of Canaan. See Stanley's *Sinai and Palestine*, p. 305. "The strategy displayed by the Israelites under Joshua

they went, and came *into* a harlot's house, named Rahab, and
lodged there. And it was told the king of Jericho, saying, 2
Behold, there came men in hither to night of the children of
Israel to search out the country. And the king of Jericho 3

—considering it only as an ordinary historical event—is worth notice.
Had Israel advanced on Palestine from the South, however victorious
they might have been, they would have driven before them an ever-
increasing mass of enemies, who after each repulse would gain fresh
reinforcements, and could fall back on new fortifications and an un-
touched country, more and more difficult at each step. The Canaanites,
if defeated on the heights of Hebron, would have held in succession those
of Jerusalem and Mount Ephraim; and it is unlikely that the invaders
would ever have reached the district of Gilboa, and Tabor, or the Sea
of Tiberias. In all probability Israel would have been compelled to
turn off to the low country—the land of the Philistines—and with the
Canaanites on the vantage ground of the mountains of Judah and
Ephraim, the nation would in its infancy have been trodden down by
the march of the Assyrian and Egyptian armies, whose military road this
was. By crossing Jordan, destroying Jericho, occupying the heights by
a night-march, and delivering the crushing blow of the battle of Beth-
horon, Joshua executed the favourite manœuvre of the greatest captain
by sea or land, since the days of Nelson and Napoleon; he broke through
and defeated the centre of the enemies' line, and then stood in a position
to strike with his whole force successively right and left."—Note to
Lenormant's *Manual of Oriental History*, I. p. 111.

and came into a harlot's house] The spies traversed successfully the
space which separated them from Jericho, crossing the fords or swimming,
and entered the city towards evening (Jos. ii. 2). There was no one in
the place to receive them, and it would have been perilous to have gone
to a public khan or caravanserai. They, therefore, followed one of the
courtesans, of whom there would be many in a Canaanitish city, to her
home.

named Rahab] The name of this courtesan was Rahab. She probably, too, carried on the trade of lodging-keeper for wayfaring men.
It would seem also that she was engaged in the manufacture of linen, and
practised the art of dyeing, for which the Phœnicians were early famous,
for we find the flat roof of the house covered with stalks of flax put there to
dry, and a stock of scarlet or crimson line in her possession. Her name
is mentioned in the genealogy of our Lord (Matt. i. 5). There she
appears as the wife of Salmon, the son of Naasson, by whom she became
the mother of Boaz, the grandfather of Jesse. See Ruth iv. 20, 21;
1 Chron. ii. 11, 51, 54. Her faith and works are glorified in (*a*) the
Epistle to the Hebrews (xi. 31), and (*b*) in the Epistle of St James
(ii. 25).

2. *it was told the king*] Jericho was the residence of a "king" or
"chief," a fenced city, enclosed by walls of considerable breadth, and
not only contained sheep and oxen, but abounded in "silver and gold,"
and "vessels of brass and iron" (Jos. vi. 24).

sent unto Rahab, saying, Bring forth the men that are come to thee, which are entered into thine house: for they be
4 come to search out all the country. And the woman took the two men, and hid them, and said thus, There came men
5 unto me, but I wist not whence they *were:* and it came to pass *about the time* of shutting of the gate, when it was dark, that the men went out: whither the men went I wot not:
6 pursue after them quickly; for ye shall overtake them. But she had brought them up to the roof of the house, and hid

3. *sent unto Rahab*] "In modern Europe the officers of the government would have entered the house without wasting the previous time in parley. But formerly, as now, in the East, the privacy of a woman was respected, even to a degree that might be called superstitious, and no one will enter the house in which she lives, or the part of the house she occupies, until her consent has been obtained, if, indeed, such consent be ever demanded. In this case it was not asked. Rahab was required not to let the messengers in, but to bring out the foreigners she harboured." Kitto's *Bible Illustrations*, II. 243.

4. *And the woman took the two men*] Instead of timidly surrendering them to the king she resolved to shield and protect them.

I wist not] For this meaning of "wist," comp. Exod. xvi. 15, "And they said one to another, It is manna, for they *wist* not what it was;" Exod. xxxiv. 29, and in many other passages both in the Old and New Testament. See *Commentary on St Mark*, ch. ix. 6, p. 100.

5. *shutting of the gate*] A necessary precaution owing to the absence of all artificial light from the streets of Oriental towns.

when it was dark] In the East, night comes on soon after sundown, and the evening twilight is of very short duration.

I wot not] Strict truth was a virtue but little known or practised in ancient times, and Rahab must not be judged by the same standard of morality as we should apply to our own days. "By faith the harlot Rahab perished not with them that believed not" (Heb. xi. 31). "It would be a mistake, an anachronism, to apply to a dweller in one of the old Canaanite cities, amidst the worshippers of false and cruel deities, destitute of one ray either of Law or Gospel light, principles of conduct and character which we owe to the Revelation of all truth and all duty by our Lord Jesus Christ. The Epistle is content to say only this, Behold in the example of this woman the working of that faith which grasps the unseen. Behold the action of faith upon evidence presented and upon an alternative of conduct. Behold the inference of truth honestly drawn, and the preference, on the strength of it, of the future to the present. Behold, St James adds (ii. 25), how faith differs from opinion, and evidences its existence by the sign of work. The hearts of other inhabitants of Jericho were melting, she tells us, with the terror of Israel,—she alone acted upon the conviction, and added another element to the 'great cloud of witnesses.'" Dr Vaughan's *Heroes of Faith*, pp. 263, 264.

them with the stalks of flax, which she had laid in order upon the roof. And the men pursued after them the way 7 to Jordan unto the fords: and as soon as they which pursued after them were gone out, they shut the gate.

8—21. *Reception of the Spies by Rahab.*

And before they were laid down, she came up unto them 8 upon the roof; and she said unto the men, I know that the 9 LORD hath given you the land, and that your terror is fallen upon us, and that all the inhabitants of the land faint because of you. For we have heard how the LORD dried up the 10 water of the Red sea for you, when you came out of Egypt;

6. *the roof of the house*] The roofs of Eastern houses were flat (St Mark ii. 4), and were made useful for various purposes, as drying corn, hanging up linen, and preparing figs and raisins. They were also used as (*a*) places of recreation in the evening; (*b*) sleeping-places at night, when the interior apartments were too hot or sultry for refreshing repose; (*c*) places for devotion and even idolatrous worship. Comp. 1 Sam. ix. 25, 26; 2 Sam. xi. 2, xvi. 22; 2 Kings xxiii. 12; Dan. iv. 29; Acts ii. 1, x. 9. The Jewish Law required that they should have a battlement, in order that guilt of blood might not come upon the house through any one falling from it (Deut. xxii. 8). "Parts of Roman houses were also furnished with such roofs called *solaria*, because they lay exposed on all sides to the sun, and also *mæniana*, as the Italians now also call them *altana*." Lange's *Commentary*.

the stalks of flax] "stubble of flaxe," Wyclif. Unbroken flax is here meant, the stalks of which, about Jericho and in Egypt, reached a height of more than three feet and the thickness of a reed. It was anciently one of the most important crops in Palestine (Hos. ii. 5, 9).

8—21. RECEPTION OF THE SPIES BY RAHAB.

9. *the Lord*] The name is remarkable as used by Rahab. But the Israelites had long been encamped in the neighbourhood, and she might easily have become acquainted with the name of their God.

your terror] i.e. "the terror of you." The prophetic words of triumph in Moses' song were now fulfilled (Exod. xv. 14—16; comp. also Deut. xi. 25).

faint] Heb. **melt.** "Oure hearte basshade, ne spirit bood in us at youre yncomynge," Wyclif. See verse 24.

10. *dried up the water*] The inhabitants of the land had heard of two important events, which filled them with alarm; (*a*) the drying up of the Red Sea before the Israelites (cp. Ps. cvi. 7. 9, 22, cxxxvi. 13); (*b*) the defeat at Jahaz of Sihon king of the Amorites, who refused the Israelites a passage through the territory between the Arnon and the Jabbok (Num. xxi. 21—31; Deut. ii. 30—37), and at Edrei of Og, the giant king of the district which, under the name of "Bashan," extended

and what you did unto the two kings of the Amorites, that *were* on the *other* side Jordan, Sihon and Og, whom ye
11 utterly destroyed. And as soon as we had heard *these things*, our hearts did melt, neither did there remain any more courage in any man, because of you: for the LORD your God, he *is* God in heaven above, and in earth beneath.
12 Now therefore, I pray you, swear unto me by the LORD, since I have shewed you kindness, that ye will also shew kindness unto my father's house, and give me a true token:
13 and *that* ye will save alive my father, and my mother, and my brethren, and my sisters, and all that they have, and de-
14 liver our lives from death. And the men answered her, Our life for yours, if ye utter not this our business. And it shall be, when the LORD hath given us the land, that we will deal
15 kindly and truly with thee. Then she let them down by a cord through the window: for her house *was* upon the
16 town wall, and she dwelt upon the wall. And she said unto them, Get you to the mountain, lest the pursuers meet you;

from the Jabbok up to the base of Hermon (Num. xxi. 33—35; Deut. iii. 1—7).

whom ye utterly destroyed] Or, **devoted.** The word here used denotes (i) *to separate for God, devote to Him* (Lev. xxvii. 21, 28; Jos. vi. 17, 18; 1 Sam. xv. 21), (ii) *to devote to utter destruction, utterly destroy* (Deut. iv. 26). The objects of such a doom might be (*a*) *persons*, as here (and comp. 1 Kings xx. 42; Rom. ix. 3; Gal. i. 8, 9, iii. 13), or (*b*) *things* (Josh. vi. 17, 18, vii. 1).

11. *he is God in heaven above*] Rahab expressly acknowledges God as Almighty, a knowledge which is possible to the heathen, for the "invisible things of God from the creation of the world are clearly seen, being understood by the things that are made, even His *eternal power and Godhead*" (Rom. i. 20).

12. *a true token*] "a verrey tokne," Wyclif; i.e. *a token of truth, a sign;* comp. Exod. iii. 12, "And this shall be *a token unto thee*, that I have sent thee;" 1 Sam. ii. 34; Isai. vii. 11; Luke ii. 12.

14. *Our life for yours*] Literally, **Our soul instead of yours for death, or instead of yours to die,** as in the margin. "Oure soule be for you into deth," Wyclif.

15. *she let them down by a cord*] Comp. the escape of St Paul from Damascus (Acts ix. 25).

her house was upon the town wall] i.e. her chamber was in the upper story of the house, which rose above the wall, as may be seen even now in old cities along the Rhine.

16. *Get you to the mountain*] i.e. probably the caverns in "the jagged range of the white limestone mountains" (of Judæa) which rise to the north of the city, "the same which in later ages afforded shelter

and hide yourselves there three days, until the pursuers be
returned: and afterward may ye go your way. And the 17
men said unto her, We *will be* blameless of this thine oath
which thou hast made us swear. Behold, *when* we come 18
into the land, thou shalt bind this line of scarlet thread in
the window which thou didst let us down (by): and thou
shalt bring thy father, and thy mother, and thy brethren, and
all thy father's household, home unto thee. And it shall be, 19
that whosoever shall go out of the doors of thy house into
the street, his blood *shall be* upon his head, and we *will be*
guiltless: and whosoever shall be with thee in the house,
his blood *shall be* on our head, if *any* hand be upon him.
And if thou utter this our business, then we will be quit of 20
thine oath which thou hast made us to swear. And she 21
said, According unto your words, so *be* it. And she sent
them away, and they departed: and she bound the scarlet
line in the window.

22—24. *Return of the Spies to Joshua.*

And they went, and came unto the mountain, and abode 22
there three days, until the pursuers were returned: and the
pursuers sought *them* throughout all the way, but found
them not. So the two men returned, and descended from 23

to the hermits who there took up their abode, in the belief that this
was the mountain of the Forty Days' Fast of the Temptation—the
'*Quarantania*,' from which it still derives its name." Stanley, *Sinai
and Palestine*, p. 308.

17. *We will be blameless*] Or, "We are blameless." We must supply
"unless you do what we shall now say unto you." Comp. Gen. xxiv.
41, "Then shalt thou be clear from this my oath, when thou comest to
my kindred; and if they give not thee one, thou shalt be clear from my
oath." Wyclif renders it "we schulen be giltles of this oath."

18. *this line of scarlet thread*] The line was spun out of crimson thread,
the crimson colour produced by the *coccus ilicis*, Linn., a cochineal
insect, living on the holm oak, the larvæ of which yield the crimson dye.

19. *his blood*]=his "bloodguiltiness," his "responsibility for blood."
Compare 2 Sam. xxi. 1, "It is for Saul, and his *bloody* (="blood-
thirsty") house, because he slew the Gibeonites;" Ezek. xxii. 2, "Wilt
thou judge the *bloody* (="bloodguilty") city? yea thou shalt shew her
all her abominations."

22—24. RETURN OF THE SPIES TO JOSHUA.

22. *the mountain*] See above, verse 16.

the mountain, and passed over, and came to Joshua the son
24 of Nun, and told him all *things* that befell them: and they
said unto Joshua, Truly the LORD hath delivered into our
hands all the land; for even all the inhabitants of the
country do faint because of us.

1—13. *The Preparation for the Passage of Jordan.*

3 And Joshua rose early in the morning; and they removed
from Shittim, and came to Jordan, he and all the children
2 of Israel, and lodged there before they passed over. And it
came to pass after three days, that the officers went through
3 the host; and they commanded the people, saying, When
ye see the ark of the covenant of the LORD your God, and

23. *and passed over*] Probably by swimming, for the water at this season was too high to allow them to ford; compare the coming to David of the eleven mighty men from the uplands of Gad, who swam the river when it had overflowed all its banks (1 Chron. xii. 15).
all things that befell them] Compare the words of the sons of Jacob to their father, Gen. xlii. 29; of Moses to his father-in-law, Exod. xviii. 8.
24. *all the inhabitants*] This was the most important part of their communication, that the inhabitants of the land were utterly dispirited and cast down.

CH. III. 1—13. THE PREPARATION FOR THE PASSAGE OF JORDAN.

1. *they removed from Shittim*] They descended from the upper terraces of the valley of Jordan, from "the Grove of Acacias," to the level of the river.
to Jordan] Speaking strictly, Jordan has a threefold bank:—
(a) The lowest, at the edge of the river, which in spring is frequently inundated, owing to the melting of the snow on Hermon;
(b) The middle bank, which is covered with a rich vegetation;
(c) An upper bank, which overhangs the river.
2. *after three days*] See above, i. 11.
the officers went through the host] Or, overseers: Vulg. *præcones*. The word denotes (i) *the head man of the people* (Exod. v. 6—19; Num. xi. 16); (ii) the magistrates in the towns (Deut. xvi. 18; 1 Chron. xxiii. 4).
3. *the ark of the covenant*] called sometimes (i) "the Ark of God," 1 Sam. iii. 3; sometimes (ii) "the Ark of the Testimony," Exod. xxv. 22. Here it means "the Ark of the Covenant of Jehovah," the Sacred Ark, an oblong chest of acacia wood, overlaid with the purest gold within and without, 2½ cubits in length, 1½ in breadth, 1½ in height. It contained the two stone tables, on both sides of which the Decalogue had been inscribed. Round the top ran a crown or wreath of pure gold, and upon it was the *Mercy Seat*, at either end of which were two

the priests the Levites bearing it, then ye shall remove from your place, and go after it. Yet there shall be a space 4 between you and it, about two thousand cubits by measure: come not near unto it, that ye may know the way by which ye must go: for ye have not passed *this* way heretofore. And Joshua said unto the people, Sanctify yourselves: 5 for to morrow the LORD will do wonders among you. And 6 Joshua spake unto the priests, saying, Take up the ark of the covenant, and pass over before the people. And they took up the ark of the covenant, and went before the people.

And the LORD said unto Joshua, This day will I begin to 7 magnify thee in the sight of all Israel, that they may know that, as I was with Moses, *so* I will be with thee. And thou 8 shalt command the priests that bear the ark of the covenant, saying, When ye are come to the brink of the water of Jordan, ye shall stand still in Jordan. And Joshua said 9 unto the children of Israel, Come hither, and hear the words of the LORD your God. And Joshua said, Hereby ye shall 10 know that the living God *is* among you, and *that* he will

golden Cherubim, with outspread wings and faces turned towards each other, and eyes bent downwards, as though desirous to look into its mysteries (1 Pet. i. 12).

and go after it] In the wilderness the Pillar of Cloud had led the way, now the Ark of the Covenant takes its place.

4. *there shall be a space*] Partly for the sake of reverence, partly that it might be observed and marked as it led the way.

two thousand cubits] a Sabbath day's journey (Acts i. 12) = 3000 feet.

5. *Sanctify yourselves*] Compare the instructions of Moses before the giving of the Law (Exod. xix. 10—15). This would consist partly in ceremonial purification, partly in turning to the Lord in a spirit of expectant faith in "the wonders" which "the Lord would do" amongst them. Wyclif renders the verse: "Be ye hallowid; forsothe to morrowe the Lord shall do among yow marveylis."

to morrow] the tenth of Nisan (iv. 19), the anniversary of the day on which forty years before the Israelites had " taken to them " (Exod. xii. 3) "every man a lamb" as a Paschal victim.

6. *And they took up*] i. e. on the day following.

9. *And Joshua said*] Verses 9—13 contain the substance of an address to a solemn assembly of the people, in which a fuller explanation is given of what has been stated generally in verses 7 and 8.

10. *the living God*] Comp. Deut. v. 26, " For who is there of all flesh, that hath heard the voice of *the living* God?" This title is applied

without fail drive out from before you the Canaanites, and the Hittites, and the Hivites, and the Perizzites, and the
11 Girgashites, and the Amorites, and the Jebusites. Behold,

to God to indicate that He is not *dead*, like the "lying vanities" of heathenism (Lev. xix. 4; Deut. xxxii. 21; Jon. ii. 8), but the source of all life.

the Canaanites] Seven nations are here enumerated, as also, though in varying order, in Deut. vii. 1; Josh. ix. 1, xi. 3, xxiv. 11.
(i) *The Canaanites* (Deut. i. 7), or " Lowlanders " properly so called, occupied (*a*) the sea-coast as far north as Dan; (*b*) a considerable portion of the plain of Esdraelon; and (*c*) of the Valley of the Jordan (Num. xiii. 29).
(ii) *The Hittites*, descended from Heth, the second son of Canaan, and settled in the time of Abraham in and round Hebron (Gen. xxiii. 19, xxv. 9), then called *Kirjath-Arba*. At that time the tribe was as yet but small and not important enough to be noticed beside the "Canaanite" and the "Perizzite." Afterwards they acquired greater strength, and took their place as equal allies with the other nations.
(iii) *The Hivites* are omitted (*a*) in the first enumeration of the nations, who, at the time of the call of Abraham, occupied the Promised Land (Gen. xv. 19—21); (*b*) in the report of the spies (Num. xiii. 29). We first hear of them when Jacob returned to Canaan (Gen. xxxiv. 2). A peaceful and commercial people (Gen. xxxiv. 10, 23, 28, 29), they were mainly located "under Hermon, in the land of Mizpeh" (Josh. xi. 3), in "mount Lebanon, from mount Baal-hermon unto the entering in of Hamath" (Judg. iii. 3; 2 Sam. xxiv. 7).
(iv) *The Perizzites*, which word is thought to denote "rustics," "dwellers in the open, unwalled towns," were located partly in the south (Judg. i. 4, 5), partly in the forest country "on the western flanks of mount Carmel."
(v) *The Girgashites* are conjectured to have been a large family of the Hivites, as they are omitted in nine out of the ten places in which the nations or families of Canaan are mentioned, while in the tenth they are mentioned and the Hivites omitted. They are supposed to have been settled in that part of the country which lay to the east of the Lake of Gennesareth.
(vi) *The Amorites*, or "Mountaineers," occupied (Gen. xiv. 7) the barren heights west of the Dead Sea, and stretched west to Hebron (Gen. xiii. 18, xiv. 13); thence, tempted probably by the high tablelands on the east, they crossed the Jordan, and occupied the country from the Arnon to the Jabbok (Num. xxi. 13, 26). In the genealogical table of Gen. x. "the Amorite" is given as the fourth son of Canaan.
(vii) *The Jebusites* are uniformly placed last in the formula, by which the Promised Land is often designated. They were a mountain tribe, and occupied the strong fortress of Jebus (*Jerusalem*).

the ark of the covenant, *even* the Lord of all the earth passeth over before you into Jordan. Now therefore take ye twelve 12 men out of the tribes of Israel, out of every tribe a man. And it shall come to pass, as soon as the soles of the feet 13 of the priests that bear the ark of the LORD, the Lord of all the earth, shall rest in the waters of Jordan, *that* the waters of Jordan shall be cut off *from* the waters that come down from above; and they shall stand *upon* a heap.

14—17. *Jordan turned backwards.*

And it came to pass, when the people removed from their 14 tents, to pass over Jordan, and the priests bearing the ark *of* the covenant before the people; and as they that bare the 15 ark were come unto Jordan, and the feet of the priests that bare the ark were dipped in the brim of the water, (for Jordan overfloweth all his banks all the time of harvest,) that 16

11. *the Lord of all the earth*] A significant title of the Most High, at a time when the conquest of the Land was contemplated.
13. *shall be cut off*] See below, verse 16.

14—17. JORDAN TURNED BACKWARDS.

14. *when the people removed*] i.e. on the 10th day of Abib or Nisan, the same month they before witnessed the departure from Egypt, corresponding to our April or May.
15. *for Jordan overfloweth all his banks all the time of harvest*] In the deeply sunken, tropical valley of the Jordan, the harvest had already commenced, and the snow on Hermon having begun to melt, the "yellow" water of the river stood high and had overflowed its lower bank. "We were on the banks of the Jordan.... Muddy, swollen, and turbid, the stream was far too formidable and rapid for the most adventurous to attempt their intended bathe.... Had we arrived a few days sooner, we could not have approached the river at all; for it had been overflowing its banks and filling the lower level, to which we had descended from the plain, and which was still a deep slimy ooze. Under our tree, however, the drift had formed a sandbank, on which we could sit. By measurement we found that the river had lately been fourteen feet higher than its present margin, and yet it was still many feet above its ordinary level." Tristram's *Land of Israel*, p. 223.

Observe: (*a*) The feet of the priests were dipped in the brim of the water. This is explained by the season being that of a periodical inundation of the Jordan, which overflowed its banks all the time of harvest;

(*b*) The *barley* harvest is here meant, for the wheat harvest was not fully completed till Pentecost, or fifty days later in the year, and the Israelites crossed the Jordan on the 10th day of Abib or Nisan, i.e. four days before the Passover;

the waters which came down from above stood *and* rose up upon a heap very far, from the city Adam, that *is* beside Zaretan: and those that came down toward the sea of the plain, *even* the salt sea, failed, *and* were cut off: and the

(*c*) Now in Exodus we learn that at the Plague of Hail, which was but a day or two before the Passover, "the *flax* and the *barley* were smitten, for *the barley was in the ear* and the flax was bolled. But the wheat and the rye were not smitten, for they were not grown up;"

(*d*) It would seem then that the flax and the barley were crops which ripened about the same time in Egypt, and as the climate of Canaan did not differ materially from that of Egypt, especially in the sunken *Ghôr* of the Jordan, this was, no doubt, the case in Canaan too; there also these two crops would come in at the same time, and this also must have been the season of the *flax* harvest;

(*e*) Now Rahab hid the spies in the *stalks of flax* (Josh. ii. 6) laid on the roof doubtless to steep and season. Here we have a strikingly undesigned coincidence in the passage of the Israelites at the time of *harvest*, and that the *barley harvest*, which coincides with the *Passover*, and the ripening of the *flax harvest*. Blunt's *Undesigned Coincidences*, pp. 105—107.

16. *the waters which came down from above*] Let us try to realise the scene:—

(*a*) At a distance of about 2000 cubits, or a mile, from the river stood the great mass of the army (Josh. iii. 4).

(*b*) On the broken edge of the river were the priests bearing on their shoulders the sacred Ark;

(*c*) As soon as the feet of the priests were "dipped in the brim of the water," the flow of the stream was arrested;

(*d*) Far up, beyond where they stood, at the city of Adam, that is beside Zaretan, about 30 miles from the place where the host was encamped, the waters which rushed down from above "*stood and rose upon an heap*," drawn up by the Divine Hand;

(*e*) At the same moment the waters that came down toward the Salt Sea "failed and were cut off" (Josh. iii. 16), and thus from north to south the waters were "driven backwards" (Ps. cxiv. 3), and the dry river-bed was exposed to view.

from the city Adam] is a correction of the text. The Hebrew has, **at the city Adam**, which was situated, it is thought, where now we find the ford *Damieh* with remains of a bridge of the Roman period (Van de Velde, *Narrative*, II. 322).

beside Zaretan] Or, more correctly, *Zarthan* (1 Kings iv. 12, vii. 46), the situation of which is unknown, but it is thought to have been near Succoth, at the mouth of the Jabbok (1 Kings vii. 46). By some it has been identified with the modern *Surtabeh*, an isolated hill some 17 miles above Jericho, where high rocks compress the Jordan Valley within its narrowest limits, and seem almost to throw a barrier across it.

the sea of the plain] This name, which also occurs in Deut. iii. 17, iv.

people passed over right against Jericho. And the priests 17 that bare the ark *of* the covenant of the LORD stood firm on dry *ground* in the midst of Jordan, and all the Israelites passed over on dry *ground*, until all the people were passed clean over Jordan.

1—18. *Completion of the Passage.*

And it came to pass, when all the people were clean 4 passed over Jordan, that the LORD spake unto Joshua, saying, Take you twelve men out of the people, out of every 2 tribe a man, and command you them, saying, Take you 3 hence out of the midst of Jordan, out of the place where the priests' feet stood firm, twelve stones, and ye shall carry

49, is used for the Dead Sea, the waters of which are clear, but strongly tinctured with salt, and fatal to fish.

failed] "The scene presented is of the 'descending stream,' not 'parted asunder,' as we generally fancy, but as the Psalm (cxiv. 3) expresses it, '*turned backwards;*' the whole bed of the river left dry from north to south, through its long windings; the huge stones lying bare here and there, imbedded in the soft bottom; or the shingly pebbles drifted along the course of the channel." Stanley's *Lectures*, p. 232.

17. *all the Israelites passed over*] Where the passage exactly took place cannot now be determined, but the typical significance of the narrative is very impressive. Whether we consider (i) the solemn inauguration of Joshua to his office; or (ii) his attestation by the waters of the Jordan; or (iii) the choice of twelve men, one from each tribe, to be the bearers of the twelve stones, and the builders of the monument founded therewith (1 Cor. iii. 10; Rev. xxi. 14), we see types of the other "Joshua," Who was solemnly inaugurated and divinely attested by the rushing waters of the same stream, and Who ordained His twelve Apostles to be the Pillars of His Church, and the builders of the Spiritual Temple. See above, Introduction, p. 25.

CH. IV. 1—18. COMPLETION OF THE PASSAGE.

1. *when all the people were clean passed over*] Below the spot, where the priests stood firm and motionless, the host, probably at various points, "*hasted and passed over*" (Josh. iv. 10).

3. *twelve stones*] We find on several occasions large stones set up to commemorate remarkable events, as (*a*) by Jacob in memory of the vision of the Angels at Beth-el (Gen. xxviii. 18); (*b*) by the same patriarch on his return from Padan-aram (Gen. xxxv. 14); (*c*) by the same patriarch again as a "heap of witness" between him and Laban (Gen. xxxi. 45—47); (*d*) by Samuel at "Eben-ezer" to mark the site of the victory over the Philistines (1 Sam. vii. 12). Such stones were sometimes consecrated by anointing with oil (Gen. xxviii. 18).

them over with you, and leave them in the lodging place,
4 where you shall lodge *this* night. Then Joshua called the
twelve men, whom he had prepared of the children of Israel,
5 out of every tribe a man: and Joshua said unto them, Pass
over before the ark of the LORD your God into the midst of
Jordan, and take ye up every man of you a stone upon his
shoulder, according unto the number of the tribes of the
6 children of Israel: that this may be a sign among you, *that*
when your children ask *their fathers* in time to come, saying,
7 What mean you by these stones? then ye shall answer them,
That the waters of Jordan were cut off before the ark of the
covenant of the LORD; when it passed over Jordan, the
waters of Jordan were cut off: and these stones shall be for
8 a memorial unto the children of Israel for ever. And the
children of Israel did so as Joshua commanded, and took
up twelve stones out of the midst of Jordan, as the LORD
spake unto Joshua, according to the number of the tribes of
the children of Israel, and carried them over with them unto
the place where they lodged, and laid them down there.
9 And Joshua set up twelve stones in the midst of Jordan, in
the place where the feet of the priests which bare the ark
of the covenant stood: and they are there unto this day.
10 For the priests which bare the ark stood in the midst of

 6. *when your children*] Comp. Exod. xii. 26, xiii. 14; Deut. vi. 20.
 8. *unto the place*] "On the upper terrace of the plain of the Jordan,
which became the centre of the first sanctuary of the Holy Land—the
first place pronounced 'holy,' the sacred place of the Jordan valley
(Josh. v. 10—15), where the Tabernacle remained till it was fixed at
Shiloh" (Josh. xviii. 1).
 9. *And Joshua set up twelve stones in the midst of Jordan*] "Alios
quoque duodecim lapides," Vulg. Another set of stones is here
intended than that just mentioned. The latter were set up by the
direct command of God to mark the spot where they passed the night;
the former Joshua set up, apparently without the Divine suggestion, to
mark the spot where the feet of the priests rested, while they bare
upwards the Ark during the passage of the people. The expression
"midst of Jordan" does not necessarily imply that the priests stood,
and that the stones were built up, in the middle channel; but only that
they were in the midst of the water when it flowed as it did before
the occurrence of the miracle. Comp. Josh. iii. 8 with iii. 15.
 unto this day] This phrase recurs again and again in the Book of
Joshua. Comp. Josh. v. 9, vi. 25, vii. 26, viii. 28, 29, ix. 27, x. 27, xiii.
13, xiv. 14, xv. 63, xvi. 10.
 10. *the priests which bare the ark stood*] Their patient attitude,

Jordan, until every thing was finished that the LORD commanded Joshua to speak unto the people, according to all that Moses commanded Joshua: and the people hasted and passed over. And it came to pass, when all the people were 11 clean passed over, that the ark of the LORD passed over, and the priests, in the presence of the people. And the 12 children of Reuben, and the children of Gad, and half the tribe of Manasseh, passed over armed before the children of Israel, as Moses spake unto them: about forty thousand 13 prepared for war passed over before the LORD unto battle, to the plains of Jericho. On that day the LORD magnified 14 Joshua in the sight of all Israel; and they feared him, as they feared Moses, all the days of his life.

And the LORD spake unto Joshua, saying, Command the 15, 16 priests that bear the ark of the Testimony, that they come up out of Jordan. Joshua therefore commanded the priests, 17 saying, Come ye up out of Jordan. And it came to pass, 18 when the priests that bare the ark of the covenant of the LORD were come up out of the midst of Jordan, *and* the soles of the priests' feet were lift up unto the dry *land*, that the waters of Jordan returned unto their place, and flowed over all his banks, as *they did* before.

19—24. *Erection of the Monument at Gilgal.*

And the people came up out of Jordan on the tenth *day* of 19 the first month, and encamped in Gilgal, in the east border of

standing still and motionless, was eminently calculated to impart courage to the people.

12. *passed over armed before the children of Israel*] Contrary to the usual order (Num. xxxii. 20), as if to secure that they should fulfil their vow.

18. *the waters of Jordan returned*] Thus the history of the crossing is related in sections: (*a*) first briefly, iii. 14—17; (*b*) then more completely, iv. 1—11; (*c*) some supplementary notices, iv. 12—17; (*d*) finally, the conclusion, concerning the return of the water, till Jordan "flowed over all his banks," as it did before.

19—24. ERECTION OF THE MONUMENT AT GILGAL.

19. *the tenth day of the first month*] Notice the exactness of the narrative. The first month is elsewhere called Abib, i. e. "the month of green ears" (Exod. xiii. 4, xxiii. 15; Deut. xvi. 1), and subsequently "Nisan" (Neh. ii. 1; Esth. iii. 7).

encamped] The site was doubtless fortified by Joshua "as a frontier

20 Jericho. And those twelve stones, which they took out of
21 Jordan, did Joshua pitch in Gilgal. And he spake unto the
children of Israel, saying, When your children shall ask their
22 fathers in time to come, saying, What *mean* these stones? then
ye shall let your children know, saying, Israel came over this
23 Jordan on dry *land*. For the LORD your God dried up the
waters of Jordan from before you, until ye were passed over,
as the LORD your God did to the Red sea, which he dried
24 up from before us, until we were gone over: that all the
people of the earth might know the hand of the LORD, that
it *is* mighty: that ye might fear the LORD your God for
ever.

fortress, such as the Greeks under the name of *epitichisma*, and the Romans under the name of *colonia*, always planted as their advanced posts in a hostile country, such as at Kufa the Arab conquerors founded before the building of Bagdad, and at Fostal before the building of Cairo." Stanley's *Lectures*, p. 233.

in Gilgal] situated apparently on a hillock or rising ground in the Arboth-Jericho, or, as it is rendered in our Version, "the plains of Jericho," the more level district of the "Ghôr" which lay between the town and the river. We find Gilgal mentioned again, (*a*) in the time of Saul (1 Sam. vii. 16, x. 8), and (*b*) some sixty years later in the history of David's return to Jerusalem (2 Sam. xix. 15). The name is here mentioned by anticipation, Josh. v. 9.

20. *those twelve stones*] which seem to have been invested with a reverence which came to be regarded at last as idolatrous (Hos. iv. 15, ix. 15; Amos iv. 4, v. 5).

21. *When your children*] Nothing is more carefully inculcated in the Law than the duty of parents to teach their children not only its precepts and principles, but the meaning of all the great historical events in their national existence. (Comp. Exod. xii. 26, xiii. 8, 14; Deut. iv. 5, 9, 10.)

24. *that all the people of the earth might know*] The miracle made the passage possible and easy for the Elect Nation, but it was intended also to have its effect on the nations around, and impart to them a knowledge of the power of Jehovah, the God of Israel.

that ye might fear] The tribes of Israel were now in the enemy's country, and they had learnt afresh, as their fathers had done before them at the Red Sea, three important lessons; (i) that the power of Jehovah was unlimited; (ii) that it would be exerted on their behalf so long as they were obedient to His commands; (iii) that their leader was acting under the direct command and guidance of their Invisible Protector. These lessons were of universal application and were to be impressed on generation after generation.

1—9. *Renewal of the Rite of Circumcision.*

And it came to pass, when all the kings of the Amorites, 5 which *were* on the side of Jordan westward, and all the kings of the Canaanites, which *were* by the sea, heard that the LORD had dried up the waters of Jordan from before the children of Israel, until we were passed over, that their heart melted, neither was there spirit in them any more, because of the children of Israel.

At that time the LORD said unto Joshua, Make thee sharp 2 knives, and circumcise again the children of Israel the second time. And Joshua made him sharp knives, and cir- 3 cumcised the children of Israel at the hill of the foreskins.

CH. V. 1—9. RENEWAL OF THE RITE OF CIRCUMCISION.

1. *when all the kings of the Amorites*] This verse stands in close connection with the last verse of the preceding Chapter. All the peoples of the earth were "to know the Name of the Lord" and to fear Him. A first example of this is seen in the case of the Canaanite nations.

which were by the sea] See note above on iii. 10.

their heart melted] The terror which, as Rahab had told the spies, had already seized them was greatly increased by the news of the marvellous passage of the Jordan. Wyclif renders it, "the herte of hem is discomfortid, and abood not in hem spiryte of hem."

2. *Make thee sharp knives*] Or, as in margin, **knives of flint**. "Stonen knyues," Wyclif. In Exod. iv. 25 we read that Zipporah, the wife of Moses, took a "sharp stone," or "knife of flint," and circumcised her son. Joshua followed the custom of antiquity on this occasion, for they had no other knives with them. Herodotus, II. 86, mentions "stone knives" as used by the Egyptian embalmers, and with such the priests of Cybele mutilated themselves. A representation of the Egyptian flint knife from the Museum at Berlin is given in Smith's *Biblical Dictionary*.

and circumcise] For forty years in the wilderness the nation had been under judgment, and those born there had not received the covenant mark of circumcision. To renew that rite in their case was the first necessity, that Israel might be restored to its full position as the Covenant-people of God.

the second time] All, it is to be remembered, who, having come out from Egypt, were at the time of the sentence at Kadesh under twenty years old (Num. xiv. 29), i. e. all at Gilgal, who were 38 years old and upwards, *had been* circumcised. The rite, therefore, now applies only to the residue.

3. *the hill of the foreskins*] or "*Gibeah-haaraloth*," probably so named from this transaction. Comp. Col. ii. 11—13, iii. 1—6.

4—2

4 And this *is* the cause why Joshua did circumcise: All the people that came out of Egypt, *that were* males, *even* all the men of war, died in the wilderness by the way, after they 5 came out of Egypt. Now all the people that came out were circumcised: but all the people *that were* born in the wilderness by the way as they came forth out of Egypt, *them* they 6 had not circumcised. For the children of Israel walked forty years in the wilderness, till all the people *that were* men of war, which came out of Egypt, were consumed, because they obeyed not the voice of the LORD: unto whom the LORD sware that *he* would not shew them the land, which the LORD sware unto their fathers that he would give us, a 7 land that floweth with milk and honey. And their children, *whom* he raised up in their stead, them Joshua circumcised: for they were uncircumcised, because they had not circumcised 8 them by the way. And it came to pass, when they had done circumcising all the people, that they abode in their 9 places in the camp, till they were whole. And the LORD said unto Joshua, *This* day have I rolled away the reproach of Egypt from off you. Wherefore the name of the place is called Gilgal unto this day.

6. *forty years*] See Num. xiv. 33; Deut. i. 3, ii. 7, 14.

a land that floweth with milk and honey] For this expression compare Exod. iii. 8, 17, xiii. 5; Lev. xx. 24; Num. xiii. 27, xvi. 14; Deut. vi. 3. "Milk and honey are productions of a land rich in grass and flowers. Both articles were abundantly produced in Canaan, even in a state of devastation. Milk, eaten partly sweet and partly curdled, that of cows as well as of goats and sheep (Deut. xxxii. 14), was prominent in the diet of the ancient Hebrews, as in that of the Orientals of the present day. The land yielded great quantities of honey also, especially that from wild bees (Judg. xiv. 8; 1 Sam. xiv. 26; Matt. iii. 4), and still yields it in its wasted condition." Keil.

8. *they abode in their places*] Keil observes that those for whom the rite was not now needed, would be sufficient to defend the camp at Gilgal, although the terror consequent upon the passage of the Jordan would have been sufficient to ensure their safety against all hostile attacks.

9. *the reproach of Egypt*] This may be explained as (i) the reproach, which had attached to the people all the way from Egypt, where the nation had been a people of slaves; comp. Gen. xxxiv. 14; 1 Sam. xvii. 26; as (ii) referring to the taunts and reproaches actually levelled by the Egyptians against the Israelites, because of their long wanderings in the desert, and the disappointment of their hopes to obtain a "rest" in Canaan. (Comp. Exod. xxxii. 12; Num. xiv. 13—16; Deut. ix. 28.)

10—12. *Celebration of the Passover. Cessation of the Manna.*

And the children of Israel encamped in Gilgal, and kept 10 the passover on the fourteenth day of the month at even in the plains of Jericho. And they did eat of the old corn of 11

Gilgal] i.e. **the Rolling**. "And þe name of þat place is clepid Galgala," Wyclif. It would seem that this was the name of the place before the Exodus, for the Canaanites are described as living "over against Gilgal" in Deut. xi. 30. Its site is fixed by Josephus 50 furlongs from the Jordan and 10 from Jericho (*Antiq.* v. 1. 4), which would be at or near the modern village of *er-Riha*. It does not seem that a new name was given to the place now; but rather that a new meaning and significancy were attached to the old name, the word *Gilgal* denoting a "circle," and also a "rolling away."

10—12. CELEBRATION OF THE PASSOVER. CESSATION OF THE MANNA.

10. *And the children of Israel encamped in Gilgal*] The camp became permanent, and probably in grateful memorial of the many associations connected with the place, the people made it for centuries the great gathering-place of the tribes (Josh. ix. 6, x. 6, 43). The following notices of its subsequent history are deserving of attention. (*a*) It was the site of the Tabernacle during the continuance of the wars and until its removal to Shiloh; (*b*) It was one of the three assize towns, where Samuel administered justice (1 Sam. vii. 16); (*c*) It was here that Samuel and Saul held solemn assemblies, as also David on his return from exile (comp. 1 Sam. x. 8, xi. 14, xv. 12; 2 Sam. xix. 15); (*d*) after the building of the Temple, it became more and more neglected, but was the site of a school of the prophets, who remained there till a late period (2 Kings ii. 5).

and kept the passover] Their "reproach" having been "rolled away," the people of God would renew the festive remembrance of their deliverance from Egypt.

on the fourteenth day] Comp. Exod. xii. 6, 18; Deut. xvi. 6. As the night of the first Passover was one of terror and judgment to Egypt, so now, while within view of the camp at Gilgal, Israel was keeping the first Passover on the soil of Palestine, "Jericho was straitly shut up because of the children of Israel, none went out, and none came in." (Josh. vi. 1.)

11. *of the old corn*] Rather, **of the produce of the land**. "And thei eten of the fruytis of the lond in the tothir day, therf looues, and potage of the same 3eer, *etin cornys seengid and frotid in the hond.*" Wyclif. It could not have been other than the new corn just ripening at the season of the Passover (Lev. xxiii. 11), not "the old corn," of which no sufficient supply could have been procurable.

11, the land on the morrow after the passover, unleavened *cakes*,
12 and parched *corn* in the selfsame day. And the manna
1 ceased on the morrow after they had eaten of the old corn
of the land; neither had the children of Israel manna any
more; but they did eat of the fruit of the land of Canaan
that year.

13—15; VI. 1—5. *Appearance of the Prince of the Host of Jehovah.*

13 And it came to pass, when Joshua was by Jericho, that he
lift up his eyes and looked, and behold, there stood a man

on the morrow after the passover] In Num. xxxiii. 3 these words denote the 15th of Nisan. Here, however, they must apparently mean the 16th. For the people could not lawfully eat of the new corn, till the firstfruits had been "waved before the Lord," which was done "on the morrow after the Sabbath," i.e. the morrow after the first day of unleavened bread; this, though not necessarily the seventh day of the week, was to be observed as a Sabbath, and therefore is so called. (Comp. Lev. xxiii. 7, 11, 14.)
unleavened cakes] according to the requirements of the Law, Exod. xii. 8, 15.
parched corn] i.e. roasted harvest ears.
12. *the manna ceased*] For the first time since leaving Sinai the Passover cakes were not made of manna, for the people had now arrived in Canaan, and no longer needed this "Bread of the Wilderness." Day after day, for forty years, there had appeared "on the face of the wilderness a small round thing, as small as the hoar frost, white, like coriander seed," the taste of which "was like wafers made with honey" (Exod. xvi. 14—36). Day by day, except on the Sabbath, it had been gathered, and had been found sufficient for their daily wants. Now it suddenly ceased. The people no longer needed this "angels' food" (Ps. lxxviii. 25), but "they did eat of the fruit of the land of Canaan." Comp. John vi. 31, 49, 58; Rev. ii. 17.

13—15; VI. 1—5. APPEARANCE OF THE PRINCE OF THE HOST OF JEHOVAH.

13. *when Joshua was by Jericho*] having as yet received no special instructions as to the mode in which he was to attack Jericho, though the people, whom he led, were altogether untrained for such a work,
he lift up his eyes and looked] Compare the expression used in Gen. xviii. 2 of Abraham as "he sat in the tent door in the heat of the day" under the terebinth of Mamre, and "he *lift up his eyes* and looked and lo."
a man] Some have supposed He was a created being, others, with far greater reason, that He was none other than HE, Who had already "manifested Himself" to Abraham (Gen. xii. 7, xviii. 2), and to Moses

vv. 14, 15; 1.]   JOSHUA, V. VI.   55

over against him with his sword drawn in his hand: and
Joshua went unto him, and said unto him, *Art* thou for us,
or for our adversaries? And he said, Nay; but *as* captain 14
of the host of the LORD am I now come. And Joshua fell
on his face to the earth, and did worship, and said unto him,
What saith my lord unto his servant? And the captain of 15
the LORD'S host said unto Joshua, Loose thy shoe from off
thy foot; for the place whereon thou standest *is* holy. And
Joshua did so. Now Jericho was straitly shut up because of 6

in the "Burning Bush" (Exod. iii. 2, 6), "the Word of God," Who
"alone hath ever declared" or revealed the Father (John i. 18).

with his sword drawn in his hand] Compare the appearance of the
Cherub at the Gate of Paradise (Gen. iii. 24), and of the Angel who
meets Balaam in the way (Num. xxii. 31).

and Joshua went unto him] This shews that the appearance was not
a mere waking vision. Joshua goes up to the mysterious Warrior and
addresses him.

14. *as captain*] or rather, **Prince of the host of Jehovah**, i.e. of the
Angelic Host, the Host of heaven. "I am prince of þe oost of þe Lord,"
Wyclif. Compare the expressions "Jehovah of hosts," or more fully
"Jehovah, Lord of hosts" (Jer. v. 14, xv. 16; Isai. vi. 3; Ps. xxiv. 10,
lxxx. 7, 19). "Not as mingling with these earthly hosts, but as they fol-
low in a higher order; as the mighty ONE in heavenly places of whom thou
art here and now on earth the type and shadow; as He whom all the
Angels worship, as the Uncreated Angel of the Covenant, as the Captain
of the heavenly host of God, have I come to thee." Bp Wilberforce's
Heroes of Hebrew History, p. 148. Comp. 1 Sam. i. 3; 1 Kings xxii. 19.
The Prince of the Angels of heaven had come to lead Israel in the
impending strife.

And Joshua fell on his face] Compare the attitude (*a*) of Abraham
before God (Gen. xvii. 3); (*b*) of his brethren before Joseph (Gen. xlii. 6);
(*c*) of Moses at the Burning Bush (Exod. iii. 6). It does not *necessarily
and of itself* imply worship, though such is intended here.

What saith my lord...?] The revelation, with which Joshua was now
favoured, forcibly recalls the incident of the "Burning Bush" at Horeb.
Not however in fiery flame, but in the person of a seemingly human
warrior, was the Divine Presence manifested to the leader of the armies
of Israel. Thus the first and the second Joshua met, and the Type fell
prostrate before the Antitype.

15. *Loose thy shoe*] "Vnlace thi schoo fro thi feet," Wyclif. Comp.
Exod. iii. 5. It was a mark of reverence to cast off the sandals in ap-
proaching a place or person of eminent sanctity.

VI. 1. *Now Jericho*] This verse is strictly parenthetical, and states
the Historical circumstance which gave occasion for this Divine inter-
vention.

was straitly shut up] Vulg. "clausa erat atque munita." "Was closid
and waardid," Wyclif. Straitly = **strictly, closely**. Comp. Gen. xliii. 7,

the children of Israel: none went out, and none came in. 2 And the LORD said unto Joshua, See, I have given into thine hand Jericho, and the king thereof, *and* the mighty 3 men of valour. And ye shall compass the city, all *ye* men of war, *and* go round about the city once. Thus shalt thou do 4 six days. And seven priests shall bear before the ark seven trumpets of rams' horns: and the seventh day ye shall

"The man asked us *straitly* of our state." Shakespeare, *Richard III.* I. 1. 85, 86:

"His majesty hath *straitly* given in charge,
That no man shall have private conference."

2. *And the Lord said*] The interview between the Hebrew leader and "the Prince of Jehovah's host" is here resumed.

See, I have given] Compare for a similar expression Josh. xi. 6. As Israel had stood on the shores of the Red Sea and seen "the salvation of God," so now they were themselves to adopt no warlike measures for the capture of the city, everything was to be done *for* them, not *by* them: the victory when achieved was to be one, "into which no feeling of pride or self-exaltation could enter."

3. *ye shall compass the city*] The scene to be witnessed from the walls of Jericho, was calculated in the most striking manner to appeal to the consciences of all who should see it:

(*a*) First in solemn procession were to advance armed men:
(*b*) Then would follow seven priests blowing continually, not the customary silver trumpets, but large horns:
(*c*) Thus heralded, was to follow the Ark of Jehovah borne by the priests:
(*d*) Then were to follow "the rereward" of Israel.

Six days was this strange procession to encompass the walls of Jericho, passing round in solemn silence, save for the long-drawn blasts of the horns. But on the seventh day, the city was to be encompassed seven times, and at the seventh the people were to shout, and it was promised that the city should "fall down flat," and its destruction would be complete. "The ark of God, with the tables of stone from Sinai hidden within, was the genius, I had almost said the general, of that mysterious march: it was made plain by every token, that God, not man, was at work. Their priests were officiating, with the emblems of festival, not of warfare —"the trumpets of jubilee"—in their hands; before them armed hosts heralding, behind them armed hosts attending, the progress of the true Champion, the representative of the God of battles, to whose presence alone the coming victory was to be due." Dr Vaughan's *Heroes of Faith*, p. 253.

4. *trumpets of rams' horns*] Rather, **trumpets of soundings**, or, of **jubilee**; "seuen trompes, vhose use is in the jubile." Not the long straight trumpets generally used, but the same kind that were to be employed on the first day of the seventh month (Lev. xxiii. 24), and to announce the year of Jubilee (Lev. xxv. 9). This instrument was

compass the city seven times, and the priests shall blow with the trumpets. And it shall come to pass, *that* when *they* make a long blast with the ram's horn, *and* when ye hear the sound of the trumpet, all the people shall shout *with* a great shout; and the wall of the city shall fall down flat, and the people shall ascend up every man straight before him.

6—21. *Capture and Destruction of Jericho.*

And Joshua the son of Nun called the priests, and said unto them, Take up the ark of the covenant, and let seven priests bear seven trumpets of rams' horns before the ark of the LORD. And he said unto the people, Pass on, and compass the city, and let him that is armed pass on before the ark of the LORD. And it came to pass, when Joshua had spoken unto the people, that the seven priests bearing the seven trumpets of rams' horns passed on before the LORD, and blew with the trumpets: and the ark of the covenant of

curved, and would be more accurately rendered "**cornet**," as in 1 Chron. xv. 28; 2 Chron. xv. 14; Ps. xcviii. 6; Hos. v. 8; Dan. iii. 5.

seven] Observe the significance here of the number: *seven* priests; *seven* horns; *seven* days of compassing the walls; *seven* repetitions of it on the *seventh* day. The influence of the number "seven" was not restricted to the Hebrews. It prevailed among the Persians (Esth. i. 10, 14), among the ancient Indians, to a certain extent among the Greeks and Romans, and probably among all nations where the week of seven days was established, as in Egypt, Arabia, China. Amongst the Hebrews seven days were appointed as the length of the Feasts of Passover and Tabernacles; seven days for the ceremonies of the consecration of priests; seven victims were to be offered on any special occasion; and at the ratification of a treaty, the notion of *seven* was embodied in the very term signifying to swear, literally meaning *to do seven times* (Gen. xxi. 28). The number seven was thus impressed with the seal of sanctity as the symbol of all connected with the Deity, with the subordinate notions of perfection or completeness. See Smith's *Bibl. Dict.* Art. "Seven."

5. *every man straight before him*] Over the prostrate walls the Israelites were to advance into Jericho, and "each one straight forward," so that, as far as possible, their order should be preserved. Compare the march of the locusts as described by Joel ii. 7, "like men of war they climb a wall, and every one marches *on his way.*"

6—21. CAPTURE AND DESTRUCTION OF JERICHO.

6. *And Joshua*] In obedience to the commands thus received Joshua implicitly carries out the instructions given him and issues the needful orders to the host.

9 the LORD followed them. And the armed men went before the priests that blew *with* the trumpets, and the rereward came after the ark, *the priests* going on, and blowing with the 10 trumpets. And Joshua had commanded the people, saying, Ye shall not shout, nor make any noise with your voice, neither shall *any* word proceed out of your mouth, until the 11 day I bid you shout; then shall ye shout. So the ark of the LORD compassed the city, going about *it* once: and they 12 came *into* the camp, and lodged in the camp. And Joshua rose early in the morning, and the priests took up the ark of 13 the LORD. And seven priests bearing seven trumpets of rams' horns before the ark of the LORD went on continually, and blew with the trumpets: and the armed men went before them; but the rereward came after the ark of the LORD, *the* 14 *priests* going on, and blowing with the trumpets. And the second day they compassed the city once, and returned *into* 15 the camp: so they did six days. And it came to pass on the seventh day, that they rose early about the dawning of the day, and compassed the city after the same manner

9. *the rereward*] The remaining warriors were to act as a rearguard. During the march through the wilderness this duty devolved on the tribe of Dan (see Num. x. 25). "Rereward" means the "rearguard" of an army; *guard* and *ward* being related as *guise* and *wise*, Fr. *guerre*, and E. *war*. It is a corruption of the Fr. *arrière-garde*, as *vanguard* for *avant-garde;* or rather the first part of the word is formed from the O. Fr. *riere* (Lat. *retro*). Comp. 1 Sam. xxix. 2, "but David and his men passed on *in the rereward* with Achish;" Isai. lii. 12, "the God of Israel will be your *rereward;*" Isai. lviii. 8, "the glory of the Lord shall be *thy rereward;*" Shakespeare, *I. Hen. VI.* III. 3,

"Now in the *rearward* comes the duke, and his;"

Rom. and Jul. III. 2,

"But with a *rearward* following Tybalt's death,
Romeo is banished."

10. *Ye shall not shout*] These instructions demanded the exercise of the utmost self-control, and the exercise also of signal trust in Him, Who had appointed such a mysterious method for the capture of the city.

11. *and they came into the camp*] On the evening of the first day and the six succeeding days they returned to their encampment at Gilgal to spend the night.

15. *about the dawning of the day*] On this day the circuit had to be made seven times, and therefore the march had to be commenced very early.

seven times: only on that day they compassed the city seven times. And it came to pass at the seventh time, when the 16 priests blew with the trumpets, Joshua said unto the people, Shout; for the LORD hath given you the city. And the city 17 shall be accursed, *even* it, and all that *are* therein, to the LORD: only Rahab the harlot shall live, she and all that *are* with her in the house, because she hid the messengers that we sent. And you, in any wise keep *yourselves* from the 18 accursed thing, lest ye make *yourselves* accursed, when ye

17. *the city shall be accursed*] "be this cyte cursid" (Wyclif), or, as in margin, *devoted*. The verb from which the word comes denotes (i) *to cut off*, (ii) *to devote*, to withdraw from common use and consecrate to God=*sacrare*. (i) The word itself, used actively, means the devotement of anything by Jehovah, His putting it under a ban, the result of which is destruction; comp. 1 Kings xx. 42, "Because thou hast let go out of thy hand a man whom *I appointed to utter destruction;*" Isai. xxxiv. 5, "Behold, it (my sword) shall come down upon Idumea, and upon the people of *my curse*, to judgment;" Zech. xiv. 11, "there shall be no more *utter destruction;* but Jerusalem shall be safely inhabited." (ii) And passively, the word denotes *the thing devoted*, doomed, laid under the ban, i. e. devoted to Jehovah without the possibility of being redeemed; comp. Lev. xxvii. 21, "But the field, when it goeth out in the jubilee, shall be holy unto the Lord, as a field *devoted;*" Lev. xxvii. 29, "None devoted, which shall be *devoted* of men, shall be redeemed." The word is used here in the latter sense, and in verses 17, 18, with which compare Josh. vii. 1, "Achan......took of *the accursed* thing," and 1 Sam. xv. 3—9. The Greek word with the same meaning, *Anathema*, frequently occurs in St Paul's writings, comp. Rom. ix. 3, "I could wish that myself were *accursed* from Christ for my brethren;" 1 Cor. xvi. 22, "If any man love not the Lord Jesus Christ, let him be *Anathema;*" comp. also 1 Cor. xii. 3; Gal. i. 9. We find similar instances of devotion to utter destruction amongst other nations; comp. (*a*) the *Ver sacrum* of the Romans, so frequently alluded to in Livy, as XXII. 9, 10; XXXIV. 44; (*b*) Cæsar's testimony concerning the Gauls, *Bell. Gall.* VI. 17, "Huic (Marti), cum prælio dimicare constituerunt, ea quæ bello ceperint, plerumque *devovent;* cum superaverunt, animalia capta *immolant;*" (*c*) Tacitus (*Ann.* XIII. 57) tells us of the Hermunduri that they were successful in a war against the Catti, "quia victores diversam aciem *Marti ac Mercurio sacravere*, quo voto equi, viri, cuncta victa occidioni dantur;" (*d*) Livy III. 55 mentions a law passed under the consuls L. Valerius and M. Horatius, "ut qui tribunis plebis, ædilibus, judicibus, decemviris nocuisset, ejus caput *Jovi sacrum esset;* familia ad ædem Cereris Liberi Liberæque venum iret."

only Rahab the harlot] See above, ii. 1, 18, 19.

18. *in any wise keep yourselves*] A warning, which Achan neglected to the destruction of himself and his family. See chap. vii.

take of the accursed thing, and make the camp of Israel a
19 curse, and trouble it. But all the silver, and gold, and
vessels of brass and iron, *are* consecrated unto the LORD:
20 they shall come *into* the treasury of the LORD. So the
people shouted when *the priests* blew with the trumpets: and
it came to pass, when the people heard the sound of the
trumpet, and the people shouted *with* a great shout, that the
wall fell down flat, so that the people went up into the city,
21 every man straight before him, and they took the city. And
they utterly destroyed all that *was* in the city, both man and

19. *are consecrated*] Or, as in the margin, **are holiness unto the Lord**: "to ye Lord be it halowid," Wyclif.
into the treasury of the Lord] Comp. Num. xxxi. 22, 23, 50—54. In the case of Jericho, the whole city, with all that it contained, was *cherem* or "devoted."
20. *the wall fell down flat*] No hand of man interposed to bring about this catastrophe, no merely natural causes precipitated the fall; "*by faith*," as the author of the Epistle to the Hebrews declares, "the walls of Jericho fell down" (Heb. xi. 30). "When we examine the operation of faith in this instance, we shall see the point of the example to be in the refraining from action at the bidding of God. The impulse of nature was to attack the city; to try upon its bulwarks the skill of military science, as then understood, as by them possessed. The power of faith was shown in curbing that impulse; in submitting to an unexplained, unintelligible, severely trying, edict of inactivity; nay in consenting to play what must have seemed a ridiculous part, in the face of a warlike and disciplined host, waiting to see what this intrusive, this presumptuous horde of rovers had to say for itself." To escort the Ark, "day after day for a whole week, round and round the ramparts of Jericho, crowded doubtless with armed spectators; to do this with a ceremonial which could be imposing only to themselves—which must have been not so much mysterious as ludicrous to the established ideas of the world, and even to those 'thoughts of the heart' which are busy in all of us, and which are the peculiar property neither of Jew nor Greek—must have taxed to the uttermost farthing the loyalty, the religion, and the moral courage of Israel; we can scarcely explain it otherwise than by saying that it was 'by faith,' in other words, that their apprehension of the invisible rose above the counteracting influences of the present, and enabled them to say within themselves, 'We ought to obey God rather than man.'" Dr Vaughan's *Heroes of Faith*, p. 257.
21. *they utterly destroyed*] In the instance of the other cities of Canaan, as in those of Sihon and Og, the inhabitants were destroyed, but the cattle were preserved. Comp. (*a*) Josh. viii. 26, x. 28; (*b*) Deut. ii. 34, iii. 6. In the case of Jericho not only the inhabitants, but the cattle also were destroyed.

woman, young and old, and ox, and sheep, and ass, with the edge of the sword.

22—25. *The Rescue of Rahab.*

But Joshua had said unto the two men that had spied out 22 the country, Go *into* the harlot's house, and bring out thence the woman, and all that she hath, as ye sware unto her. And the young men that were spies went in, and brought 23 out Rahab, and her father, and her mother, and her brethren, and all that she had; and they brought out all her kindred, and left them without the camp of Israel. And they burnt 24 the city with fire, and all that *was* therein: only the silver, and the gold, and the vessels of brass and of iron, they put *into* the treasury of the house of the LORD. And Joshua 25 saved Rahab the harlot alive, and her father's household, and all that she had; and she dwelleth in Israel *even* unto this day; because she hid the messengers, which Joshua sent to spy out Jericho.

the edge of the sword] Comp. Gen. xxxiv. 26, and many places in Joshua.

22—25. THE RESCUE OF RAHAB.

22. *Go into the harlot's house*] We are told that Rahab's house was *upon the town wall*, and that she dwelt *upon the wall*. But though the walls of Jericho fell down flat, her house was preserved. They fell by *faith*, and she was saved by *faith* (Heb. xi. 30, 31).

as ye sware unto her] See above, ii. 14.

23. *the young men*] Vulg. *juvenes*. Comp. Gen. xxii. 3, "And Abraham rose up early......and took *two* of *his young men* with him;" Judg. viii. 20, "And he said unto Jether his firstborn, Up, and slay them. But *the youth* drew not his sword."

all her kindred] Heb. **families**.

without the camp of Israel] Comp. Lev. xxiv. 14; Num. xxxi. 19. As heathen, they were unclean, and must therefore remain a specified time, probably seven days, "without the camp."

25. *she dwelleth in Israel*] These words do not *necessarily* imply that she was alive at the time the Book of Joshua was written, but that the family of strangers, of which she was reckoned the head, continued to dwell among the children of Israel. She married Salmon, of the tribe of Judah, and became the ancestress of Boaz, the husband of Ruth. See Matt. i. 5. Her reception into the Jewish Church, and her mention in the genealogy of Christ, were a pledge and earnest of the reception of the Gentile world, and of the grafting of the wild olive into the good olive-tree (Rom. xi. 24).

26, 27. *The Curse upon Jericho.*

26 And Joshua adjured *them* at that time, saying, Cursed *be* the man before the LORD, that riseth up and buildeth this city Jericho: he shall lay the foundation thereof in his firstborn, and in his youngest *son* shall he set up the gates of it. 27 So the LORD was with Joshua; and his fame was [*noised*] throughout all the country.

26, 27. THE CURSE UPON JERICHO.

26. *adjured them*] i. e. "put an oath upon them."

Cursed be the man] A city, which was *cherem* or "devoted," could not be rebuilt, Deut. xiii. 15, 16, 17. Joshua therefore pronounces an imprecation on the foundation of Jericho. The words "have a rhythmical and antistrophical form; which was probably adopted for greater solemnity, and to impress them more deeply on the memories of the people." Bp Wordsworth.

and buildeth] So Agamemnon is said to have uttered a curse upon Ilium, and Scipio upon Carthage. Here the curse is to be understood as extending only to the walls and gates of Jericho, or a *fortified place*, on which, as bidding proud defiance to the host, the attention of Joshua, as a military leader, would chiefly fasten. Comp. 1 Kings xv. 17; 2 Chron. xi. 5. He himself gave it to the Benjamites (Josh. xviii. 21), and it was inhabited in the time of the Judges (Judg. iii. 13; 2 Sam. x. 5).

he shall lay the foundation] What the prophecy foretells is that the beginning of the building would be marked by the death of the builder's eldest son, and the end of it by the death of his youngest. Comp. Jos. *Antiq.* v. 1. 8. In the ungodly reign of Ahab the prophecy was fulfilled; Hiel, a native of Bethel, "built Jericho; he laid the foundation thereof in Abiram his firstborn, and set up the gates thereof in his youngest son Segub, according to the word of the Lord, which he spake by Joshua" (1 Kings xvi. 34). Observe the incidents connected with Jericho in the life of the Antitype of the first Joshua. Here He entered into the house of Zacchæus (Luke xix. 5, 9); here He healed blind Bartimæus (Mark x. 46, 52); He mentioned Jericho in the parable of "the Good Samaritan" (Luke x. 30); in the vicinity of the city He repeated the announcement of His coming sufferings (Luke xviii. 31).

27. *So the Lord was with Joshua*] He and He alone had achieved the victory for His people, and they had "stood still" and "seen the salvation of Jehovah" (Exod. xiv. 13; 2 Chron. xx. 17):—

(*a*) The entrance into Canaan itself had been effected by the miraculous receding of the waters of the Jordan;

(*b*) The walls of the city had fallen down flat, not before Israel, but before the Ark of Jehovah, Whose presence was ever connected with its golden Mercy-Seat;

(*c*) When it had been bestowed upon the people as *a free gift*, without any effort on their part, all that it contained was devoted

1—5. *The Sin of Achan, and Assault on Ai.*

But the children of Israel committed a trespass in the 7 accursed thing: for Achan, the son of Carmi, the son of Zabdi, the son of Zerah, of the tribe of Judah, took of the accursed thing: and the anger of the LORD was kindled against the children of Israel. And Joshua sent men from 2 Jericho *to* Ai, which *is* beside Beth-aven, on the east side of

entirely to the Lord, nothing in the way of *gain* was to be made out of it;
(*d*) The means they had been allowed to employ as preliminary to the capture were such as could not fail to make them a scorn and derision to the proud warriors of the Doomed City, and so called into exercise, in a striking degree, their faith, patience, and obedience.

CH. VII. 1—5. THE SIN OF ACHAN, AND ASSAULT ON AI.

1. *committed a trespass*] The word used here in the Septuagint Version is very striking. It is the same as that employed in Acts v. 1, 2 to describe the sin of Ananias and Sapphira. They *took for themselves, appropriated to themselves, sequestered from God*, a portion of what had been devoted to Him at Jericho. Wyclif renders it "mystoken of the halewid thing."
for Achan] Or, *Achar*, as he is called in 1 Chron. ii. 7.
the son of Zabdi] Or, *Zimri*, as his name is given in 1 Chron. ii. 6.
took of the accursed thing] What he took is more fully described in verse 21. His sin was rendered more heinous by the fact that he knew full well the ban which had been pronounced upon the doomed city, a ban extending to all time, and including even the whole family of any who should dare to restore the fortifications of Jericho. Cæsar in his account of the devotion of conquered towns to the gods amongst the Gauls, alluded to above, VI. 17, goes on to say, "Multis in civitatibus harum rerum exstructos tumulos locis consecratis conspicari licet: neque sæpe accidit, ut neglecta quispiam religione, aut *capta apud se occultare, aut posita tollere auderet; gravissimumque ei rei supplicium cum cruciatu constitutum est*" (*Bell. Gall.* VI. 17).
2. *from Jericho to Ai*] The country of Canaan seems in the time of Joshua to have been broken up into a number of small territories, each governed by an independent chief or "king," who extended his rule from his fortified citadel to the district round. In Josh. xii. 7—24, we find mention of no less than 32 such "kings." A series of sieges, therefore, rather than of pitched battles, might be expected to characterise the campaigns of Joshua.
which is beside Beth-aven] Ai had been already mentioned in Gen. xii. 8, in connection with the history of Abraham, who is said to have removed from Shechem "to a mountain on the east of Bethel, and pitched his tent, having Bethel on the west, and *Hai* on the east." Though

64   JOSHUA, VII.   [vv. 3—5.

Beth-el, and spake unto them, saying, Go up and view the
3 country. And the men went up and viewed Ai. And they
returned to Joshua, and said unto him, Let not all the
people go up;˙ *but* let about two or three thousand men go
up and smite Ai; *and* make not all the people to labour
4 thither; for they *are but* few. So there went up thither
of the people about three thousand men: and they fled
5 before the men of Ai. And the men of Ai smote of them
about thirty and six men: for they chased them *from* before
the gate *even* unto Shebarim, and smote them in the going

smaller than Jericho, Ai was a position of great importance; (*a*) It
dominated the road to Jerusalem, then called Jebus, and was situated only
a few hours distant; (*b*) It commanded the approaches into the heart of
the country, and especially the fertile district of Samaria; (*c*) Its fall
virtually involved that of Bethel. Beth-aven lay between Bethel and
Michmash (1 Sam. xiii. 5, xiv. 23). In Hos. iv. 15, v. 8, x. 5, the
name is transferred, with a play upon the word characteristic of the
prophet, to the neighbouring Bethel, once the "house of God," but
then the house of idols, or "naught."

the east side of Beth-el] Bethel, formerly Luz (Gen. xxviii. 19), was an
ancient Canaanitish royal city. The name Bethel existed, it would
seem, as early as the time of Abraham, who removed from the oaks of
Mamre to the "mountain on the east of *Bethel*" (Gen. xii. 8).
Here he built an altar, and hither he returned from Egypt with Lot
before their separation (Gen. xiii. 3, 4). Even in those early times a
distinction seems to have been drawn between the "city" of Luz and
the consecrated "place" in its neighbourhood (Gen. xxxv. 7) called
"Bethel" by Jacob (*a*) Gen. xxviii. 19, (*b*) Gen. xxxv. 14, 15, which
name does not appear to have been appropriated to the city itself till
after the conquest by Joshua (Josh. xvi. 1, 2; Judg. i. 22—26).

Go up and view the country] So important did the Hebrew leader
deem the position of Ai that he resolved to repeat the tactics already
pursued at Jericho, and to send spies to "view the country." For the
use of "view"=to "survey," "review," comp. Ezra viii. 15, "and I
viewed the people and the priests, and found there none of the sons of
Levi;" and Hall, *Henry V*., "Before whose arriuall the kyng was departed from Wyndsor to Winchester, entending to haue gone to Hamp-
ton and to haue *vewed* his nauie." Shakespeare, *Henry V*. II. 4. 21,

" Therefore, I say, 'tis meet we all go forth
To *view* the sick and feeble parts of France."

See *Bible Word Book*, pp. 511, 512.
5. *unto Shebarim*] So called, perhaps, from the **mines**, or **stone
quarries**, which lay in the neighbourhood. The LXX. translates "*till
they had crushed* or *annihilated them*."

mouth of the LORD. And Joshua made peace with them, 15 and made a league with them, to let them live: and the princes of the congregation sware unto them.

And it came to pass at the end of three days after they 16 had made a league with them, that they heard that they *were* their neighbours, and *that* they dwelt among them. And the children of Israel journeyed, and came unto their 17 cities on the third day. Now their cities *were* Gibeon, and Chephirah, and Beeroth, and Kirjath-jearim. And the chil- 18 dren of Israel smote them not, because the princes of the congregation had sworn unto them by the LORD God of

Joshua by means of the Sacred Oracle, the Urim and Thummim; "at his word shall they go out, and at his word they shall come in, both he, and all the children of Israel with him" (Num. xxvii. 21). See also Exod. xxviii. 30. Against any league with the inhabitants of Canaan they had been specially warned (Exod. xxiii. 32, xxxiv. 12; Num. xxxiii. 55; Deut. vii. 2).

17. *on the third day*] A three days' journey it might well be "according to the slow pace of eastern armies and caravans." Stanley's *S. & P.* p. 209.

Chephirah] "a village," afterwards allotted to Benjamin (Josh. xviii. 26). It was an inhabited city in the times of Ezra and Nehemiah (Ezra ii. 25; Neh. vii. 29). On the western declivity of the mountain range, 11 miles from Jerusalem, and 4 from Kirjath-jearim, is a ruined village called *Kefir*, which doubtless marks the site of the old city of Chephirah. After remaining unknown, or at least unnoticed, for more than 2000 years, its site was discovered by Dr Robinson in 1852. See Robinson, *Bible Res.* III. 146.

Beeroth] Mentioned afterwards along with other Benjamite cities among the places whose inhabitants returned with Zerubbabel (Ezra ii. 25; Neh. vii. 29). It is commonly identified with the large village of *El-Bireh* between Jerusalem and Bethel.

Kirjath-jearim] i.e. "*the city of woods,*" or "*groves,*" written *Kirjath-arim* in Ezra ii. 25, and *Kiriathiarius* in 1 Esdr. v. 19. It derived its name from its olive, fig, and other plantations, as its modern representative, *Kuriet-el-Enab*, "the city of grapes," does from its vineyards. It was afterwards allotted to Judah, and here the Ark remained from the time of its return from the Philistines to the reign of David (1 Sam. vii. 2; 2 Sam. vi. 2; 1 Chron. xiii. 5, 6; Ps. cxxxii. 6), where David is said to have found the Ark in "the fields of the wood." Before the Israelitish conquest it was known as Baalah and Kirjath-baal (Josh. xv. 9, 60), names which point to its early sanctity as one of the special seats of the worship of Baal.

18. *had sworn unto them*] The remembrance of the league was kept up through the whole course of the subsequent history. A terrible trial befell the nation because Saul had massacred certain of the Gibeonites

Israel. And all the congregation murmured against the
19 princes. But all the princes said unto all the congregation,
We have sworn unto them by the LORD God of Israel: now
20 therefore we may not touch them. This we will do to
them; we will even let them live, lest wrath be upon us,
21 because of the oath which we sware unto them. And the
princes said unto them, Let them live; but let them be
hewers of wood and drawers of water unto all the congrega-
22 tion; as the princes had promised them. And Joshua
called for them, and he spake unto them, saying, Wherefore
have ye beguiled us, saying, We *are* very far from you; when
23 ye dwell among us? Now therefore ye *are* cursed, and
there shall none of you be freed from being bondmen, and
hewers of wood and drawers of water for the house of my
24 God. And they answered Joshua, and said, Because it was
certainly told thy servants, how that the LORD thy God
commanded his servant Moses to give you all the land, and
to destroy all the inhabitants of the land from before you,
therefore we were sore afraid of our lives because of you,
25 and have done this thing. And now, behold, we *are* in
thine hand: as it seemeth good and right unto thee to do
26 unto us, do. And so did he unto them, and delivered them
out of the hand of the children of Israel, that they slew

(2 Sam. xxi. 1, 2; 1 Sam. xxii. 18, 19), and David remained faithful to
the vow which Joshua had made.
   21. *hewers of wood and drawers of water*] "trees thei kutten and watris
thei beren," Wyclif. They were devoted to the sanctuary, called at a
later period *Nethinims = Deo dati, donati*, and were bound to discharge
menial duties which usually devolved upon the lowest classes. Comp.
Deut. xxix. 10, 11, "Ye stand this day all of you before the Lord
your God; your captains of your tribes, your elders, and your officers,
with all the men of Israel, your little ones, your wives, and thy stranger
that is in thy camp, from *the hewer of thy wood unto the drawer of thy
water*." Compare also 1 Chron. ix. 2; Ezra ii. 43, 70; Neh. vii. 46, 60.
   23. *ye are cursed*] Comp. Gen. ix. 25.
   24. *the Lord thy God commanded*] See Deut. vii. 1, 2.
   we were sore afraid] Fear had been their sole motive in seeking an
alliance with Israel. Theirs was not the faith, which had prompted
Rahab to save the spies.
   25. *we are in thine hand*] Compare the words of Abraham to Sarah,
"Behold, thy maid *is in thy hand; do to her as it pleaseth thee*"
(Gen. xvi. 6).

them not. And Joshua made them that day hewers of wood 27 and drawers of water for the congregation, and for the altar of the LORD, *even* unto this day, in the place which he should choose.

1—6. *Confederacy of the Five Kings against Gibeon.*

Now it came to pass, when Adoni-zedek king of Jerusa- 10 lem had heard how Joshua had taken Ai, and had utterly

26. *delivered them out of the hand of the children of Israel*] who would have certainly been glad to destroy them.

27. *made them that day*] It is deserving of notice that the Gibeonites never appear to have betrayed their trust, or enticed Israel into idolatry.

CH. X. 1—6. CONFEDERACY OF THE FIVE KINGS AGAINST GIBEON.

1. *Now it came to pass*] The surrender of such a place as Gibeon would naturally fill the kings of southern Canaan with alarm. "It was, so to speak, treason within their own camp." The invaders had obtained a strong position in the very heart of the country, while the possession of the passes from Gibeon would expose the whole south of Canaan to their incursions. The retaking and punishment of Gibeon was the first object of the chieftains of the south.

Adoni-zedek] i.e. "*Lord of righteousness.*" It is no longer Melchizedek, "My king righteousness." The alteration of the name marks a change of dynasties.

king of Jerusalem] "the habitation of peace," or "the possession of peace."

(i) This world-famous city was (*a*) sometimes called after its original inhabitants "*Jebus*" (Judg. xix. 10, 11; 1 Chron. xi. 4); (*b*) sometimes "*the city of the Jebusites*" (Judg. xix. 11), or "*Jebusi*" (Josh. xviii. 16, 28; 2 Sam. v. 8); (*c*) sometimes "Salem"="peace" (Gen. xiv. 18; Ps. lxxvi. 2); (*d*) once "*the city of Judah*" (2 Chron. xxv. 28); (*e*) finally "*Jerusalem*" (Josh. x. 1, xii. 10; Judg. i. 7, &c.).

(ii) It stands in latitude 31° 46′ 39″ North, and longitude 35° 14′ 42″ East of Greenwich, and is 32 miles distant from the sea, and 18 from the Jordan; 20 from Hebron, and 36 from Samaria.

(iii) Its situation is in several respects singular. Its elevation is remarkable, but is occasioned not from its being on the summit of one of the numerous hills of Judæa, but on the edge of one of the highest table-lands of the country. From every side, except the south, the ascent to it is perpetual, and it must always have presented the appearance, beyond any important city that has ever existed on the earth, of a "*mountain city, enthroned on a mountain fortress.*"

(iv) But besides being thus elevated more than 2500 feet above the level of the sea, it was separated by deep and precipitous ravines from the rocky plateau of which it formed a part. These slopes surround it on the southern, south-eastern, and western sides, and out of them the

destroyed it; as he had done to Jericho and her king, so he had done to Ai and her king; and how the inhabitants of Gibeon had made peace with Israel, and were among them; 2 that they feared greatly, because Gibeon *was* a great city, as one of the royal cities, and because it *was* greater than Ai, 3 and all the men thereof *were* mighty. Wherefore Adonizedek king of Jerusalem sent unto Hoham king of Hebron, and unto Piram king of Jarmuth, and unto Japhia king of 4 Lachish, and unto Debir king of Eglon, saying, Come up unto me, and help me, that we may smite Gibeon: for it hath made peace with Joshua and with the children of 5 Israel. Therefore the five kings of the Amorites, the king of Jerusalem, the king of Hebron, the king of Jarmuth, the king of Lachish, the king of Eglon, gathered themselves together, and went up, they and all their hosts, and en-6 camped before Gibeon, and made war against it. And the

city rose "like the walls of a fortress out of its ditches." Hence its early strength and subsequent greatness. See Stanley's *Sinai and Palestine*, p. 172; Ritter's *Geography of Palestine*, III. 1—33, IV. 3; Robinson's *Bibl. Res.* I. 258—260.

2. *as one of the royal cities*] See above, ix. 3.

3. *king of Hebron*] Situated amongst the mountains, 20 Roman miles, about 7 hours, south of Jerusalem; one of the most ancient cities in the world, rivalling even Damascus, being a well-known town even when Abraham first entered Canaan (Gen. xiii. 18). Its original name was Kirjath-Arba (Judg. i. 10), "the city of Arba," the father of Anak, and progenitor of the giant Anakims (Josh. xxi. 11, xv. 13, 14). Hoham denotes "Jehovah of the multitude."

Piram king of Jarmuth] the present *Yarmûk*, about 1½ miles from *Beit-Netif*, on the left of the road to Jerusalem. Near it is an eminence called *Tell-Ermûd*. It was visited by Robinson.

Japhia king of Lachish] Lachish has been identified with (1) *Um-Lâkis*, (2) *Zukkarijeh*, 2½ hours south-west of *Beit-Jibrîn*. It was afterwards fortified by Rehoboam (2 Chron. xi. 9). Here Amaziah died (2 Kings xiv. 19). It was besieged by Sennacherib, who moved thence to Libnah (Isai. xxxvi. 2, xxxvii. 8).

Debir king of Eglon] Lachish and Eglon are mentioned in several other passages (Josh. xii. 11, 12, xv. 39), in such a way as shews they were not far apart. Eglon has been identified with *'Ajlan*.

4. *for it hath made peace*] The enterprise was directed primarily not against Joshua, but against Gibeon which had made peace with him. Comp. ix. 15.

5. *the five kings*] The names of the kings are not given here a second time, but of the cities over which they held sway, and they are mentioned in the same order.

men of Gibeon sent unto Joshua to the camp to Gilgal, saying, Slack not thy hand from thy servants; come up to us quickly, and save us, and help us: for all the kings of the Amorites that dwell in the mountains are gathered together against us.

7—15. *The Battle of Beth-horon.*

So Joshua ascended from Gilgal, he, and all the people of 7 war with him, and all the mighty *men* of valour. And the 8 LORD said unto Joshua, Fear them not: for I have delivered them into thine hand; there shall not a man of them stand before thee. Joshua therefore came unto them suddenly, 9 *and* went up from Gilgal all night. And the LORD discom- 10 fited them before Israel, and slew them *with* a great slaughter

6. *Slack not thy hand*] The climax in the message is very noticeable; (1) slack not thy hand; (2) come up to us quickly; (3) save us; (4) help us. Compare the prayer of the persecuted Christians (Acts iv. 24—30). *Slack* = "slacken," "relax;" A. S. *slæcan* from the adjective *slæc*. It occurs in an intransitive sense in Deut. xxiii. 21, "When thou shalt vow a vow unto the Lord thy God, thou shalt not *slack* to pay it." Comp. Latimer, *Serm.* p. 231, "What a remorse of conscience shall ye have, when ye remember how ye have *slacked* your duty."

all the kings of the Amorites] This is a common designation of the five chiefs. Their march had evidently been very rapid, and the danger was urgent.

7—15. THE BATTLE OF BETH-HORON.

7. *So Joshua ascended*] "Not a moment was to be lost. As in the battle of Marathon, everything depended on the suddenness of the blow which should break in pieces the hostile confederation." Stanley's *Sinai and Palestine*, p. 209.

8. *Fear them not*] Comp. Josh. xi. 6; Judg. iv. 14.

9. *came unto them suddenly*] He marched the whole night, and in the morning, "when the sun rose behind him, he was already in the open ground at the foot of the heights of Gibeon, where the kings were encamped."

10. *And the Lord discomfited them*] "As often before and after," so now, "not a man could stand before the awe and the panic of the sudden sound of the terrible shout, the sudden appearance of that undaunted host who came with the assurance not to fear, nor to be dismayed, but to be strong and of a good courage, for the Lord had delivered their enemies into their hands." Comp. Judg. iv. 15; 1 Sam. vii. 10; 2 Sam. xxii. 15.

discomfited] Comp. Exod. xvii. 13, "And Joshua *discomfited* Amalek and his people with the edge of the sword;" 1 Sam. vii. 10, "but the Lord thundered with a great thunder on that day upon the Philistines, and *discomfited* them;" 2 Sam. xxii. 15, "he sent out

at Gibeon, and chased them *along* the way that goeth up to Beth-horon, and smote them to Azekah, and unto Makkedah. And it came to pass, as they fled from before Israel, *and* were in the going down to Beth-horon, that the LORD cast down great stones from heaven upon them unto Azekah, and they died: *they were* moe which died with hailstones than *they* whom the children of Israel slew with the sword.

arrows, and scattered them; lightning, and *discomfited* them." Discomfit comes from Fr. *déconfire*, It. *sconfiggere*, to rout, whence the substantive *sconfitta*, the original of all being the Latin *configere*, to fasten together; whence *discomfit* primarily signifies to *unfasten*; then to *disintegrate*, or break up a mass into the parts of which it is composed. Hence to break up an army, to disperse it.

before Israel] In Exod. xxiii. 27, the promise is given that God will always do so before the foes of Israel.

up to Beth-horon] or *"the House of caves."* Notice the expression "along the way that *goeth up* to Beth-horon." It was the first stage of the flight—in the long *ascent* from Gibeon towards Beth-horon the upper.

to Azekah] which lay in the Shephelah or rich agricultural plain. It was near Shochoh, and between the two places the Philistines encamped before the battle in which Goliath was killed (1 Sam. xvii. 1). It was afterwards fortified by Rehoboam (2 Chron. xi. 9), was still standing at the time of the Babylonish invasion (Jer. xxxiv. 7), and was reoccupied by the Jews after their return from the Captivity (Neh. xi. 30).

unto Makkedah] Porter would identify it with a ruin on the northern slope of the *Wady es Sunt*, bearing the somewhat similar name of *el-Klediah*. Van de Velde would place it at *Sumeil*, a village standing on a low hill 6 or 7 miles N.W. of *Beth-Jebrin*.

11. *were in the going down to Beth-horon*] This was the second stage in the flight. The Amorite host had gained the height before their pursuers, and were hurrying down the pass of nether Beth-horon, "a rough, rocky road, sometimes over the upturned edges of the limestone strata, sometimes over sheets of smooth rock, sometimes over loose rectangular stones, sometimes over steps cut in the rock" (Stanley's *Lectures*, I. 242), when

the Lord cast down great stones from heaven upon them] As afterwards in the great fight of Barak against Sisera (Judg. v. 20), one of the fearful tempests, which from time to time sweep over the hills of Palestine, burst upon the disordered army, and hailstones of enormous size fell upon their shattered ranks.

they were moe which died with hailstones] Some have explained these as meteoric stones, but it was rather a fearful storm, "thunder, lightning, and a deluge of hail," Jos. *Ant.* v. 1. 17. "By a very similar mischance the Austrians were overtaken in 1859 at the battle of Solferino." Even ordinary hailstones in Syria are often of enormous size. "I have seen some that measured two inches in diameter; but sometimes irregularly shaped pieces are found among them weigh-

v. 12.] JOSHUA, X. 87

Then spake Joshua to the LORD in the day when the 12
LORD delivered up the Amorites before the children of
Israel, and he said in the sight of Israel,

ing alone twenty drams." Russell's *Natural History of Aleppo*, I. 76. "During a storm at Constantinople in 1831, many of the hailstones, or rather masses of ice, weighed from half a pound to above a pound. Under this tremendous fall, the roofs of houses were beaten in, trees were stripped of their leaves and branches, many persons who could not soon enough find shelter were killed, animals were slain, and limbs were broken. In fact, none who know the tremendous power which the hailstones of the East sometimes exhibit, will question, as some have questioned, the possibility that any hail could produce the effect described." Kitto's *Bible Illustrations*, II. p. 293.

they were moe] "and ben deed manye *mo* with stones of haiul, than whom with swerd had smyten the sons of Yrael." Wyclif. In the edition of 1611, "moe" is the comparative of "many," and is altered to "more" in the later editions. Compare

"For elles hadde I dweld with Theseus
I-fetered in his prisoun for ever moo."
                    Chaucer, *Knight's Tale*, 1231.

Bru.   "Is he alone?
Lu. No, sir, there are *moe* with him."
                    Shakespeare, *Jul. Cæs.* II. 1. 71.

12. *Then spake Joshua to the Lord*] The quotation probably com‍mences with the 12th verse and extends to the end of the 15th. It ?
begins as follows:—

"Then spake Joshua unto Jehovah,
In the day Jehovah delivered up the Amorites before the sons of Israel."

Then] The crisis of the battle had now arrived. The day had far advanced since Joshua had emerged after his night-march through the passes of Ai. It was noon, and the sun stood high in the midst of heaven above the hills which hid Gibeon from his sight. "In front, over the western vale of Ajalon, was the faint figure of the crescent moon visible above the hailstorm (Jos. *Ant.* v. 1. 17), which was fast driving up from the sea in the valleys below." Beneath him was the Amorite host rushing in wild confusion down the western passes. The furious storm was obscuring the light of day, and the work was but half accomplished. Was the foe to make good his escape? Was the speed, with which he had "come up quickly, and saved, and helped" the defenceless Gibeonites, to be robbed of half its reward? Oh that the sun would burst forth once more from amidst the gloom that had obscured it! Oh that the day, all too short for his great undertaking, could be prolonged "until the people had avenged themselves upon their enemies"! See Stanley's *Sin. and Pal.* p. 210; Edersheim's *Israel in Canaan*, pp. 81, 82.

spake Joshua] Then it was, standing on the lofty eminence above

Sun, stand thou still upon Gibeon;
And thou, Moon, in the valley of Ajalon.
13 And the sun stood still, and the moon stayed,
Until the people had avenged themselves upon their enemies.

Gibeon, "doubtless with outstretched hand and spear," that Joshua burst forth into that ecstatic prayer of faith, which has been here incorporated into the text from the "Book of Jasher."
and he said in the sight of Israel] literally, **before the eyes of Israel**, in the sight or presence of Israel, who were witnesses of his words,
Sun, stand thou still] Literally, as in the margin, "**be silent,**" comp. Lev. x. 3, "And Aaron *held his peace.*" The word denotes (i) *to be dumb with astonishment;* (ii) *to be silent;* (iii) *to rest,* or, *be quiet.* Comp. 1 Sam. xiv. 9, "If they say thus unto us, Tarry (or *be still* as in marg.) until we come to you;" Job xxxi. 34, "Did I fear a great multitude, or did the contempt of families terrify me, *that I kept silence?*" Keil would translate it "*wait.*" The Vulgate renders it, "*Sol contra Gabaon ne movearis et luna contra vallem Ajalon;*" Wyclif thus, "Sunne, a3ens Gabaon be thow not meued, and mone, a3ens the valey of Haylon."
Gibeon...Ajalon] These spots are named as stations of the sun and moon "because Joshua, when he engaged in the battle, was probably west of Gibeon, in a place where he saw the sun shining in the east over that city, and the moon in the far west over Ajalon." The hour of utterance contemplated was probably still in the forenoon.
in the valley of Ajalon] i. e. "the valley of the gazelles." It is represented by the modern *Merj Ibn Omeir,* "a broad and beautiful valley" running in a westerly direction from the mountains towards the great western plain. The town of Ajalon was afterwards, the conquest being concluded, in the territory of Dan (Josh. xix. 42), and was assigned to the Levites (Josh. xxi. 24; 1 Chron. vi. 69). Here the Philistines were routed by Saul and Jonathan (1 Sam. xiv. 31), and the place is often mentioned in the wars with that people (1 Chron. viii. 13; 2 Chron. xxviii. 18).

13. *And the sun stood still*] God hearkened to the voice of Joshua. Once more the sunlight burst forth, and the day was miraculously protracted till the end was gained. For expressions similar to those here used compare what is said in Judg. v. 20, of the *stars* "fighting (not *in* but *out of*) their courses against Sisera;" in Isai. xxxiv. 3; Amos ix. 13; Mic. i. 4, of the *melting down* of the mountains; in Isai. lxiv. 1, of the *rending of the heavens;* in Ps. xxix. 6, of the *skipping of Lebanon;* in Isai. lv. 12, of the *clapping of hands* by the trees in the field; in Ps. xviii. 9, of the *bowing* of the heavens. How or in what way this protraction of the light was brought about we are not told.
Is not this written in the book of Jasher?] The Book here quoted is also alluded to in 2 Sam. i. 18, "Also he—David—bade them teach the children of Israel the Bow (i.e. '*the Song of the Bow*'); behold, it is written *in the Book of Jasher,*" or, as it is rendered in the margin, "*the*

Is not this written in the book of Jasher? So the sun stood still in the midst of heaven, And hasted not to go down about a whole day. And there was no day like that before it or after it, that the 14 LORD hearkened unto the voice of a man: for the LORD fought for Israel. And Joshua returned, and all Israel with him, unto the 15 camp to Gilgal.

16—27. *Flight and Execution of the Five Kings.*

But these five kings fled, and hid themselves in a cave at 16

Book of the Upright," or "*Righteous.*" It was in all probability a collection, rhythmical in form and poetical in diction, of various pieces celebrating the heroes of the Hebrew nation and their achievements. The word itself, *Jasher,* or *Jashar,* is considered to be an appellation of the Elect Nation, nearly equivalent to "*Jeshurun*" in Deut. xxxii. 15. The Book was naturally compiled only by degrees, and gradually any ode or song deemed worthy of preservation was added to it, "so that the quotation of it here is no proof at all that the Book of Joshua was composed after the date of the reference to the 'Book of Jasher' in 2 Sam. i. 18, and as little is the quotation there a proof that the 'Book of Jasher' was not extant until, at any rate, the time of David."

And hasted not to go] Edersheim would translate this, "And hasted not to go—like (as on) a complete day."

14. *And there was no day*] This is still a quotation from the Book of Jashar, or "of ristwise men," as Wyclif translates it.

"And so stood the sunne in the mydil of heuene,
And hyede not to goo doun the space of o day;
There was not before ne afterward so loong a day;
For the Lord obeide to the vois of man,
And fau3t for Israel."

Compare the returning of the shadow on the dial of Ahaz in the time of Hezekiah, 2 Kings xx. 11; Isai. xxxviii. 8.

for the Lord fought for Israel] Compare the account of Josephus, "He then heard that God was helping him, by the signs of thunder, lightning, and unusual hailstones; and that the day was increased lest the night should check the zeal of the Hebrews......That the length of the day did then increase, and was longer than usual, is told in the books laid up in the temple." *Ant.* v. i. 17.

15. *And Joshua returned*] This is still apparently part of the quotation from the "Book of Jasher," for it is evident that Joshua did *not* return to Gilgal immediately after the battle of Gibeon. In the historical narrative this finds place in verse 43.

16—27. FLIGHT AND EXECUTION OF THE FIVE KINGS.

16. *But these five kings*] Here the regular historical narrative is resumed. The second stage in the flight was over. "In the length-

17 Makkedah. And it was told Joshua, saying, The five kings
18 are found hid in a cave at Makkedah. And Joshua said,
Roll great stones upon the mouth of the cave, and set men
19 by it for to keep them: and stay you not, *but* pursue after
your enemies, and smite the hindmost of them; suffer them
not to enter into their cities: for the LORD your God hath
20 delivered them into your hand. And it came to pass, when
Joshua and the children of Israel had made an end of slaying them *with* a very great slaughter, till they were consumed,
that the rest *which* remained of them entered into fenced
21 cities. And all the people returned to the camp to Joshua

ened day granted to Joshua's prayer" now commences the third stage. The tide of fugitives rolled on, hotly pursued by the Israelites through the pass of Lower Beth-horon to Azekah, and thence to Makkedah.

17. *in a cave*] "lurkinge in the spelunk," Wyclif; in one of the numerous limestone caves, with which the district abounds, though the article here, both in the Hebrew and the LXX., seems to intimate that it was a well-known cave, overshadowed probably by a grove of trees (comp. Josh. x. 26). Many such caves, large and dry, and often branching out into chambers, are found in the lime and chalk rocks of Palestine. Comp. (i) the cave in which Lot dwelt after the destruction of Sodom (Gen. xix. 30); (ii) the cave at Rimmon (Judg. xx. 47), which could contain six hundred men in its spacious recess; (iii) David's cave of Adullam, where he concealed "his brethren, and all his father's house" (1 Sam. xxii. 1); (iv) the cave of Engedi, which Saul entered, and in the sides of which "David and his men remained" (1 Sam. xxiv. 3); (v) Obadiah's cave, in which he concealed "an hundred prophets" (1 Kings xviii. 4). "The caves of Syria and Palestine are still used, either occasionally or permanently, as habitations....The shepherds near Hebron leave their villages in the summer to dwell in caves and ruins, in order to be nearer to their flocks and fields. Almost all the habitations at *Om-keis*, Gadara, are caves." See Smith's *Bible Dict.* Art. *Caves.*

18. *And Joshua said*] The victory was not yet won. The conqueror would not be diverted from his object. The mouth of the cave was blocked with huge stones, and armed men were stationed to guard it, while the pursuit was still continued.

20. *the rest*] i.e. broken remnants of the fugitives.

fenced cities] "the strengthid citees," Wyclif, = the fortified towns of great strength and impregnable position. Comp. Num. xxxii. 17; Deut. iii. 5, ix. 1; Josh. xiv. 12; 1 Sam. vi. 18, &c. The fortifications of the cities of Palestine regularly fenced, consisted of one or more walls crowned with battlemented parapets, having towers at regular intervals (2 Chron. xxxii. 5; Jer. xxxi. 38), on which in later times engines of war were placed,

at Makkedah in peace: none moved his tongue against any
of the children of Israel. Then said Joshua, Open the 22
mouth of the cave, and bring out those five kings unto me
out of the cave. And they did so, and brought forth those 23
five kings unto him out of the cave, the king of Jerusalem,
the king of Hebron, the king of Jarmuth, the king of
Lachish, *and* the king of Eglon. And it came to pass, when 24
they brought out those kings unto Joshua, that Joshua
called for all the men of Israel, and said unto the captains
of the men of war which went with him, Come near, put
your feet upon the necks of these kings. And they came
near, and put their feet upon the necks of them. And 25
Joshua said unto them, Fear not, nor be dismayed, be
strong and of good courage: for thus shall the LORD do to

and in time of war watch was kept night and day (Judg. ix. 46, 47;
2 Kings ix. 17; 2 Chron. xxvi. 9, 15). The earlier Egyptian fortifications
consisted of a quadrangular and sometimes double wall of sun-dried brick,
fifteen feet thick, and often fifty feet in height, with square towers at
intervals of the same height as the walls, both crowned with a parapet,
and a round-headed battlement in shape like a shield. See Smith's
Bib. Dict. I. 616.

21. *to the camp*] Which had been already formed round the royal
hiding-place.

none moved his tongue] "And no man ajens the sones of Yrael was
hardy to grucche, ether to make priuy noise," Wyclif. Comp. Exod. xi.
7, "But against any of the children of Israel shall not a *dog move his
tongue*, against man or beast."

22. *Then said Joshua*] Probably this was on the morning after the
victory.

23. *the king of Jerusalem*] Observe the rhythmic roll of the enumeration of the kings and the cities over which they ruled.

24. *put your feet upon the necks*] According to the usage portrayed
on the monuments of Assyria and Egypt, which seems also to have
been practised by the Byzantine emperors long after the Christian era.
For this symbol of complete subjection comp. Ps. cx. 1; 1 Cor. xv.
25.

25. *Fear not*] "Take je coumfort (*con* and *fortis*), and be je
stronge," Wyclif. The proud foes they had so lately seen in all the
pomp and circumstance of war lay prostrate at their feet.

for thus] Even as, after the defeat of Sihon and Og, Moses had
assured Joshua would be the case, saying, "Thine eyes have seen all
that the Lord your God hath done unto these two kings; so shall the
Lord do unto all the kingdoms whither thou passest. Ye shall not fear
them: for the Lord your God he shall fight for you," Deut. iii. 21, 22;
Exod. xiv. 14.

26 all your enemies against whom ye fight. And afterward Joshua smote them, and slew them, and hanged them on five trees : and they were hanging upon the trees until the 27 evening. And it came to pass at the time of the going down of the sun, *that* Joshua commanded, and they took them down off the trees, and cast them into the cave wherein they had been hid, and laid great stones in the cave's mouth, *which remain* until this very day.

28—39. *The Conquest of Southern Palestine.*

28 And that day Joshua took Makkedah, and smote it with the edge of the sword, and the king thereof he utterly destroyed, them, and all the souls that *were* therein; he let none remain : and he did to the king of Makkedah as he 29 did unto the king of Jericho. Then Joshua passed from Makkedah, and all Israel with him, *unto* Libnah, and fought

26. *Joshua smote them*] The actual execution of the kings he reserved for his own hands.
hanged them] "Hongide upon fiue stokkis," Wyclif; or suspended their bodies after death. Comp. Deut. xxi. 23; Josh. viii. 29. In like manner Joshua had done to the king of Ai ; Josh. viii. 29.
on five trees] Each body on its own tree.
27. *at the time of the going down of the sun*] According to the strict command in Deut. xxi. 23.
into the cave wherein they had been hid] "Into the spelonk, in the which thei lorkiden," Wyclif, which then became a royal sepulchre, while the stones "which on the self-same day had cut them off from escape, closed the mouth of the tomb." See Keil on Josh. x. 27.

28—39. THE CONQUEST OF SOUTHERN PALESTINE.

28. *And that day*] The victory of Beth-horon did not stand alone. It involved other consequences in its train. It inaugurated a campaign, which may have lasted some weeks or even months, during which the whole of southern Canaan was swept into the hands of Israel.
took Makkedah] The cities distinctly specified as now subdued are Makkedah, Libnah, Lachish, Eglon, Hebron, Debir.
and smote it with the edge of the sword] As before at Ai (Josh. viii. 24). Four times does this expression occur in the present section.
he let none remain] This expression also occurs four times in the section.
as he did] See chap. vi. 21.
29. *unto Libnah*] In a westerly direction. Libnah belonged to

against Libnah: and the LORD delivered it also, and the 30 king thereof, into the hand of Israel; and he smote it with the edge of the sword, and all the souls that *were* therein; he let none remain in it; but did unto the king thereof as he did unto the king of Jericho. And Joshua passed from 31 Libnah, and all Israel with him, unto Lachish, and encamped against it, and fought against it: and the LORD delivered 32 Lachish into the hand of Israel, which took it on the second day, and smote it with the edge of the sword, and all the souls that *were* therein, according to all that he had done to Libnah. Then Horam king of Gezer came up to help 33

the district of the Shephelah, the maritime lowland of Judah, and we find it enumerated among the cities of this district (Josh. xv. 42). With its suburbs it was appropriated to the priests (Josh. xxi. 13; 1 Chron. vi. 57), but revolted from Judah in the reign of Jehoram the son of Jehoshaphat (2 Kings viii. 22; 2 Chron. xxi. 10). On account of the accordance of the name Libnah ("*white*") with the "Blanche-garde" of the Crusaders, Dean Stanley would place it at *Tell es-Safieh*, about 5 miles north-west of *Beit-Jibrin*. Others would place it 4 miles west of the same spot, at *Arak el Menshiyeh*.

31 *unto Lachish*] See above, verse 3. The Israelitish leader moved in a south-westerly direction.

32. *which took it on the second day*] Observe: 1. All the other cities seem to have fallen before Joshua at once except Lachish. Of Lachish, and Lachish alone, is it said that he took it *on the second day*.

2. When Sennacherib invaded Judah, he attacked and took "the fenced cities," but Lachish appears to have foiled him, and he was constrained to raise the siege (2 Kings xix. 8; 2 Chron. xxxii. 9).

3. When Nebuchadnezzar came up against Jerusalem, he fought against all "the cities of Judah *that were left*, against *Lachish*, and against Azekah: *for these defenced cities remained of the cities of Judah*," i. e. they had strength to stand out, when the others had fallen (Jer. xxxiv. 7).

4. When in describing the assault on Lachish the writer of the Book of Joshua tells us it was *the second day* before it succeeded, he *undesignedly* leads us to suspect that Lachish was a stronghold; and on consulting other portions of the history of the Jews we discover that suspicion to be confirmed; and on the whole a coincidence results very characteristic of truth and accuracy, and this in a narrative full of the miraculous. Blunt's *Undesigned Coincidences*, pp. 107, 108.

33. *Then Horam*] His city lay at no great distance from Lachish.

Gezer] or, as it is called later, *Gazara* (2 Macc. x. 32), *Gadara* (Jos. *Ant.* v. i. 22), was an ancient city of Canaan. It was afterwards allotted with its suburbs to the Kohathite Levites (Josh. xxi. 21; 1 Chron. vi. 67); but the original inhabitants were not dispossessed (Judg. i. 29), and even down to the reign of Solomon the Canaanites

Lachish; and Joshua smote him and his people, until *he* had
34 left him none remaining. And from Lachish Joshua passed
unto Eglon, and all Israel with him; and they encamped
35 against it, and fought against it: and they took it on that
day, and smote it with the edge of the sword, and all the
souls that *were* therein he utterly destroyed that day, accord-
36 ing to all that he had done to Lachish. And Joshua went
up from Eglon, and all Israel with him, unto Hebron; and
37 they fought against it: and they took it, and smote it with
the edge of the sword, and the king thereof, and all the
cities thereof, and all the souls that *were* therein; he left
none remaining, according to all that he had done to Eglon;
but destroyed it utterly, and all the souls that *were* therein.
38 And Joshua returned, and all Israel with him, to Debir; and

were still dwelling there, and paying tribute to Israel (1 Kings ix. 16). Its site has lately been identified with *Tel el Jezar*, about four miles from *Amwâs*, on the road to *Ramlah* and *Lydd*. "The position of the Levitical city of Gezer (Josh. xii. 12; 1 Chron. vi. 67; Judges i. 29), which Pharaoh gave to his daughter—Solomon's queen—as a dowry, has been a subject of prolonged controversy. M. Clermont Ganneau discovered the ancient site, with the very name itself still lingering on the spot. Not only that, but he found the Levitical boundaries. In no other case have these been found. They were cut in the rock itself—not on movable stones—in two separate places, in Greek and square Hebrew characters, signifying the 'boundary of Gezer.' The date seems to be Maccabean." (*Quarterly Statement* of the "Palestine Exploration Fund," 1874.)

and Joshua smote him] Joshua seems to have been content with repulsing his attack, slaying the king, and inflicting a severe defeat upon his people. Gezer itself lay too far northward of his present line of operations to justify its capture.

34. *Eglon*] See on verse 3. He now marches eastward from Lachish to Eglon on the road from Jerusalem to Gaza; invests, takes, and destroys it with all its inhabitants.

36. *unto Hebron*] which lay next in a tolerably direct line. He is said to have "gone up" to it, for, in order to invest it, he had to march from the plain to the hill country.

37. *and the king thereof*] The successor doubtless of the chief who fell at Makkedah. See above, verse 23.

all the cities thereof] i.e. all the smaller towns dependent upon it; "alle the *burgh touns* of that region," Wyclif.

38. *returned*] or *turned*. "Turnyde in," Wyclif. The words indicate a change in the direction of the march. Comp. Exod. v. 22, "and Moses *returned* unto the Lord." From Hebron he turned in to the south-west, and attacked Debir.

fought against it: and he took it, and the king thereof, and 39 all the cities thereof; and they smote them with the edge of the sword, and utterly destroyed all the souls that *were* therein; he left none remaining: as he had done to Hebron, so he did to Debir, and to the king thereof; as he had done also to Libnah, and to her king.

40—43. *Survey of the Results of the Campaign in Southern Canaan.*

So Joshua smote all the country of the hills, and of the 40 south, and of the vale, and of the springs, and all their kings:

Debir] The early name of this city was Kirjath-sepher = "*the town of the book*" (Josh. xv. 15; Judg. i. 11), or Kirjath-sannah = "*the town of palm*" ("of the law"?) (Josh. xv. 49). We find it afterwards given with its "suburbs" to the priests (Josh. xxi. 15; 1 Chron. vi. 58). "About three miles to the west of Hebron is a deep and secluded valley called the *Wady Nunkûr*, enclosed on the north by hills, of which one bears a name certainly suggestive of Debir, *Dewîr-ban*. The name supplies some evidence that the Canaanites were acquainted with writing and books. The town probably contained a noted school, or was the site of an oracle, and the residence of some learned priests." This accounts for the Hebrew name, Debir, which Jerome renders "oraculum." The same term was used to denote the adytum of Solomon's temple.

40—43. SURVEY OF THE RESULTS OF THE CAMPAIGN IN SOUTHERN CANAAN.

40. *all the country*] Rather, **all the land, the hill country**, &c. The entire region is comprehensively surveyed, and then treated with special detail: (*a*) *The Hills;* (*b*) *The South;* (*c*) *The Vale;* (*d*) *The Springs*.
   (*a*) *The Hills*, i.e. *the mountain* district of Judah extending southward from Jerusalem. It consists of calcareous limestone, and forms the water-parting between the Mediterranean and the Dead Sea, rising to the height of 3000 feet. It is generally, especially in the southern portion, an uneven and rocky district.
   (*b*) *The South = the Negeb*, the "land of the south," the dry, parched land, where the mountain-brooks fail in the summer (Ps. cxxvi. 4). It is a limestone district, a land intermediate between wilderness and cultivated land, like the steppes of southern Russia. Because it lay in the south of Palestine, "Negeb" comes to mean generally "*south*" (comp. Num. xxxv. 5; Exod. xl. 24; Josh. xvii. 9, 10). It must, however, have once been fertile, for Palmer and Drake found grape-mounds all round the western border. "Almost sudden was the transition to the upland wilderness, the 'Negeb,' or south country—a series of rolling hills, clad with scanty herbage here and

he left none remaining, but utterly destroyed all that breath-
41 ed, as the LORD God of Israel commanded. And Joshua
smote them from Kadesh-barnea even unto Gaza, and all the
42 country of Goshen, even unto Gibeon. And all these kings
and their land did Joshua take *at* one time, because the

> there, especially on their northern faces; and steadily rising, till the barometer, falling three and a half inches, told us that we had mounted 3,200 feet above our camp of the morning."—Tristram's *Land of Israel*, pp. 365, 366.
>
> (*c*) *The Vale*, i.e. *the Lowlands*, or *Shephêlah*, a strip of land in southern Palestine stretching along from Joppa to Gaza, "the plain of the Philistines." "Viewed from the sea this maritime region appears as a long low coast of white or cream-coloured sand, its slight undulations rising occasionally into mounds or cliffs, which in one or two places almost aspire to the dignity of headlands."
>
> (*d*) *The Springs*, rather *the Slopes* or *Declivities*. The verb from which the original word is formed, denotes *to pour*, *to rush down*. Hence it means (i) an *outpouring;* (ii) *a place, upon which something pours out*. Comp. Deut. iii. 17, "from Chinnereth even unto the sea of the plain, even the salt sea, under Ashdoth-pisgah" =*the springs* or *slopes of Pisgah* (see margin), where the LXX. and English Version treat the word as a proper name. The word here denotes the district of undulating ground between the *Shephêlah* or "lowlands," just mentioned, and the hill or "mountain" of the centre.

as the Lord] See Deut. xx. 16, 17.

41. *from Kadesh-barnea*] i. e. from the wilderness in which Kadesh-barnea lay. This place, the scene of Miriam's death, was the furthest point which the Israelites reached in their direct road to Canaan. From it also the spies were sent forth (Num. xiii. 17, 26), and there also, on their return, the people broke out into murmuring, and upon this their penal term of wandering began (Num. xiv. 29—33; Deut. ii. 14).

even unto Gaza] In the *Shephêlah*, and only about one hour from the Mediterranean Sea. This defines the limits of Joshua's conquests on the west, Gaza being the last town in the S.W. of Palestine on the frontier towards Egypt. This town, properly *Azzah*, the name of which means "*the strong*," appears even before the call of Abraham (Gen. x. 19), as a "border" city of the Canaanites. We shall find the territory of Gaza mentioned afterwards, as one which Joshua was not able to subdue (Josh. xi. 22, xiii. 3), and though assigned to the tribe of Judah (Josh. xv. 47), they did not obtain possession of it (Judg. i. 18, 19).

all the country of Goshen] "Alle the lond of Josson," Wyclif. This is not to be confounded with the province of Goshen (*frontier*) in Egypt. It was a district in the south of Judah, and probably derived its appellation from a town of that name, mentioned in company with Debir, Socoh, and others in the mountains of Judah (Josh. xv. 48—51).

even unto Gibeon] This marks the extent of the Conquest on the east.

down: wherefore the hearts of the people melted, and became as water.

6—15. *The Defeat before Ai. Joshua's Prayer.*

And Joshua rent his clothes, and fell to the earth upon 6 his face before the ark of the LORD until the eventide, he and the elders of Israel, and put dust upon their heads. And Joshua said, Alas, O Lord GOD, wherefore hast thou 7 at all brought this people over Jordan, to deliver us into the hand of the Amorites, to destroy us? would to God we had been content, and dwelt on the *other* side Jordan! O Lord, 8 what shall I say, when Israel turneth *their* backs before their enemies! For the Canaanites and all the inhabitants of the 9 land shall hear *of it*, and shall environ us round, and cut off

in the going down] Or, as in the margin, *in Morad*. If we retain the translation in the text, "the going down" would point to a spot, about a mile distant, "where the wâdies, descending from Ai, take their final plunge eastwards."

the hearts of the people melted] Comp. Deut. i. 28; Josh. ii. 11. "And the herte of the puple myche dredde, and at the lickenesse of water is molten," Wyclif.

6—15. THE DEFEAT BEFORE AI. JOSHUA'S PRAYER.

6. *And Joshua rent his clothes*] in token of sorrow and distress (comp. Lev. x. 6, xxi. 10). The clothes were torn in front over the breast, yet for not more than a handbreadth. In Patriarchal times we read of Reuben *rending his clothes*, because "Joseph was not in the pit" (Gen. xxxvii. 29); of Jacob *rending his clothes*, and "mourning for his son many days" (Gen. xxxvii. 34); of Joseph's brethren that they *rent their clothes*, when they found the cup in Benjamin's sack (Gen. xliv. 13). For the same custom among the Romans compare Juvenal XIII. 131,

"Nemo dolorem
Fingit in hoc casu, vestem diducere summam
Contentus."

and put dust upon their heads] Likewise a sign of mourning. Comp. the young man of Benjamin running to Shiloh with tidings of the battle, his clothes rent, and with *earth upon his head* (1 Sam. iv. 12); the man coming from the camp to David with his clothes rent, and *earth upon his head* (2 Sam. i. 2). See also 2 Sam. xiii. 19, xv. 32. Comp. Hom. *Il.* XVIII. 25, XXIV. 164.

7. *would to God we had been content*] Or perhaps better as the LXX. have rendered it, "would that we had remained and dwelt on the other side Jordan."

our name from the earth: and what wilt thou do unto thy
10 great name? And the LORD said unto Joshua, Get thee
11 up; wherefore liest thou thus upon thy face? Israel hath
sinned, and they have also transgressed my covenant which
I commanded them: for they have even taken of the accursed thing, and have also stolen, and dissembled also,
12 and they have put *it* even amongst their own stuff. Therefore the children of Israel could not stand before their enemies, *but* turned *their* backs before their enemies, because
they were accursed: neither will I be with you any more,
13 except ye destroy the accursed from amongst you. Up,
sanctify the people, and say, Sanctify yourselves against to
morrow: for thus saith the LORD God of Israel, *There is
an accursed thing in the midst of thee, O Israel*: thou canst
not stand before thine enemies, until ye take away the ac-
14 cursed thing from among you. In the morning therefore ye
shall be brought according to your tribes: and it shall be,
that the tribe which the LORD taketh shall come according

10. *Get thee up*] Joshua might well infer that the people had in-
curred the Divine displeasure, but it was no time for unavailing remorse
—he must be up and trying to detect and put away the sin.

12. *except ye destroy the accursed from among you*] The LXX. translate, "Except ye remove the accursed thing, the Anathema, from among
you," using the identical word for *remove* that St Paul uses respecting
the incestuous Corinthian, "therefore *put away from among yourselves*
that wicked person," 1 Cor. v. 13.

13. *sanctify the people*] "Rise, halwe the puple," Wyclif. Compare
the instructions to Moses before the giving of the Law, Exod. xix. 10.

14. *according to your tribes*] Each tribe was divided into *families;*
each family into *houses;* each house into *persons.*

the tribe which the Lord taketh] i.e. by the sacred lot. We find the
lots used (*a*) for the detection of a criminal here, and in the case of
Jonathan (1 Sam. xiv. 42, and Jonah i. 7); (*b*) in the choice of men for
an invading force (Judg. i. 1, xx. 10); (*c*) in the partition of land (Num.
xxvi. 55; Josh. xviii. 10; 1 Macc. iii. 36); (*d*) in the assignment to
foreigners or captors of spoils or prisoners (Joel iii. 3; Nah. iii. 10); (*e*)
in the selection of the scapegoat on the day of Atonement (Lev. xvi.
8); (*f*) in the settlement of doubtful questions (Prov. xvi. 33, xviii.
18). The custom was of great antiquity and widely spread, and "recommended itself as a sort of appeal to the Almighty, secure from all influence of passion or bias." In Homer we find it employed by the gods
themselves (*Il.* XXII. 209; Cic. *de Div.* I. 34, II. 41), and the Romans
had their lots in divisions (*sortes divisoriæ*) and elections (*sors urbana*
and *peregrina*) in the choice of a prætor.

to the families *thereof;* and the family which the LORD shall take shall come by households; and the household which the LORD shall take shall come man by man. And it shall 15 be, *that* he that is taken with the accursed thing shall be burnt with fire, he and all that he hath: because he hath transgressed the covenant of the LORD, and because he hath wrought folly in Israel.

16—26. *The Discovery and Punishment of Achan.*

So Joshua rose up early in the morning, and brought 16 Israel by their tribes; and the tribe of Judah was taken: and he brought the family of Judah; and he took the family of the Zarhites: and he brought the family of the Zarhites 17 man by man; and Zabdi was taken: and he brought his 18 household man by man; and Achan, the son of Carmi, the son of Zabdi, the son of Zerah, of the tribe of Judah, was taken. And Joshua said unto Achan, My son, give, I pray 19 thee, glory to the LORD God of Israel, and make confession

15. *shall be burnt with fire*] Achan by his conduct had become *cherem* or *devoted*, and is so called in verse 12, and everything devoted to punishment for the reparation of the Divine honour was to be burnt. Comp. Lev. xx. 14, xxi. 9; Josh. vi. 24; 2 Kings xxiii. 16.

folly] Or, as in margin, *wickedness;* "and hath do• sacrilege in Ysrael," Wyclif.

16—26. THE DISCOVERY AND PUNISHMENT OF ACHAN.

16. *brought Israel by their tribes*] Joshua first caused the heads of the tribes to come before the Ark, and lots were cast for them, and the lot fell upon Judah; then the heads of the clans of Judah were brought, and the lot fell upon the Zarhites; then the heads of the houses of the Zarhites were brought before the Ark, and the lot fell upon Zabdi; then the men of his house were brought, and the lot fell upon Achan, the son of Carmi.

18. *and Achan...was taken*] (*a*) Sometimes in taking the sacred lot dice were thrown; comp. the expression *"to cast lots"* (Josh. xviii. 10); to *"throw"* them (Josh. xviii. 6); "the *lot falls*" (Jonah i. 7; Ezek. xxiv. 6); (*b*) sometimes *tesseræ* were flung into a vessel and then drawn out; comp. the expressions "the lot *came forth*" Num. xxxiii. 54; "*came up*" Lev. xvi. 9.

19. *My son*] "Not said ironically but earnestly, *My son;* an example of the pity for the Sinner which Justice feels even in punishing the sin." Bp Wordsworth.

give...glory] Comp. 1 Sam. vi. 5, "Wherefore ye shall make images of your emerods, and images of your mice that mar the land; and ye *shall*

5—2

unto him; and tell me now what thou hast done; hide *it* not from me. And Achan answered Joshua, and said, Indeed I have sinned against the LORD God of Israel, and thus and thus have I done: when I saw among the spoils a goodly Babylonish garment, and two hundred shekels *of* silver, and a wedge of gold of fifty shekels weight, then I coveted them, and took them; and behold, they *are* hid in the earth in the midst of my tent, and the silver under it. So Joshua sent messengers, and they ran unto the tent; and behold, *it was* hid in his tent, and the silver under it. And they took them out of the midst of the tent, and brought them unto Joshua, and unto all the children of Israel, and laid them out before the LORD. And Joshua, and all Israel with him, took Achan the son of Zerah, and

give glory unto the God of Israel; peradventure He will lighten His Hand from off you;" Jer. xiii. 16, "*Give glory to the Lord your God,* before He cause darkness, and before your feet stumble upon the dark mountains;" John ix. 24, "Then again called they the man that was blind, and said unto him, *Give God the praise;* we know that this man is a sinner." "The Omniscience of Jehovah is proved by this discovery. Give Him the praise, therefore, by a full confession of thy sin."

21. *a goodly Babylonish garment*] Literally, **a goodly mantle of Shinar**, i.e. Babylonia. Comp. Gen. xi. 2, "They found a plain in the land of *Shinar*, and they dwelt there," 9, "therefore is the name of it called *Babel*." The word here translated "garment," means a long robe, such as was worn by kings on state occasions; comp. Jonah iii. 6, and by prophets, 1 Kings xix. 13; 2 Kings ii. 13, 14; Zech. xiii. 4. Probably it was stuff embroidered, made in the loom with many colours, and wrought of gold and silk threads. On the elaborate and beautiful products of the Babylonian looms see Heeren's *Asiatic Nations* I. 2, ff. 22; Layard's *Nineveh* II. 319; Kitto's *Bible Illustrations* II. 204. The word employed points to the existence of a trade already between Canaan and Mesopotamia. Wyclif renders it "a reed mentil ful good."

a wedge of gold] Literally, **a tongue of gold**. Vulg. *regula aurea*, "a golden bar," or "a tongue-shaped jewel made of gold," "a golden rewle of fifti siclis," Wyclif. The name *lingula* was given by the Romans to a spoon, and to an oblong dagger made in the shape of a tongue. The weight of the wedge was 50 shekels=about 25 ounces. See *The Speaker's Commentary* in loc.

the silver under it] The mantle would naturally lie at the top, then the tongue of gold, and the silver lowest.

23. *laid them out*] Literally, **poured them out**.

before the Lord] i.e. before the ark of Jehovah, where He was enthroned. Comp. vi. 8.

24. *son of Zerah*] Strictly, his great-grandson.

vv. 25, 26] JOSHUA, VII. 69

the silver, and the garment, and the wedge of gold, and his sons, and his daughters, and his oxen, and his asses, and his sheep, and his tent, and all that he had: and they brought them *unto* the valley of Achor. And Joshua said, Why hast 25 thou troubled us? the LORD shall trouble thee this day. And all Israel stoned him *with* stones, and burned them with fire, after they had stoned them with stones. And they 26 raised over him a great heap of stones unto this day. So the LORD turned from the fierceness of his anger. Wherefore the name of that place was called, The valley of Achor, unto this day.

and his sons, and his daughters] Some have thought they were brought to the valley merely as spectators, that they might have a terrible warning: others think they must have been accomplices in his sin, and as he by his own act had placed himself under a ban (vi. 18), so all that he had was treated as coming under the same law. (Comp. Deut. xiii. 15—17.)

the valley] Henceforth known by the name of "*Achor*," i. e. causing trouble and sorrow. Comp. Josh. xv. 7, "And the border went up toward Debir from the valley *of Achor*;" Isai. lxv. 10, "And Sharon shall be a fold of flocks, and the *valley of Achor* a place for the herds to lie down in;" Hos. ii. 15, "And I will give her her vineyards from thence, and the *valley of Achor* for a door of hope." The exact site of the valley is unknown, but it was somewhere on the northern border of the tribe of Judah, among the ridges to the south of Jericho.

25. *Why hast thou troubled us?*] Compare the question of Ahab to Elijah, "Art thou he that *troubleth* Israel?" (1 Kings xviii. 17). "For thou disturblidist us, the Lord schall disturble the in this dai," Wyclif.

And all Israel stoned him] The use of the singular here and in the following verse is deserving of notice. It suggests that it does not necessarily follow that the sons and daughters of Achan were burned with him. In this case "the plural number used would refer only to the oxen, asses, and sheep, and all that Achan possessed." Edersheim. Stoning was the ordinary mode of execution (Exod. xvii. 4), especially for idolatry and blasphemy (1 Kings xxi. 10).

and burned them with fire] This was a terrible aggravation of the ordinary punishment of death, Lev. xx. 14.

26. *a great heap of stones*] As a memorial and a warning of his sin and its punishment. The custom of casting stones on certain graves was not unknown among other nations also, as the Arabs and the Romans. Compare Propertius IV. 5. 74.

So the Lord turned] "Even to Achan himself," remarks Bp Wordsworth, "the valley of Achor may have been made a door of hope (Hos. ii. 15), because he confessed his sin, and there is reason to hope and believe that he listened to the words of Joshua, 'My son, give

1—29. *The Capture of Ai.*

8 And the LORD said unto Joshua, Fear not, neither be thou dismayed: take all the people of war with thee, and arise, go up *to* Ai: see, I have given into thy hand the king 2 of Ai, and his people, and his city, and his land: and thou shalt do to Ai and her king as thou didst unto Jericho and her king: only the spoil thereof, and the cattle thereof, shall ye take for a prey unto yourselves: lay thee an ambush for 3 the city behind it. So Joshua arose, and all the people of war, to go up *against* Ai: and Joshua chose out thirty thousand mighty *men* of valour, and sent them away by night.

glory to the Lord God of Israel,' and submitted to the punishment due to his sin."

CH. VIII. 1—29. THE CAPTURE OF AI.

1. *And the Lord said unto Joshua*] The same encouraging address, and one much needed after all that had taken place, is now given as that recorded in i. 9. The sin of Israel having been removed, the Almighty once more assures Joshua of His presence to give success in the reduction of Ai.

all the people of war] Not three thousand men only as at the first attempt.

2. *the spoil thereof*] unlike the case of Jericho, is formally conceded to the Israelites.

an ambush] "Put busshementis to the citye bihynde it," Wyclif. Literally a *weaver*, a lier in wait, from *arab*, to weave = "nectere insidias, struere dolos."

for the city behind it] High up, probably in the main ravine between Ai and Bethel. "Ai must be somewhere between Michmash and Rimmon, a region greatly cut up with gorges and ravines; and as I passed from Beit-în toward Michmash, I could easily understand how Joshua's ambush of 5000 men could lie hid between Ai and Bethel." Thomson's *Land and the Book*, p. 671.

3. *Joshua chose out thirty thousand mighty men of valour*] There is an apparent discrepancy between this statement and that in verses 10—12. But possibly (*a*) while 30000 were selected for the ambush, 5000 were actually employed when the decisive moment came; or (*b*) Joshua may have sent two distinct bodies of men, one of 30000, the other of 5000; or (*c*) as Bp Wordsworth suggests, on the day after the 30000 had taken up their position the 5000 may have been sent from Joshua's own force to encourage and assure them.

sent them away by night] The force detached might easily reach the neighbourhood of Ai before daybreak, since the distance from Gilgal thither is not more than five to six hours. See Robinson, Vol. II. 307—312.

And he commanded them, saying, Behold, ye shall lie in 4 wait against the city, *even* behind the city: go not very far from the city, but be ye all ready: and I, and all the people 5 that *are* with me, will approach unto the city: and it shall come to pass, when they come out against us, as at the first, that we will flee before them, (for they will come out after 6 us) till we have drawn them from the city; for they will say, *They* flee before us, as at the first: therefore we will flee before them. Then ye shall rise up from the ambush, and 7 seize upon the city: for the LORD your God will deliver it into your hand. And it shall be, when ye have taken the 8 city, *that* ye shall set the city on fire: according to the commandment of the LORD shall ye do. See, I have commanded you. Joshua therefore sent them forth: and they went to 9 lie in ambush, and abode between Beth-el and Ai, on the west side of Ai: but Joshua lodged that night among the people. And Joshua rose up early in the morning, and 10 numbered the people, and went up, he and the elders of Israel, before the people *to* Ai. And all the people, *even the* 11 *people* of war that *were* with him, went up, and drew nigh, and came before the city, and pitched on the north side of Ai: now *there was* a valley between them and Ai. And he 12 took about five thousand men, and set them to lie in ambush between Beth-el and Ai, on the west side of the city. And when they had set the people, *even* all the host that 13

4. *go not very far from the city*] They would station themselves high up in the Wâdy Harith, at no great distance from the city, and between it and Bethel.

5. *will approach unto the city*] Joshua himself took up his position on the north side of "the ravine," apparently the deep chasm through which the Wâdy Harith descends to the Wâdy Kelt. Stanley's *Sinai and Palestine*, pp. 202, 203.

8. *See, I have commanded you*] Comp. the words of Jehovah to Joshua, i. 9, "Have not *I commanded thee?* Be strong, and of a good courage;" and of Absalom to his servants, 2 Sam. xiii. 28, "Have not I *commanded you?* Be courageous and be valiant."

10. *numbered the people*] Rather, **mustered** or **arrayed** them. The day after the despatch of the ambush would be naturally occupied with the marshalling of the army, and the march from Gilgal to Ai, where they would arrive in the evening.

12. *he took*] Or rather, **had taken**.
between Beth-el and Ai] Comp. ch. vii. 2 with Gen. xii. 8 and xiii. 3.

was on the north of the city, and their liers in wait on the west of the city, Joshua went that night into the midst of 14 the valley. And it came to pass, when the king of Ai saw *it*, that they hasted and rose up early, and the men of the city went out against Israel to battle, he and all his people, at a time appointed, before the plain; but he wist not that 15 *there were* liers in ambush against him behind the city. And Joshua and all Israel *made as if they* were beaten before 16 them, and fled *by* the way of the wilderness. And all the people that *were* in Ai were called *together* to pursue after them: and they pursued after Joshua, and were drawn away 17 from the city. And there was not a man left in Ai or Beth-el, that went not out after Israel: and they left the 18 city open, and pursued after Israel. And the LORD said unto Joshua, Stretch out the spear that *is* in thy hand toward Ai; for I will give it into thine hand. And Joshua stretched out the spear that *he had* in his hand toward the 19 city. And the ambush arose quickly out of their place, and they ran as soon as *he* had stretched out his hand: and they entered *into* the city, and took it, and hasted and set the

14. *when the king of Ai saw it*] It was early on the following morning that the king of Ai discovered the advance of the army against him. The words apply to the forces of Joshua, the ambush was of course hidden from his view. Ai was a "royal" city. Comp. Josh. viii. 23, 29, x. 1, xii. 9.

at a time appointed] Rather, **at the place appointed**, at some spot before agreed upon suitable for marshalling his forces. It was "before the plain," i.e. before the "ambush," at the entrance of the depressed tract which runs down to the Jordan valley, probably = "the wilderness of Beth-aven," Josh. xviii. 12.

he wist not] Comp. Judg. xx. 34, "And there came against Gibeah ten thousand chosen men—but they *knew not* that evil was near them." For "wist," see above, ch. ii. 4.

17. *or Beth-el*] The inhabitants of Bethel would seem on this occasion to have sent help to the people of Ai in resisting the attack of Joshua.

18. *the spear*] Heb. *Cidôn*, a *dart*, or *javelin* which is hurled, lighter than the *Chanith*, or spear of the largest kind like that of Goliath, 1 Sam. xvii. 7, 45, or king Saul, 1 Sam. xxvi. 7, 8. The *Cidôn* could easily be held outstretched for some considerable time and was probably furnished with a flag. When not in action, it was carried on the back of the warrior between the shoulders (1 Sam. xvii. 6). The LXX. renders the word by *Gaison*, a short javelin or lance, the Vulg. by *sceptrum*.

city on fire. And when the men of Ai looked behind them, 20 they saw, and behold, the smoke of the city ascended up to heaven, and they had no power to flee this way or that way: and the people that fled *to* the wilderness turned back upon the pursuers. And when Joshua and all Israel saw that the 21 ambush had taken the city, and that the smoke of the city ascended, then they turned again, and slew the men of Ai. And the other issued out of the city against them; so they 22 were in the midst of Israel, some on this side, and some on that side: and they smote them, so that *they* let none of them remain or escape. And the king of Ai they took alive, 23 and brought him to Joshua. And it came to pass, when 24 Israel had made an end of slaying all the inhabitants of Ai in the field, in the wilderness wherein they chased them, *when* they were all fallen on the edge of the sword, until they were consumed, that all the Israelites returned *unto* Ai, and smote it with the edge of the sword. And *so* it was, 25 *that* all that fell that day, both of men and women, *were* twelve thousand, *even* all the men of Ai. For Joshua drew 26 not his hand back, wherewith he stretched out the spear, until *he* had utterly destroyed all the inhabitants of Ai. Only the cattle and the spoil of that city Israel took for 27 a prey unto themselves, according unto the word of the LORD which he commanded Joshua. And Joshua burnt Ai, 28 and made it a heap for ever, *even* a desolation unto this day.

20. *they had no power*] no **hand**. Comp. Judg. xviii. 10 (Heb.).
that fled to the wilderness] See above, ver. 15, and below, ver. 24.
22. *so they were in the midst of Israel*] "The host of Israel now turned again, while those who had set Ai on fire advanced in an opposite direction. Between these two forces the men of Ai were literally crushed."
27. *which he commanded Joshua*] See ver. 2, and comp. Num. xxxi. 22—26.
28. *a heap*] "an everlasting toumbe," Wyclif. Heb. a "*Tel*," always with the article, *The Tel*, or *Heap*. "For a long time modern explorers in vain sought for the site of Ai, where they knew it must have stood. "The inhabitants of the neighbouring villages," writes Canon Williams, "declared repeatedly and emphatically that this was *Tel* and nothing else. I was satisfied that it should be so when, on subsequent reference to the original text of Josh. viii. 28, I found it written that 'Joshua burnt Ai, and made it a *Tel* for ever, even a desolation unto this day.' There are many *Tels* in modern Palestine, that land of *Tels*, even *Tel* with some other name attached to it to

29 And the king of Ai he hanged on a tree until eventide: and as soon as the sun was down, Joshua commanded that they should take his carcase down from the tree, and cast it at the entering of the gate of the city, and raise thereon a great heap of stones, *that remaineth* unto this day.

30—35. *The Altar of Blessing and of Cursing.*

30 Then Joshua built an altar unto the LORD God of Israel
31 in mount Ebal, as Moses the servant of the LORD com-

mark the former site. But the site of Ai has no other name 'unto this day.' It is simply *et-Tel=the Heap*, 'par excellence.'"

29. *he hanged on a tree*] "He hongid in a gybet," Wyclif. Hanging is mentioned as a distinct punishment, Num. xxv. 4. In Deut. xxi. 22 we read that in certain cases the criminal was put to death, and *after that*, his dead body was hung on a tree till eventide; the king of Ai was probably slain and then hanged on a cross or gallows.

as soon as the sun was down] This was in accordance with the Mosaic Law, which directed, Deut. xxi. 23, that a man's body should "not remain all night upon the tree." Comp. also Josh. x. 27.

and raise thereon a great heap of stones] Comp. Josh. vii. 26. Two words are used for "heap" in verses 28, 29. The first (*Tel*) indicates the ruins of the city itself, the second (*Gal*) the cairn over the king's grave.

30—35. THE ALTAR OF BLESSING AND OF CURSING.

30. *Then Joshua built*] The passes being now secured, and the interior of the country rendered accessible, Joshua resolved to take advantage of the terror which the success of his arms had inspired in the hearts of the Canaanites, and to carry out the command of Moses respecting the ratification of the Law with solemn ceremonies (Deut. xxvii. 2—8). By a grand national act it was to be declared "in what character Israel meant to hold what it had received of God." This act was to consist of three parts:—

(*a*) The Law was to be inscribed on "great stones" (Deut. xxvii. 2) which had been "plaistered with plaister;" and these as Memorial Stones were to be set up on "mount Ebal" (Deut. xxvii. 4);

(*b*) An altar of "whole stones" (Deut. xxvii. 5, 6) was to be erected on the same spot and solemn sacrifices offered thereon;

(*c*) The priests with the Ark were to occupy the valley between Ebal and Gerizim, surrounded by the elders, officers, and judges; the curses of the Law were then to be read aloud by the Levites, to which half the tribes on Ebal were to respond with a loud *Amen*, and to the blessings of the Law the other half on Gerizim were similarly to testify their acquiescence.

in mount Ebal] To carry out this solemn function, the first step taken by Joshua was to advance with the people from Ai and Beth-el

manded the children of Israel, as it is written in the book of the law of Moses, an altar of whole stones, over which no *man* hath lift up *any* iron : and they offered thereon burnt offerings unto the LORD, and sacrificed peace offerings. And 32 he wrote there upon the stones a copy of the law of Moses, which he wrote in the presence of the children of Israel. And all Israel, and their elders, and officers, and their 33 judges, stood on this side the ark and on that side before the priests the Levites, which bare the ark of the covenant of the LORD, as well the stranger, as he that was born among them ; half of them over against mount Gerizim, and half of

northwards towards Shechem, to the valley bounded on the south by the range of Gerizim, and on the north by that of Ebal, "the most beautiful, perhaps it might be said the only very beautiful spot in central Palestine." Two events consecrated the valley in the memory of every Israelite. (*a*) It was here that Abraham halted on his journey from Chaldæa and erected his first altar to the Lord (Gen. xii. 6, 7) ; (*b*) It was here that Jacob settled on his return from the same region of Mesopotamia, and bought the parcel of the field, where he had spread his tent, of the children of Hamor, the father of Shechem, for a hundred pieces of money (Gen. xxxiii. 19).

31. *an altar of whole* (or, "unhewn") *stones*] Thus the Law required in general (Exod. xx. 25), and in this case it had been specially ordained.

32. *a copy of the law*] " Short declaracioun of the lawe of Moyses," Wyclif. This has been variously interpreted as meaning (*a*) the whole Law; (*b*) the Decalogue; (*c*) the Book of Deuteronomy; (*d*) the "commandments" proper, the "statutes" and "rights" contained in the Pentateuch, "six hundred and thirteen in number, according to the Jewish reckoning, not including all the narratives also, and warnings, admonitions, discourses, reasons, and the like."

he wrote in the presence] The Law was probably "written upon or in the plaster with which these pillars were coated. This could easily be done; and such writing was common in ancient times. I have seen numerous specimens of it certainly more *than two thousand years old*, and still as distinct as when they were first inscribed on the plaster." Thomson's *Land and the Book*, p. 471. "The investigation of the Egyptian monuments has shewn that it was an ancient Egyptian custom first to plaster the stone walls of buildings, and also monumental stones that were to be painted with figures and hieroglyphics, with a plaster of lime and gypsum, into which the figures were worked ; thus it was possible in Egypt to engrave on the walls the most extensive pieces of writing. And in this manner Deut. xxvii. 4—8 must be understood, and in this manner it was accomplished by Joshua." Oehler's *Theology of the Old Testament*, p. 121 n.

33. *as well the stranger*] See Deut. xxxi. 12.

half of them over against mount Gerizim] viz., those which had sprung

them over against mount Ebal; as Moses the servant of the LORD had commanded before, that they should bless the
34 people of Israel. And afterward he read all the words of the law, the blessings and cursings, according to all that is
35 written in the book of the law. There was not a word of

from the lawful wives of Jacob, Simeon, Levi, Judah, Issachar, Joseph, Benjamin (Deut. xxvii. 12).
and half of them over against mount Ebal] viz., Reuben, Gad, Asher, Zebulun, Dan, and Naphtali (Deut. xxvii. 13). Five of these had sprung from the handmaids of Leah and Rachel, to whom Reuben is added probably on account of his great sin.

34. *the blessings and cursings*] "The twelve curses are directed against idolatry (Deut. xxvii. 15), contempt of parents (verse 16), removing a neighbour's land-mark (verse 17), inhumanity towards the blind, strangers, orphans, widows (verses 18, 19), incest and unnatural crimes (20—23), murder (verses 24, 25), and finally, in general against the transgression of the Law in any manner (verse 26). Blessings are promised in the city and on the field (Deut. xxviii. 3), on all births (xxviii. 4), on the basket and on the kneading-trough (xxviii. 5), on going out and coming in (xxviii. 6), a blessing in particular on the arms of Israel in contest with their enemies (xxviii. 7), a blessing on their position among the nations (xxviii. 9—14). A people standing as the Israelites then did on the scale of morality needed stern discipline, and not only might be allured by promises but must be alarmed by threats." Keil.

35. *There was not a word*] The acoustic properties of the valley between Ebal and Gerizim are interesting, the more so that several times they are incidentally brought before us. Comp. with this passage Judg. ix. 7, "And when they told it to Jotham, he went and stood in the *top of mount Gerizim, and lifted up his voice, and cried*, Hearken unto me, ye men of Shechem, that God may hearken unto you." "It is impossible to conceive a spot more admirably adapted for the purpose than this one, in the very centre of the newly acquired land, nor one which could more exactly fulfil all the required conditions. Let us imagine the chiefs and the priests gathered in the centre of the valley, the tribes stretching out as they stood in compact masses, the men of war and the heads of families, half on the north and half on the south, crowding the slopes on either side, the mixed multitude, the women and the children extending along in front till they spread into the plain beyond but still in sight: and there is no difficulty, much less impossibility in the problem. A single voice might be heard by many thousands, shut in and conveyed up and down by the enclosing hills. In the early morning we could not only see from Gerizim a man driving his ass down a path on Mount Ebal, *but could hear every word he uttered, as he urged it;* and in order to test the matter more certainly, on a subsequent occasion two of our party *stationed themselves on opposite sides of the valley* and with perfect ease recited the commandments antiphonally." Tristram's *Land of Israel*, pp. 149, 150. "The people in these

all that Moses commanded, which Joshua read not before all the congregation of Israel, with the women, and the little ones, and the strangers that were conversant among them.

1, 2. *The First League of the Canaanite Kings.*

And it came to pass, when all the kings which *were* on 9 *this* side Jordan, in the hills, and in the valleys, and in all the coasts of the great sea over against Lebanon, the Hittite, and the Amorite, the Canaanite, the Perizzite, the Hivite, and the Jebusite, heard *thereof;* that they gathered 2 themselves together, to fight with Joshua and with Israel, *with* one accord.

3—27. *The Embassy of the Gibeonites.*

And when the inhabitants of Gibeon heard what Joshua 3

mountainous countries are able, from long practice, so to pitch their voices as to be heard distinctly at distances almost incredible. They talk with persons across enormous wâdies, and give the most minute directions, which are perfectly understood; and in doing this they seem to speak very little louder than their usual tone of conversation." Thomson's *Land and the Book*, pp. 473, 474.

CH. IX. 1, 2. THE FIRST LEAGUE OF THE CANAANITE KINGS.

1. *And it came to pass*] Thus "that spring morning" did Israel "consecrate Palestine unto the Lord, and take sea and lake, mountain and valley—the most hallowed spots in their history—as witnesses of their covenant." It was probably on this occasion that the Egyptian coffin, containing the embalmed body of Joseph (Gen. l. 25, 26), was laid by the two tribes of the house of Joseph *in the parcel of ground* near Shechem, *which Jacob bought of the sons of Hamor* (Gen. xxxiii. 19). These important preliminaries having been carried out, the further prosecution of the campaign was possible.

the kings] Hitherto single cities had been the objects of Joshua's contention. Now leagues and confederacies were formed against him.

in the hills] i.e. the hill country of southern and central Canaan. In Num. xiii. 17, it is called "the mountain." Comp. also Deut. i. 7. The whole region of the western portion of Canaan is here described under three divisions: (*a*) the central hills, (*b*) the valleys = the *shephelah* (Deut. i. 7), (*c*) the seaboard. For the nations here enumerated see above, iii. 10.

3—27. THE EMBASSY OF THE GIBEONITES.

3. *of Gibeon*] This city was the head of the four towns occupied by the Hivites, the other three being Chephirah, Beeroth, and Kirjath-

4 had done unto Jericho and to Ai, they did work wilily, and went and made as if they had been ambassadors, and took old sacks upon their asses, and wine bottles, old, and rent, 5 and bound up; and old shoes and clouted upon their feet,

Jearim (Josh. ix. 17). It appears to have been a sort of independent republic, since we hear of elders there (Josh. ix. 11), but not of a king, and is said to have been a great city *like* a royal city (Josh. x. 2), i.e. of the same size and importance as those which the kings of the country made their capitals. The name itself signifies "pertaining to a hill," i.e. built on a hill, and describes the site, which is, by the direct route, about 5 miles north of Jerusalem, on two of the rounded hills peculiar to this neighbourhood. Placed at the head of the pass of Bethhoron, and commanding the main route from Jerusalem and the lower Jordan valley to Joppa and the sea-coast, and inhabited by a numerous and brave population, it was one of the most important cities of southern Canaan. It is still known as *El-Jib*.

4. *they did work wilily*] Rather, **they also did work wilily.** They had heard what Joshua had done in the case of Jericho and Ai, and the stratagems he had employed, and now they also resolved to do something and to meet craft with craft. " Thei thou3ten felli," Wyclif.

made as if they had been] Or, as the Ancient Versions with the change of a single consonant, reading here as in ver. 12, render, **provided themselves with victuals.**

old sacks upon their asses] These were probably the same as "the large bags, usually of hair, in which the Orientals pack up, for convenient transport on the backs of animals, all the baggage and commodities required for the journey. Beds, boxes, provisions, pots, packages of goods, all are carried in such bags, slung over the back of the animal, one hanging at each side. Being a good deal knocked about and exposed to the weather, these saddle-bags, as one might call them but for their size, suffer in a long journey; and hence the Gibeonites took old bags, to convey the impression that a long journey had been made. Kitto's *Bible Illustrations*, II. p. 286.

wine bottles] i.e. *skin bottles*, of which classical antiquity has afforded many representations. In the East the wine was preserved not in casks but in earthen jars and leathern bottles, made of the skins of goats, oxen, and buffaloes, turned inside out, washed, and rubbed over with warm mineral tar or naphtha. The wine is drawn out at one of the feet, by opening or closing the cord with which it is tied. This explains how the bottles could be "old," "rent," and "bound up," and also the caution of our Lord against pouring new wine into old bottles, lest they should be burst by the wine (Mark ii. 22).

5. *old shoes*] " and ful olde shoon," Wyclif, i.e. *sandals*, made of (1) hide, or (2) palm-leaves and papyrus stalks. Comp. Mark vi. 9.

clouted] i.e. **patched,** "sowid with patchis," Wyclif; from clout, A. S. *cleot*, *clút*, "a patch," properly a swelling from a blow, connected with Du. *klotsen*, to strike, as "botch" with Du. *botsen*. Comp. Jer. xxxviii. 11, 12, "So Ebed-melech took...thence old cast *clouts*, and old

and old garments upon them; and all the bread of their
provision was dry *and* mouldy. And they went to Joshua 6
unto the camp *at* Gilgal, and said unto him, and to the men

rotten rags...and said unto Jeremiah, Put now these old cast clouts and
rotten rags under thine armholes under the cords." Shakespeare, *II.
Henry VI.*, IV. 2,

"Spare none, but such as go in *clouted* shoon;"

and Latimer, *Serm.* p. 110, "Paul, yea and Peter too, had more skill in
mending an old net, and in *clouting* an old tent, than to teach law-
yers what diligence they should use in the expedition of matters." Sandals were seldom mended, being of so little value, that they could
easily be renewed when the worse for wear. "We have seen a man
make himself a new pair out of a piece of skin in a few minutes. The
mere fact, that articles so easily renewed, were patched in this instance,
was well calculated to suggest the idea of a long journey, in which the
convenience of purchasing new ones, or materials for making them, had
not been found, for which reason they had been obliged to make their
old ones serve by patching. It was a singular thing to see sandals
clouted at all, and only a journey would explain the fact." Kitto's
Bible Illustrations, II. p. 288.

old garments] It behoved ambassadors to appear in clean and decent,
if not in splendid, raiment. This was so essential, that the appearance
of these Gibeonites with old and travel-stained clothes could only be explained, upon any common principle, by the assigned reason, that they
had come direct from a long journey.

dry and mouldy] "Harde and 'brokun into gobetis," Wyclif. The
Hebrew word translated "mouldy" is the same which is rendered by
"cracknels" in 1 Kings xiv. 3. This word (*nikuddim*) denotes a kind
of crisp cake. The ordinary bread, baked in thin cakes, is not made
to keep more than a day or two, a fresh supply being baked daily. If
kept longer it dries up, and becomes at last excessively hard. It was
this kind of bread that the Gibeonites produced, and they indicated its
hardness—*hard as biscuits*—in evidence of the length of the journey
they had taken. Kitto's *Bible Illustrations*, II. p. 289.

6. *unto the camp at Gilgal*] Where was this Gilgal? (i) According
to some it was the Gilgal, of which we have already heard (v. 10), in
the Jordan valley, whither Joshua had returned after his successful
expedition against Ai, in order thence to undertake fresh enterprises, and
where the women, children, and property were left under a sufficient
guard, while he was absent with the host. (ii) Others think it is impossible to suppose that Joshua marched back from Shechem to the banks
of Jordan (ix. 6, x. 6, 7, 9), and, again, that he did so a second time,
after the battles in the north, to make the final apportionment of the
land among the people, and that the spot is that alluded to in Deut. xi.
30, as being situated "beside the oaks of Moreh," i.e. near the site of
Abraham's first altar (Gen. xii. 6, 7). If this is so, it would correspond
with the modern *Jilgiliah*, a few miles from Bethel.

of Israel, We be come from a far country: now therefore
7 make ye a league with us. And the men of Israel said unto
the Hivites, Peradventure ye dwell among us; and how
8 shall we make a league with you? And they said unto
Joshua, We *are* thy servants. And Joshua said unto them,
9 Who *are* ye? and from whence come ye? And they said
unto him, From a very far country thy servants are come
because of the name of the LORD thy God: for we have
10 heard the fame of him, and all that he did in Egypt, and all
that he did to the two kings of the Amorites, that *were* beyond Jordan, to Sihon king of Heshbon, and to Og king of
11 Bashan, which *was* at Ashtaroth. Wherefore our elders and
all the inhabitants of our country spake to us, saying, Take
victuals with you for the journey, and go to meet them, and
say unto them, We *are* your servants: therefore now make
12 ye a league with us. This our bread we took hot for our
provision out of our houses on the day we came forth to go
13 unto you; but now, behold, it is dry, and it is mouldy: and
these bottles of wine, which we filled, *were* new; and behold, they be rent: and these our garments and our shoes
14 are become old by reason of the very long journey. And
the men took of their victuals, and asked not *counsel* at the

a far country] Far beyond the boundaries of Palestine.
7. *the Hivites*] Comp. Josh. xi. 19; 2 Sam. xxi. 2.
8. *Who are ye?*] To this is to be noticed that they made no direct reply. They adroitly evaded the question by dwelling on the fact that they were Joshua's "servants" (comp. Gen. xxxii. 4, l. 18).
9. *we have heard the fame of him*] Comp. Josh. ii. 10, vi. 27.
10. *to Og, king of Bashan*] They prudently omit all mention of the late capture of Jericho and Ai, lest the revelation of what had recently occurred should betray them.
14. *the men took of their victuals*] "thei token thanne of the meetis of hem," Wyclif. "The men" here denote the elders of Israel, the heads of the tribes. Comp. verses 18—21. Some think it means they took and tasted of their provisions by way of test to see if their story was true, so Keil and Rosenmüller. Others interpret the words as denoting that the princes of the people took of the provisions, and by thus eating, according to the usages of Oriental nations, pledged themselves to friendship and amity. Compare the eating together as a sign of friendship of Jacob and Laban, Gen. xxxi. 46; and the expression "covenant of salt," Lev. ii. 13; 2 Chron. xiii. 5.
and asked not counsel] This was a transgression of an explicit command that the priest should seek a revelation of the Divine will for

vv. 43; 1, 2.] JOSHUA, X. XI. 97

LORD God of Israel fought for Israel. And Joshua returned, 43 and all Israel with him, unto the camp to Gilgal.

1—15. *Confederacy of the Kings of Northern Canaan.*

And it came to pass, when Jabin king of Hazor had heard 11 *those things*, that he sent to Jobab king of Madon, and to the king of Shimron, and to the king of Achshaph, and to the 2 kings that *were* on the north of the mountains, and of the plains south of Cinneroth, and in the valley, and in the

42. *at one time*] i.e. in one campaign, or in one expedition, which doubtless lasted some days or even weeks.
43. *unto the camp to Gilgal*] See note above on verse 15.

CH. XI. 1—15. CONFEDERACY OF THE KINGS OF NORTHERN CANAAN.

1. *And it came to pass*] We now enter upon a different scene in the conquests of Joshua. Just as before Adoni-Zedek, the king of Jerusalem, had summoned the five kings of southern Canaan, so now Jabin, the king of Hazor, summons the chiefs of the north against the Israelitish leader.

Jabin] This was an hereditary and official title of the chief of Hazor. It denotes "*the wise*" or "*intelligent.*" Here we find a king of the same name at a considerably later date (Judg. iv. 2).

Hazor]="*enclosed,*" "*fortified,*" was an important, and apparently almost impregnable, stronghold of the Canaanites of the north, situated in the mountains, north of the waters of Merom. We find it afterwards fortified by Solomon (1 Kings ix. 15), and its inhabitants were carried away captive by Tiglath-pileser (2 Kings xv. 29). The most probable site is *Tell Khuraibeh*. It lay apparently between Ramah and Kedesh, on the high ground overlooking the Lake of Merom.

Jobab king of Madon] The three places here mentioned, Madon, Shimron, and Achshaph, were probably in the neighbourhood of Hazor, but their sites cannot be determined. Schwarz on very slight grounds proposes to identify Madon with *Kefr Menda*, a village at the western end of the Plain of *Buttauf*, four or five miles N. of Sepphoris.

the king of Shimron] Its full name appears to have been Shimron-Meron. It was afterwards included in the tribe of Zebulun (Josh. xix. 15).

the king of Achshaph] This place was afterwards included within the territory of Asher (Josh. xii. 20, xix. 25). It has been identified with *Chaifa*, a place which, from its situation, must always have been of great importance.

2. *that were on the north*] Or, that were "northwards in the mountains," i.e. "the mountains of Naphtali" (Josh. xx. 7), the mountainous region of Galilee.

the plains south of Cinneroth] Literally, "in the **Arabah**, south of

JOSHUA 7

3 borders of Dor on the west, *and to* the Canaanite on the east and on the west, and *to* the Amorite, and the Hittite, and the Perizzite, and the Jebusite in the mountains, and *to*
4 the Hivite under Hermon in the land of Mizpeh. And they

Chinneroth," i.e. the "Ghôr" of the Jordan, the northern portion of the depressed tract which extends along the Jordan from the Lake of. Gennesareth southwards.
Cinneroth] or Chinnereth, or Chinneroth, was the name of a fortified town in Naphtali (Josh. xix. 35), situated on the shore of the Sea of Galilee, and giving its earliest name to that lake (Num. xxxiv. 11).
and in the valley] "In the wild feeldis," Wyclif; i.e. "the lowlands," the level plain bordering the sea between Akko and Sidon.
in the borders of Dor] Rather, **the highlands of Dor**. Dor was an ancient royal city of the Canaanites (Josh. xii. 23), situated on the coast of the Mediterranean, 14 miles south of the promontory of Carmel, and 7 north of Cæsarea. The district, of which it was the capital, was afterwards within the allotted territory of Asher, but was assigned to Manasseh (Josh. xvii. 11), but the Israelites could never obtain possession of this strong city (Josh. xvii. 12; Judg. i. 27), though they made the inhabitants pay tribute in the days of Solomon (1 Kings iv. 11). What is here rendered *"the borders of Dor,"* is rendered *"the coast of Dor"* Josh. xii. 23, and the *"region of Dor"* 1 Kings iv. 11. The original word *Napheth*, thus variously translated, means an "elevated tract," and hence a coast as being raised above the water. Dor stood on a rocky promontory, behind which lies a beautiful and fertile plain, extending southward to Sharon, and northward to Carmel. This plain is the "coast" or "region" of Dor. Dor was one of the Phœnician seats of commerce, deriving its importance from (i) its well-sheltered haven, (ii) the abundance amidst its rocks of the *murex*, a shell-fish yielding the famous purple dye. It was still a flourishing town in the Roman age, and afterwards became the seat of a bishop, who was, in the days of the Crusades, a suffragan in the province of Cæsarea. The modern *Tantûra* or *Dandora* is a corruption of the ancient name. It is now represented by a little fishing village, consisting of some thirty houses, while the site of the old city lies to the north of it, covered for a space of half a mile with massive ruins.
3. *and to the Canaanite*] Not satisfied with summoning to his banner the tribes of the north, Jabin extended his "war-token" to the remnants of the defeated tribes of the south too; (*a*) the Canaanites, or "lowlanders" of the east and west; (*b*) the Amorites, or "highlanders" of the south; (*c*) the Hittites; (*d*) the Perizzites; (*e*) the Jebusites, from the still unconquered Jebus; (*f*) the Hivites under the snowy heights of Hermon, the most beautiful and conspicuous mountain in Palestine or Syria. For the distribution of these various nations see note above, ch. iii. 10.
in the land of Mizpeh} Mizpeh means "prospect" or "watch-tower." It has the article here = "*the Land of the Watch-Tower.*" There were several places in Palestine bearing this name. This Mizpeh was

went out, they and all their hosts with them, much people, *even* as the sand that *is* upon the sea shore in multitude, with horses and chariots very many. And when all these 5 kings were met together, they came and pitched together at the waters of Merom, to fight against Israel.

And the LORD said unto Joshua, Be not afraid because of 6 them: for to morrow about this time will I deliver them up all slain before Israel: thou shalt hough their horses, and

probably in a plain stretching south-west at the foot of Hermon, where now is situated the village of *Metullah*, which also means "the lookout," or "look-down," perched on a hill 200 feet high, south of Lake Merom, and commanding a splendid view. This Mizpeh (= "*Belle Vue*" amongst ourselves) must not be confounded with the Mizpeh of Gilead (Josh. xiii. 26); nor with the Mizpeh of Judah (Josh. xv. 38); nor yet with that of Moab (1 Sam. xxii. 3).

4. *And they went out*] "As the British chiefs were driven to the Land's End before the advance of the Saxon, so at this Land's End of Palestine were gathered for this last struggle, not only the kings of the north in the immediate neighbourhood, but from the desert valley of the Jordan south of the Sea of Galilee, from the maritime plain of Philistia, from the heights above Sharon, and from the still unconquered Jebus." Stanley, *Lectures*, I. 259.

as the sand] "as the grauel that is in the brenk of the see," Wyclif. Comp. the description (*a*) of the hosts of the Midianites and Amalekites in the time of Gideon (Judg. vii. 12); and (*b*) of the Philistines in the time of Saul (1 Sam. xiii. 5).

with horses and chariots very many] These now for the first time appear in Canaanite warfare, and "it was the use of these which probably fixed the scene of the encampment by the lake, along whose level shores they could have full play for their force."

5. *at the waters of Merom*] i.e. "the Upper Waters;" the uppermost of the three lakes in the Jordan valley, called by the Greeks "Semechonitis," or Samochonitis (Jos. *Ant.*v. 5. 1), and by the Arabs "*Hûleh*." The lake is formed by the expansion of the descending Jordan, about 7 miles long by 5 in breadth, of a triangular shape, the point being at the south, where the Jordan, which enters it on the north, again quits it. It is surrounded by marshes and numberless streams bordered with thickets of papyrus. For the fullest and most graphic description of this lake, and the surrounding morasses, see Macgregor's *Rob Roy on the Jordan*, xii.—xvii.

6. *And the Lord said*] We may believe that Joshua was already some way on the march when these encouraging words were addressed to him. The distance from his encampment to the waters of Merom was too great for him to reach the latter place between one day and the next.

thou shalt hough their horses] So especially formidable to the Israelites, who had none. The word "hough" also occurs in 2 Sam. viii. 4, where we read that David "*houghed* all the chariot horses." It comes from

7—2

7 burn their chariots with fire. So Joshua came, and all the people of war with him, against them by the waters of 8 Merom suddenly; and they fell upon them. And the LORD delivered them into the hand of Israel, who smote them, and chased them unto great Zidon, and unto Misrephoth-maim, and unto the valley of Mizpeh eastward; and they

the A. S. *hoh*, and means to cut the ham-strings or back sinews of cattle, so as to disable them and render them utterly unfit for use, since the sinew, once severed, can never be healed again, and as a rule the arteries are cut at the same time, so that the horses bleed to death. In the late version of Wyclif the verse is rendered, "Thou shalt *hoxe* the horsis of hem," while in the earlier version it runs, "The hors of hem thow shalt *kut of the synewis at the knees*." "Hox" is the form found in Shakespeare,

"If thou inclin'st that way, thou art a coward;
Which *hoxes* honesty behind, restraining
From course requir'd." *Winter's Tale*, I. 2. 243.

The Scotch *hoch* is used in the same way.

and burn their chariots] of which it is said (Josh. xvii. 18) that they were iron chariots, i.e. had wheels with iron tires. Scythe-chariots were first introduced by Cyrus: Xen. *Cyrop.* VI. i. 30.

7. *So Joshua came*] With the suddenness and rapidity which characterized all his movements, he did not wait for the northern confederacy to attack him at Gilgal, but marched against them with the intention of coming upon them before their army could be got into order.

against them suddenly] He *fell* upon them, like a thunderbolt, so the word is to be literally understood as in the corresponding passage in Job i. 15, "the Sabeans *fell* upon them, and took them away." Without a word of warning he burst upon them in the mountain slopes of the plain, before they had time to rally on the level ground.

8. *and chased them*] The rout was complete, and the fugitives seem to have divided into three parts—

(*a*) *unto great Zidon*] One party took the road north-west over the mountains above the gorge of the Leontes "to Sidon," or, as it is distinguished here and in Josh. xix. 28, "the great Sidon," as being the metropolis of Phœnicia. This it had ceased to be before the reign of David, by which time its sister city Tyre had eclipsed it in splendour, and taken the first place amongst the cities of Phœnicia. At the present day Sidon, *Saida*, is again larger than Tyre. The former contains 5000 or 6000 inhabitants and many large houses built of stone, whereas the present Sur is nothing but a market town, the houses of which are little more than huts.

(*b*) *unto Misrephoth-maim*] A second party took the road, west, and south-west, to Mizrephoth-maim, which is interpreted either (i) as "*the warm springs*," or (ii) "*the salt-pits*," or (iii) "*the smelting-pits by the*

smote them, until *they* left them none remaining. And 9
Joshua did unto them as the LORD bade him: he houghed
their horses, and burnt their chariots with fire. And Joshua 10
at that time turned back, and took Hazor, and smote the
king thereof with the sword: for Hazor beforetime *was* the
head of all those kingdoms. And they smote all the souls 11
that *were* therein with the edge of the sword, utterly destroying *them:* there was not any left to breathe: and he burnt
Hazor with fire. And all the cities of those kings, and all 12
the kings of them, did Joshua take, and smote them with
the edge of the sword, *and* he utterly destroyed them, as
Moses the servant of the LORD commanded. But *as for* the 13
cities that stood still in their strength, Israel burned none of
them, save Hazor only; *that* did Joshua burn. And all the 14
spoil of these cities, and the cattle, the children of Israel
took for a prey unto themselves; but every man they smote
with the edge of the sword, until they had destroyed them,

waters," the glass-houses, of which there were several in the neighbourhood of Sidon.

(*c*) *and unto the valley of Mizpeh*] A third party fled eastward unto
the *Buka'a* or "valley" of Mizpeh at the foot of Hermon. The eastward
direction is spoken of in reference to Sidon.

and they smote them] But wherever they fled, they were hotly pursued
by the Israelites, who captured their cities one by one, put the inhabitants to death, and carried away the booty and cattle.

9. *he houghed their horses*] "he kuttide the sinewis at the knee,"
Wyclif. The command, to render the horses useless, was intended to
lead Israel not to place its confidence in horses and chariots (Ps. xx. 7,
cxlvii. 10), and wisely incapacitated them from extending their conquests
beyond the borders of Canaan. See Deut. xvii. 16.

10. *turned back*] Far over the western hills Joshua pursued the flying
hosts before he "turned back," and took Hazor, and because of its
prominence as the chief city of these petty northern kingdoms, burned it
with fire.

12. *as Moses the servant of the Lord commanded*] See Deut. vii. 2,
xx. 16, 17.

13. *the cities that stood still in their strength*] Rather, **the cities which
stood each on its own hill,** or **mound,** "the citees that weren in the hillis,
and in the hillockis set," Wyclif. Comp. Jer. xxx. 18, "and the city
shall be builded upon her own heap" ("*little hill*" margin). With the
exception of Hazor, Joshua did not burn the cities, but left them standing,
each on its own hill, the ordinary site for cities in Canaan. Comp.
Matt. v. 14.

14. *all the spoil*] This was not devoted as at Jericho, but divided as
at Ai. Comp. Josh. viii. 2, 27.

15 neither left they any to breathe. As the LORD commanded Moses his servant, so did Moses command Joshua, and so did Joshua; he left nothing undone of all that the LORD commanded Moses.

16—20. *General Retrospect of the Conquest of Palestine.*

16 So Joshua took all that land, the hills, and all the south *country*, and all the land of Goshen, and the valley, and the plain, and the mountain of Israel, and the valley of the same; 17 *even* from the mount Halak, that goeth up *to* Seir, even unto Baal-gad in the valley of Lebanon under mount Hermon:

15. *As the Lord commanded Moses*] For this command of God to Moses comp. (*a*) Exod. xxxiv. 11—16; (*b*) Num. xxxiii. 51—54; (*c*) Deut. xx. 16; and for the transference of the command to Joshua comp. (*a*) Num. xxvii. 18—23; (*b*) Deut. iii. 21.

he left nothing undone] "he passide not beside of alle the maundementis," Wyclif. Conscientiousness in carrying out the Divine commands is thus represented as a prominent feature in Joshua's character.

16—20. GENERAL RETROSPECT OF THE CONQUEST OF PALESTINE.

16. *So Joshua took*] The sacred writer pauses to survey and sum up the conquests of the Israelitish leader.

the hills] The country is contemplated under a sevenfold division, (i) the cities; (ii) the south country; (iii) the land of Goshen (comp. x. 41); (iv) the valley; (v) the plain; (vi) the mountain of Israel; (vii) the valley of the same.

17. *even from the mount Halak*] Or, as it is rendered in the margin, "*the smooth mountain*," or "*the bald mountain*." We find this name only once again, viz. in xii. 7, and there, as here, it seems to mark the southern limit of Joshua's conquests. Several ranges near the southern border of Canaan might be thus described. (*a*) Some would identify it with the modern *Jebel-el-Mukrah*, 60 miles south of the Dead Sea; (*b*) others with the mountain *Madurah*, or *Maderah*; (*c*) while others would identify it with the range of white cliffs, which cuts the *Arabah* obliquely at about eight English miles to the south of the Dead Sea, and divides the great valley into the two parts *El Ghor* and *El Arabah*. This row of cliffs, which is about 60 to 80 feet high, might very well be called "*the bald mountain which ascends to Seir*," for it was a point well adapted to form the southern boundary of Canaan, since it both touches the territory of Kadesh-Barnea, and joins in the east the upper chain of the mountains of Seir.—See Keil *in loc.*

even unto Baal-Gad] This was a town dedicated to Baal, under the aspect of "Gad" or the "god of good fortune" (Josh. xii. 7, xiii. 5), probably the same as Baal-Hermon (Judg. iii. 3; 1 Chron. v. 23). In later times it was known as *Panium* or *Paneas*, and when enlarged and embellished by Herod Philip, *Cæsarea Philippi*, to distinguish it from

and all their kings he took, and smote them, and slew them. Joshua made war a long time with all those kings. There was not a city that made peace with the children of Israel, save the Hivites the inhabitants of Gibeon: all *other* they took in battle. For it was of the LORD to harden their hearts, that *they* should come against Israel *in* battle, that *he* might destroy them utterly, *and* that they might have no favour, but that *he* might destroy them, as the LORD commanded Moses.

Cæsarea "*Palestinæ*" or Cæsarea "*on the sea*" (Mark viii. 27). Dean Stanley calls it a Syrian Tivoli, and certainly there is much in the rocks, caverns, cascades, and the natural beauty of the scenery, to recall the Roman Tibur. Behind the village, in front of a great natural cavern, a river bursts forth from the earth, the "upper source" of the Jordan. Inscriptions and niches in the face of the cliff tell of the old idol worship of Baal and of Pan. Tristram's *Land of Israel*, p. 581.

18. *a long time*] "Myche time," Wyclif. Five years at least. Caleb was 40 years old when Moses sent him out of Kadesh-Barnea as a spy, and 80 years old when, on the conquest of the land, he received his portion at the hands of Joshua. Thus 45 years had elapsed since the former date, of which 40, or 38, had been spent in the wanderings of the wilderness. The campaigns of Joshua must therefore have occupied at least five or seven years for their accomplishment.

19. *save the Hivites*] Gibeon had surrendered peacefully (Josh. ix. 3, 7, 15, x. 1, 6). All the rest were taken in battle.

20. *For it was of the Lord*] "Forsothe the sentence of the Lord it was," Wyclif. Compare Exod. iv. 21, "When thou goest to return into Egypt, see that thou do all those wonders before Pharaoh, which I have put in thine hand: *but I will harden his heart*, that he shall not let the people go;" and Exod. vii. 3, "And *I will harden* Pharaoh's heart, and multiply my signs and my wonders in the land of Egypt;" xiv. 4; Rom. ix. 17. Here, as everywhere in Scripture where such hardening is spoken of, it is to be carefully borne in mind, that it is always inflicted as a judgment on those who had previously acted contrary to the Divine will. This is true of

(*a*) *Pharaoh*, who had grievously and cruelly oppressed the Israelites for his own selfish ends;

(*b*) *The Canaanites*, who had persisted in the lowest and most degrading idolatry and sensuality;

(*c*) *The Israelites*, who in spite of warning and example fell away into idolatry in like manner, and forgat the Lord, Who had done such great things for them (Isai. vi. 10; Matt. xiii. 12—15).

The same is in a measure said of Sihon king of the Amorites (Deut. ii. 30); of Samson (Judg. xiv. 4); of the sons of Eli (1 Sam. ii. 25); of Solomon (1 Kings xii. 15); of Ahaziah (2 Chron. xxii. 7); of Amaziah (2 Chron. xxv. 16, 20). It is expressed also in the Latin proverb, "Quem Deus vult perdere, prius dementat."

21—23. Extermination of the Anakims.

21   And at that time came Joshua, and cut off the Anakims from the mountains, from Hebron, from Debir, from Anab, and from all the mountains of Judah, and from all the

21—23. EXTERMINATION OF THE ANAKIMS.

21. *at that time*] That is, in the course of the "long time," the seven years spoken of in verse 18. We have now a supplementary notice of the destruction of the Anakims, and a general conclusion substantially as given in verse 16.

the Anakims] In Num. xiii. 22 we are told of the spies that they "ascended by the south and came unto Hebron; where Ahiman, Sheshai, and Talmai, the children of Anak, were," and when this was reported to the Israelites, and they heard of "the giants, the sons of Anak, which come of the giants, in whose sight the spies seemed as grasshoppers" (Num. xiii. 33), "all the congregation lifted up their voice, and cried, and murmured against Moses and against Aaron" (Num. xiv. 1, 2). The sacred writer therefore now goes back to record pointedly this terrible race, who had inspired such faithless murmuring and complaint (comp. Deut. ix. 2). It has been concluded by some that these giants were a tribe of Cushite wanderers from Babel, and of the same race as the Philistines, the Phœnicians, and the Egyptian shepherd-kings, representing one or more families of Amorite descent, distinguished for their lofty stature and physical powers. Thus Og, king of Bashan, is described as of the "remnant of the giants" (Deut. iii. 11). In Abraham's time (Gen. xiv. 5, 6) they inhabited the territories afterwards known as Edom and Moab, and the region east of Jordan, under the names of (*a*) Rephaims, (*b*) Zuzims or Zamzummims, (*c*) Emims, and (*d*) Horites. Here they were attacked by Chedorlaomer, the Elamite king, who also smote the Amorites of Engedi in the Jordan valley. Subsequently the Horites were conquered by the Edomites, the Emims and the Zuzims by the Moabites and Ammonites, while the remnant, to which Og king of Bashan belonged, was destroyed by the Israelites under Moses. Now, as under Moses on the east, so under Joshua on the west of Jordan, the Anakims were driven forth before the arms of Israel.

from Hebron] Which from the progenitor of this race received its original name of Kirjath-Arba. See above on x. 3.

from Debir] See x. 38.

from Anab] A town in the mountains of Judah (Josh. xv. 50). It has retained its ancient name, and lies among the hills about 10 miles S.S.W. of Hebron, close to Shoco and Eshtemoa. See Robinson's *Bib. Researches*, I. 494 and II. 195, who from *Main* (the Maon of Scripture) observed a place of this name, distinguished by a small tower.

the mountains of Judah] A distinction is here made between "the mountains of Judah," and "the mountains of Israel." This, strange as

mountains of Israel: Joshua destroyed them utterly with their cities. There was none of the Anakims left in the land 22 of the children of Israel: only in Gaza, in Gath, and in Ashdod, there remained. So Joshua took the whole land, 23 according to all that the LORD said unto Moses; and Joshua gave it for an inheritance unto Israel according to their divisions by their tribes. And the land rested from war.

it may seem, affords one of the undesigned evidences of the early composition of the Book of Joshua. "When Judah entered on his possession, all the other tribes were still in Gilgal (Josh. xiv. 6, xv. 1). Afterwards, when Ephraim and Manasseh entered on theirs, all Israel, except Judah, were camped in Shiloh (Josh. xvi. 1, xviii. 1), these two possessions being separated by the still unallotted territory which later was given to Benjamin (Josh. xviii. 11). What more natural than that the mountain given to 'the children of Judah' should have been called 'the mountain of Judah,' and that where all the rest of Israel camped 'the mountain of Israel,' and also 'the mountain of Ephraim' (Josh. xix. 50, xx. 7), because it was afterwards given to that tribe?" Dr Edersheim's *Israel in Canaan*, p. 86.

22. *only in Gaza*] See above, x. 41.

in Gath] One of the five royal cities of the Philistines (Josh. xiii. 3; 1 Sam. vi. 17), and the native place of the giant Goliath, who, though doubtless of the old stock of the Anakims (1 Sam. xvii. 4; 2 Sam. xxi. 18—20), is called a Philistine, shewing that in David's time the two races had coalesced and become one. Gath occupied a strong position (2 Chron. xi. 8), on the border of Judah and Philistia (1 Sam. xxi. 10; 1 Chron. xviii. 1) near Shoco and Adullam (2 Chron. xi. 8), and from its strength and resources formed the key of both countries.

and in Ashdod] Ashdod or Azotus (Acts viii. 40) was situated about 30 miles from the southern frontier of Palestine, three from the Mediterranean Sea, and nearly midway between Gaza and Joppa. It was assigned to the tribe of Judah (Josh. xv. 47), but was never subdued by the Israelites, and even down to Nehemiah's age it preserved its distinctiveness of race and language (Neh. xiii. 23, 24). It was the city of Dagon (1 Sam. v. 1—7), and against it, as against Gaza, the prophets often direct their denunciations (Jer. xxv. 20; Amos i. 8; Zeph. ii. 4; Zech. ix. 6).

23. *And the land rested from war*] But this does not denote a permanent cessation. It rather implies that the Israelites no longer needed to war *unitedly* against the Canaanites. There was yet much land to be possessed, but the time had arrived for the occupation of the country by the different tribes, and the completion of the work of conquest was now to be left to the separate action of each.

1—6. *Catalogue of the Kings conquered in Eastern Palestine.*

12 Now these *are* the kings of the land, which the children of Israel smote, and possessed their land on the *other* side Jordan toward the rising of the sun, from the river Arnon 2 unto mount Hermon, and all the plain on the east: Sihon king of the Amorites, who dwelt in Heshbon, *and* ruled from

CH. XII. 1—6. CATALOGUE OF THE KINGS CONQUERED IN EASTERN PALESTINE.

1. *Now these*] This Chapter may be termed an official summary, suitable to a public record, of the whole territory conquered by Moses and by Joshua. "It contains no new matter, except that certain cities and their rulers are specified by name, which have previously been included in more general statements of Joshua's wars."

from the river Arnon] The first province described is the southeastern, previously the territory of the Amorite king, Sihon, "from the river Arnon unto Mount Hermon." The Arnon (*the rushing river*), now the *Wady el-Mojeb*, flows in part, through a deep rocky bed, into the Dead Sea. "As far as we could calculate by observation, the width of the ravine is about 3 miles from crest to crest; the depth by our barometers 2150 feet from the south side, which runs for some distance nearly 200 feet higher than the northern edge." Tristram's *Land of Moab*, p. 126.

unto mount Hermon] Called by the Sidonians Sirion = "breastplate," a name suggested by its rounded glittering top, when the sun's rays are reflected by the snow that covers it (Deut. iii. 9; Cant. iv. 8). It was also called Sion = "the elevated," and is now known as *Jebel-es-Sheikh*, "the chief mountain," which rises over 9000 feet. "In whatever part of Palestine the Israelite turned his eye northward, Hermon was there terminating the view. From the plain along the coast, from the mountains of Samaria, from the Jordan valley, from the heights of Moab and Gilead, from the plateau of Bashan, the pale blue, snow-capped cone forms the one feature in the northern horizon." In Ps. xlii. 6 we have a vivid description of the mountain landscape on Hermon, but "the land of splendour, of heaven-towering mountains, and of glorious streams, offers no compensation to the heart of the Psalmist for the humbler hills of Zion where his God abides."

all the plain on the east] "al the est coost that beholdith the wildernes," Wyclif; i.e. part of the great valley, now called *the Ghor*, from the Sea of Galilee to the Ælamitic Gulf, along the east bank of the Jordan.

2. *Sihon king of the Amorites*] See Num. xxi. 24; Deut. ii. 33, iii. 6, 16.

who dwelt in Heshbon] On the western border of the high plain (*Mishor*, Josh. xiii. 17), and on the boundary line between the tribes of Reuben and Gad. "The ruins of *Hesbân*, 20 miles east of the Jordan, on the parallel of the northern end of the Dead Sea, mark the

JOSHUA, XII.

Aroer, which *is* upon the bank of the river of Arnon, and *from* the middle of the river, and *from* half Gilead, even unto the river Jabbok, *which is* the border of the children of Ammon; and *from* the plain to the sea of Cinneroth on the east, and 3 unto the sea of the plain, *even* the salt sea on the east, the way to Beth-jeshimoth; and from the south, under Ashdoth-pisgah: and the coast of Og king of Bashan, *which was* of 4

site, as they bear the name, of the ancient Heshbon." "There is little, of a place once famed in olden story, for the traveller to see. A large piece of walling at the west end of the bold isolated hill, on which the old fortress stood; with a square block house, and a pointed archway adjoining; a temple on the crest of the hill, with the pavement unbroken and the bases of four columns still *in situ;* on the east, in the plain, just at the base of the hill, a great cistern, called by some 'the fish-pools of Hesbon,' but more probably only the reservoir for the supply of the city—these are all that remain." Tristram's *Land of Moab*, pp. 338, 339.

from Aroer] "which is set on the brenke of the stronde of Arn̥on," Wyclif. Aroer lay partly on and partly in the Arnon, i.e. on an island, now '*Arâir*. It was allotted to Reuben (Josh. xiii. 16), but later came into the possession of Moab (Jer. xlviii. 19). Bochardt found ruins with the name 'Arâir on the old Roman road, upon the very edge of the precipitous north bank of the *Wady Mojeb*.

half Gilead] Properly Gilead denotes (i) a mountain on the south bank of the Jabbok (Gen. xxxi. 21—48) with a city of the same name; (ii) the immediate neighbourhood of this mountain (Num. xxxii. 1; Deut. ii. 36, 37); (iii) the whole mountain district between the Arnon and the Jabbok, now called *Belka* (see Deut. xxxiv. 1; 1 Kings iv. 19).

the river Jabbok] "The streem of Jabuch," Wyclif, = "the gushing-brook," now the *Wady Zurka*.

3. *and from the plain*] Rather, **and the plain**, the Arabah, i.e. the eastern part of the Jordan valley, as far as the Sea of Chinneroth.

the sea of Cinneroth] So called after the city of this name. See above, ch. xi. 2. In the New Testament it is called (*a*) the "Sea of Galilee" (Matt. iv. 18, xv. 29; Mark i. 16); (*b*) the "lake of Gennesaret" (Luke v. 1); (*c*) the "sea of Tiberias" (John vi. 1, xxi. 1); and sometimes (*d*) simply "the sea."

and unto the sea of the plain] i.e. of the Arabah. While the Lake of Gennesareth forms the northern boundary of the eastern part of the Jordan valley, it is in like manner bounded on the south by the Salt Sea, i.e. the Dead Sea. Near which lay

Beth-jeshimoth]="the House of the Wastes." It was one of the limits of the encampment of Israel before crossing the Jordan (Num. xxxiii. 48, 49).

under Ashdoth-pisgah] See above, x. 40.

4. *the coast of Og*] See Num. xxi. 33, 35; Deut. iii. 4, 10.

the remnant of the giants, that dwelt at Ashtaroth and at
5 Edrei, and reigned in mount Hermon, and in Salcah, and
in all Bashan, unto the border of the Geshurites and the
Maachathites, and half Gilead, the border of Sihon king of
6 Heshbon. Them did Moses the servant of the LORD and

at Ashtaroth] The residence of Og. It is now called *Tel Ashterah*, or *Asherah*. The Tel (*hill*) rises to a height of between fifty and a hundred feet from the level of the plain, in which ruins lie scattered. At the foot of the hill are ancient foundations of walls and copious springs.

at Edrei] = *Strength*. Here, "in the Thermopylæ of his kingdom," Og was slain. See Num. xxi. 33—35; Deut. iii. 1—3. On a rocky promontory, 1½ miles wide, and 2½ miles long, south-west of the basaltic district of Argob, rose the city, "without water, without access save over rocks, and through defiles almost impracticable. Strength and security seem to have been the great objects kept in view, and to these all other advantages were sacrificed." By the Greeks it was called *Adraa*; by the Crusaders *Adratum*, also *Civitas Bernardi de Stampis*, now *Edr'a*. In A.D. 1142 the Crusaders under Baldwin III. made a sudden attack upon it, but without success. The historian of the Crusades, in his account of this incident, refers to the immense subterranean cisterns that abound in the neighbourhood of the city, among the rocks, and the modern traveller is astonished at the extent and number of reservoirs, not only here but in all the other towns and villages in the *Lejah*, and in Jebel Haurân. Porter's *Handbook*, II. 533, 534.

5. *and in Salcah*] Identical with the town of *Sûlkhad* at the southern extremity of the *Jebel Haurân*. It was conquered by the Israelites, Deut. iii. 10. The town is of considerable size, two or three miles in circumference, surrounding a castle on a lofty isolated hill. "The country is stony and undulating; but the soil is rich, and traces of former cultivation are everywhere visible. The view from the top of the castle is extensive and strangely interesting.... On the segment of the plain, extending from the south to the east, I counted the towns or large villages, none of them more than 12 miles distant, and almost all of them, so far as I could see by the aid of a telescope, still habitable like *Sulkhad*, but entirely deserted. Well may we exclaim with the prophet, as we look over this mournful scene of utter desolation, 'Moab is confounded; for it is broken down; howl and cry; tell ye it in Arnon, that Moab is spoiled, *and judgment is come upon the plain country* ... upon *Beth-gamul*, and upon *Beth-meon*, and upon *Kerioth*, and upon *Bozrah*, and upon *all the cities* of the land of Moab, far or near' (Jer. xlviii. 19—24)." Porter's *Handbook*, II. 522.

the border of the Geshurites] Geshur was a little principality in the N.E. corner of Bashan, adjoining the province of Argob (Deut. iii. 14), and the kingdom of Aram or Syria (2 Sam. xv. 8). Hither Absalom fled after the murder of Amnon (2 Sam. xiii. 37).

the Maachathites] The people of Maacha dwelt on the south-west slope of Hermon at the sources of the Jordan (Deut. iii. 14).

the children of Israel smite: and Moses the servant of the LORD gave it *for* a possession unto the Reubenites, and the Gadites, and the half tribe of Manasseh.

7—24. *Catalogue of the Kings vanquished on the West of the Jordan.*

And these *are* the kings of the country which Joshua and 7 the children of Israel smote on *this* side Jordan on the west, from Baal-gad in the valley of Lebanon even unto the mount Halak, that goeth up to Seir; which Joshua gave unto the tribes of Israel *for* a possession according to their divisions; in the mountains, and in the valleys, and in the plains, and 8 in the springs, and in the wilderness, and in the south *country;* the Hittites, the Amorites, and the Canaanites, the Perizzites, the Hivites, and the Jebusites: the king of 9 Jericho, one; the king of Ai, which *is* beside Beth-el, one; the king of Jerusalem, one; the king of Hebron, one; the 11 king of Jarmuth, one; the king of Lachish, one; the king of 12 Eglon, one; the king of Gezer, one; the king of Debir, oue; 13 the king of Geder, one; the king of Hormah, one; the king 14 of Arad, one; the king of Libnah, one; the king of Adullam, 15

7—24. CATALOGUE OF THE KINGS VANQUISHED ON THE WEST OF THE JORDAN.

7. *And these are the kings*] This and the following verse coincide with ch. xi. 16, and x. 40—42. They introduce the following narrative.

9. *the king of Jericho*] The kings are enumerated generally in the order in which they were conquered. For the overthrow of the kings of Jericho, Ai, Jerusalem, Hebron, Jarmuth, Lachish, Eglon, and Gezer see (*a*) Josh. vi. 2 ff.; (*b*) viii. 29; (*c*) x. 1—5, 33.

12. *Gezer*] The situation of this royal city has lately (see above, x. 33) been discovered by M. Clermont Ganneau at *Tel-el-Jezar*, about four miles from *Amwâs* (Emmaus), and on the western boundary of the territory of Ephraim. The ruins are extensive, with rock-hewn tombs, quarries, and remains of an aqueduct.

13. *the king of Debir*] See Josh. x. 39.

the king of Geder] Somewhere in the lowland of Judah. Possibly the same place as the Gedor mentioned in 1 Chron. iv. 39.

14. *the king of Hormah*] or Zephath, see Judg. i. 17. Robinson would place it near the pass of *Es-Sufah*, W.S.W. of the Dead Sea, where the Israelites were defeated by the Canaanites (Num. xiv. 44, 45), and subsequently the Canaanites by the Israelites (Num. xxi. 1—3).

16 one; the king of Makkedah, one; the king of Beth-el, one;
17 the king of Tappuah, one; the king of Hepher, one; the
18
19 king of Aphek, one; the king of Lasharon, one; the king of
20 Madon, one; the king of Hazor, one; the king of Shimron-
21 meron, one; the king of Achshaph, one; the king of
22 Taanach, one; the king of Megiddo, one; the king of

Arad] Near the wilderness of Kadesh, 20 Roman miles S. of Hebron. It is also mentioned in Num. xxi. 1—3; Judg. i. 16, 17. Now probably *Tell' Arâd*.
15. *Libnah*] See Josh. x. 29, 30.
Adullam] In the low country of Judah, a place of great antiquity (Gen. xxxviii. 1, 12, 20). The limestone cliffs of the locality are pierced with extensive caverns, one of which is famous as the refuge of David (1 Sam. xxii. 1; 2 Sam. xxiii. 13). The city was fortified by Rehoboam (2 Chron. xi. 7). Adullam has been traditionally identified with a place called *Khureitun*, where is a great cave which has been explored by Captain Warren and Lieutenant Conder. Later writers are inclined to place it at Deir Dubbân, about six miles north of *Beit Jibrîn* (Eleutheropolis). M. Clermont Ganneau, however, was the first to discover the site of Adullam and the existing name of *Ayd el Mieh*, which preserves all the essential letters of the Hebrew. Lieutenant Conder has now made a careful survey of the spot. He finds the ruins of an ancient town (Gen. xxxviii. 1, 12, 20), strongly situated (Josh. xii. 15, and 2 Chron. xi. 7) on a height commanding the broad valley of Elah, which was the highway by which the Philistines invaded Judah (1 Sam. xvii. 19), and where David killed Goliath. Roads connect it with Hebron, Bethlehem, and Tell es Safiyeh—the probable site of Gath. There are terraces of the hill for cultivation, scarped rock for fortification, tombs, wells, and aqueducts. The "Cave" is a series of caves, some of moderate size and some small, but quite capable of housing David's band of followers.
16. *Makkedah*] See Josh. x. 10, 16, 17, 21.
Beth-el] Earlier, Luz, famous for (i) Jacob's dream (Gen. xxviii. 11—19); (ii) the worship of the calves in Jeroboam's reign (1 Kings xii. 28—33), hence called Beth-aven = "the house of naught."
17. *Tappuah*] In the Shephelah, or lowland of Judah, on the lower slopes of the mountains of the N.W. portion of Judah, about 12 miles W. of Jerusalem. Now called *Teffûh*.
Hepher] Mentioned in 1 Kings iv. 10. Situation not known.
18. *Aphek*] A royal city of the Canaanites, probably the same as the Aphekah of Josh. xv. 53.
Lasharon] Only mentioned here. The site is unknown.
19. *Madon*] See ch. xi. 1.
Hazor] Ch. xi. 1, 10.
20. *Shimron-meron*] Ch. xi. 1. *Achshaph*] xi. 1.
21. *Taanach*] Almost always in company with Megiddo, one of the chief towns of the rich district which forms the western portion

Kedesh, one; the king of Jokneam of Carmel, one; the 23
king of Dor in the coast of Dor, one; the king of the nations
of Gilgal, one; the king of Tirzah, one: all the kings thirty 24
and one.

1—7. *The Divine Command to Joshua to distribute the Land.*

Now Joshua was old *and* stricken in years; and the LORD 13

of the great plain of Esdraelon (1 Kings iv. 12). It was a city of the
Levites (Josh. xxi. 25), and was famous for the victory of Barak
(Judg. v. 19). Under the form Ta'annuk it retains its old name with
hardly the change of a letter.

Megiddo] which commanded one of those passes from the north
into the hill country, which were of such critical importance in the
history of Judæa. It does not seem to have been really occupied by
the Israelites till the time of Solomon, and is famous as the place
(i) where Ahaziah died in his flight from Jehu (2 Kings ix. 27), and
(ii) where Josiah was fatally wounded in the battle against Necho
king of Egypt (2 Chron. xxxv. 22—24). The modern name is *el-
Lejjûn*, the "Legio" of Eusebius and Jerome.

22. *Kedesh*] in Issachar, allotted to the Gershonite Levites (1 Chron.
vi. 72). Sometimes called Kishon or Kishion (Josh. xxi. 28).

Jokneam of Carmel] Or, on Carmel, a city of the tribe of Zebulun,
allotted with its suburbs to the Merarite Levites (Josh. xxi. 34). The
modern site *Tell Kaimon* stands just below the eastern termination of
Carmel.

Carmel] = "the park," or "the well-wooded place," almost always
with the definite article. Rightly does it bear its name, being covered
below with laurels and olive trees, above with pines and oaks, and full
of the most beautiful flowers, "hollyhocks, jasmine, and various flower-
ing creepers." It is famous for its connection with the history of the
two great prophets Elijah and Elisha (1 Kings xviii. 19, 20, 42; 2 Kings
ii. 25, iv. 25, xix. 23; Isai. xxxiii. 9, xxxv. 2).

23. *Dor*] See Josh. xi. 2.

the nations of Gilgal] "The kyng of the Gentils (folkis) of Galgal,"
Wyclif. For the word here rendered "nations" comp. Gen. x. 5,
"every one after his tongue, after their families, in their *nations*;" Gen.
xiv. 1, "Tidal king of *nations*." The Gilgal here mentioned is not the
Gilgal on the Jordan, but the modern *Jiljilieh*, west of Ebal and
Gerizim, in the plain along the Mediterranean. See above, ch. ix. 6.

24. *Tirzah*] Three miles from the city of Samaria, now called *Tellûzah*,
of proverbial beauty. Cant. vi. 4, "Thou art beautiful, O my love, *as
Tirzah*." It was to Shechem afterwards "what Windsor is to London,"
and became the residence of Jeroboam and his successors (1 Kings xiv.
17). Here Zimri was besieged by Omri, and perished in the flames of
his palace (1 Kings xvi. 18).

CH. XIII. 1—7. THE DIVINE COMMAND TO JOSHUA TO
DISTRIBUTE THE LAND.

1. *Now Joshua*] With the thirteenth chapter begins the Second Part

said unto him, Thou art old *and* stricken in years, and there
2 remaineth *yet* very much land to be possessed. This is the
land that *yet* remaineth : all the borders of the Philistines,
3 and all Geshuri, from Sihor, which *is* before Egypt, even

of the Book of Joshua. It describes the division of the Land, and rests
no doubt on definite records which lay before the writer. "There is
one document in the Hebrew Scriptures to which probably no parallel
exists in the topographical records of any other ancient nation. In the
Book of Joshua we have what may without offence be termed the
Domesday Book of the conquest of Canaan. Ten chapters of that
Book are devoted to a description of the country, in which not only are
its general features and boundaries carefully laid down, but the names
and situations of its towns and villages enumerated with a precision of
geographical terms which encourages and almost compels a minute investigation." Stanley's *Sinai and Palestine*, p. xiii.

Now Joshua was old] The Hebrew leader was now about ninety
years of age. Much land still remained to be occupied. Strong
fortresses—like Jerusalem, Gezer, and Bēthshean—still remained in the
hands of the defeated Canaanites. Their reduction by ordinary means
would require time and entail difficulty. The command, therefore,
is now given to wait no longer, but proceed to the division of the
Land.

and stricken in years] "Thou hast woxe eld, and art of loong age,"
Wyclif. Comp. Gen. xviii. 11, xxiv. 1; Josh. xxiii. 1, 2.

2. *the land that yet remaineth*] It is described as lying partly (*a*) *in
the south* (*vv.* 3, 4), and partly (*b*) *in the north* (*vv.* 5, 6). The cities
still occupied by the Canaanites were left for reduction by the tribes into
whose allotment they might severally fall.

all the borders of the Philistines] Literally, **all the circles of the
Philistines.** Vulgate, "*Galilæa Philisthiim;*" "*Galilee of the Philistines*," Luther. "Galile Philistym," Wyclif. The unsubdued district
commences on the south with the Shephêlah and the maritime plain.
The Philistines are now first prominently mentioned. Since the time
of Abraham (Gen. xxi. 32, 34, xxvi. 1, 8), this people had been transformed from a pastoral tribe to a settled and powerful nation, and had
advanced northwards into "the plain of Philistia" or the " Shephêlah,"
so well suited for war chariots, and offering by its occasional elevations
secure sites for towns and strongholds.

and all Geshuri] The Geshurites, not the country mentioned in chs.
xii. 5, xiii. 13, but an ancient tribe, which dwelt in the desert between
Arabia and Philistia. See 1 Sam. xxvii. 8.

3. *from Sihor*]="*the Black Stream*," the usual name of the Nile.
Here probably it is "the river of Egypt," the *Wady el Arish* (1 Chron.
xiii. 5), the Rhinokolura or Rhinokorura. Wyclif, following the Vulg.,
"*a fluvio turbido qui irrigat Ægyptum*," renders it, "the trubli flood
that weetith Egipt."

which is before Egypt] The "brook of Egypt" flows actually *before*,

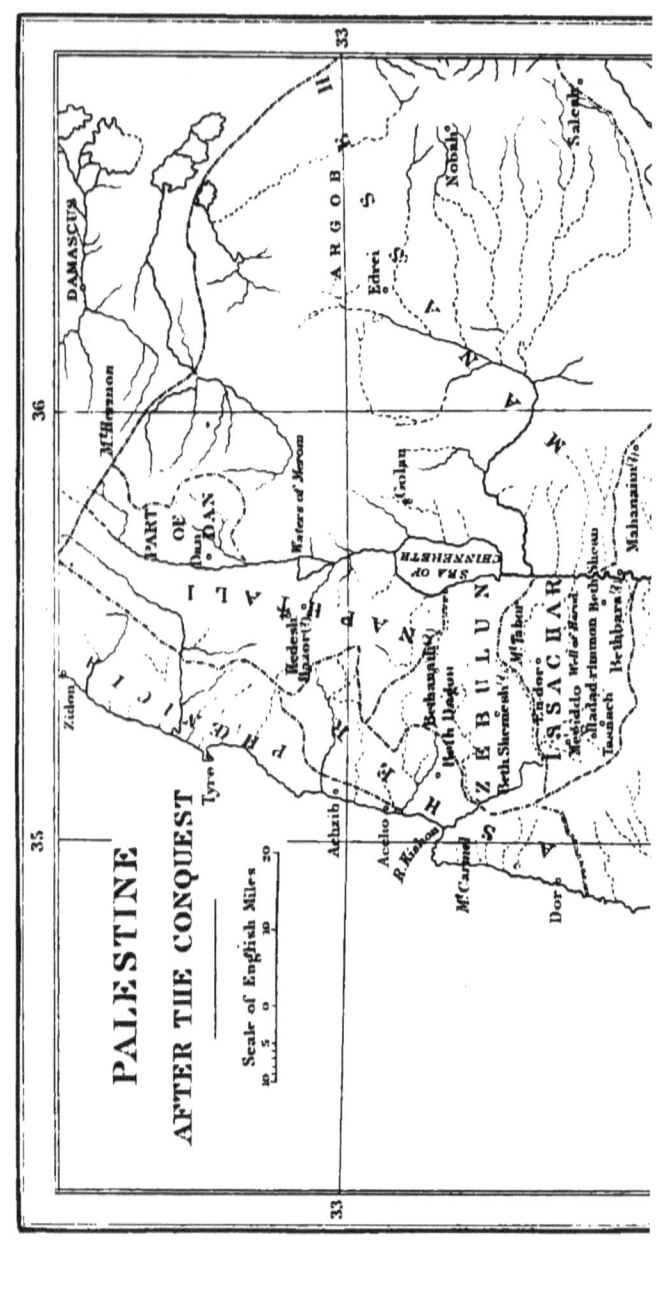

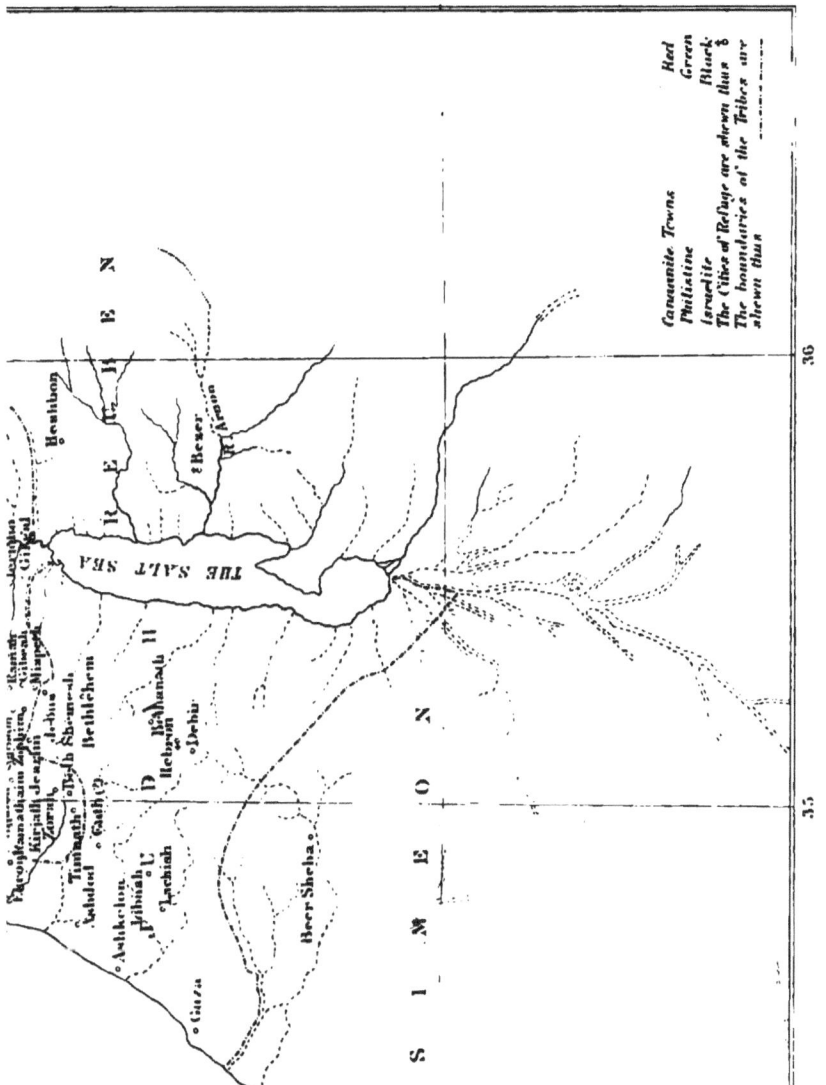

unto the borders of Ekron northward, *which* is counted to
the Canaanite: five lords of the Philistines; the Gazathites,
and the Ashdothites, the Eshkalonites, the Gittites, and the
Ekronites; also the Avites: from the south, all the land of 4
the Canaanites, and Mearah that *is* beside the Sidonians,

i. e. in a N. E. direction from Egypt, while the Nile takes its course through the middle of that country.

unto the borders of Ekron] The most northerly of the five towns belonging to the lords of the Philistines. The city of the fly-god Beelzebub. In the Apocrypha it appears as *Accaron* (1 Macc. x. 89).

which is counted to the Canaanite] Or better, **shall it be counted to the Canaanites**. The western strip of country beginning at Sihor, and extending northward to Ekron, was to be regarded as Canaanitish, and so subject to conquest; although the Philistines were not Canaanites, but were sprung from Mizraim (Gen. x. 13) and had dispossessed the Canaanite Avites or Avim.

five lords] A special word is here used, and the cities over which they held sway are enumerated as (i) Gaza; (ii) Ashdod; (iii) Ashkelon; (iv) Gath; (v) Ekron.

the Gazathites] See above, x. 41, xi. 22.

the Ashdothites] See above, xi. 22.

the Eshkalonites] Or Ashkalonites of Ashkelon, which is mentioned nowhere else in the book of Joshua. Next to Gaza it was probably the most important city of the Philistines. Hither Samson repaired from Timnath (Judg. xiv. 19); there David would not have the deaths of Saul and Jonathan proclaimed (2 Sam. i. 20), lest the daughters of the Philistines should rejoice. Like the other Philistine cities, it was threatened by the prophets with the Divine judgment (see Jer. xxv. 20, xlvii. 5, 7; Amos i. 8; Zeph. ii. 7; Zech. ix. 5). Near the town afterwards rose the celebrated temple of Derceto, the Syrian Venus. It played a conspicuous part in the struggles of the Crusades, and within the walls and towers now standing Richard I. held his court. See Smith's *Dictionary of the Bible*, sub voc.

the Gittites] i.e. the people of Gath, the home of Goliath (1 Sam. xvii. 4); connected with Ashkelon in David's lamentation (2 Sam. i. 20); conquered by David (1 Chron. xviii. 1). See above, xi. 22.

also the Avites] *Avim*, or *Avims*. These people, a portion of the early inhabitants of Palestine, are mentioned in Deut. ii. 23 as dwelling in the villages in the southern part of the great western lowland as far as Gaza. Here they were attacked by the invading Philistines, who drove them northwards and occupied their rich possessions.

4. *from the south*] The LXX. here gives a proper name, "from Teman." This was the former southern limit of the Avites' territory.

all the land of the Canaanites] Here some would insert a full stop, as though the words summed up what had gone before.

and Mearah] "Mara of Sydonys," Wyclif. This place is only mentioned in this passage. The word meârâh means in Hebrew "*a cave*" (see

5 unto Aphek, to the borders of the Amorites: and the land of the Giblites, and all Lebanon, *toward* the sunrising, from Baal-gad under mount Hermon unto the entering into 6 Hamath. All the inhabitants of the hill country from

margin), and it has been commonly supposed that the reference is to a remarkable cavern near Zidon. A village called *el-Mughâr* has been found in the mountains of Naphtali some 10 miles west of the northern extremity of the Sea of Galilee, which it has been thought may possibly represent the ancient Mearah. See Menke's *Bible Atlas*, Plate iii.

unto Aphek] A city in the extreme north of Asher, now *Afka*, N.E. of Beyrout, and apparently beyond Sidon. It was called by the Greeks *Aphaca*, and was noted for a temple of Venus destroyed by Constantine.

to the borders of the Amorites] i.e. on the extreme north border of the Amorites, or the land once inhabited by them, and which afterwards passed to Og, king of Bashan.

5. *the land of the Giblites*] i.e. the land of the inhabitants of Gebal, a name which occurs in Ps. lxxxiii. 7,

"*Gebal*, and Ammon, and Amalek;
The Philistines with the inhabitants of Tyre;"

and Ezek. xxvii. 8, 9, "The inhabitants of Zidon and Arvad were thy mariners: thy wise men, O Tyrus, that were in thee, were thy pilots. The ancients of *Gebal* and the wise men thereof were in thee thy calkers." It was a maritime town of Phœnicia. Its inhabitants are written "Giblians" in the Vulgate, and "Byblians" in the LXX. (while in 1 Kings v. 18 the word is rendered "stone-squarers"), whence we may infer the identity of the city with the Byblus of classical literature. Byblus was a seat of the worship of Adonis or Syrian Tammuz. The modern name is *Jebail*, about 22 miles north of Beyrout. The coins of Byblus have frequently the type of Astarte, also of Isis, who came here in search of the body of Osiris. "At *Jebail* and in other ancient Phœnician cities there are traces of the same large bevelled stones clamped with iron, which appear in the foundations of Solomon's temple. These are probably the work of the Giblites." See Ritter's *Geog. Pal.* II. 214, 215.

all Lebanon, toward the sunrising] i.e. Anti-Lebanon.

from Baal-gad] See above, note on xi. 17.

the entering into Hamath] The extreme northern boundary point of Palestine whither the spies originally penetrated (Num. xiii. 21), and to which the kingdom of David and Solomon once actually extended (2 Sam. viii. 3—12; 1 Chron. xiii. 5, xviii. 3—11; 2 Chron. viii. 3, 4). In the time of the Crusades it was called Epiphaneia, a town situated on the western bank of the Orontes, lower down the stream than Emesa. It is called "Hamath the Great" (Amos vi. 2), and commanded the whole of the Orontes valley, from the low screen of hills which forms the watershed between the Orontes and the *Litâny*—"the entrance of Hamath"—to the defile of Daphne below Antioch.

vv. 7—10.]   JOSHUA, XIII.   115

Lebanon unto Misrephoth-maim, *and* all the Sidonians, them will I drive out from before the children of Israel: only divide thou it *by lot* unto the Israelites for an inheritance, as I have commanded thee. Now therefore divide this land 7 for an inheritance unto the nine tribes, and the half tribe of Manasseh,

8—14. *The Territory of the Two Tribes and a Half East of the Jordan. Its Boundaries.*

With whom the Reubenites and the Gadites have 8 received their inheritance, which Moses gave them, beyond Jordan eastward, *even* as Moses the servant of the LORD gave them; from Aroer, that *is* upon the bank of the river Arnon, 9 and the city that *is* in the midst of the river, and all the plain of Medeba unto Dibon; and all the cities of Sihon 10

6. *All the inhabitants*] In addition to those already enumerated there remained to be conquered all the inhabitants of the mountains from Lebanon unto Mizrephoth-maim, which has been already mentioned above, ch. xi. 8. "May it not be the place," asks Mr Grove, "with which we are familiar in the later history as Zarephath?" Smith's *Bibl. Dict.*

only divide thou it by lot] These words connect themselves with verse 1.

7. *Now therefore divide*] Here we have a more definite statement of the tribes amongst whom western Palestine was to be divided.

8—14. THE TERRITORY OF THE TWO TRIBES AND A HALF EAST OF THE JORDAN. ITS BOUNDARIES.

8. *With whom*] i.e. with Manasseh. It alludes to the other half of that tribe.

the Reubenites and the Gadites] These statements are the same as in ch. xii. 1—6.

9. *and all the plain of Medeba*] Instead of "half Gilead," as in ch. xii. 2, we have here "all the plain (=Mishor="table-land" or "downs") of Medeba unto Dibon," "the wijld feeldis of Medeba," Wyclif. Medeba is first mentioned in th fragment of a populare song of the time of the conquest, Num. xxi. 30, "Heshbon is perished even unto Dibon, and we have laid them waste even unto Nophah, which reacheth unto *Medeba.*" It is in the pastoral district of the *Belka*, four miles S. E. of *Heshbon*, and like it lying on a rounded but rocky hill. In Christian times it was a noted bishopric of the patriarchate of Becerra. Dibon, or *Dibon-Gad*, from its being taken possession of and rebuilt by the children of Gad (Num. xxxii. 3, 34), or *Dimon* (in Isai. xv. 9), has been discovered with the name *Dhiban* on the Roman road three miles north of

8—2

king of the Amorites, which reigned in Heshbon, unto the
11 border of the children of Ammon; and Gilead, and the
border of the Geshurites and Maachathites, and all mount
12 Hermon, and all Bashan unto Salcah; all the kingdom of
Og in Bashan, which reigned in Ashtaroth and in Edrei, who
remained of the remnant of the giants: for these did Moses
13 smite, and cast them out. (Nevertheless the children of
Israel expelled not the Geshurites, nor the Maachathites:
but the Geshurites and the Maachathites dwell among the
14 Israelites until this day.) Only unto the tribe of Levi he gave
none inheritance; the sacrifices of the LORD God of Israel
made by fire *are* their inheritance, as he said unto them.

15—23. *The Possession of the Tribe of Reuben.*

15 And Moses gave unto the tribe of the children of Reuben
16 *inheritance* according to their families. And their coast was

the Arnon (*Wady el-Mojeb*). Here the inscribed block of basalt, known as "the Moabite stone," was discovered in 1868.

12. *all the kingdom of Og in Bashan*] "With respect to the two tribes and a half beyond the Jordan, nothing is more striking at the first glance than their wide extent, compared with the narrow space into which the western tribes were compressed...it is certainly a domain which, taken in its entire superficies, would not yield in extent to the whole region on the west of the Jordan." Ewald's *History of Israel*, II. 294, 295.

13. *expelled not the Geshurites*] "Valiant as was the contest long kept up against their enemies, Israel could not prevent two little kingdoms in the north-east from maintaining their independence within her own borders. One of these was the Aramean Maachah, probably extending to the sources of the Jordan; and the other belonged to the aborigines, and was called Geshur. These two little kingdoms are generally mentioned together, and they existed till after David's time." Ewald, p. 302.

14. *Only unto the tribe of Levi*] The Levites not being destined for agriculture, but being intended to become the regular teachers of the people, received no inheritance. See *v*. 33, and ch. xiv. 3, 4.

the sacrifices of the Lord God] "the sacryfices, and the slayn offryngis of the Lord God of Yrael," Wyclif. The offerings of Jehovah were to be their portion (Num. xviii. 20; Deut. x. 9, xviii. 2).

15—23. THE POSSESSION OF THE TRIBE OF REUBEN.

15. *the tribe of the children of Reuben*] The historian now gives us, on the faith of the ancient registers, the several boundaries of the tribes east of the Jordan.

Reuben] Reuben naturally comes first. His boundaries are more briefly given, Num. xxxii. 33—42.

from Aroer, that *is* on the bank of the river Arnon, and the city that *is* in the midst of the river, and all the plain by Medeba; Heshbon, and all her cities that *are* in the plain; 17 Dibon, and Bamoth-baal, and Beth-baal-meon, and Jahazah, 18 and Kedemoth, and Mephaath, and Kirjathaim, and Sibmah, 19 and Zareth-shahar in the mount of the valley, and Beth-peor, 20

16. *their coast*] Observe the use of the word "coast" here, without any allusion to the seaboard. The word comes from the Latin *costa*= "a rib," "side," through the Fr. "coste." Hence it="a border" generally, though now applied to the sea-coast only. Comp. "Bethlehem and in all the *coasts* thereof" (Matt. ii. 16); "the coasts of Judæa" (Matt. xix. 1); the *coasts* of Gadara (Mark v. 17); "the *coasts*" of Antioch in Pisidia (Acts xiii. 50). The portion of country this tribe selected, under its modern name of the *Belka*, is still esteemed beyond all others by the Arab sheepmasters. It was the southernmost and smallest portion of the district east of the Jordan.

from Aroer] See above, ch. xii. 2; *all the plain by Medeba*=the plateau east of Abarim or mount Pisgah. See above, xii. 3.

the city that is in the midst]=Ar of Moab, as above, verse 9.

17. *Bamoth-baal*] It was a site of the old heathen worship of Baal. It is probably mentioned under the shorter form of Bamoth, Num. xxi. 19, or "*Bamoth-in-the-ravine.*" It occurs again in Isai. xv. 2.

Beth-baal-meon] At the first approach of the Israelites to this part of Palestine (Num. xxxii. 38) it is called *Baal-Meon*, or in its contracted form *Beon* (Num. xxxii. 3). The Beth is probably a Hebrew addition, and the word denotes "*the House of Baal of the den.*" The name still clings to a ruined place of considerable size, a short distance S. W. of Heshbân, and bearing the name of the fortress of *Mi'ûn*.

18. *and Jahazah*] Also called *Jahaz* and *Jahaza* and *Jahzah*, in the Hebrew *Yahats* and *Yahtsah*. Here the decisive battle was fought between the Israelites and Sihon king of the Amorites (Num. xxi. 23).

and Kedemoth] Given to the Merarite Levites (Josh. xxi. 37).

Mephaath] Lying in the district of the Mishor (see Jer. xlviii. 21).

19. *and Kirjathaim*] In Jer. xlviii. 1, 23 and Ezek. xxv. 9 the name is given in our version as *Kiriathaim*. This place, as well as Dibon, Beth-baal-meon, and Medeba, is found among the proper names recorded on the now celebrated "Moabite stone." Canon Tristram would identify it with the modern *Kureiyat*. "The twin hills explain the Hebrew dual and plural terminations." *Land of Moab*, p. 275.

Sibmah] Hardly 500 paces from Heshbon, according to Jerome. Isaiah and Jeremiah mention it in the lament pronounced over Moab (Isai. xvi. 8, 9; Jer. xlviii. 32).

and Zareth-shahar]="the Splendour of the Dawn," in Mount Ira-Emak = "the Mountain of the Valley." Menke places it *west* of Mount Pisgah, towards the Dead Sea. "Having climbed the hills and traced the feeders of the Callirrhoe to their mountain sources, our next aim was to get down to the shore of the Dead Sea by the unvisited Zara,

21 and Ashdoth-pisgah, and Beth-jeshimoth, and all the cities of the plain, and all the kingdom of Sihon king of the Amorites, which reigned in Heshbon, whom Moses smote with the princes of Midian, Evi, and Rekem, and Zur, and Hur, and Reba, *which were* dukes of Sihon, dwelling in the country. 22 Balaam also the son of Beor, the soothsayer, did the children

the 'Zareth-shahar in the mountain of the valley' of Josh. xiii. 19...... At length we reached the Dead Sea shore at Zara, which...is really three miles south of the mouth of the Callirrhoe, and in a wide open belt of land, beyond the opening of *Wady Z'gara.* The surrounding mountain crescent is beautiful, both in form and colour. The sandstone, gilded by the sun, presents the most gorgeous colouring, red predominating, but white, yellow, and brown patches and streaks abound. Groves of tamarisk and acacia, and all the strange tropical shrubs of Engedi and the Sáfieh, gradually give place to huge tufts of a sort of Pampas-grass ten feet high; and then to impenetrable cane-brakes, which reach to within a few feet of the pebbly shore...... Of Zara, the old Hebrew town of Zareth-shahar, but little remains. A few broken basaltic columns and pieces of wall, about 200 yards back from the shore, and a ruined fort rather nearer the sea, about the middle of the coast-line of the plain, are all that are left, beyond the identity of name. Of Rome, or later work, there is not a vestige. Yet these poor relics have an interest of their own. We are looking here on, perhaps, the only surviving relic of the buildings of the semi-nomad tribe of Reuben, prior to the Babylonish captivity." Tristram's *Land of Moab,* pp. 281—284. See the photograph of the Remains, p. 283.

20. *and Beth-peor*] A place dedicated to the god Baal-peor, on the east of the Jordan opposite Jericho, about six miles above Libias or Beth-haran. Comp. Deut. iii. 29, iv. 46.

and Ashdoth-pisgah] See ch. xii. 3.

21. *all the cities*]="all the other cities of the table-land, and all the kingdom of Sihon, as far as it extended over the plain."

with the princes of Midian] They are also mentioned, and in the same order, in Num. xxxi. 8.

which were dukes of Sihon] "dukys of Sion," Wyclif, from the Vulgate "duces"=**vassals of Sihon**, and *princes.* "The word stands only in the plural, and is always used, as would seem, of native, although dependent and *subjugated,* princes, and not of installed, ordinary officials." Gesenius. From the appellation here used, "vassals of Sihon," we may clearly infer that that king, who had taken from the Moabites the greatest part of their territory, had also made them tributary. From this subjection they were delivered by the defeat of Sihon, and then fearing that they would receive from the Israelites the same treatment as the Amorites, they immediately conspired to destroy the Israelites, and thus brought destruction upon themselves. See Keil.

22. *Balaam also*] The mention of these "vassals of Sihon" leads the historian to record also at this point the death of Balaam, which

of Israel slay with the sword among them that were slain by them. And the border of the children of Reuben was 23 Jordan, and the border *thereof*. This *was* the inheritance of the children of Reuben after their families, the cities and villages thereof.

took place at the same time as that of these vassals (Num. xxxi. 8). He is here called a "soothsayer" (*kosem*); "the fals divynor" (Wyclif); like (*a*) the diviners of the Philistines (1 Sam. vi. 2), and (*b*) the necromancers (1 Sam. xxviii. 8, 9) whom Saul had "cut off."
The late Professor Blunt has drawn attention to the fact that (*a*) in the original mission to Balaam, the *elders of Midian* were concerned as much as the elders of Moab (Num. xxii. 7); that all mention of Midian is then dropped, and "the princes of Balak" and "the servants of Balak" are the titles given to the messengers, and in the prophet's fruitless struggle to curse the people whom God had blessed, Balak and the Moabites engrossed all his attention.
(*b*) Balaam then disappears, on his way apparently to his own country, Pethor in Mesopotamia (Num. xxiv. 25), while the historian pursues his narrative through several long chapters, which are taken up with entirely different matter.
(*c*) Then comes an account of an attack made upon the *Midianites* in revenge for their having seduced the people of Israel by the wiles of their women, at the close of which we find a notice that "*Balaam also the son of Beor they slew with the sword*" (Num. xxxi. 8).
(*d*) It seems, then, that the Prophet did not after all immediately return to Mesopotamia, but paid a visit to the Midianites, who were equally concerned in bringing him where he was, and there suggested the enticements of the licentious orgies of Baal-Peor, into which Israel fell. But his stay was unseasonably protracted, and Moses coming upon the Midianites slew them and him together.
(*e*) Here an undesigned coincidence lies (*a*) in the elders of Moab and the elders of *Midian* going to Balaam; (*b*) in *Midian* being then mentioned no more, while Balaam having been sent away from Moab, apparently that he might go home, is subsequently found a corpse amongst the slaughtered *Midianites*. See Blunt's *Undesigned Coincidences*, pp. 86, 87.
23. *was Jordan*] i. e. "the boundary of the children of Reuben was the Jordan and adjoining land." Comp. Num. xxxiv. 6; Deut. iii. 16, 17.
the villages thereof] = "*farm premises*," not enclosed, like a city, with walls. Thus the boundaries of the tribe of Reuben were, (*a*) On the West, *the Dead Sea*; (*b*) on the South, *the country of Moab*; (*c*) on the East, *the kingdom of Ammon*; (*d*) on the North, *the Arnon, or the Wady Mojeb*. Here the tribe settled, "preferring pasturage to agriculture." His subsequent history fulfils the prophecy of Jacob. "Unstable (or swelling) as water" (Gen. xlix. 4), he vanishes away into a mere Arabian tribe; "his men are few" (Deut. xxxiii. 6); it is all he can do "to live and not die." The only events of the

24—28. *The Possession of the Tribe of Gad.*

24 And Moses gave *inheritance* unto the tribe of Gad, *even*
25 unto the children of Gad according to their families. And
their coast was Jazer, and all the cities of Gilead, and half
the land of the children of Ammon, unto Aroer that *is* before
26 Rabbah; and from Heshbon unto Ramath-mizpeh, and
Betonim; and from Mahanaim unto the border of Debir;

subsequent history of the tribe are (*a*) the multiplication of "their cattle in the land of Gilead;" (*b*) their wars with the Bedouin "sons of Hagar" (1 Chron. v. 10); (*c*) their spoils "of camels fifty thousand, and of sheep two hundred and fifty thousand, and of asses two thousand" (1 Chron. v. 21). In the chief struggle of the nation Reuben never took part. No judge, no prophet, no hero of the tribe is handed down to us. See Stanley's *Lectures*, I. 218.

24—28. THE POSSESSION OF THE TRIBE OF GAD.

25. *their coast was Jazer*] or *Jaazer*. We first hear of it in possession of the Amorites, and as taken by Israel after Heshbon, and on their way from thence to Bashan (Num. xxi. 32). At present it is identified with *Szir*, or *Seir*, nine Roman miles west of Ammân, and about 12 from Heshbon. For *coast* see above, *v.* 16.

all the cities of Gilead] i. e. of the southern part of Gilead, which belonged to the kingdom of Sihon, for the other half, on the north of the Jabbok, which was governed by king Og, was allotted to the half tribe of Manasseh.

half the land of the children of Ammon] i. e. that portion of the land which had been taken from them by the Amorites under Sihon, for the Israelites were not allowed to attack the land of the Ammonites themselves (Deut. ii. 19; Judges xi. 13 sq.).

unto Aroer] i.e. *unto Aroer of Gad* (Num. xxxii. 34), not the Aroer near the Arnon (of *v.* 16), *that is before Rabbah*, the capital of the Ammonites, famous (*a*) in the history of Jephthah (Judg. xi. 33), and (*b*) in the history of David (2 Sam. xxiv. 5).

26. *and from Heshbon*] Thus the extension northward of the tribe is expressed, *unto Ramath-mizpeh*, which is identical with the early sanctuary at which Jacob and Laban set up their cairn of stones, and which received the names of Mizpeh, Galeed, and Jegar-Sahadutha, and which probably was the same as the famous Ramoth-gilead, where (*a*) Ahab was slain (1 Kings xxii. 1—37), (*b*) his son Joram was wounded by Hazael (2 Kings viii. 28), (*c*) Jehu was anointed king (2 Kings ix. 1—6). It is the modern *es-Salt* on the road from Jericho to Damascus.

and Betonim] a town somewhere on the northern boundary of Gad. Its site was unknown to Jerome.

and from Mahanaim] in the east, *unto Debir*, on the heights which

and in the valley, Beth-aram, and Beth-nimrah, and Succoth, 27 and Zaphon, the rest of the kingdom of Sihon king of Heshbon, Jordan and *his* border, *even* unto the edge of the sea of Cinnereth on the *other* side Jordan eastward. This *is* the 28 inheritance of the children of Gad after their families, the cities, and their villages.

border the Jordan on the west. Mahanaim (=the *two hosts*) is famous in the history (*a*) of Jacob's return from Padanaram (Gen. xxxii. 2), (*b*) of Ishbosheth's reign (2 Sam. ii. 8), (*c*) of David's flight from Absalom (2 Sam. xvii. 24, 27). The site of Debir is undetermined.

27. *and in the valley*] i. e. the valley of the Jordan. The possessions of the Gadites are now described in this valley as far north as the Sea of Galilee.

Beth-aram] or Beth-haran, the modern *Beit-haran* (Num. xxxii. 36). In later times it was known as Bethramphtha, and was called Julias or Livias by Herod Antipas in honour of the Emperor Augustus.

Beth-nimrah] or *Nimrah* (Num. xxxii. 3), which name still survives in the *Nahr Nimrîn*, close to one of the fords of Jordan just above Jericho.

and Succoth] ("*Booths*"), in the Jordan valley, between Peniel, near the ford of the torrent Jabbok, and Shechem (Gen. xxxii. 30, xxxiii. 18). It is famous (*a*) in the history of Jacob's return from Padan-aram; of (*b*) Gideon's pursuit of Zebah and Zalmunna (Judg. viii. 5—17); (*c*) as the spot at which the brass foundries were placed for casting the metal-work of the Temple (1 Kings vii. 46; 2 Chron. iv. 17). Its position has not been exactly ascertained, and no place resembling *Zaphon* also has yet been discovered.

Jordan and his border] See above, *v.* 23. For the *Sea of Chinnereth*=the "*sea of Galilee*," see above, xii. 3.

28. *This is the inheritance*] Thus, speaking roughly, the country allotted to Gad appears to have lain chiefly about the centre of the land east of the Jordan. Commencing at or about Heshbon on the south, it extended to the ancient sanctuary of Mahanaim on the north; on the east the furthest landmark was "Aroer that faces Rabbah;" while the Jordan formed the boundary on the west. The character of the tribe was throughout fierce and warlike (Gen. xlix. 19), "strong men of might, men of war for the battle, that could handle shield and buckler, their faces the faces of lions, and like roes upon the mountains for swiftness" (1 Chron. v. 18, and xii. 8). In the finest region south of the Jabbok Gad "dwelt as a lion" (Deut. xxxiii. 20), and that the civilisation attained by this tribe was of a higher order than "the mere fierceness necessary to repel the attacks of the plunderers of the desert" comes out in (*a*) the history of Jephthah (Judg. xi. 1); of (*b*) the eleven valiant chiefs who crossed the fords of Jordan in flood-time to join David—"their faces like the faces of lions, as swift as the gazelles upon the mountains" (1 Chron. xii. 8—15); in (*c*) the loyalty

29—32. *The Possession of the Half Tribe of Manasseh.*

29 And Moses gave *inheritance* unto the half tribe of Manasseh: and *this* was *the possession* of the half tribe of the 30 children of Manasseh by their families. And their coast was from Mahanaim, all Bashan, all the kingdom of Og king of Bashan, and all the towns of Jair, which *are* in Bashan, 31 threescore cities: and half Gilead, and Ashtaroth, and Edrei,

and generosity of Barzillai (2 Sam. xix. 32—39); (*d*) the marvellous career of Elijah "the Tishbite, of the inhabitants of Gilead" (1 Kings xvii. 1).

29—32. THE POSSESSION OF THE HALF TRIBE OF MANASSEH.

29. *the half tribe of Manasseh*] "The fact that it is always called a half tribe appears curious, especially on comparison with the similar, yet widely different, case of Dan, which sent out to the north an army which surprised the Phœnician town of Laish." Ewald, II. 299.

30. *from Mahanaim*] Which formed its southern border. For "the kingdom *of Og*" see above, *v.* 12.

all the towns of Jair] The whole of Bashan embraced
(i) *The Havoth-Jair*, sixty cities in the district of Argob (Deut. iii. 4), which had been captured by Jair the son of Manasseh and called after his name (Num. xxxii. 41; Deut. iii. 14).
(ii) "*half Gilead*," i.e. the northern half, together with the two capitals, *Ashtaroth* and *Edrei*.

31. *Ashtaroth*] See ch. xii. 4, so called doubtless from being a seat of the worship of Ashtoreth, the principal female divinity of the Phœnicians, the Astarte of the Greeks and Romans. The only trace of the name yet recovered is *Tell-Ashterah* or *Asherah*.

and Edrei] See above, ch. xii. 4. The northern part of Gilead was given to Machir, the eldest son of the patriarch Manasseh (1 Chron. vii. 14), or rather the half of his male descendants. They consisted of seven families, whose heads are named 1 Chron. v. 24. So great was their power, that the name of Machir occasionally supersedes that of Manasseh. They took the bold "tract of Argob...sixty great cities (Deut. iii. 14), among the most difficult, if not the most difficult, district in the whole country." Thus it is plain that the half tribe of Manasseh occupied by far the largest extent of land on the east of the Jordan. It embraced (*a*) the inaccessible heights and impassable ravines of Gilead; and (*b*) the almost impregnable tract of Argob, where "all is stone," "an ocean of basaltic rocks and boulders tossed about in the wildest confusion." "The same martial spirit, which fitted the western Manasseh to defend the passes of Esdraelon, fitted 'Machir, the firstborn of Manasseh, the father of Gilead,' to defend the passes of Haurân and Anti-Libanus; 'because he was a man of war, therefore he had Gilead and Bashan.'" Stanley's *Lectures*, I. 219. Of the development of the tribe subsequently we have a remarkable illustration at the time

cities of the kingdom of Og in Bashan, *were pertaining* unto the children of Machir the son of Manasseh, *even* to the one half of the children of Machir by their families. These *are* 32 *the countries* which Moses did distribute for inheritance in the plains of Moab, on the *other* side Jordan, *by* Jericho, eastward. But unto the tribe of Levi Moses gave not *any* 33 inheritance: the LORD God of Israel *was* their inheritance, as he said unto them.

1—5. *Distribution of the Land West of the Jordan.*

And these *are the countries* which the children of Israel 14 inherited in the land of Canaan, which Eleazar the priest, and Joshua the son of Nun, and the heads of the fathers of the tribes of the children of Israel, distributed for inheritance to them. By lot *was* their inheritance, as the 2

of the coronation of David at Hebron. On that occasion, "while the western Manasseh sent 18,000, and Ephraim itself but 20,800, the eastern Manasseh, with Gad and Reuben, mustered to the number of 120,000, thoroughly armed—a remarkable demonstration of strength, still more remarkable when we remember the fact that Saul's house, with the great Abner at its head, was then residing at Mahanaim on the border of Manasseh and Gad." See Smith's *Bib. Dict.* Art. "Manasseh."

32. *in the plains of Moab*] This distribution had been made during the lifetime of Moses in "the plains of Moab," opposite to the city of Jericho (Num. xxii. 1, xxxiv. 15).

33. *But unto the tribe of Levi*] See above, *v.* 14, and comp. Num. xviii. 20.

CH. XIV. 1—5. DISTRIBUTION OF THE LAND WEST OF THE JORDAN.

1. *And these are the countries*] In this section, from *v.* 1 to 5, we have an introduction to the division of the country west of the Jordan among the nine and a half remaining tribes.

Eleazar the priest] He was the third son of Aaron, and his successor in the highpriesthood (Num. xx. 25; Deut. x. 6). See below, ch. xxiv. 33. Both here and in Num. xxxiv. 17 he is mentioned before Joshua, "for the division by lot was presided over by the high priest as the representative of the government of the Lord in Israel." Keil.

2. *By lot was their inheritance*] See Num. xxvi. 55, xxxiii. 54, and note above on the use of "lots" ch. vii. 18.

(*a*) *The use of lots* was specially characteristic of the ancient world. Thus it was a standing custom of the Athenians to divide the land of conquered enemies to colonists by lot (Diod. XV. 23, 29), and we find it resorted to by them (*a*) in Euboea (Herod. V. 77; VI. 100), (*b*) in Lesbos (Thuc. III. 50). The Romans also assigned territory to the victorious legions by lot (Cic. *Ep. ad Div.* XI. 20).

Lord commanded by the hand of Moses, for the nine
3 tribes, and *for* the half tribe. For Moses had given the
inheritance of two tribes and a half tribe on the *other* side
Jordan: but unto the Levites he gave none inheritance
4 among them. For the children of Joseph were two tribes,
Manasseh and Ephraim: therefore they gave no part unto
the Levites in the land, save cities to dwell *in*, with their

> (*b*) *How the lot was taken* on this occasion we are not told. The
> Rabbins conjecture that there were two urns; in one had been
> placed little tablets with the names of the tribes, and in the other
> similar tablets with the names of the districts, and that one of
> each was drawn at the same time.
> (*c*) *The decision* was made by lot, not merely to prevent all disputes
> with reference to their respective possessions, and to remove every
> ground of discontent and complaint, but also in order that each
> tribe might cheerfully and thankfully accept the share awarded to
> it, as the inheritance intended for it by God. "For the cast-
> ing of lots is not regulated either by the opinion, or caprice, or
> authority of men." (Calvin.) "It is true that it seems as though
> this might have been as easily accomplished, if Joshua or the High
> Priest had been divinely inspired to give to every tribe its inherit-
> ance. But men are never so ready to submit cheerfully to the
> decisions of another man, even though they may be the result of
> Divine Inspiration, as they are to a decision arrived at by a lot
> over which the Lord presides, and thus entirely raised above
> human caprice." (See Prov. xviii. 18, xvi. 33.)
>   3. *For Moses*] In this verse the reason is stated why there were
> only nine tribes and a half, to whom the land was distributed by lot;
> viz. because two tribes and a half had already received their inheritance
> on the east of the Jordan, and no land was given to the Levites as an
> inheritance.
>   4. *For the children of Joseph*] There would have been only eight
> tribes and a half left, but the two sons of Joseph, Manasseh and
> Ephraim, had been adopted by Jacob as his sons (Gen. xlviii. 5), and
> were reckoned as tribes, and therefore there were still nine tribes and a
> half to receive their inheritance.
>   *therefore they gave*] Rather, **and they gave.** The repetition of these
> statements respecting the Levites is not due "to the redundancy of the
> Semitic style," but is intended to shew the reader that the instructions
> left by Moses (Num. xviii. 20, xxxv. 2) had been literally and exactly
> fulfilled.
>   *with their suburbs*] i.e. pasture-ground within the precincts of
> the cities, or certain districts round them in which their cattle might
> graze. These "pasture-grounds," rendered by Bunsen "commons,"
> and in Switzerland called *All-menden*, are incorrectly translated in our
> version "suburbs," from the Vulgate *suburbana*; "suburbis of hem to
> hous beestis and his feeld beestis to be fed," Wyclif.

suburbs for their cattle and for their substance. As the 5
LORD commanded Moses, so the children of Israel did, and
they divided the land.

6—15. *The Possession of Caleb.*

Then the children of Judah came unto Joshua in Gilgal: 6
and Caleb the son of Jephunneh the Kenezite said unto him,
Thou knowest the thing that the LORD said unto Moses the
man of God concerning me and thee in Kadesh-barnea. Forty 7
years old *was* I when Moses the servant of the LORD sent
me from Kadesh-barnea to espy out the land; and I brought

5. *they divided the land*] The division was not finished at once.
See below, ch. xviii. 1. But that is not the point here. The section
contains the general introduction to the distribution of the land.

6—15. THE POSSESSION OF CALEB.

6. *in Gilgal*] Where the casting of the lots commenced.

and Caleb the son of Jephunneh] Caleb was a prince of the tribe of
Judah, a descendant of Hezron, the son of Pharez, and grandson of
Judah (1 Chron. ii. 5, 18, 25). He is first mentioned in the list of the
princes who were sent to search the land of Canaan in the second year
of the Exodus (Num. xiii. 6), and he and Joshua were the only two
who on their return encouraged the Israelites to go up and take possession of the land. In the plague that ensued, these two alone were
spared, and deemed worthy to enter the Promised Land (Num. xiv. 24,
30, xxvi. 65).

the Kenezite] His younger brother Othniel, afterwards the first
Judge, is also called "the son of *Kenaz*" (Josh. xv. 17; Judg. i. 13,
iii. 9, 11). Hence (*a*) some have thought he was a foreigner by birth,
descended from the Edomite tribe spoken of in Gen. xv. 19, a proselyte
who had been incorporated into the tribe of Judah (comp. Gen. xxxvi.
15, 42); (*b*) others hold that even if Jephunneh was on the father's
side descended from this people, on the mother's he came from Judah,
and that this Kenaz probably belonged to the posterity of Judah of
whom nothing further is known. From 1 Chron. iv. 15 it appears that
one of Caleb's sons was called *Kenaz*, and it is clear that the name
was held in great affection by the family, and it was customary both
with Hebrews and Arabs to perpetuate certain family names. See
Keil's *Commentary*.

Thou knowest] Caleb begins by reminding his friend and leader of
the word which Jehovah had spoken to Moses at Kadesh-barnea concerning them both (Num. xiv. 24).

in Kadesh-barnea] Next to Sinai, the most important of all the rest-
ing-places of the children of Israel (see Deut. xxxiii. 2).

7. *to espy out the land*] "for to behold the loond," Wyclif.
"Espy" (comp. Gen. xlii. 27, "And as one of them opened his sack...

8 him word again as *it was* in mine heart. Nevertheless my
brethren that went up with me made the heart of the people
9 melt: but I wholly followed the LORD my God. And
Moses sware on that day, saying, Surely the land whereon
thy feet have trodden shall be thine inheritance, and thy
children's for ever, because thou hast wholly followed the
10 LORD my God. And now behold, the LORD hath kept me
alive, as he said, these forty and five years, *even* since the
LORD spake this word unto Moses, while *the children of
Israel wandered in the wilderness*: and now lo, I *am this*
11 day fourscore and five years old. As yet I *am as* strong *this*
day as *I was* in the day that Moses sent me: as my strength
was then, even so *is* my strength now, for war, both to go
12 out, and to come in. Now therefore give me this mountain,

he *espied* his money") comes from Fr. *espier*, Sp. *espiar*, which are
modifications of the Latin *aspicere*. The old form was *aspy* or *aspie*.
See below the quotation from Wyclif, *v.* 11, and comp.

"Securely I *espy*
Virtue with valour couched in thine eye."
Shakespeare, *Richard II.* I. 3. 97.

as it was in mine heart] i.e. "according to my thorough conviction,"
in the bold confident spirit, which spoke out exactly what it felt. "He
had neither courted the favour of any man by his words, nor feared their
anger." He had spoken out what he believed.

8. *made the heart of the people melt*] (Comp. Num. xiv. 1, 4; Deut.
i. 28), so that they murmured against Moses and Aaron, and wanted to
return again to Egypt. "Discomfortiden the herte of the puple,"
Wyclif.

9. *And Moses sware on that day*] The oath of the great Lawgiver
is not mentioned either in Num. xiv. 23, or Deut. i. 35. Caleb probably quotes an express declaration of Moses, not recorded in the Pentateuch, but familiar to Joshua, in whose hearing it may have been first
related by Moses.

Surely the land] Comp. Num. xiii. 22, xiv. 24; Deut. i. 36.

10. *And now behold*] God had fulfilled His promise, and not only
prolonged his life forty-five years, but had preserved his strength in
such full vigour, that, though now in his eighty-fifth year, he felt as
strong, and as well able to engage in war, as when he was forty years
old.

11. *As yet I am*] "To day Y am of fyue and ei3ti 3eer, so my3ti
as that tyme Y was myghti, whanne Y was sent to *aspie*," Wyclif.

12. *this mountain*] i.e. the mountain of Hebron. "The great
elevation of this country above the level of the sea is most forcibly
brought out by the journey we have made. From the moment of

whereof the LORD spake in that day; for thou heardest in that day how the Anakims *were* there, and *that* the cities *were* great *and* fenced: if so be the LORD *will be* with me, then I shall *be able to* drive them out, as the LORD said. And Joshua blessed him, and gave unto Caleb the son of 13 Jephunneh Hebron for an inheritance. Hebron therefore 14 became the inheritance of Caleb the son of Jephunneh the Kenezite unto this day, because that he wholly followed the LORD God of Israel. And the name of Hebron before 15 *was* Kirjath-arba; which *Arba was* a great man among the Anakims. And the land had rest from war.

leaving the 'Arabah has been almost a continual ascent. We mounted the great Pass of Sâfeh, and, having mounted, hardly descended at all —crossed the great tableland of Beersheba—and then mounted the barrier of the hills of Judah—and thence have been mounting ever since. Hebron is, in fact, only four hundred feet lower than Helvellyn."—Stanley's *Sinai and Palestine*, p. 102.

whereof the Lord spake] These words are a proof that it was not merely a general promise, but a special one in reference to Hebron which Caleb had received.

how the Anakims were there] The names of some are specially mentioned, Num. xiii. 22; Judg. i. 10: Sheshai, Ahiman, and Talmai.

if so be the Lord] More literally, **perhaps Jehovah will be with me, and I may drive them out, as Jehovah said.** The word "perhaps" does not indicate any doubt, but expresses a hope and desire. "If in hap the Lord is with me, and Y may do hem awai, as he bihiȝte to me," Wyclif.

13. *And Joshua blessed him*] The Hebrew leader cheerfully granted the request of his old companion in the work of espial, and emphatically prayed for a successful issue to all his efforts against his gigantic foes.

14. *Hebron therefore became*] Thus the city of Hebron passed into the possession of Caleb, to be by him ceded to the Levites (Josh. xxi. 11), while he retained the land for himself.

15. *And the name of Hebron*] "Hebron would appear to have been the original name of the city, and it was not till after Abraham's stay there that it received the name Kirjath-Arba, who was not the founder but the conqueror of the city, having led thither the tribe of the Anakim to which he belonged. It retained this name till it came into the possession of Caleb, when the Israelites restored the original name *Hebron*." Keil *in loc.* "Caleb must have seen the spot, afterwards his own, when with the spies he passed through this very valley." *S. & P.* p. 165. The translation of Wyclif here is very curious, "The name of Ebron was clepid bifore Cariatharbe. *Adam, moost greet there in the loond of Enachym was set.*"

And the land had rest from war] This formula is repeated here

1—12. *Boundaries of the Tribe of Judah.*

15 *This* then was the lot of the tribe of the children of Judah by their families; *even* to the border of Edom, the wilderness of Zin southward *was* the uttermost part of the south 2 *coast*. And their south border was from the shore of the 3 salt sea, from the bay that looketh southward: and it went out to the south side to Maaleh-acrabbim, and passed along

to furnish a point of transition to the history of the peaceful distribution of the country.

CH. XV. 1—12. BOUNDARIES OF THE TRIBE OF JUDAH.

1. *the lot of the tribe of the children of Judah*] In this Chapter we have (*a*) *the boundaries of the tribe of Judah* (1—12); (*b*) *Caleb's possession* (13—19); (*c*) *a list of the cities of Judah* (20—63). " *The lot of the tribe*"= the lot which was drawn or fell to them.

even to the border of Edom] i.e. the territory of Judah extended to Edom on the east, and was bounded on the south by the wilderness of Zin, or that part of the wilderness of Paran, in which Kadesh-barnea was situated.

2. *And their south border*] The general account of the position of the tribe of Judah is followed by a more particular description of its boundaries. And first *the southern boundary* is described.

from the shore] The southern border of Canaan has already been described in Num. xxxiv. 3—5. It is here given in still greater detail. It commenced (*a*) from the "shore (or end) of the Salt Sea," or more exactly, *the tongue which turneth southward* (see margin), "fro the tonge of it that biholdith to the south," Wyclif. By this "tongue" is meant the southern portion of the Dead Sea reaching from the peninsula, which runs at a great distance from the Sea on the west of Karah, and extends quite to the south point at the so-called Salt-hill and Salt-Marsh." Keil. " We were now in the most desolate and dreary corner of that desolate shore, without one trace of vegetable life, not even a stray salsola, or salicornia, to relieve the flat sand beds. The sand and loam of the shore was deep and heavy; our horses sank at each step above the fetlocks, and not until we were wet through, could we return to the Salt Mountains on our right......The whole ridge (of the mountain) is of pure rock-salt, perhaps 200 feet high, and covered by a layer of chalky marl and natron, about 50 or 60 feet thick....The salt deposit is similar in its nature and geological position to the salt rocks of Cheshire, and the new red sandstone of England." Tristram's *Land of Moab*, pp. 39, 40, 41.

3. *and it went out to the south*] From this point the border ran in a tolerably direct course towards the south side of Maaleh-acrabbim, "*the ascent of scorpions*," "the stiyinge vp of Scorpion," Wyclif; "the going up to Akrabbim," as it is given in Num. xxxiv. 4; Judg. i. 36, a pass in "the bald mountain" (Josh. xi. 17, xii. 7), which " goeth up to Seir."

to Zin, and ascended up on the south side unto Kadeshbarnea, and passed along *to* Hezron, and went up to Adar, and fetched a compass to Karkaa : *from thence* it passed 4 toward Azmon, and went out *unto* the river of Egypt; and the goings out of that coast werê at the sea : this shall be your south coast. And the east border *was* the salt sea, 5 *even* unto the end of Jordan. And *their* border in the north quarter *was* from the bay of the sea at the uttermost part of Jordan : and the border went up *to* Beth-hogla, and passed 6 along by the north of Beth-arabah ; and the border went up

De Saulcy suggests it was the *Wâdy Zouara*, and testifies to "the scorpions" there found under every pebble. *S. and P.* 113, n.

and passed along to Zin] Thence it passed along to Zin, i.e. a certain spot in the desert of Zin not far from Kadesh-barnea, and passed over to *Hezron*, and went up to *Adar*, and fetched a compass or turned to *Karkaa*, and thence towards *Azmon*, and went out at the water-course of Egypt, i.e. the "torrent of Egypt, the *Wady-el-Arish*, already spoken of in ch. xiii. 3. The border went directly southwards to Kadesh-barnea; south of Kadesh it turned westward, and came out finally at the "torrent of Egypt" and at the Mediterranean Sea. Hezron, Adar, Karkaa, Azmon, are unknown sites.

fetched a compass] Compare Fr. *compas*, It. *compasso*, a compass, circle; compasser, to compass, encircle ; from Latin *cum, passus*. The word is used both as (1) *a noun* and (2) *a verb*. (*a*) In the sense of "circumference" it occurs in Exod. xxvii. 5, xxxviii. 4, of "circuit" in 2 Sam. v. 23; 2 Kings iii. 9; Acts xxviii. 13. Here, to fetch a compass = simply to "turn," to "go round." Thus Fuller (*Pisgah View*, IV. ii. 43) says: "Wicked men may for a time retard, not finally obstruct our access to happiness. It is but *fetching a compass*, making two steps for one ; a little more pains and patience will do the deed;" and he says of the Jordan, "he *fetcheth* many turnings and windings, but all will not excuse him from falling into the Dead Sea" (*Holy War*, I. 18).

5. *And the east border*] "Till to the laste partis of Jordan," Wyclif. This was the Salt Sea in all its extent from south to north, even "unto the end of Jordan," i. e. to the point where it enters the Dead Sea.

their border in the north quarter was from the bay of the sea] i.e. from the embouchure of the Jordan. "The tonge of the see vnto the same flood of Jordan," Wyclif.

6. *and the border went up to Beth-hogla*] A point between Judah and Benjamin (Josh. xviii. 19). A magnificent spring and a ruin between Jericho and the Jordan still bear the names of *Ain-hajla* and *Kûsr Hajla*, and are doubtless at or near the old site.

and passed along by the north of Beth-arabah] between Beth-hogla and the highland on the west of the Jordan valley. It is mentioned below (xv. 61) as one of the six cities of Judah in the sunken valley of the Jordan and the Dead Sea.

JOSHUA 9

7 *to* the stone of Bohan the son of Reuben: and the border went up toward Debir from the valley of Achor, and so northward, looking toward Gilgal, that *is* before the going up to Adummim, which *is* on the south side of the river: and the border passed towards the waters of En-shemesh, 8 and the goings out thereof were at En-rogel: and the bor-

the stone of Bohan the son of Reuben] This "Stone" is only mentioned once more, in ch. xviii. 17, and must have lain somewhere to the west or south-west of Beth-arabah.

7. *and the border went up toward Debir*] Not the royal Canaanitish city conquered (Josh. x. 29, 38), but somewhere behind Jericho. A *Wady Dabor* is marked in *Van de Velde's* Map as close to the south of *Nêby Mûsa*, at the north-west of the Dead Sea." Smith's *Bibl. Dict.*

from the valley of Achor] south of Jericho; see ch. vii. 26.

looking toward Gilgal] Not the place where the Israelites first encamped. It is called *Geliloth*, ch. xviii. 17.

that is before the going up to Adummim]="the pass of the red," the road leading up from Jericho and the Jordan valley to Jerusalem. (*a*) Jerome ascribes the name to the blood "qui in illo loco a latronibus funditur," i.e. by the robbers who infested the pass in his day, and as they do still, and as they did in the days of our Lord, of whose parable of "the Good Samaritan" this is the scene. (*b*) But the more natural meaning of the word is "the Pass of the Red-haired Men," as if alluding to some aboriginal tribe of the country. (*c*) Others would derive it from the red colour of the rocks—"the whole pass is white limestone, with the remarkable exception of one large mass of purplish rock on the ascent from Jericho."—*S. and P.* 424, *n.*

which is on the south side of the river] more literally, **of the watercourse**, or **torrent**, the *Wady Kelt.*

the waters of En-shemesh] "and passith the waters, that ben clepid the welle of the sunne," Wyclif. This is the present *Ain el Haudr* or "Apostles' Spring," about a mile below Bethany, the only spring on the road to Jericho.

and the goings out thereof were at En-rogel] This some (*a*) would identify with *'Ain Umm ed-Daraj*, "the Fountain of the Virgin;" (*b*) others with *Bîr Eyub*, below the junction of the valleys of Kidron and Hinnom, and south of the Pool of Siloam. It was near this well that (*a*) Jonathan and Ahimaaz lay hid during the rebellion of Absalom, in order to collect and send news to David (2 Sam. xvii. 17); and (*b*) afterwards Adonijah slew sheep and oxen and fat cattle by En-rogel, when he conspired to seize the kingdom (1 Kings i. 9). "In itself it is a singular work of ancient enterprise. The shaft, sunk through the solid rock in the bed of the Kidron, is 125 feet deep. The idea of digging such a well at that precise spot may have been suggested by the fact, that, after very great rains, water sometimes rises nearly to the top, and then flows out into the valley below, a strong brook capable of driving a mill. This, however, soon ceases, and the

der went up *by* the valley of the son of Hinnom unto the south side of the Jebusite; the same *is* Jerusalem: and the border went up to the top of the mountain that *lieth* before

water in the well subsides to less than half its depth. From that point a stream seems to run constantly across it, and pass down the valley under the rock.......The water is pure and entirely sweet, quite different from that of Siloam, which proves that there is no connection between them. I have seen the water gushing out like a mill-stream, some fifteen rods south of the well; and then the whole valley was alive with people bathing in it, and indulging in every species of hilarity." Thomson's *Land and the Book*, pp. 658, 659.

8. *and the border went up*] From En-rogel the border *went up into the valley of the son of Hinnom, on the south side of the Jebusite, that is Jerusalem*. The direction accordingly runs S. S.W. of Jerusalem, where the valley mentioned lies. Nothing is known of this Hinnom. Possibly he was some ancient hero, who had encamped here, and from whom it was called " *Ge-Ben-Hinnom*," "the Ravine of the son of Hinnom," whence came "Ge-Hinnom," and so "Gehenna." It is a deep retired glen, shut in by rugged cliffs, with the bleak mountain-sides rising over all. Here (*a*) Solomon erected high places for Moloch (1 Kings xi. 7), and (*b*) in the times of Ahaz and Manasseh it became notorious as the scene of the barbarous rites of that deity and of Chemosh, when the idolatrous inhabitants of Jerusalem cast their sons and daughters into the red-hot arms of a monster idol of brass placed at the opening of the ravine (2 Kings xvi. 3; 2 Chron. xxviii. 3; Jer. vii. 31). To put an end to these abominations the place was polluted by Josiah, who spread over it human bones and other corruptions (2 Kings xxiii. 10, 13, 14), from which time it seems to have become the common cesspool for the city. These inhuman rites and subsequent ceremonial defilement caused the later Jews to regard it with horror and detestation, and they applied the name given to the valley to *the place of torment*.

the same is Jerusalem] As Bethel was in earlier times called *Luz* (Gen. xxviii. 19), and Bethlehem was called *Ephrath* (Gen. xxxv. 16; Mic. v. 2), so Jerusalem was called *Jebus* (Judg. xix. 11; 1 Chron. xi. 4). It is interpreted by some to mean a place "*dry*" or "*down-trodden like a threshingfloor*," which is thought to prove it must have been the south-western hill.

went up to the top of the mountain] From the ravine of Hinnom the border now ascended to the top of the mountain that lieth before the valley of Hinnom westward, which is at the end of "the Valley of Giants northward." The "Valley of the Giants" was "the Valley of Rephaim," an ancient settlement of this giant tribe, from which sprang Og king of Basan, possibly after they were driven from their original seats by Chedorlaomer (Gen. xiv. 5). It was a "valley-plain," extending in a S.W. direction from Jerusalem to Mar Elias, spacious enough to serve as a camp for an army. Here (*a*) David twice encountered the Philistines and inflicted a destruction upon them so signal that it gave

9—2

the valley of Hinnom westward, which *is* at the end of the
9 valley of the giants northward: and the border was drawn
from the top of the hill unto the fountain of the water of
Nephtoah, and went out to the cities of mount Ephron; and
the border was drawn *to* Baalah, which *is* Kirjath-jearim:
10 and the border compassed from Baalah westward unto
mount Seir, and passed along unto the side of mount
Jearim, which *is* Chesalon, on the north side, and went
11 down *to* Beth-shemesh, and passed on *to* Timnah: and the

the place a new name, Baal-perazim = " *the plain of Bursts* " or " *Destructions* " (2 Sam. v. 17—20). Here (*b*) too it was in all probability that the incident of the water of Bethlehem occurred (2 Sam. xxiii. 13).

the mountain] here alluded to was the slight "rock-ridge" which on the north constitutes the boundary of the valley of Hinnom.

9. *and the border was drawn*] From the summit of the mountain just alluded to, the border was drawn to "the fountain of the water at Nephtoah." Nephtoah has been identified with *Ain Lifta*, a spring situated a little distance above the village of the same name, N.W. of Jerusalem. It irrigates a strip of smiling gardens, and its excellent water is carried also to Jerusalem.

and went out to the cities of mount Ephron] Ephron is nowhere else mentioned. It is probably the range of hills on the west side of *Wâdy-Beit-Hanina*, opposite *Lifta*.

and...was drawn to Baalah] another name for Kirjath-jearim or Kirjath-Baal (Josh. xv. 60; xviii. 14). Baalah was probably the earlier or Canaanite appellation. We have already met with Kirjath-jearim as one of the four cities of the Gibeonites (above, ch. ix. 17). It is famous as the spot, (*a*) behind which the band of Danites pitched their camp before their expedition to Laish (Judg. xviii. 12); (*b*) where the Ark remained upwards of twenty years (1 Sam. vii. 2), and (*c*) whence it was removed by David to the house of Obed-Edom the Gittite (1 Chron. xiii. 5, 6). It is now known as *Kureyet el-Enab*.

10. *and the border compassed*]=it "beat round," "took a circuit;" and see above, *v.* 3.

unto mount Seir] not the Edomite range (Gen. xxxii. 3; Num. xxiv. 18), but the range, which lies between the *Wady Aly* and *the Wady Ghurab*. It may have derived its name either (*a*) from some peculiarity in the form or appearance of the spot, or (*b*) from some incursion of the Edomites, which has escaped record.

and passed along unto the side of mount Jearim] or, *unto the* **shoulder** *of mount Jearim*," which is Chesalon. Chesalon, probably now *Kesla* (see Robinson's *Later Bibl. Res.* p. 154), was also called Har-jearim = "*mountain of forests*," as Baalah was called Kirjath-jearim="city of forests" or "forest town." The region appears in early times to have been thickly covered with woods.

and went down to Beth-shemesh, and passed on to Timnah] (*a*) *Beth-shemesh*="*house of the sun*," or *Ir-shemesh* (ch. xix. 22), now

border went out unto the side of Ekron northward: and the border was drawn to Shicron, and passed along *to* mount Baalah, and went out *unto* Jabneel; and the goings out of the border were at the sea. And the west border *was* to 12 the great sea, and the coast *thereof*. This *is* the coast of the children of Judah round about according to their families.

13—19. The Request of Achsah, Daughter of Caleb.

And unto Caleb the son of Jephunneh he gave a part 13

'*Ain-Shems*, about two miles from the great Philistine plain, and seven miles from Ekron. It (*a*) was allotted to the priests (Josh. xxi. 16); was (*b*) the place whither "the kine took the straight way" from Ekron with the Ark of the Covenant (1 Sam. vi. 9); where (*c*) the people looked into the Ark and caused the severe judgment that followed (1 Sam. vi. 19); and where (*d*) Solomon had one of his commissariat districts (1 Kings iv. 9). "Here," at '*Ain-Shems*, "are the vestiges of a former extensive city, consisting of many foundations, and the remains of ancient walls of hewn stone. Both the name and the position of this spot seem to indicate the site of the ancient Beth-shemesh of the Old Testament." Robinson, *Later Bibl. Res.* p. 153. (β) *Timnah*, or *Timnath*, or *Thimnathah* (Josh. xix. 43), now *Tibnah*, a village about two miles west of '*Ain-Shems*, from which Samson fetched his wife (Judg. xiv. 1, 5), and in the vineyards of which, without anything in his hand, he killed the lion (Judg. xiv. 5, 6).

11. *unto the side of Ekron northward*] The boundary, still following a N.W. course, now tended towards a point lying near the Philistine city of Ekron (see above, ch. xiii. 3), whence it was drawn to *Shicron*, between Ekron and Jabneal (Yebna), and passed along to mount *Baalah*, "the short line of hills running almost parallel with the coast," and so "went out unto Jabneel" the modern village of Yebna or Ibna, about two miles from the Sea, 11 miles south of *Jaffa*, and four from *Ækir* (Ekron), represents the ancient Jabneel or *Jabneh* (2 Chron. xxvi. 6), or, in its Greek garb, *Jamnia* (1 Macc. iv. 5; v. 58).

12. *the west border*] was formed by the Mediterranean Sea.
to the great sea] From Jabneel the boundary continued to the Mediterranean Sea along the *Wady es Surah*.
and the coast thereof] or *borders thereof*; see above, ch. xiii. 23, 27, and comp. Num. xxxiv. 6.

13—19. THE REQUEST OF ACHSAH, DAUGHTER OF CALEB.

13. *And unto Caleb*] This section, from ver. 13—19, is repeated with slight alterations almost verbatim in Judg. i. 10—20. The two sections are probably derived from a common source. As occurring here the verses are intended to complete the history of the division of the land amongst the tribes. As Caleb had brought forward his claims to the possession of Hebron, before the casting of the lots

among the children of Judah, according to the commandment of the LORD to Joshua, *even* the city of Arba the father 14 of Anak, which *city is* Hebron. And Caleb drove thence the three sons of Anak, Sheshai, and Ahiman, and Talmai, 15 the children of Anak. And he went up thence to the inhabitants of Debir: and the name of Debir before *was* Kir-16 jath-sepher. And Caleb said, He that smiteth Kirjath-sepher, and taketh it, to him will I give Achsah my daughter 17 to wife. And Othniel the son of Kenaz, the brother of Caleb, took it: and he gave him Achsah his daughter to

commenced, and those claims had been admitted by Joshua, it was quite in order for the author, when giving here the list of the cities assigned to the tribe of Judah, to refer especially to the portion which Caleb had received, not by lot, but in fulfilment of the Divine promise made to him by Moses, and at the same time to record how fully his hopes had been fulfilled of driving out the Anakims, and thus securing the undisputed possession of Hebron and its vicinity to himself and his descendants. Keil's *Commentary*.

he gave] i. e. Joshua, by the command of Jehovah. For "the city of Arba" see above, ch. xiv. 15.

14. *the three sons of Anak*] Three chiefs of the Anakims. Comp. Num. xiii. 22.

15. *to the inhabitants of Debir*] On Debir see above, xi. 21. Joshua had conquered and devoted it.

Debir before was Kirjath-sepher] = "*the city of Books*," "citee of lettrys;" Wyclif, or (Josh. xv. 49) Kirjath-Sannah = "city of palm."

16. *to him will I give Achsah my daughter*] So Saul promised to the victor over Goliath to "give him his daughter" (1 Sam. xvii. 25), and undertook if David was valiant for him to give him to wife his elder daughter Merab (1 Sam. xviii. 17).

17. *Othniel the son of Kenaz*] The younger brother of Caleb (comp. Judg. i. 13, iii. 9; 1 Chron. iv. 13). But it is not certain from these passages whether Kenaz was his father, or, as some think, the more remote ancestor and head of the tribe, whose descendants were called "sons of Kenaz" (Num. xxxii. 12). If Jephunneh was the father of Caleb, he was probably the father of Othniel also. The next mention of him is in Judg. iii. 9, where we find him the first Judge of Israel after the death of Joshua (for his genealogy see 1 Chron. iv. 13, 14), delivering the Israelites from the tyranny of the Mesopotamian king, Chushan-rishathaim.

the brother of Caleb] There is a doubt here whether Othniel was "filius Kenasi, frat*er* Calebi," or "filius Kenasi frat*ris* Calebi." For the second explanation comp. 2 Sam. xiii. 3, 32, "Jonadab, the son of Shimeah David's brother; for the first, 1 Sam. xxvi. 6, "Abishai, the son of Zeruiah, and brother to Joab;" this is adopted by the *Maronites*, the LXX., and the Vulgate.

wife. And it came to pass, as she came *unto him*, that she 18
moved him to ask of her father a field: and she lighted off
her ass; and Caleb said unto her, What wouldest thou?
Who answered, Give me a blessing; for thou hast given me 19
a south land; give me also springs of water. And he gave
her the upper springs, and the nether springs.

and he gave him Achsah] She had probably remained with her father at Hebron.
18. *as she came unto him*] i.e. as she proceeded to the home of Othniel at Debir to become his wife. "When the parties live in different villages, the bridegroom accompanied by his friends, all well mounted and armed, and escorted with music, repair to the house of the bride, and escort her to her new home." See the picture of such a procession in Van Lenneps' *Bible Lands and Customs*, p. 550.
she moved him] The original word denotes (1) *to impel*, (2) *to incite*, *induce*. Comp. 2 Chron. xviii. 2, "And Ahab *persuaded* him to go up with him to Ramoth-Gilead." "The which, whanne she went to togidre, hir man meeued to hir for to axe of hir fader a feeld." Wyclif.
a field] more definitely, **the field**, either (*a*) which belonged to Debir, as some suppose, or (*b*) the field which was fit for cultivation, and had a sufficient supply of water.
she lighted off her ass] The original word only occurs in three places; (*a*) here; (*b*) the parallel passage in Judg. i. 14; and (*c*) in Judg. iv. 21, "Then Jael Heber's wife took a nail of the tent...and *went softly* unto him." It denotes (1) *to force oneself away from:* (2) *to descend quickly from, to sink down from*, as in Gen. xxiv. 64, "And Rebekah lifted up her eyes, and when she saw Isaac, she *lighted off the camel*." The LXX. have rendered it, apparently from a different reading, "she cried from the ass;" the Vulgate, "*suspiravitque* ut sedebat in asino;" and so Wyclif, "And she siside, as she sat in the asse."
18. *and Caleb said unto her*] It would seem as though Othniel could not be prevailed upon to make such a request himself, and that Achsah therefore determined to prefer it herself. Her action in springing from the ass so astonished Caleb, that he put to her the question, "What wouldest thou?"
19. *Give me a blessing*] Comp. the words of Jacob to Esau, Gen. xxxiii. 11, "Take, I pray thee, *my blessing* that is brought to thee;" Josh. xiv. 13, "And Joshua *blessed him*, and gave unto Caleb...Hebron for an inheritance;" and the words of Naaman to Elisha, "Now therefore, I pray thee, *take a blessing* of thy servant." 2 Kings v. 15.
a south land] He had given it to her, inasmuch as he had given her as a wife to the conqueror of Debir. The words are used in a double sense. "The south country"="the barren and dry land," "terram australem et torrentem dedisti mihi," Vulgate; "the south loond and drye," Wyclif.
springs of water] The word here used, "gulloth,"="waves" or "bubblings." "Underneath the hill on which Debir stood is a deep

20—32. *Cities of Judah in the South.*

20 This *is* the inheritance of the tribe of the children of

valley, rich with verdure from a copious rivulet, which, rising at the crest of the glen, falls, with a continuity unusual in the Judæan hills, down to its lowest depth. On the possession of these upper and lower 'bubblings,' so contiguous to her lover's prize, Achsah had set her heart. The scene of this incident was first discovered by Dr Rosen, and under his guidance I saw it in 1862." Stanley's *Lectures*, I. 264.

the upper springs, and the nether springs] Caleb responded to her wish, and gave her the higher and lower fields watered by these springs. Nether adj. = *lower*. Comp. Exod. xix. 17, "And Moses brought forth the people...and they stood at the *nether* part of the mount;" Deut. xxiv. 6, "No man shall take *the nether* or the upper millstone to pledge;" 1 Kings ix. 17, "And Solomon built Gezer, and Beth-horon *the nether;*" Job xli. 24, "His heart is as firm as a stone, yea as hard as a piece of the *nether* millstone." A. S. *nyðcra*, or *neoðra*. Comp. "the *Nether*lands"="the Lowlands;" "a foolish hanging of thy *nether* lip." Shakespeare, *I. Henry IV.* II. 4.

20—32. CITIES OF JUDAH IN THE SOUTH.

20. *This is the inheritance*] "The speech of Achsah to her father was the best reason for the slight notice of this desert tract in later times, and is the best introduction to the real territory of Judah, on which we now enter. 'Give me a blessing, *for* thou hast given me a *south* land; give me also *springs of water.*' The wells of Beersheba were enough for the Patriarchs, the Amalekites, and the Kenites, but they were not enough for the daughter of Judah and the house of the mighty Caleb." Stanley's *Sinai and Palestine*, p. 161. The territory of Judah, in average length about 45 miles and in average breadth about 50, was from a very early period divided into four main regions—(i) the South; (ii) the Lowland; (iii) the Mountain; (iv) the Wilderness.

(α) *The South* was the undulating pasture country which intervened between the hills, the proper possession of the tribe, and the desert country which marks the lower part of Palestine.

(β) *The Lowland*, or, to give it its proper name, the *Shephelah*, was a broad strip of land lying between the central mountains and the Mediterranean Sea. From the edge of the sandy tract which fringes the immediate shore it stretched up to the bases of the hills of Judah—the garden and granary of the tribe—and formed the lower part of the maritime plain which extended along the whole seaboard of Palestine from "the river of Egypt" to Sidon.

(γ) *The Mountain*, or "the Hill Country," though not the richest, was at once the largest and the most important of the four. "Beginning a few miles below Hebron, where it attains its highest level, it stretches eastward to the Dead Sea and westward to *the Shephelah*, and forms an elevated district or plateau, which, though thrown into considerable undulations, yet preserves a general level in both directions."

Judah according to their families. And the uttermost cities 21
of the tribe of the children of Judah toward the coast of
Edom southward were Kabzeel, and Eder, and Jagur, and 22
Kinah, and Dimonah, and Adadah, and Kedesh, and Hazor, 23
and Ithnan, Ziph, and Telem, and Bealoth, and Hazor, 24
Hadattah, and Kerioth, *and* Hezron, which *is* Hazor, Amam, 26
and Shema, and Moladah, and Hazar-gaddah, and Hesh- 27
mon, and Beth-palet, and Hazah-shual, and Beersheba, and 28

(δ) *The Wilderness, Midbah,* which here, and here only, is synonymous with *Arâbah,* represents the sunken district adjoining the Dead Sea. See Mr. Grove's article in Smith's *Bibl. Dict.*
21. *And the uttermost cities*] The writer commences with the cities at the extremity of the territory of Judah, the S.E. point of the Dead Sea, on the Edomite frontier.
toward the coast of Edom southward] For *"coast,"* see above, ch. xiii. 16. (*a*) *First* we have a group of *nine cities* within the *Negeb* at the south-east :—
(1) *Kabzeel* = *"which God gathers,"* the birth-place of Benaiah, one of David's heroes (2 Sam. xxiii. 20) ; (2) *Eder* and (3) *Jagur* are altogether unknown ; (4) *Kinah,* possibly the territory of the Kenites who settled at Arad; (5) *Dimonah* = *Dibon* (Neh. xi. 25) ; (6) *Adadah,* identified by Robinson with *Sudeid ;* (7) *Kedesh,* (8) *Hazor,* and (9) *Ithnan* are unknown.
24. *Ziph*] (*b*) With this town commences a *second group* of *five cities* :—
(1) *Ziph,* not identified ; (2) *Telem,* not identified—not to be confounded with *Telaim,* where Saul collected and numbered his forces before his attack on Amalek (1 Sam. xv. 4); (3) *Bealoth* = Bealoth-beer, on the road towards Hebron ; (4) *Hazor-hadattah* = *"New Hazor;"* (5) *Kerioth-Hezron,* which is *Hazor;* the names here are to be joined together, like Kirjath-arba and Kirjath-jearim.
26. *Amam* (*c*) *Third group* of *nine cities* :—
(1) *Amam,* unknown ; (2) *Shema,* a place of the Simeonites (ch. xix. 2); (3) *Moladah,* called *Malatua* by the Greeks and Romans = the modern *El-Milh,* four English miles from *Tell Arad* and nine or ten due east of Beersheba ; (4) *Hazar-gaddah,* unknown ; (5) *Heshmon,* unknown ; (6) *Beth-palet,* unknown ; (7) *Hazar-shual* = *"village of jackals,"* inhabited after the Captivity by men of Judah (Neh. xi. 27) ; (8) *Beer-sheba* = either (*a*) *" Well of Seven"* or (*b*) *" Well of the Oath"* (Gen. xxi. 28—32). We find Beer-sheba visited by Abraham, who dug the well (Gen. xxi. 31); the place where Samuel's sons judged Israel (1 Sam. viii. 2) ; constituting, with Dan in the north, the established formula for the whole of the Promised Land—"Dan to Beer-sheba" (2 Sam. xxiv. 2) ; the seat of an idolatrous worship in the time of Amos (Amos v. 5, viii. 14). It still retains as nearly as possible its ancient name, *Bîr-es-Sebâ.* There are at present two principal wells and five smaller ones. The curb-stones round the mouth are worn into deep grooves by the action of the ropes of

138   JOSHUA, XV.   [vv. 29—35.

²⁹₃₀ Bizjothjah, Baalah, and Iim, and Azem, and Eltolad, and
31 Chesil, and Hormah, and Ziklag, and Madmannah, and
32 Sansannah, and Lebaoth, and Shilhim, and Ain, and Rimmon : all the cities *are* twenty and nine, with their villages.

33—47. Cities in the Lowland.

³³₃₄ And in the valley, Eshtaol, and Zoreah, and Ashnah, and
35 Zanoah, and Engannim, Tappuah, and Enam, Jarmuth, and

so many centuries, and look as if "frilled or fluted all round"; (9) *Bizjothjah,* unknown.

29. *Baalah*] A *fourth group* is added of *thirteen places* which lay to the *west* and *south-west*:—
(1) *Baalah,* called *Balah* (ch. xix. 3) and *Bilhah* (1 Chron. iv. 29); (2) *Iim,* unknown ; (3) *Azem* = "firmness" or "strength" (ch. xix. 3); (4) *Eltolad* = *Tolad* (1 Chron. iv. 29), unknown ; (5) *Chesil* = *Bethul* (Josh. xix. 4) = *Bethuel* (1 Chron. iv. 30) ; (6) *Hormah,* or *Zephath* (comp. xii. 14) ; (7) *Ziklag* = "wilderness of destruction" (Gesenius), which afterwards came into the possession of Achish, king of Gath, who presented it to David (1 Sam. xxvii. 6), and was burnt by the Amalekites (1 Sam. xxx. 1) ; (8) *Madmannah* = possibly to *el-Minyây,* south of Gaza, on the route of the pilgrims during the fifteenth and sixteenth centuries ; (9) *Sansannah,* unknown; (10) *Lebaoth* = Beth-lebaoth (Josh. xix. 6 ; 1 Chron. iv. 31), perhaps *Lebhem,* eight hours south of Gaza ; (11) *Shilhim* = *el-Scheriat,* about midway between Gaza and Beer-sheba ; (12) *Ain ;* (13) *Rimmon;* in ch. xix. 7, 1 Chron. iv. 32, these are treated as one place, and comp. Neh. xi. 29. Rimmon has been supposed to be represented by *Um er-Rumamim,* about three hours north of Beersheba.

32. *all the cities are twenty and nine*] Thirty-six, however, are actually given, viz., (1) *the first group* = 9 ; (2) the *second group* = 5 ; (3) the *third group* = 9 ; (4) the *fourth group* = 13 = 36 in all. The discrepancy has been variously explained by supposing (*a*) that some of the places were merely hamlets or villages, and were therefore not counted with the rest; (*b*) that in some cases two names may have belonged to the same city ; (*c*) that there is an error in the numeral letters ; (*d*) that the author originally wrote fewer names, and "that others were added by a later hand without a corresponding alteration being made in the number." (See Keil *in loc.*)

33—47. CITIES IN THE LOWLAND.

33. *in the valley*] i. e. the Lowland. See above, ver. 20, and also Josh. x. 40, xi. 16. The places mentioned are arranged in *four groups.* The first of these lies in the *north-eastern* portion of the *Shephêlah*:—
Group I. 1. *Eshtaol* = *Yeshûa;* 2. *Zoreah* = *Sûrah,* the residence of Manoah (Judg. xiii. 2, 25) and the native place of Samson. It lay close to Eshtaol. Here Samson spent his boyhood, and to a spot between the two places his dead body was brought after his last great exploit (Judg. xiii. 25; xvi. 31); 3. *Ashnah,* unknown; 4. *Zanoah,*

Adullam, Socoh, and Azekah, and Sharaim, and Adithaim, 36
and Gederah, and Gederothaim; fourteen cities with their
villages. Zenan, and Hadashah, and Migdal-gad, and Di- 37
lean, and Mizpeh, and Joktheel, Lachish, and Bozkath, and 39
Eglon, and Cabbon, and Lahmam, and Kithlish, and Gede- 40
roth, Beth-dagon, and Naamah, and Makkedah; sixteen
cities with their villages. Libnah, and Ether, and Ashan, 42
and Jiphtah, and Ashnah, and Nezib, and Keilah, and Ach- 43
zib, and Mareshah; nine cities with their villages. Ekron, 45

now *Zânû'a*; 5. *En-gannim*, and 6. *Tappuah* are unknown; 7. *Enam*
is mentioned Gen. xxxviii. 14, 21; 8. *Jarmuth* (*Yarmuk*), a Canaanitish
capital, see above xv. 35; 9. *Adullam*, see above xv. 35; 10. *Socoh*,
now *Shuweikeh*; 11. *Azekah* (see above, x. 10), the beautiful vale, "the
valley of Elah," between it and Socoh, was celebrated for the combat
between David and Goliath; 12. *Sharaim*, see 1 Sam. xvii. 52; 13.
Adithaim, site unknown; 14. *Gederah*, with the article, properly="*the
wall*," undiscovered; 15. *Gederothaim*, unknown.
36. *fourteen cities*] The LXX. omits Gederothaim, which makes
fourteen instead of fifteen cities.
37. *Zenan*] *Group II.* comprises the cities of the actual plain in
its whole extent from north to south, between the hilly region on the
west and the Philistine coast on the east. It includes *sixteen cities*:—
1. *Zenan* = Zaanan (Mic. i. 11), site unknown; 2. *Hadashah*, site
unknown; 3. *Migdal-gad*, site unknown; 4. *Dilean*, site unknown;
5. *Mizpeh*, not the Mizpeh of Benjamin (ch. xviii. 26); 6. *Joktheel*,
site unknown; 7. *Lachish* (see above x. 3); 8. *Bozkath*, uncertain;
9. *Eglon* (see above, x. 3); 10. *Cabbon*; 11. *Lahmam*; 12. *Kithlish*;
13. *Gederoth*, all undetermined; 14. *Beth-dagon*, indicating by its name
the Philistine worship of Dagon; 15. *Naamah*, undetermined; 16.
Makkedah, a royal city of the Canaanites, already spoken of x. 16.
42. *Libnah*] *Group III.* consists of the places in the southern part
of the hill region, and includes *nine cities*:—
1. *Libnah*, conquered by Joshua, see above, x. 29, 30; 2. *Ether*, and
3. *Ashan*, see 1 Chron. iv. 32; 4. *Jiphtah*; 5. *Ashnah*, sites unknown;
6. *Nezib* = the modern *Nûsib*; 7. *Keilah*, to the north of *Nezib*, the
modern *Kila*; this was the town (*a*) which David rescued from the
attack of the Philistines (1 Sam. xxiii. 7); (*b*) which became the reposi-
tory of the sacred ephod after the massacre of the priests at Nob (1 Sam.
xxiii. 6); (*c*) which David left, warned of the intention of the inhabitants to deliver him to Saul (1 Sam. xxiii. 13); 8. *Achzib*, see Gen.
xxxviii. 5; Mic. i. 14; 9. *Mareshah*, afterwards fortified by Rehoboam
(2 Chron. xi. 8), and the scene of the victory of king Asa (2 Chron. xiv.
9—13). It was subsequently called *Maresa*, and was famous in the contests of the Maccabees (1 Macc. v. 65—68). It was restored by the
Roman general Gabinius, and destroyed by the Parthians. The modern
name is *Merash*.

46 with her towns and her villages: from Ekron even unto the 47 sea, all that *lay* near Ashdod, with their villages: Ashdod *with* her towns and her villages, Gaza *with* her towns and her villages, unto the river of Egypt, and the great sea, and the border *thereof.*

48—60. *The Cities in the Mountains.*

48 And in the mountains, Shamir, and Jattir, and Socoh, 49 50 and Dannah, and Kirjath-sannah, which *is* Debir, and Anab, 51 and Eshtemoh, and Anim, and Goshen, and Holon, and 52 Giloh; eleven cities with their villages. Arab, and Dumah, 53 and Eshean, and Janum, and Beth-tappuah, and Aphekah, 54 and Humtah, and Kirjath-arba, which *is* Hebron, and Zior;

45. *Ekron. Group IV.* includes the Philistine line of coast, and includes three chief cities:—
1. *Ekron,* see ch. xiii. 3, with her *towns,* or rather "*daughter towns,*" and *villages;* 2. *Ashdod,* with her "*daughter towns*" and *villages,* see above, ch. xi. 21; 3. *Gaza,* with her "*daughter towns*" and *villages,* see above, ch. x. 41; as far as the "river of Egypt," see above, xiii. 3, and "the great sea."

48—60. THE CITIES IN THE MOUNTAINS.

48. *And in the mountains*] This section treats of the Cities in the Mountains or "the Hill Country," (see above, *v.* 20), and includes *five groups.*
Shamir] *Group I.* consists of *eleven cities* on the south-western portion of the "hill Country:"—
1. *Shamir,* still unknown; 2. *Jattir,* probably the modern '*Attir,* 10 miles south of Hebron; 3. *Socoh,* not *Shocoh* in "the Lowland," but like it now called *Suweikeh;* 4. *Dannah,* still unknown; 5. *Kirjath-sannah,* i. e. Debir, see above, x. 38, xv. 15; 6. *Anab,* a town of the Anakims (ch. xi. 21), still existing under its old name; 7. *Eshtemoh,* one of the places frequented by David and his followers during his life as an outlaw (1 Sam. xxx. 28). Now *Semua,* seven miles south of Hebron; 8. *Anim,* close to Eshtemoa, nine miles south of Hebron; 9. *Goshen,* not determined; 10. *Holon,* a priest's city (1 Chron. vi. 58); 11. *Giloh,* the site of which has not yet been discovered, but it was (*a*) the birthplace of Ahithophel (2 Sam. xv. 12); (*b*) and the place where the traitor hanged himself (2 Sam. xvii. 23).
52. *Arab. Group II.* includes *nine cities* to the north of those just enumerated in the country round Hebron:—
1. *Arab;* 2. *Dumah,* a ruined village not far from Hebron, now *Ed-Daumeh;* 3. *Eshean,* site unknown; 4. *Janum,* not discovered; 5. *Beth-tappuah* = "House of Apples." The name has been preserved in *Teffûh,* a place about 5 miles west of Hebron; 6. *Aphekah,* not the

nine cities with their villages. Maon, Carmel, and Ziph, 55
and Juttah, and Jezreel, and Jokdeam, and Zanoah, Cain, 56
Gibeah, and Timnah; ten cities with their villages. Halhul, 58
Beth-zur, and Gedor, and Maarath, and Beth-anoth, and 59
Eltekon; six cities with their villages. Kirjath-baal, which 60
is Kirjath-jearim, and Rabbah; two cities with their villages.

61—63. *Cities in the Wilderness.*

In the wilderness, Beth-arabah, Middin, and Secacah, 61

Aphek of ch. xii. 18, xiii. 4, but on the mountains of Judah; 7. *Humtah*, not yet discovered; 8. *Kirjath-Arba*, see above, xiv. 15, xv. 13; 9. *Zior*, unknown.

55. *Maon*] *Group III.* consists of ten cities, on the south-east of the two preceding groups, towards the desert:—

1. *Maon*, to the east of Eshtemoa, now *Main;* here David hid himself during his life as an outlaw (1 Sam. xxiii. 24), and here he met Nabal, the churl (1 Sam. xxv. 2); 2. *Carmel* (*Kurmul*), a name familiar in the history (*a*) of Saul (1 Sam. xv. 12); (*b*) of David (1 Sam. xxv. 2, 5, 7); (*c*) of Uzziah (2 Chron. xxvi. 10); 3. *Ziph* (*Tell Zif*), about five miles south-east of Hebron, where (*a*) David hid himself (1 Sam. xxiii. 19; Ps. liv. title); which (*b*) Rehoboam fortified (2 Chron. xi. 8); 4. *Juttah*, west of Ziph, now *Yütta*, a priests' city (ch. xxi. 16); 5. *Jezreel*, the home of Ahinoam the second wife of David (1 Sam. xxv. 43); 6. *Jokdeam;* 7. *Zanoah*, these places are undiscovered, and not elsewhere named; 8. *Cain*, likewise unknown; 9. *Gibeah*="hill," a very common name; 10. *Timnah*, not the Timnah between Beth-shemesh and Ekron (xv. 10), but the place whither Judah went up to his sheepshearing (Gen. xxxviii. 12—14).

58. *Halhul*] *Group IV.* consists of *six cities* on the north of Hebron:—

1. *Halhul*, still called *Hŭlhŭl*, north of Hebron, on the way to Jerusalem, in a well-cultivated region of fields and vineyards; 2. *Bethzur*, to the north of Halhul, now *Beit Sur*, fortified by Rehoboam (2 Chron. xi. 7), and one of the strongest fortresses afterwards in all Judæa (1 Macc. iv. 29, 61; vi. 7, 26); 3. *Gedor*, north-west of Bethzur, now *Jedûr;* see 1 Chron. xii. 7, on the brow of a high mountain, north-west of the road between Jerusalem and Hebron; 4. *Maarath*, unknown; 5. *Beth-anoth* = "house of Echo" (Gesenius), now *Beit Ainûn;* 6. *Eltekon*, site unknown.

60. *Kirjath-baal*] *Group V.* consists of *two cities* on the west of Jerusalem:—

1. *Kirjath-baal* = *Kirjath-jearim*, see above, v. 9; 2. *Rabbah*, unknown.

61—63. CITIES IN THE WILDERNESS.

This section relates to the cities in "the Wilderness" between the Mountain and the Dead Sea, and includes one Group of *six cities*:—

62 and Nibshan, and the city of salt, and En-gedi; six cities 63 with their villages. As for the Jebusites the inhabitants of Jerusalem, the children of Judah could not drive them out: but the Jebusites dwell with the children of Judah at Jerusalem unto this day.

1. *Beth-arabah*, see above, v. 6; 2. *Middin*; 3. *Secacah*; 4. *Nibshan*, sites unknown, places not mentioned elsewhere; 5. *The city of Salt*, "*Civitas Salis*," Vulgate, probably near the Valley of Salt, at the southern end of the Dead Sea, where the Edomites suffered several defeats (2 Sam. viii. 13; 2 Kings xiv. 7; 1 Chron. xviii. 12); 6. *Engedi*, "the spring of the wild goat" or "gazelle," from the numerous ibexes or Syrian chamois which inhabit these cliffs, now *Ain Jidy*. "Here," remarks Canon Tristram, "a copious warm fresh spring bursts forth amidst an oasis of tropical vegetation. Here that quaint asclepiad the osher, the jujube, the beautiful parasite *Lonicera indica*, and a host of strange semi-tropical plants send our botanist into an ecstacy of delight." *Land of Moab*, p. 27. "Relics of its grove of palms"(whence its name Hazazon Tamar = "the felling of palm-trees") "are still to be seen, in the trunks of palms washed up on the shores of the Dead Sea, preserved by the salt with which a long submersion in those strange waters has impregnated them." Stanley's *S. and P.*, p. 144. Here (*a*) the settlements of the Amorites were attacked by the army of Chedorlaomer (Gen. xiv. 7), immediately before its descent into the plain, and final victory over the five kings; here (*b*) the Kenites had their "nest" in the cliff (Num. xxiv. 21); here (*c*) David took refuge from the pursuit of Saul (1 Sam. xxiv. 1); here (*d*) the solitary sect of the Essenes had their chief seat." See Stanley, *S. and P.*, pp. 295, 296.

In the wilderness] The wilderness of Judæa. "A true wilderness it is, but no desert, with the sides of the limestone ranges clad with no shrubs larger than a sage or a thyme—brown and bare on all the southern and western faces, where the late rains had not yet restored the life burnt out by the summer's sun, but with a slight carpeting of tender green already springing up on their northern sides. Not a human habitation, not a sign of life, meets the eye for twenty miles; and yet there seems no reason why, for pasturage at least, the country might not be largely available. But there are no traces of the terraces which furrow the hills of the rest of Palestine; and one small herd of long-eared black goats were all we saw till we reached the plains of Jericho." Tristram's *Land of Israel*, p. 197.

63. *As for*] The Author closes the catalogue of the cities of Judah with an announcement that the children of this royal tribe failed to drive out the Jebusites from Jerusalem.

the Jebusites] The Jebusites are noticed above, ch. x. 1, and ch. xi. 3. They were a strong mountain-tribe, and as long as the "Upper City" remained in their hands they practically had possession of the whole. The children of Judah, as also the children of Benjamin, took and burnt the "Lower City," but relinquished the attempt to capture the "Upper City." (See Judg. i. 8, 21.)

1—4. *The Lot of the Children of Joseph.*

And the lot of the children of Joseph fell from Jordan by 1
Jericho, unto the water of Jericho on the east, *to* the wilderness that goeth up from Jericho throughout mount Beth-el,
and goeth out from Beth-el to Luz, and passeth along unto 2
the borders of Archi *to* Ataroth, and goeth down westward 3

unto this day] It is plain from this that the Book of Joshua was written before the reign of David (1 Chron. xi. 3—9).

CH. XVI. 1—4. THE LOT OF THE CHILDREN OF JOSEPH.

1. *the lot of the children of Joseph*] Having described the inheritance of the royal tribe of Judah, the Author proceeds to relate the distribution of the descendants of the great house of Joseph.

fell] Heb. *went forth*, i.e. "came out of the urn or chest." See above, ch. vii. 16, and xiv. 2.

from Jordan by Jericho] We have first the southern boundary, which coincided for part of its length with the northern boundary of Benjamin. It began at the Jordan, at the port, or reach, exactly opposite to Jericho. Compare for the expression, above ch. xiii. 32, and below xx. 8.

unto the water of Jericho] From this point it ran to "the water of Jericho," i.e. to the one brook, which is found in the neighbourhood of Jericho. It rises at the fountain *Ain es Sultân*, the waters of which were healed by Elisha (2 Kings ii. 19), and flows into the Jordan.

to the wilderness that goeth up] i.e. by one of the ravines, the *Wâdy Harith* or *Wâdy Suweinît*, to the wilderness or uncultivated waste hills (*Midbah*), to the mountains in the vicinity of Bethel.

2. *and goeth out*] Thence it passed on to Luz. It seems impossible to determine exactly whether Bethel and Luz were the same town, *Luz* being the Canaanite and *Bethel* the Hebrew name, or whether they were distinct places close to one another.

(*a*) This verse, xviii. 13, and Gen. xxviii. 19, seem to favour the last interpretation.

(*b*) Gen. xxxv. 6, Judg. i. 23, favour the former.

The conclusion of Mr Grove is "that the two places were distinct during the times preceding the conquest, Luz being the city, and Bethel the pillar and altar of Jacob; but after the destruction of Luz by the tribe of Ephraim the town of Bethel arose." See his Article in Smith's *Bibl. Dict.*

unto the borders of Archi] Comp. 2 Sam. xvi. 16, 1 Chron. xxvii. 33, where we read of Hushai *the Archite*. The precise locality is unknown.

to Ataroth] See below v. 5, and comp. xviii. 13.

3. *and goeth down westward*] Hence the boundary passed unto the "coast" of Beth-horon the nether, i.e. the "Lower Beth-horon," and Gezer, to the Mediterranean Sea at Jaffa.

to the coast of Japhleti, unto the coast of Beth-horon the nether, and to Gezer: and the goings out thereof are at the 4 sea. So the children of Joseph, Manasseh and Ephraim, took their inheritance.

5—10. *The Inheritance of the Tribe of Ephraim.*

5 And the border of the children of Ephraim according to their families was *thus*: even the border of their inheritance on the east side was Ataroth-addar, unto Beth-horon the 6 upper; and the border went out toward the sea *to* Michmethah on the north side; and the border went about eastward *unto* Taanath-shiloh, and passed by it on the east 7 *to* Janohah; and it went down from Janohah to Ataroth,

Japhleti] is unknown.
Beth-horon] See above, ch. x. 10, 11.
Gezer] See above ch. x. 33. It probably lay between Beth-horon and Lydda. "The territory assigned to 'the house of Joseph' may be roughly estimated at 55 miles from east to west, by 70 from north to south, a portion about equal in extent to the counties of Norfolk and Suffolk combined."

5—10. THE INHERITANCE OF THE TRIBE OF EPHRAIM.

5. *And the border*] The border given is not traced out with the same completeness as that given above of the tribe of Judah. No mention, it will be observed, is made of the northern boundary line of the tribes descended from Joseph, although the eastern and western boundaries are implied, viz. the Jordan and the Mediterranean.

on the east side] It is to be borne in mind that the border traced above in verses 1—3 is here presupposed. The boundary is not drawn *de novo*, but is based upon the other.

Ataroth-addar] Comp. ch. xviii. 13. It is a little remarkable that the "Upper Beth-horon" is mentioned in this verse instead of Lower Beth-horon, as in *v*. 3. But both places were situated close to each other.

6. *and the border went out*] The line appears to run north towards the Beth-horons, where it meets the southern boundary common to both tribes. Then it went north-westward (or toward the sea) to Michmethah, which lay "facing Shechem" (Josh. xvii. 7), but which has not been discovered by any travellers.

Taanath-shiloh] identified by some with *Ain Tâna*, which lay between Shechem and the Jordan.

Janohah] Doubtless identical with the modern *Yanûn*, about 10 miles south-east of Shechem, where extensive ruins of great antiquity exist.

7. *went down*] The border "*went down*," because it descended along the slopes in the direction of the Jordan valley.

and to Naarath, and came to Jericho, and went out *at* Jordan. The border went *out* from Tappuah westward *unto* the 8 river Kanah; and the goings out thereof were at the sea. This *is* the inheritance of the tribe of the children of Ephraim by their families. And the separate cities for the 9 children of Ephraim *were* among the inheritance of the children of Manasseh, all the cities with their villages. And 10 they drave not out the Canaanites that dwelt in Gezer: but the Canaanites dwell among the Ephraimites unto this day, and serve under tribute.

1—6. *The Inheritance of Western Manasseh.*

There was also a lot for the tribe of Manasseh; for he 17

to Ataroth] which place, it is thought, is to be sought somewhere in this valley, "at the point where the border makes an angle in turning southward."

and to Naarath] Eusebius and Jerome mention it as well known to them. It is mentioned in 1 Chron. vii. 28, and was, it is thought, about five miles north of Jericho.

came to Jericho] i.e. to the region in the neighbourhood of Jericho (which belonged to Benjamin), where the eastern border formed an angle with the southern.

8. *The border*] In this verse the western half of the northern border is described.

from Tappuah] It ran from Tappuah, which has not yet been met with at all in the central district of Palestine, south of Shechem, "westward unto the river Kanah," or rather "the brook of reeds." This is probably the modern *Nahr el Khassab*, which reaches the Sea between Joppa and Cæsarea, under the name of *Nahr Falaik*, or as some think, the *Nahr el Aujeh*, just below the last-mentioned city.

9. *And the separate cities*] Or, the *places which were portioned off*.

were] This verb, introduced into our Version, should be omitted, and the full stop at the end of verse 8 should be replaced by a colon. The author intended us to add to "the inheritance of the children of Ephraim" the "separate" or "single" cities allotted to the tribe within the borders of Manasseh. It is supposed that after their relative boundaries had been fixed—though the subdivision of the territory assigned to the two brother tribes does not seem to have been very definite—it was found that the territory of Ephraim was too small in proportion to its strength.

10. *that dwelt in Gezer*] Comp. above, x. 33 and xii. 12.

CH. XVII. 1—6. THE INHERITANCE OF WESTERN MANASSEH.

1. *There was also a lot for the tribe of Manasseh*] Although the tribe of Manasseh had already, as we have seen, obtained an extensive in-

JOSHUA 10

was the firstborn of Joseph; *to wit*, for Machir the firstborn of Manasseh, the father of Gilead: because he was a man 2 of war, therefore he had Gilead and Bashan. There was also *a lot* for the rest of the children of Manasseh by their families; for the children of Abiezer, and for the children of

heritance east of the Jordan, where a portion of the warlike descendants of Machir had left their families, the rest of the tribe now claimed a further grant of land in addition to what they had acquired by force of arms.

for he was the firstborn of Joseph] Comp. Gen. xli. 51, "And Joseph called the name of the *firstborn Manasseh* (*a forgetter*); for God, said he, hath made me *forget* all my toil, and all my father's house." And again, xlviii. 14, "And Israel stretched out his...left hand, and laid it upon Manasseh's head, guiding his hands wittingly; for Manasseh was *the firstborn*." The birth of this child in Egypt, before the commencement of the famine, was the first alleviation of Joseph's sorrows since he left his home and his father, who loved him with such passionate affection.

for Machir] The eldest son of the patriarch Manasseh. His mother was an Aramæan or Syrian concubine (1 Chron. vii. 14, 15). Her name is not preserved, but her children are commemorated as having been caressed by Joseph before his death; "the children also of *Machir*, the son of Manasseh, were brought up (*borne*, marg.) upon Joseph's knees (Gen. l. 23).

the father of Gilead] The word "Gilead" here in the original has the article. This denotes not a person, but the province, or district of Gilead, and the word rendered father="lord," or "possessor." The expression "father of Gilead" therefore="lord" or "possessor of Gilead."

therefore he had Gilead and Bashan] Machir is here used for his family, for it was not he himself, but his descendants Jair and Nobah, who conquered the territory east of the Jordan. Jair captured the whole of the tract of Argob (Deut. iii. 14), and in addition took possession of some nomad villages in Gilead, which he called after his own name, *Havoth-Jair* (Num. xxxii. 41; 1 Chron. ii. 23). Nobah possessed himself of the town of Kenath and the hamlets dependent upon it, and gave them his own name (Num. xxxii. 42). For the territory of the half tribe of Manasseh east of the Jordan, see above, ch. xiii. 29—32. The district called "Gilead" is also sometimes called "Mount Gilead" (Gen. xxxi. 25); sometimes "the land of Gilead" (Num. xxxii. 1); and sometimes simply "Gilead" (as here, and Gen. xxxvii. 25; Ps. lx. 7). The name signifies the physical aspect of the country=a "hard rocky region." It extended from the parallel of the south end of the Sea of Galilee to that of the north end of the Dead Sea, about 60 miles, and its average breadth scarcely exceeded 20. See Smith's *Bibl. Dict.*

2. *for the rest of the children of Manasseh*] The descendants of Machir received their inheritance on the east of the Jordan, the descendants of Gilead on the west side, along with Ephraim. These—*the rest of the children of Manasseh*—were divided into six families.

Helek, and for the children of Asriel, and for the children of Shechem, and for the children of Hepher, and for the children of Shemida: these *were* the male children of Manasseh the son of Joseph by their families. But Zelophehad, 3 the son of Hepher, the son of Gilead, the son of Machir, the son of Manasseh, had no sons, but daughters: and these *are* the names of his daughters, Mahlah, and Noah, Hoglah, Milcah, and Tirzah. And they came near before Eleazar 4 the priest, and before Joshua the son of Nun, and before the princes, saying, The LORD commanded Moses to give us an inheritance among our brethren. Therefore according to the commandment of the LORD he gave them an inheritance among the brethren of their father. And there fell ten por- 5 tions to Manasseh, beside the land of Gilead and Bashan, which *were* on the *other* side Jordan; because the daughters 6 of Manasseh had an inheritance among his sons: and the rest of Manasseh's sons had the land of Gilead.

3. *But Zelophehad*] He seems to have been the second son of his father, Hepher. He had been born during the bondage in Egypt, and came out thence with Moses, but died in the wilderness, as did the whole of that generation (Num. xiv. 35, xxvii. 3). He died without male heirs.

4. *And they came*] In place of sons, Zelophehad had five daughters, and they, anxious that their father's name should not perish, present themselves before Eleazar and Joshua, with a request for an inheritance.

The Lord commanded Moses] They remind the high-priest, Joshua, and the princes, of the command of Moses in the wilderness in their favour. They had then reminded the great lawgiver (Num. xxvii. 1—4) that their father had no share in the sin of those who rose up against the Lord "in the company of Korah," but died "in his own sin." It was an injustice, therefore, that, because he had no son, "his name should be done away from among his family." Moses brought their cause before the Lord (Num. xxvii. 5), and by the Divine command granted them an inheritance amongst their brothers.

5. *And there fell*] The inheritance they claimed was now allotted them.

ten portions] The land allotted to the Manassites had to be divided into ten portions. The male descendants consisted of five families, and these five received five shares. The sixth family, that of Hepher, was again subdivided into five families, viz., those of his five granddaughters, the daughters of Zelophehad. They married husbands from the other families of their tribe (Num. xxxvi. 1—12), and each now received her special share of the land. See Keil's *Commentary*.

6. *the rest of Manasseh's sons*] i.e. the descendants of Machir.

7—13. *Boundaries of Western Manasseh.*

7 And the coast of Manasseh was from Asher *to* Michmethah, that *lieth* before Shechem; and the border went *along* on the right hand unto the inhabitants of En-tappuah. 8 *Now* Manasseh had the land of Tappuah : but Tappuah on the border of Manasseh *belonged* to the children of Ephraim; 9 and the coast descended *unto* the river Kanah, southward of the river: these cities of Ephraim *are* among the cities of Manasseh : the coast of Manasseh also *was* on the north side of the river, and the outgoings of it were at the sea: 10 southward *it was* Ephraim's, and northward *it was* Manasseh's, and the sea is his border; and they met together in 11 Asher on the north, and in Issachar on the east. And Manasseh had in Issachar and in Asher Beth-shean and her

7—13. BOUNDARIES OF WESTERN MANASSEH.

7. *And the coast*] We now have a description of the boundaries of Manasseh. And first (*a*), *vv.* 7—10, of the *southern* boundary towards Ephraim; and (*b*), second, *vv.* 10, 11, of the *northern* and *eastern* boundaries.

was from Asher] The description of the southern boundary commences at the eastern end. The *Asher* here spoken of is not the tribe of Asher, but a city on the east of Shechem. Eusebius places it on the road from Shechem to Bethshean. "Three quarters of an hour from *Tûbâs* is the hamlet of *Teyâsîr*, which may probably be identified with Asher, a town of Manasseh." Porter's *Handbook*, II. 348.

to Michmethah] See ch. xvi. 6. It is described as facing Shechem (*Nablûs*).

the border went along] The boundary now turned towards the right in a northerly direction, to the inhabitants of En-tappuah.

8. *the land of Tappuah*] The "land" of Tappuah fell to the lot of Manasseh, the "city" to Ephraim.

9. *unto the river Kanah*] From Tappuah the border descended to the river of Kanah, or "the Brook of Reeds" (see above, xvi. 8), southward of the watercourse.

these cities of Ephraim] See above, xvi. 9.

10. *southward*] Southward of the brook the land belonged to Ephraim, northward of the same it belonged to Manasseh, and the sea constituted the western border.

they met] or "struck upon" Asher in the north and on Issachar in the east. Thus the two tribes were bounded (*a*) on the *east* by Issachar; (*b*) on the *north* by Asher; (*c*) on the *west* by the sea; (*d*) and on the *south* by Benjamin and Dan.

11. *And Manasseh had*] Six cities are now enumerated, which

towns, and Ibleam and her towns, and the inhabitants of Dor and her towns, and the inhabitants of Endor and her towns, and the inhabitants of Taanach and her towns, and

Manasseh received beyond the borders of his own country in Issachar and Asher, but from which he failed to expel the Canaanites.

Beth-shean] or *Beth-shan* (1 Sam. xxxi. 10) lies in the *ghôr*, or Jordan valley, about 12 miles south of the Sea of Galilee, and four miles west of the Jordan. See a picture of it in Thomson's *Land and the Book*, p. 454. "It is naturally," he says, "one of the strongest places even in this country of strongholds......The ancient city consisted of several distinct quarters, or wards, separated by deep ravines, with noisy cascades leaping over ledges of black basalt......The tell is very strong, and it rises about 200 feet high, with the sides nearly perpendicular. A strong wall was carried round the summit......and on this wall the bodies of Saul and his sons were fastened by the Philistines after the battle of Gilboa, and this supposition enables us to understand how the men of Jabesh-Gilead could execute their daring project of carrying them away. Jabesh-Gilead was on the mountain east of the Jordan, in full view of Beth-shean, and these brave men could creep up to the tell, along *Wady Jalûd*, without being seen, while the deafening roar of the brook would render it impossible for them to be heard." In Solomon's time it appears to have given its name to a district, and "all Beth-shan" was placed under one of his commissariat officers. It is mentioned in the Book of Maccabees (1 Macc. v. 52, xii. 40, 41). In later times it was called *Scythopolis*, in consequence of its capture by the Scythians, who after their occupation of Media passed through Palestine on their way to Egypt (Herod. I. 104—106), about B.C. 600. It afterwards became the seat of a Christian bishop, and the name of Scythopolis is found as late as the Council of Constantinople, A.D. 536. It has now regained its ancient name, and is known as *Beisan* only.

and her towns = and her "daughter towns."

and Ibleam] Afterwards a Levitical city (Josh. xxi. 25). Here Ahaziah was mortally wounded by Jehu "at the going up to Gur, which is by Ibleam" (2 Kings ix. 27).

Dor] See above, xi. 2, xii. 23.

Endor] is described by Eusebius as a large village four miles south of Tabor, at the N.E. corner of *Jebel ed Dûhy*, facing Tabor, and overlooking the valley between them. The declivity of the mountain is everywhere perforated with caves, and most of the habitations are merely walls built round the entrances to them. It was one of these caves, which "the witch of Endor" inhabited, whither came King Saul, crossing in his agony of despair the shoulder of the very hill, on which the Philistines were entrenched, to consult her before the disastrous battle of Gilboa (1 Sam. xxviii. 7). It was long held in memory by the Jews in connection with the famous victory over Sisera and Jabin (Ps. lxxxiii. 10). See Thomson's *Land and the Book*, p. 446. Van de Velde, II. 383.

Taanach] See above, xii. 21.

the inhabitants of Megiddo and her towns, *even* three
12 countries. Yet the children of Manasseh could not drive
out *the inhabitants of* those cities; but the Canaanites would
13 dwell in that land. Yet it came to pass, when the children
of Israel were waxen strong, that they put the Canaanites to
tribute; but did not utterly drive them out.

14—18. *Complaint of the Children of Joseph.*

14 And the children of Joseph spake unto Joshua, saying,
Why hast thou given me *but* one lot and one portion to

Megiddo] See above, xii. 21. "Whenever the Israelites in aggressive movements could choose their arena, they selected their own element, the mountains and the mountain-passes. The battles of Esdraelon, on the other hand, were almost all forced upon them by adverse or invading armies: and though some of their chief victories were won here, yet this plain is associated in the mind of an Israelite with mournful at least as much as with joyful recollections; two kings perished on its soil; and the two saddest dirges of the Jewish nation were evoked by the defeats of Gilboa and Megiddo."—Stanley's *S. and P.*, p. 338.

even three countries] Rather, **the three heights**, or the **triple hill.** The LXX. and Vulgate translate the word as a proper name. The term brings the three cities lying on hills, Endor, Taanach, and Megiddo, into close connection with each other.

12. *Yet the children of Manasseh*] Comp. Judg. i. 27, 28.

13. *put the Canaanites to tribute*] Comp. above, xvi. 10. They made them *tributary servants*, but could not drive them out.

14—18. COMPLAINT OF THE CHILDREN OF JOSEPH.

14. *And the children of Joseph*] The descendants of Joseph, i.e. the patriarchs of the tribes of Ephraim and Manasseh, were not satisfied with the portion which Joshua had assigned them. The preponderating tribe from the earliest times, and since the Egyptian period the dominant one, they did not deem it sufficient that they had been divided into two, and so obtained a double voice in the national assembly, they claimed more than "one lot and one portion to inherit."

seeing I am a great people] At the census in the wilderness of Sinai (Num. i. 32, 33, ii. 19) the numbers of Ephraim were 40,500, which placed it at the head of the children of Rachel. The number of Manasseh was 32,200. But forty years later, on the eve of the conquest, while Ephraim had decreased to 32,500, Manasseh had advanced to 52,700. How much they subsequently increased, we can form some estimate by comparing the number of warriors they sent to the coronation of David at Hebron.

inherit, seeing I *am* a great people, forasmuch as the LORD hath blessed me hitherto? And Joshua answered them, If 15 thou *be* a great people, *then* get thee up to the wood *country*, and cut down for thyself there in the land of the Perizzites

forasmuch as the Lord hath blessed me hitherto] Comp. the words of the dying Jacob, "And he blessed them that day, saying, In thee shall Israel bless, saying, *God make thee as Ephraim and as Manasseh*; and he set Ephraim before Manasseh" (Gen. xlviii. 20); and again (Gen. xlix. 25, 26; with which comp. Deut. xxxiii. 13—17),

"The Almighty, who shall *bless* thee
With *blessings* of heaven above,
Blessings of the deep that lieth under,
Blessings of the breasts, and of the womb;
The *blessings* of thy father have prevailed above the *blessings*
   of my progenitors
Unto the utmost bound of the everlasting hills:
They shall be on the head of Joseph,
And on the crown of the head of him that was separate from his
   brethren."

15. *And Joshua answered them*] They expected of their fellow-tribesman a better guardianship of their interests.

If thou be a great people] There is a kind of delicate irony in Joshua's reply. "Yes, it is true that thou art a numerous people, and hast great strength, and oughtest to have more than one share. But if thou wouldest have it, procure it for thyself! Rely on thine own power and resources!"

get thee up to the wood country] i.e. the forest of the "mountain of Ephraim." This was a district, which extended as far south as Ramah and Bethel (1 Sam. i. 1, vii. 17; 2 Chron. xiii. 19). It is an elevated district of limestone, consisting of rounded hills separated by valleys of denudation, but much less regular and monotonous than that part more to the south, about and below Jerusalem; with wide plains in the heart of the mountains, streams of running water, and continuous tracts of vegetation. That the "mount" was then covered with woods is clear from 1 Sam. xiv. 25; 2 Sam. xviii. 6, and even now travellers have found wooded heights, and forests of oak trees, between Carmel and the mountains of Samaria. To these mountain heights even the members of other tribes resorted for shelter and for power. "Ehud the Benjamite, when he armed his countrymen against Moab, 'blew his trumpet *in the mountain of Ephraim*' (Judg. iii. 27, 28); Deborah, though, as it would seem, herself of the northern tribes, 'dwelt between Ramah and Bethel in *Mount Ephraim*' (Judg. iv. 5). Tola, of Issachar, judged Israel in Shamir, in Mount Ephraim (Judg. x. 1). Samuel, too, was of Ramathaim-zophim of *Mount Ephraim*." Stanley, *S. and P.*, p. 231. The name, "Mount Ephraim," is applied here, in anticipation, to the mountain which afterward received it as a standing name, from the tribe of Ephraim, to which it was first assigned.

cut down for thyself] "Cut down for thyself there," says the great

152   JOSHUA, XVII.   [vv. 16, 17.

and of the giants, if mount Ephraim be too narrow for thee.
16 And the children of Joseph said, The hill is not enough for
us: and all the Canaanites that dwell in the land of the
valley have chariots of iron, *both they* who *are* of Beth-shean
and her towns, and *they* who *are* of the valley of Jezreel.
17 And Joshua spake unto the house of Joseph, *even* to Ephraim

Captain, "in the land of the Perizzites (see above, iii. 10) and of the giants" or Rephaim (see above, ch. xii. 4), "if Mount Ephraim is too narrow."

16. *have chariots of iron*] The iron chariots of the Canaanites were objects of terror to the Israelites, see above, ch. xi. 6—9. They were the main reason why the Israelites could not establish themselves in the plain, on which Beth-shean, Taanach, and Megiddo were situated. The forest they could occupy, but the plain, where the "chariot-cavalry" of their foes were so effective though powerless in the mountains, they could not reduce. Comp. Judg. i. 19, iv. 3; 1 Sam. xiii. 5. Compare as to the insecurity of the plains the remarks of Tristram: "No matter how wide, how rich, how well cultivated a plain may be, like Acre or Esdraelon, its tame monotony is never relieved by a single village. These are all hidden in the nooks of the mountains; for no fellâhin or cultivators would venture to dwell where any night they might be harried by a party of Bedouin troopers, and to this risk they gladly prefer an hour or two's weary climb added to their daily toil: while no traveller would dream of encamping even for a night in the open plain." *Land of Israel*, p. 421.

the valley] As the "hill" here denotes Mount Ephraim, so the valley country includes both (*a*) the valley or *ghôr* of the Jordan near Bethshean, and (*b*) the wide plain of Jezreel, between Gilboa and little Hermon, to which, in its widest extent, the name of Esdraelon has been applied in modern times; a name first used in Judith i. 8. "It was only this plain of Jezreel, and that north of Lake *Huleh*, that was then accessible to the chariots of the Canaanites. It was in this plain of Jezreel that Joram king of Israel and Ahaziah king of Judah went forth *in chariots* to meet the enemy (2 Kings ix. 21). It was here that Jehu passed in *a chariot* to Samaria, to meet the faithful Jehonadab (2 Kings x. 15). And Wilson (*Lands of the Bible*, II. 303), in leaving the hilly district of Judæa, wholly unfitted for vehicles, and entering the plain of Esdraelon at *Jenin*, was surprised to see how entirely it differed from the country which he had previously traversed, and how easily it might be crossed by excellent highways, if the custom of the country admitted of the use of vehicles. In the days of the Jews, the plain was so associated with the use of the chariot, that this term became to a certain extent an exponent of the power of the people inhabiting the plain. The *chariot* was the glory of Ephraim, as the horse was of Judah (Zech. ix. 9, 10). Carl Ritter's *Geography of Palestine*, II. 327, 328.

17. *And Joshua spake*] The reply of the descendants of Joseph betrayed a spirit of discontent mingled with cowardice and unbelief.

and to Manasseh, saying, Thou *art* a great people, and hast great power: thou shalt not have one lot *only:* but the mountain shall be thine; for it *is* a wood, and thou shalt cut it down: and the outgoings of it shall be thine: for thou shalt drive out the Canaanites, though they have iron chariots, *and* though they *be* strong. 13

1—10. *Erection of the Tabernacle at Shiloh.*

And the whole congregation of the children of Israel 18

Joshua therefore contents himself, "with no less wisdom than patriotism," by telling them that what more they won must be by their own exertions.

18. *the mountain*] i.e. "the mountain of Ephraim," shall be thine, for it is a forest. It should fall to their lot because the house of Joseph was strong and able, and could clear the woodland.

the outgoings of it] i.e. the fields and plains bordering upon the wood.

though they have] Though they have war chariots, and are so formidable, yet wilt thou who art a great people and hast great power, drive them out. None of the tribes of Israel can compete with thee in strength! Use it then, and thou wilt gain not only the mountain, but the "outgoings" beyond, and as at the waters of Merom (Josh. xi. 7), the iron chariots and the military strength of thy foes will avail them nothing. "The long range of mountains running from Carmel south-eastward across central Palestine appeared like a frowning rampart defended by Canaanite foes." But this was the very reason why the great house of Joseph should prove themselves worthy of their great power by scaling that rampart. It is plain from this passage that "at the time of the Israelitish invasion the mountains of Gilboa and the country adjacent were covered with dense forests, of which not a trace now remains, and which made them a more secure asylum for those who sought protection, than open fields could be. And it seems to have been a shrewd device of the great Hebrew chieftain, the counselling the descendants of Joseph to go up into the mountain land; for it would lead to the laying bare of the whole country, and would compel the adjacent inhabitants to come out from their places of refuge, and make open resistance to the invaders." Ritter, II. 328. Observe in the discontent now expressed by the "house of Joseph," the mutterings of the louder complaints we afterwards hear them making against Gideon (Judg. viii. 1—3), against Jephthah (Judg. xii. 1—7), and against David (2 Sam. xx. 1—5).

CH. XVIII. 1—10. ERECTION OF THE TABERNACLE AT SHILOH.

1. *And the whole congregation of the children of Israel*] The descendants of Judah and of Joseph had now taken up their re-

assembled together *at* Shiloh, and set up the tabernacle of the congregation there. And the land was subdued before

spective inheritances, the one in the south, the other in the north of the country. But "the murmuring," it has been remarked, "of the children of Joseph, and the spirit from which it proceeded, gave sad indications of danger in the near future. National disintegration, tribal jealousies, coupled with boastfulness and unwillingness to execute the work given them of God, were only too surely foreboded in the conduct of the children of Joseph. If such troubles were to be averted, it was high time to seek a revival of religion." Dr Edersheim's *Israel in Canaan under Joshua and the Judges*, p. 94. The camp at Gilgal, therefore, was broken up, and the people removed to Shiloh, which was situated within the territory of Ephraim, Joshua's own tribe.

The whole congregation of the children of Israel. This formula often recurs. Thus in Exod. xvi. 1 we read, "And they took their journey from Elim, and all *the congregation of the children of Israel* came unto the wilderness of Sin ;" and again, Exod. xvi. 9, "And Moses spake unto Aaron, Say unto all *the congregation of the children of Israel*." Sometimes it is more brief, "*the congregation of Israel*," as in Exod. xii. 3, "Speak ye unto all *the congregation of Israel*." Sometimes more briefly still, "*the congregation*," as in Lev. iv. 15, "And the elders of *the congregation* shall lay their hands upon the head of the bullock before the Lord." The Greek word here used is the same as that used by our Lord, Matt. xvi. 18, "Upon this rock I will build My *Church*." Originally it denoted an assembly of persons *called out* from among others by the voice of a herald, as, at Athens, for the purpose of legislation. It is applied to the Israelites, as being a nation *called out* by God from the rest of the world, to bear witness to His unity, to preserve His laws, to keep alive the hope of Redemption, and to exhibit the pattern of a people living in righteousness and true godliness. Hence, St Stephen says of Moses, that he was "in the *Church* (or *congregation*) in the wilderness with the angel which spake to him in the mount Sina" (Acts vii. 38); again, David says in Ps. xxii. 22, quoted in Hebrews ii. 12, "I will declare Thy name unto my brethren, in the midst of the *church* (or *congregation*) will I sing praise unto Thee;" and again he says in Ps. xxvi. 12, "My foot standeth in an even place: in *the congregations* will I bless the Lord."

assembled together at Shiloh] Few places in respect to situation are described so accurately as Shiloh. In Judg. xxi. 19 it is said to have been situated "on the north side of Bethel, on the east side of the highway that goeth up from Bethel to Shechem, and on the south of Lebonah." "In agreement with this, the traveller at the present day, going north from Jerusalem, lodges the first night at *Beitîn*, the ancient Bethel; the next day, at the distance of a few hours, turns aside to the right, in order to visit *Seilûn*, the Arabic for Shiloh; and then passing through the narrow Wady, which brings

them. And there remained among the children of Israel 2 seven tribes, which had not *yet* received their inheritance.

him to the main road, leaves *el-Lebbân*, the Lebonah of Scripture, on the left, as he pursues the 'highway' to *Nâblus*, the ancient Shechem." Smith's *Bibl. Dict.* It was one of the earliest and most sacred of the Hebrew sanctuaries. "Its selection," observes Dean Stanley, "may partly have arisen from its comparative seclusion, still more from its central situation. The most hallowed spot of that vicinity, Bethel, which might else have been more naturally chosen, was at this time still in the hands of the Canaanites (Judg. i. 23—27); and thus, left to choose the encampment of the Sacred Tent, not by old associations, but according to the dictates of convenience, the conquerors fixed on this retired spot in the heart of the country, where the allotment of the territory could be most conveniently made, north, south, east, and west, to the different tribes; and there the Ark remained down to the fatal day when its home was uprooted by the Philistines." *S. and P.* p. 232. "It was a central point for all Israel, equidistant from north and south, easily accessible to the trans-Jordanic tribes, and in the heart of that hill-country which Joshua first subdued, and which remained, to the end of Israel's history, the district least exposed to the attacks of Canaanitish or foreign invaders." Tristram's *Land of Israel*, p. 162. Here (*a*) "the daughters of Shiloh" were seized by the Benjamites (Judg. xxi. 19—23); here (*b*) Samuel spent his boyhood in the service of the Lord, and as an attendant upon the aged Eli (1 Sam. iii. 19—21); here (*c*) the wicked conduct of the sons of that pontiff occasioned the loss of the Ark of the Covenant, and Shiloh from that day forward sank into insignificance (1 Sam. ii. 17, iv. 12), for the Lord "forsook the tabernacle" there, "the tent that He had pitched among men; *He refused the tabernacle of Joseph, and chose not the tribe of Ephraim*" (Ps. lxxviii. 60, 67). "Shiloh is a mass of shapeless ruins, scarcely distinguishable from the rugged rocks around them...... No one relic could we trace which in any way pointed to earlier times among all the wasted stone-heaps which crowded the broken terraces. So utterly destroyed is the house of the ark of God, the home of Eli and of Samuel. 'Go ye now unto My place which was *in Shiloh*, where I set My Name at the first, and see what I did to it for the wickedness of My people Israel' (Jer. vii. 12)." Tristram's *Land of Israel*, p. 161.

the tabernacle of the congregation] i.e. **the tabernacle, or, tent of meeting.** The phrase has the meaning of *a place of or for a fixed meeting*. This thought comes out in Exod. xxv. 22, "there *I* will *meet with thee*, and I will commune with thee from above the mercy seat;" in Exod. xxx. 6, "before the mercy seat that is over the testimony, where *I will meet with thee*;" and especially in Exod. xxix. 42, 43, "This shall be a continual burnt offering throughout your generations at the door of the tabernacle of the congregation before the Lord; where *I will meet you*, to speak there unto thee: and there I will *meet* with the children of Israel, and the tabernacle shall be sanctified by My glory."

156 JOSHUA, XVIII. [vv. 3, 4.

3 And Joshua said unto the children of Israel, How long *are*
you slack to go to possess the land, which the LORD God of
4 your fathers hath given you? Give out from among you
three men for *each* tribe: and I will send them, and they
shall rise, and go through the land, and describe it according
to the inheritance of them; and they shall come *again* to

"Not the gathering of the worshippers only, but the meeting of
God with His people, to commune with them, to make Himself
known to them, was what the name embodied." See Smith's *Bibl.
Dict.* After the catastrophe when the Ark fell into the hands of
the Philistines, the Tabernacle was removed (i) to Nob (1 Sam. xxi.
1), and (ii) when that place was destroyed by Saul (1 Sam. xxii. 19),
to Gibeon (1 Kings iii. 4).

was subdued before them] The word rendered "subdued" denotes
to "*tread* under the feet." Comp. Gen. i. 28, "Be fruitful and
multiply, and replenish the earth, and *subdue it*;" and Jer. xxxiv. 16,
"But ye turned and polluted My name, and caused every man his
servant......to return, and *brought them into subjection*, to be unto
you for servants and for handmaids." The verse seems to imply that
immediately after the conquest of the land, it was the intention of
the Israelites to set up the sacred Tent, but that this purpose could
not be carried into effect until the tribe, in the midst of which the
Lord had intended it to stand, had received its inheritance. See
Keil's *Commentary*.

3. *And Joshua said*] No particulars are given of the solemn and
impressive ceremonies which doubtless marked the setting up of the
time-honoured monument of the wanderings, and the resumption of
the regular sacrifices and other ceremonies, which must have been
imperfectly observed during the years of warfare now ended. The
history passes on to the distribution of the yet unoccupied territory.

How long are you slack] These seven tribes appear to have been
backward and indolent not only in conquering the land still unsubdued,
but even in sharing it out amongst them.

4. *Give out from among you*] If the territory was to be distributed,
it was necessary that the more distant portions of the country should
be surveyed. Joshua therefore directs the tribes to appoint a commission of twenty-one members, three from each tribe, who should
undertake the duty and report to him at Shiloh. Their duty apparently was not so much to carry out an actual measurement of
the country, as the preparation of a list of the cities (see *v.* 9), and
the procuring information respecting the peculiar characteristics of different districts, such as, "what lands were barren and what fertile,
whether a district was hilly or flat, whether well-watered or destitute
of springs, and anything else which served to shew the goodness
of the soil, and the comparative worth of different localities." Rosenmüller.

vv. 5—10.]   JOSHUA, XVIII.   157

me. And they shall divide it into seven parts: Judah shall 5
abide in their coast on the south, and the house of Joseph
shall abide in their coasts on the north. Ye shall therefore 6
describe the land *into* seven parts, and bring *the description*
hither to me, that I may cast lots for you here before the
LORD our God. But the Levites have no part among you; 7
for the priesthood of the LORD *is* their inheritance: and
Gad, and Reuben, and half the tribe of Manasseh, have received their inheritance beyond Jordan on the east, which
Moses the servant of the LORD gave them. And the men 8
arose, and went away: and Joshua charged them that went
to describe the land, saying, Go and walk through the land,
and describe it, and come again to me, that I may here cast
lots for you before the LORD in Shiloh. And the men went 9
and passed through the land, and described it by cities into
seven parts in a book, and came *again* to Joshua to the host
at Shiloh. And Joshua cast lots for them in Shiloh before 10

5. *Judah shall abide*] The division, which had secured by lot their territory to the tribes of Judah and Joseph, was still to be respected.

6. *before the Lord our God*] i.e. before the "Tabernacle of Meeting," where Jehovah manifested His presence to the people, enthroned above the Cherubim of the Ark of the Covenant.

7. *But the Levites*] See above, ch. xiii. 33; Num. xviii. 20.

the priesthood of the Lord] Notice the change here as compared with ch. xiii. 14. There "the sacrifices of Jehovah" are said to be the portion of Levi, and in xiii. 33, "Jehovah, God of Israel" is said to be their portion. Here we have "the priesthood of Jehovah," as in Num. iii. 10, xvi. 10, xviii. 1—7.

9. *and passed through the land*] How long they were absent we are not told. Josephus tells us it was seven months, *Ant.* V. I. 21. The Rabbis tell us it was seven years. Both suppositions are equally devoid of foundation.

and described it] Although the survey was connected chiefly with a general estimate of the resources and characteristics of the several districts, yet it is to be remembered that the Israelites had acquired a knowledge of the art of mensuration in Egypt, where, on account of the annual overflowing of the Nile, it had been practised from the earliest times.

by cities into seven parts] i.e. they surveyed it so as to divide the cities and then the land itself into seven parts.

10. *And Joshua cast lots*] After their return the Hebrew leader proceeded to a formal apportionment of the land by the sacred lot. This mode of assignment, it has been remarked, "places the conquest of Palestine, even in that remote and barbarous age, in a favourable

the LORD: and there Joshua divided the land unto the children of Israel according to their divisions.

11—20. *Boundaries of the Tribe of Benjamin.*

11 And the lot of the tribe of the children of Benjamin came up according to their families: and the coast of their lot came forth between the children of Judah and the children 12 of Joseph. And their border on the north side was from Jordan; and the border went up to the side of Jericho on the north side, and went up through the mountains westward; and the goings out thereof were at the wilderness of 13 Beth-aven. And the border went over from thence toward Luz, to the side of Luz, which *is* Beth-el, southward; and the border descended *to* Ataroth-adar, near the hill that *lieth*

contrast with the arbitrary caprice, by which the lands of England were granted away to the Norman chiefs." Stanley's *Lectures*, I. p. 265.

in Shiloh] Shiloh was appropriate, we have already seen, from its central situation, for the site of the Tabernacle and this apportionment of the tribes. But it has been noticed that it was appropriate also from its name, "which recalled *rest* (Shiloh=*rest*), and the promised *Rest-giver*" (Gen. xlix. 10).

11—20. BOUNDARIES OF THE TRIBE OF BENJAMIN.

11. *between the children of Judah and the children of Joseph*] When the lots were now cast "before the Lord," the lot of Benjamin came forth first, and we have an account of (*a*) the boundaries, and then (*b*) of the cities of this tribe, which, we are here told, lay between the sons of Judah on the south and the sons of Joseph on the north.

12. *And their border on the north side*] The northern boundary of Benjamin mainly coincided with the southern boundary.of Ephraim.

from Jordan] Commencing from the Jordan on the east, their boundary ascended to the mountains west and north-west of Jericho as far as "the wilderness of Beth-aven," i.e. the bare and rocky heights to the east and north of Michmash. The situation of Beth-aven has been already described, above, ch. vii. 2.

13. *toward Luz*] See above, ch. xvi. 2. The border next went to the south of the ridge of Bethel, and thence descended, in a north-westerly direction, toward Ataroth-adar.

descended] We understand the appropriateness of this word when we remember that Bethel lay 3000 feet above the level of the Mediterranean Sea.

Ataroth-adar] See above, ch. xvi. 5.

near the hill] Or, **over the mountain that lieth on the south side of the nether Beth-horon.** Thus the north border of Benjamin, as far as lower Beth-horon, coincides with the southern border of Ephraim.

on the south side of the nether Beth-horon. And the border 14 was drawn *thence*, and compassed the corner of the sea southward, from the hill that *lieth* before Beth-horon southward; and the goings out thereof were at Kirjath-baal, which *is* Kirjath-jearim, a city of the children of Judah: this *was* the west quarter. And the south quarter *was* from the end 15 of Kirjath-jearim, and the border went out on the west, and went out to the well of waters of Nephtoah: and the border 16 came down to the end of the mountain that *lieth* before the valley of the son of Hinnom, *and* which *is* in the valley of the giants on the north, and descended *to* the valley of Hinnom, to the side of Jebusi on the south, and descended *to* En-rogel, and was drawn from the north, and went forth *to* 17 En-shemesh, and went forth toward Geliloth, which *is* over against the going up of Adummim, and descended *to* the stone of Bohan the son of Reuben, and passed along toward 18 the side over against Arabah northward, and went down unto Arabah: and the border passed along to the side of 19 Beth-hoglah northward: and the outgoings of the border were at the north bay of the salt sea at the south end of Jordan: this *was* the south coast. And Jordan was the 20 border of it on the east side. This *was* the inheritance of the children of Benjamin, by the coasts thereof round about, according to their families.

Beth-horon] See above (*a*) x. 11; (*b*) xvi. 3—5. An upper and a lower Beth-horon are still recognised. The upper is now called *Beit-'ûr El-Fôka*, the lower *Beit-'ûr El-Tahta*. The pass between the two places was called *the ascent* and *the descent* of Beth-horon. Comp. 1 Macc. iii. 15—24. "The ascent," remarks Robinson, "is very rocky and rough: but the rock has been cut away in many places and the path formed into steps, shewing that this is an ancient road." *Bibl. Res.* III. 58.

14. *And the border was drawn thence*] From the mountain south of Beth-horon the boundary line of Benjamin trended in a southerly direction towards "Kirjath-baal, which is Kirjath-jearim, a city of the children of Judah."

compassed] On "compass," see above, note on ch. xv. 3.

Kirjath-jearim] See above, note on ix. 17.

this was the west quarter] The word here rendered *quarter*, = (i) *a mouth*, then (ii) *a side*, which is turned to any quarter of the heavens. The Eastern boundary was formed by the Jordan, see *v.* 20.

15. *And the south quarter*] This coincides exactly with the northern border of Judah, for which see above, xv. 5—9.

21—28. *The Cities of Benjamin.*

21 Now the cities of the tribe of the children of Benjamin according to their families were Jericho, and Beth-hoglah, 22 and the valley of Keziz, and Beth-arabah, and Zemaraim, 23 and Beth-el, and Avim, and Parah, and Ophrah, and Che- 24 phar-haammonai, and Ophni, and Gaba; twelve cities with 25 26 their villages. Gibeon, and Ramah, and Beeroth, and Mizpeh, 27 and Chephirah, and Mozah, and Rekem, and Irpeel, and

21—28. THE CITIES OF BENJAMIN.

21. *Now the cities*] The cities here enumerated fall into two groups, (*a*) *the first* of *twelve* lying on the *east*, (*b*) *the second* of *fourteen* lying on the *west*.
1. *Jericho*] see note above, ii. 1. 2. *Beth-hoglah*, see note above, xv. 6. 3. *The valley of Keziz*, this is not exactly known.
22. 4. *Beth-arabah*] See note above, xv. 6. 5. *Zemaraim* is unknown. 6. *Bethel*, see verse 13.
23. 7. *Avim*] Some have regarded this as identical with Ai, which is also called Aija (Neh. xi. 31) and Aiath (Is. x. 28). 8. *Parah* is unknown. 9. *Ophrah* appears to be mentioned again in 1 Sam. xiii. 17 in describing the spoilers who issued from the Philistine camp at Michmash. Robinson would identify it with *El-Taiyibeh*, a small village 4 miles E.N.E. of *Beitin* (Bethel). This was not the Ophrah of Gideon (Judg. vi. 11, 15).
24. 10. *Chephar-haammonai*] is quite unknown, so also is 11. *Ophni;* 12. *Gaba*, or *Geba* = "height," "hill," not the *Geba* or *Gibeah* of Saul, is mentioned in 2 Kings xxiii. 8; Zech. xiv. 10.
25. *Gibeon*] We have now enumerated the second group of fourteen cities lying on the west of Benjamin. 1. *Gibeon*, see note above, ch. ix. 3; 2. *Ramah*, not the Ramah of Samuel or *Ramathaim*. In Isai. x. 28—32, the king of Assyria is described as crossing the ravine at Michmash, and successively dislodging or alarming *Geba*, Ramah, *and Gibeah of Saul*. This Ramah is the modern *er-Râm*, a wretched village on an elevation. It was the place where Jeremiah was set free (Jer. xxxi. 15, xl. 1). It was inhabited again after the exile (Ez. ii. 26; Neh. vii. 30). 3. *Beeroth, el-Bireh*, mentioned above, ix. 17, where see note. It belonged to or was in alliance with Gibeon. It was the home of (*a*) the murderers of Ishbosheth (2 Sam. iv. 2), and (*b*) of Joab's armourbearer (2 Sam. xxiii. 37).
26. 4. *Mizpeh*] Not the same as the Mizpeh of ch. xv. 38, but either (*a*) the modern *Neby Samwîl*, or (*b*) the tower of *Scopus*. Here (*a*) the war against Benjamin was resolved on (Judg. xx.); here (*b*) Samuel judged the people (1 Sam. vii. 5—15), and (*c*) chose Saul as king (1 Sam. x. 17). 5. *Chephirah*, see note above, ix. 17; 6. *Mozah* and
27. 7. *Rekem* unknown. 8. *Irpeel*, Lieut. Conder thinks that this may be recognised in the modern *Râfât*, N. of El Jib, being the same from which the name Rephaim is derived. 9. *Taralah* is unrecognised.

Taralah, and Zelah, Eleph, and Jebusi, which *is* Jerusalem, 28
Gibeath, *and* Kirjath; fourteen cities with their villages.
This *is* the inheritance of the children of Benjamin according to their families.

1—9. *The Territory of the Tribe of Simeon.*
And the second lot came forth to Simeon, *even* for the 19

28. 10. *Zelah*]=*Beit Jala*, S. of the plain of Rephaim, is afterwards mentioned as the burial-place of Saul and Jonathan (2 Sam. xxi. 14). 11. *Eleph* is unknown; 12. *Jebusi, which is Jerusalem*, see note above, xv. 8. 13. *Gibeath* is the *Gibeah of Saul*, now *Tuleil-el-Fûl*, about one hour and 25 minutes north of Jerusalem. Here (*a*) occurred the outrage recorded in Judg. xix.; here (*b*) was Jonathan with a thousand chosen warriors when he made his victorious onslaught on the garrison of the Philistines (1 Sam. xiii. 2, 3). 14. *Kirjath* is at present unrecognised.

This is the inheritance of the children of Benjamin] The situation of the territory of this tribe was highly favourable, forming almost a parallelogram, of about 26 miles in length by 12 in breadth. The smallness of the district, hardly larger than the county of Middlesex, was compensated for by the excellence of the land.

(*a*) The general level of this part of Palestine is very high, being 2000 feet above the level of the Mediterranean on the western side, and 3000 feet above the deep valley of the Jordan on the eastern side. This plateau is surmounted by a large number of eminences (Gibeon, Gibeah, Geba, all = "*hill;*" Ramah = "*eminence;*" Mizpeh = "*a watch-tower*"), which presented favourable sites for strong fortresses.

(*b*) No less important than these eminences are the torrent-beds and ravines by which the upper country looks down into the deep tracts on each side of it, forming then, as they do now, the only mode of access from either the plains of Philistia and of Sharon on the west, or the *Ghôr* of the Jordan on the east.

(*c*) In the broken and hilly country, "little Benjamin" (Ps. lxviii. 27), famous above the rest for skill in archery (2 Sam. i. 22), for its slingers (Judg. xx. 16) and left-handed warriors (Judg. iii. 15), became warlike and indomitable. "In his mountain passes—the ancient haunt of beasts of prey, he 'ravined as a wolf in the morning,' descended into the rich plains of Philistia on the one side, and of the Jordan on the other, and 'returned in the evening to divide the spoil' (Gen. xlix. 27). In the troubled period of the Judges, the tribe of Benjamin maintained a struggle, unaided and for some time with success, against the whole of the rest of the nation (Judg. xx., xxi.). And to the latest times they never could forget that they had given birth to the first king." Stanley's *Sinai and Palestine*, pp. 200, 201.

CH. XIX. 1—9. THE TERRITORY OF THE TRIBE OF SIMEON.

1. *And the second lot*] drawn at Shiloh, fell to the tribe of Simeon, which, during the journey through the wilderness, marched on the south side of the Sacred Tent, with Reuben and Gad for its associates.

tribe of the children of Simeon according to their families: and their inheritance was within the inheritance of the children of Judah. And they had in their inheritance Beersheba, or Sheba, and Moladah, and Hazar-shual, and Balah, and Azem, and Eltolad, and Bethul, and Hormah, and Ziklag, and Beth-marcaboth, and Hazar-susah, and Beth-lebaoth, and Sharuhen; thirteen cities and their villages: Ain,

for the tribe of the children of Simeon] Two groups of cities are here enumerated. (*a*) First a *group* of *thirteen* or *fourteen* cities *in the south*, (*b*) a *second group* of four cities, of which two were situated in the south, two in the *Shephêlah* or "Lowlands" of Judah on the west.

within the inheritance of the children of Judah] Judah discovered that the tract allotted to him was too large (see verse 9), and too much exposed to marauders on the west and south even for his great powers. To Simeon accordingly was allotted a district out of the territory of his kinsman, whose ancestor like his had been the child of Leah (Gen. xxxv. 23).

2. *And they had in their inheritance*] First Group. 1. *Beersheba*, see note ch. xv. 28; or *Shema*, so ch. xv. 26: comp. 1 Chron. iv. 28 with Gen. xxvi. 33; 2. *Moladah* = *el-Milh*, see ch. xv. 26, about four English miles from *Tel Arad*, eighteen from Hebron, and nine or ten due east of Beersheba;

3. 3. *Hazar-shual*] Between Beer-sheba and Hazar-gaddah; see 1 Chron. iv. 28; 4. *Balah*, see ch. xv. 29; in 1 Chron. iv. 29 it is called *Bilhah*; 5. *Azem*, elsewhere called *Ezem*, 1 Chron. iv. 29;

4. 6. *Eltolad*] See ch. xv. 30 and 1 Chron. iv. 29; 7. *Bethul*, which in the parallel lists, ch. xv. 30 and 1 Chron. iv. 30, appears under the forms of *Chesil* or *Bethuel*; 8. *Hormah*, or Zephath (Judg. i. 17), reduced by Joshua, was originally included in the territory of Judah, see above, ch. xv. 30;

5. 9. *Ziklag*] See ch. xv. 31, identified by Rowlands and Wilton (*Negeb*, p. 209) with *Asloodg* or *Kasloodg;* (*a*) Achish bestowed the town upon David; (*b*) here David resided upwards of one year and four months (1 Sam. xxvii. 7, xxx. 14, 26); (*c*) here he received the news of Saul's death (2 Sam. i. 1, iv. 10); 10. *Beth-marcaboth* = "*house of chariots*," and 11. *Hazar-susah* = "*village of horses*," appear to be the old names of Madmannah and Sansannah (see ch. xv. 31). These names indicate, remarks Dean Stanley, "that they were stations of passage, like those which now are to be seen on the great line of Indian transit between Cairo and Suez," we recognise in them "the dépôts and stations for the 'horses' and 'chariots,' such as those which in Solomon's time went to and fro between Egypt and Palestine." *Sinai and Palestine*, p. 160;

6. 12. *Beth-lebaoth*] contrasted with *Lebaoth* above, xv. 32, is called *Beth-birei* in 1 Chron. iv. 31; 13. *Sharuhen* = *Shilhim* in xv. 32 = *Shaaraim*, 1 Chron. iv. 31.

Remmon, and Ether, and Ashan; four cities and their villages: and all the villages that *were* round about these cities 8 to Baalath-beer, Ramath of the south. This *is* the inheritance of the tribe of the children of Simeon according to their families. Out of the portion of the children of Judah 9 *was* the inheritance of the children of Simeon: for the part

7. *Second Group.* 1. *Ain*=an "*eye*," and also in the vivid imagery of the East, a spring or natural burst of living water, always distinguished from the artificial "well" or "tank"=*Beer* or *Bor*. It generally occurs in combination with other words, defining the locality as *En-gedi, En-gannim, En-hakkore, En-rogel*. In two cases it stands alone, (*a*) here, and (*b*) in Num. xxxiv. 11. Mr Wilton (*Negeb*, pp. 229—234) would here also connect it with the next name; 2. *Remmon*, as the name of a single city, *Ain* or *En-Remmon* = *the spring of the pomegranate*, and in the catalogue of the places re-occupied by the Jews after the return from the Captivity the two are joined, and appear in our Version as *En-Rimmon*, see Neh. xi. 29; 3. *Ether*, see ch. xv. 42 Van de Velde heard of a Tel Athar in the desert country below Hebron; 4. *Ashan*, see above, ch. xv. 42.

8. *and all the villages that were round about*] i.e. Simeon, not merely certain cities in the territory of Judah, but the whole country round the cities named, together with all the villages that were situated near them.

to Baalath-beer] See above, ch. xv. 24 or 29, = *Baal* in 1 Chron. iv. 33.

Ramath of the south] Ramath, like Ramah and Ramoth, = a "height." This Ramath of *the Negeb*, or *the South*, is thought to be another name for *Baalath-beer*, and has been by some identified with the present ruins of *Kurnub*, situated on the slope of a low range of hills about 20 miles south-east of Beer-sheba.

9. *of the children of Simeon*] In this "*Negeb*" or "*land of the south*," Simeon now took up his abode. Like Reuben on the east of Jordan, the tribe was destined to have little influence on the subsequent history, to be *divided in Jacob and scattered in Israel* (Gen. xlix. 5—7). In the prophecy of Moses he is not even mentioned (Deut. xxxiii.), nor are we told what part he took at the time of the division of the kingdom. "As time rolled on, the tribe gradually crossed the imperceptible boundary between civilisation and barbarism, between Palestine and the Desert, and, in 'the days of Hezekiah' (1 Chron. iv. 28—43), they wandered forth to the east to seek pasture for their flocks, and 'smote the tents' of the pastoral tribes who had 'dwelt there of old;' and roved along across the '*Arabah* till they arrived at the 'Mount Seir'—the range of Petra—and 'smote the rest of the Amalekites, and dwelt there unto this day.'" Stanley, *Sinai and Palestine*, p. 161. "It is startling to find that a tribe professing to be" of the "sons of Israel," and holding no connection with the

of the children of Judah was too much for them: therefore the children of Simeon had their inheritance within the inheritance of them.

10—16. *The Territory of the Tribe of Zebulun.*

10 And the third lot came up for the children of Zebulun according to their families: and the border of their inherit- 11 ance was unto Sarid: and their border went up toward the sea, and Maralah, and reached to Dabbasheth, and reached 12 to the river that *is* before Jokneam; and turned from Sarid eastward *toward* the sunrising unto the border of Chisloth-tabor, and *then* goeth out to Daberath, and goeth up *to*

Arabs of the district, is still to be found in the country around Petra, literally fulfilling an ancient prediction:—" They of the South (= the *Negeb*) shall possess the mount of Esau." See Pusey's *Commentary* on Obad. 19.

10—16. THE TERRITORY OF THE TRIBE OF ZEBULUN.

10. *And the third lot came up for the children of Zebulun*] The tribe descended from the tenth of the sons of Jacob (Gen. xxx. 19, 20), and the sixth and last of the sons of Leah (Gen. xxxv. 23, xlvi. 14). During the journey from Egypt to Palestine, the tribe of Zebulun formed one of the first camp, with Judah and Issachar, also sons of Leah, marching under the standard of Judah. Its numbers at the census of Sinai were 57,000, surpassed only by Simeon, Dan, and Judah.

the border of their inheritance was unto Sarid] A spot unknown, but believed to be somewhere inland, in the plain of Esdraelon, and west of Chisloth-tabor (= "*the loins of Tabor*") (see ver. 12).

11. *and went up*] From Sarid the southern border *went up toward the sea in a westerly direction, and that as far as Maralah*, somewhere on the mountains of Carmel, *and touched upon Dabbasheth* (= *Camel's hump*), the site of which is unknown, *the stream which is before Jokneam*. In ch. xii. 22, Jokneam is said to have been by Carmel, and is identified with the modern *Tell Kaimon*, an eminence which stands just below the eastern end of Carmel. "The stream," therefore, is in all probability the *Kishon* (= "*twisted*" or "*winding*"), famous (*a*) in the history of Deborah and Barak (Judg. iv. 7, 13, v. 21), and (*b*) in that of Elijah and the prophets of Baal (1 Kings xviii. 40). See Menke's map in his *Bibel-atlas*.

12. *and turned from Sarid eastward*] As the border turned from Sarid westward, so also it turned from the same point *toward the east, toward the sunrising*, unto the border of

Chisloth-tabor] now *Iksâl*, a rocky height two miles and a half to the west of Mount Tabor. Robinson's *Bib. Res.* III. 182. For Tabor, see below, *v.* 22.

Japhia, and from thence passeth on along on the east to 13
Gittah-hepher, to Ittah-kazin, and goeth out *to* Remmon-
methoar *to* Neah; and the border compasseth it on the 14
north side *to* Hannathon: and the outgoings thereof are *in*
the valley of Jiphthah-el: and Kattath, and Nahallal, and 15

Daberath] Thence it went on to *Daberath*, a Levitical city, Josh. xxi.
28; 1 Chron. vi. 72, now *Debûrieh*, a small village "lying on the
side of a ledge of rocks directly at the foot of Tabor."
and goeth up to Japhia] "and stieth up ajens Jasie;" Wyclif.
Japhia (=*glancing*) is two miles south of Nazareth, the modern *Yâfa*.
Note the words "*goeth up*," and compare the following words of
Porter: "For three quarters of an hour more we wind through
picturesque glens, their beds green with corn, and their banks dark
with the foliage of the dwarf oak, hawthorn, and wild pear. *Yâfa*
now appears *on the top of a tell*, down in a glen on the right." *Handbook*, II. p. 385. It was fortified by Josephus, and afterwards captured
by Trajan and Titus under the orders of Vespasian; and in the storm
and sack of the place 15000 of the inhabitants were put to the sword,
and 2130 taken captive. The valley of Nazareth lies 400 feet higher
than the plain at the western foot of Tabor.

13. *to Gittah-hepher*] From Japhia the border ran still in an
easterly direction, "toward the rising of the sun," "to Gittah-
hepher, to Ittah-kazin, and went out unto Remmon, which stretches
to Neah."

Gittah-hepher] or *Gath-hepher*, was not far from *Yâfa*, and has
been identified with the modern *el-Meshhad*, about five miles from
Nazareth on the north-east. It is celebrated as the birthplace of the
prophet Jonah (2 Kings xiv. 25).

Ittah-kazin] is unknown.

Remmon-methoar] See the margin here, "*which is drawn;*" it
means that the border went out unto Remmon, which is "*marked
off to*," or "*stretched out to*" Neah. Remmon or Rimmon is marked
on Mr Grove's map at *Rummâneh*, about seven miles to the north
of Nazareth. See Robinson's *Bib. Res.* III. 195. Neah has not yet
been identified.

14. *and the border compasseth it*] The meaning seems to be "and
the border went round it (Neah) northward to Hannathon; and the
outgoings thereof were in the valley of Jiphthah-el."

compasseth it] For "compass" see above, note on ch. xv. 3.

Hannathon] (="pleasant"), which some have identified with the
Cana of the New Testament (John ii. 1), the present *Kana-el-Jelil*.

the valley of Jiphthah-el] Dr Robinson suggests that it was
identical with Istapata, and that both names survive in the modern
Jefât, a village in the mountains of Galilee half way between the bay
of Acre and the lake of Gennesareth. But the northern boundary
of Zebulun is not easy to trace.

15. *and Kattath*] The account of the cities here appears to be
imperfect. We have only the names of five cities given, though there

Shimron, and Idalah, and Beth-lehem: twelve cities with
16 their villages. This *is* the inheritance of the children of
Zebulun according to their families, these cities with their
villages.

17—23. *Inheritance of the Tribe of Issachar.*

17 *And* the fourth lot came out to Issachar, for the children
18 of Issachar according to their families. And their border
19 was toward Jezreel, and Chesulloth, and Shunem, and

are said to have been "twelve cities and their villages.". There is
nothing to which the list of terms here given, introduced by *and*, can
be attached.

Kattath] This also has been supposed to be "Cana of Galilee."
Nahallal, Shimron (ch. xi. 1), *Idalah*, are all as yet unknown.
Beth-lehem] This Beth-lehem in Zebulun is not to be confounded
with Beth-lehem Ephratah in Judah (Gen. xxxv. 19).

16. *This is the inheritance of the children of Zebulun*] It is evidently
impossible in the present state of our knowledge exactly to define
the limits of this tribe. But it seems to have reached on the one
side nearly to the lake of Gennesareth, and on the other to Carmel
and the Mediterranean. It enclosed one of the fairest portions of
Palestine. Besides the fertile plain near the fisheries of the lake of
Gennesareth, and the rich mountain-valleys, the tribe possessed the
goings out, the outlet, of the plain of Akka (Deut. xxxiii. 18), where
he could "dwell at the shore," and "suck of the abundance of the
seas" (Gen. xlix. 13; Deut. xxxiii. 19). But though possessing a district excelling in natural beauty and fertility, Zebulun, like the other
northern tribes, occupies quite a subordinate position in Old Testament History. We read of it as emerging from its obscurity only on two
occasions; (*a*) *first*, when side by side with Naphtali the men of the
tribe "jeoparded their lives unto the death" upon "the high places"
of Tabor in the contest with Sisera; and (*b*) *secondly*, when fifty
thousand "expert in war," with "all instruments of war," came up to
the coronation of David at Hebron (1 Chron. xii. 33).

17—23. INHERITANCE OF THE TRIBE OF ISSACHAR.

17. *And the fourth lot*] came forth to the tribe of Issachar, whose
place during the journey to Canaan had been on the east of the
tabernacle, side by side with his brothers Judah and Zebulun, the
group moving foremost in the march (Num. ii. 5, x. 15).

18. *And their border*] lay above that of Manasseh, and, according
to Josephus, "extended in length from Carmel to the Jordan, and
in breadth to Mount Tabor."

was toward Jezreel] Observe in this verse that the description of
the boundaries of this tribe, though begun, is not continued. Instead,
the names of the cities are given, which were included in it.

Hapharaim, and Shion, and Anaharath, and Rabbith, and 20
Kishion, and Abez, and Remeth, and En-gannim, and En- 21
haddah, and Beth-pazzez; and the coast reacheth to Tabor, 22
and Shahazimah, and Beth-shemesh; and the outgoings of

Jezreel] (=*the planting*, or *seed-plot, of God*, now *Zerin*), stood in the celebrated plain of the name between Gilboa and little Hermon on the brow of a very steep rocky slope of at least 100 feet in a strong and central position, commanding the view towards the Jordan on the east (2 Kings ix. 17), and visible from Carmel on the west (1 Kings xviii. 46). The splendid site induced Ahab to make it his chief residence. Here (*a*) he had his palace and "ivory house" (1 Kings xxi. 1, xxii. 39); here (*b*) he had a watch-tower whence sentinels were able to give timely notice of danger (2 Kings ix. 17); here (*c*) Jezebel lived, and from her high window facing eastward watched the entrance of the conquering Jehu (2 Kings ix. 30).

Chesulloth] (="*the loins*") was probably so called from its position on the slopes of some mountain, possibly between Jezreel and Shunem. On Mr Grove's map it is marked direct north of Jezreel, and is identified with Chisloth-tabor, the "Xaloth" of Josephus (*B. J.* III. 3. 1), the "Chasalus" of Jerome.

and Shunem] Now *Solâm*, three miles to the N.E. of Jezreel in the Esdraelon plain, "full in view of the sacred spot on Mount Carmel, and situated in the midst of the finest corn-fields in the world." Here (*a*) the Philistines encamped before the fatal battle of Gilboa (1 Sam. xxviii. 4); here (*b*) was the native place of Abishag (1 Kings i. 3); here (*c*) Elisha often lodged in the house of the "Shunammite woman," and here (*d*) he raised her son to life (2 Kings iv. 8—37, viii. 1—6).

19. *Hapharaim*] is mentioned above as the residence of a Canaanitish king, see ch. xii. 17; *Shion* is not found; *Anaharath*, too, has not been identified.

20, 21. *Rabbith, Kishion* (1 Chron. vi. 72), *Abez, Remeth* (1 Chron. vi. 73), are all unknown.

En-gannim]=*the spring of the gardens*, the modern *Jenîn*. Even now it justifies its ancient name; for the village lies, according to Robinson, *Bib. Res.* III. 155, "in the midst of gardens of fruit trees, which are surrounded by hedges of the prickly pear." But its most remarkable feature is a flowing, public fountain, rising in the hills at the back of the town, and brought down so that it issues in a copious stream in the midst of the place. Ahaziah was driving towards the mountain-pass by En-gannim (2 Kings ix. 27—the *Bethgan* of the LXX.=*En-gannim*), when he was overtaken by Jehu, and fled to die of his wounds at Megiddo.

En-haddah and *Beth-pazzez* are not known.

22. *and the coast reacheth to Tabor*] Not the mountain, but a town upon the mountain, given to the Levites (1 Chron. vi. 77), and to *Shahazimah* and *Beth-shemesh*. The site of neither of these places is known, for the Beth-shemesh here mentioned is not the town of that name in the tribe of Judah (ch. xv. 10).

their border were *at* Jordan : sixteen cities with their
23 villages. This *is* the inheritance of the tribe of the children
of Issachar according to their families, the cities and their
villages.

the outgoings of their border] The Jordan formed the eastern boundary of the tribe, but how far its territory extended down into the Jordan Valley is not stated.

sixteen cities] Which number is correct, if Tabor is taken as a city. Being a border town, it is not remarkable that here it is reckoned to Issachar, and in 1 Chron. vi. 77 to Zebulun.

23. *This is the inheritance of the tribe of the children of Issachar*] Then, as it still is, among the richest land in Palestine. "Westward was the famous plain which derived its name from its fertility. On the north is Tabor, which even under the burning sun of the climate is said to retain the glades and dells of an English wood. On the east, behind Jezreel, is the opening which conducts to the plain of the Jordan—to the Bethshean, which was proverbially among the Rabbis the Gate of Paradise for its fruitfulness." The soil yielded corn and figs, wine and oil (1 Chron. xii. 40); the stately palm waved over the villages; and the very weeds testify to the extraordinary fertility of the Esdraelon plain. Here Issachar *rejoiced in his tents* (Deut. xxxiii. 18), couched down as the strong he-ass (Gen. xlix. 14, 15), used for burden and field-work, and "*seeing that rest was good, and the land that it was pleasant, bowed his shoulder to bear, and became a servant unto tribute,*" which various marauders, Canaanites (Judg. iv. 3, 7), Midianites, Amalekites (Judg. vi. 3, 4), Philistines (1 Sam. xxix. 1), exacted, bursting through his frontier, open both on the east and the west, and tempted by his luxuriant crops. See Porter's *Handbook*, II. 352; Stanley's *S. and P.*, p. 348. "Two things strike us forcibly in looking over the plain of Esdraelon, and in wandering through it:

(*a*) *First, its wonderful richness.* After the grey hills of Judah, and the rocky mountains of Ephraim, the traveller looks with admiration over this unbroken extent of verdure. The luxuriant grass, and the exuberance of the crops on the few spots where it is cultivated, amply prove the fertility of the soil. It was the frontier of Zebulun. 'Rejoice, O Zebulun, in thy *goings out*' (Deut. xxxiii. 18).

(*b*) *Second, its desolation.* If we except its eastern branches there is not a single inhabited village on its whole surface, and not more than one-sixth of its soil is cultivated. It is the home of the wandering Bedawy, who can scour its smooth turf on his fleet mare in search of plunder, and when hard pressed can speedily remove his tents and his flocks beyond the Jordan, and beyond the reach of a weak government. In its condition, thus exposed to every hasty incursion, and to every shock of war, we read the fortunes of that tribe which for the sake of its richness consented to sink into a half nomadic state. 'Rejoice, O Issachar, in thy *tents*' (Gen. xlix. 14, 15; Deut. xxxiii. 18). Their exposed position and valuable possessions made them eager for the succession of David to the throne,

24—31. *The Inheritance of the Tribe of Asher.*

And the fifth lot came out for the tribe of the children of 24 Asher according to their families. And their border was 25 Helkath, and Hali, and Beten, and Achshaph, and Alamme- 26 lech, and Amad, and Misheal; and reacheth to Carmel westward, and to Shihor-libnath; and turneth *toward* the 27 sunrising *to* Beth-dagon, and reacheth to Zebulun, and to the

as one under whose sceptre they would enjoy the peace and rest they loved." See 1 Chron. xii. 32, 40. Porter's *Handbook*, II. pp. 352, 353.

24—31. THE INHERITANCE OF THE TRIBE OF ASHER.

24. *And the fifth lot came out for the tribe of the children of Asher*] who were descended from the eighth son of Jacob, and in the march through the desert closed the long procession side by side with Dan and Naphtali, with the standard of Dan, an "eagle with a serpent in its talons."

25. *And their border*] The general position of the tribe was on the slope of the Galilean mountains from Carmel northwards, with Manasseh on the south, Zebulun and Issachar on the south-east, and Naphtali on the north-east, a narrow, but beautiful and fertile region.

And their border was Helkath] The first boundary given us is that formed by the cities of *Helkath*, afterwards given to the Levites (ch. xxi. 31), *Hali, Beten*, and *Achshaph* (ch. xii. 20), of none of which cities is the situation known to us.

26. *Alammelech, and Amad*, are at present unknown. *Misheal* has been identified with *Misalli* at the northern extremity of the plain of Sharon.

and reacheth to Carmel] This boundary struck Carmel on the west and Shihor-libnath, somewhere to the south of that range.

Shihor-libnath] Not, as some have supposed, the Belus, which falls into the Mediterranean near to Acre or Ptolemais, but south of Carmel, and probably the *Nahr Zerka*, or "Crocodile Brook," which rises in the Carmel range, and flows into the Mediterranean just above Cæsarea. For the existence of crocodiles still in the *Zerka*, see Macgregor's *Rob Roy on the Jordan*, p. 387, who also found a crocodile in the Kishon, which is only about 20 miles north of the *Zerka*, pp. 400—403. "I suspect," writes Dr Thomson, "that long ages ago, some Egyptians, accustomed to worship this ugly creature, settled here (Cæsarea), and brought their gods with them. Once here, they would not easily be exterminated; for no better place could be desired by them than this vast jungle and impracticable swamp." See *Land and the Book*, p. 497.

27. *and turneth toward the sunrising*] From the *Shihor-libnath*, the border, still keeping to the south of Carmel, turned in an easterly direction towards *Beth-dagon*, of which we know as little as of the Beth-dagon of Judah, above, xv. 41.

and reacheth to Zebulun] Thence it trended in a north-easterly direc-

valley of Jiphthah-el toward the north side *of* Beth-emek,
28 and Neiel, and goeth out to Cabul on the left hand, and
Hebron, and Rehob, and Hammon, and Kanah, *even* unto
29 great Zidon; and *then* the coast turneth *to* Ramah, and to
the strong city Tyre; and the coast turneth *to* Hosah; and
the outgoings thereof are at the sea from the coast to Achzib:
30 Ummah also, and Aphek, and Rehob: twenty and two cities

tion, and "touched the border of Zebulun," and the valley, or ravine, of *Jiphthah-el*, where, according to v. 14, were "the outgoings" of the north-western boundary of the latter tribe; and passed on north of *Beth-emek* and *Neiel* (which has been identified with *Mi'ar*), "and went out to Cabul on the left hand," i.e. on the north side of it.

Cabul] it is thought, may be considered as still existing in the modern *Kâbûl*, found about eight or nine miles east of *Akka*, and thus on the very borders of Galilee. It is possible, therefore, that there may be some connection between this place and the district containing twenty cities, which was presented by Solomon to Hiram, king of Tyre (1 Kings ix. 11—13). See Smith's *Bibl. Dict.* under *Cabul*.

28. *and Hebron*] The main portion of Asher having been described, the northern portion is now defined more particularly.

Hebron] Instead of Hebron we find Abdon in ch. xxi. 30, and 1 Chron. vi. 74. But twenty MSS. and all the ancient versions read *Hebron*. See Keil's *Commentary*.

Rehob, Hammon, are at present unknown. *Kanah* may possibly be identified with *Ain-Kana*, about eight miles south-east of *Saida* (Zidon).

unto great Zidon] On *Zidon*, or Sidon, see above, ch. xi. 8.

29. *and then the coast turneth to Ramah*] Having reached Zidon by Kanah, the boundary bent southward by Ramah, and so turned to the "strong," or "fortified city" of Tyre. Robinson would identify Ramah with *Rameh*, south-east of Tyre, on a solitary hill in the midst of a basin of green fields, and surrounded by greater heights (*Bib. Res.* III. 63).

the strong city Tyre] "The most strengthened citie Tyruns" (Wyclif) here alluded to is not the island of Tyre, but the city standing on the mainland, now *Sûr*.

turneth to Hosah] From Tyre the border turned toward Hosah, the site of which is unknown, and finally ran towards the sea in the region of *Achzib*, the modern *es-Zib*, on the sea-shore, little more than two hours from Acre. The Canaanites, we are told (Judg. i. 31), were afterwards not expelled from it by the tribe of Asher, and in classical times it was known as Ecdippa. It is to be noted that both the fortified city Tyre and great Zidon were included in Asher's inheritance, but no effort was made by the Israelites to obtain possession of these Phœnician cities.

30. *Ummah also*] Of the three cities here mentioned, *Ummah, Aphek*, and *Rehob*, the first and third are unknown. Aphek apparently lay in the extreme north of Asher, and is probably the same place as that alluded to above, ch. xiii. 4, beyond Sidon, the Aphaca of classical, and the Afka of modern, times.

with their villages. This *is* the inheritance of the tribe of 31 the children of Asher according to their families, these cities with their villages.

32—39. *The Territory of the Tribe of Naphtali.*

The sixth lot came out to the children of Naphtali, *even* 32 for the children of Naphtali according to their families.

twenty and two cities] Which number does not correspond with the cities given, and at present the explanation is not clear.

31. *the inheritance of the tribe of the children of Asher*] The territory of Asher extended from the *Nahr Zerka* on the south, to Zidon on the north, and contained some of the richest soil of the country, and the maritime portion of the fertile plain of Esdraelon, and commanded all approaches to Palestine from the sea on the north. Its soil well fulfilled the prophetic dèscriptions of Jacob and Moses. Here Asher could "dip his foot" in the *oil* of his luxuriant olive-groves (Deut. xxxiii. 24) such as still distinguish this region, and fatten on the *bread*, the fruit of the rich plain of Phœnicia and his fertile upland valleys (Gen. xlix. 20). Here he could "yield royal dainties" (Gen. xlix. 20), "oil and wine from his olives and vineyards, and milk and butter from his pastures;" while *under his shoes* (Deut. xxxiii. 25) was the *iron ore* of the southern slopes of Lebanon, and the *brass* or copper of the neighbouring Phœnician territory. See Stanley's *S. and P.*, p. 362; Pusey's *Lectures on the Book of Daniel*, p. 294; Porter's *Handbook of Sinai and Palestine*, II. p. 363. But to the richness of his soil and the proximity of the Phœnician towns the degeneracy and subsequent obscurity of Asher may be mainly traced. At the numbering of Israel at Sinai, the tribe was more numerous than either Ephraim, Manasseh, or Benjamin (Num. i. 32—41), "but in the reign of David, so insignificant had it become, that its name is altogether omitted from the list of the chief rulers" (1 Chron. xxvii. 16—22). "The Asherites dwelt among the Canaanites" (Judg. i. 32), and "though not nominally, or even really, a subject people, they were so thoroughly checked in their plans of conquest, and dashed their strength so uselessly against the strong rock of Phœnician power, that in the shock of failure they settled down as a people admitted to be strong, and allowed to exist side by side with the Phœnicians, under certain statutes and arrangements mutually entered into." Ritter's *Compar. Geo. of Palestine*, III. 187, 188. With the exception of the aged widow, "Anna, the daughter of Phanuel" (Luke ii. 36), no name "shines out of the general obscurity" of the tribe. "The contemptuous allusion in the Song of Deborah sums up this whole history, when in the great gathering of the tribes against Sisera, *Asher continued on the sea-shore and abode in his creeks.*" So insignificant was the tribe to which was assigned the fortress which Napoleon called the key of Palestine. Stanley's *S. and P.*, p. 265.

32—39. THE TERRITORY OF THE TRIBE OF NAPHTALI.

32. *The sixth lot*] fell out to the tribe descended from Naphtali,

33 And their coast was from Heleph, from Allon to Zaanannim, and Adami, Nekeb, and Jabneel, unto Lakum; and the 34 outgoings thereof were *at* Jordan : and *then* the coast turneth westward *to* Aznoth-tabor, and goeth out from thence to

the fifth son of the patriarch Jacob, which, during the march through the wilderness, occupied a position north of the Tabernacle, side by side with Dan and Asher (Num. ii. 25—31), and at the census taken at Mount Sinai numbered upwards of 53400 fighting men (Num. i. 43, ii. 30).

33. *And their coast*] The territory appropriated to the tribe was bounded (*a*) on the *west* by Asher, (*b*) on the *south* by Zebulun and Issachar, (*c*) on the *east* by the Sea of Gennesaret and the Jordan, while (*d*) on the *north* it reached far up into Cœle-Syria, "the splendid valley which separates the two ranges of Lebanon."

from Heleph] Apparently the west border towards Asher is first described, with the north and east boundary. The southern border is defined in *v.* 34. *Heleph* is unknown.

Allon to Zaanannim]=**the oak**, or **terebinth, by Zaanannim**. It is the same place, on the N.W. of Lake Merom, as that mentioned in Judg. iv. 11, where Sisera was slain by Jael, "the wife of Heber the Kenite," and derived its name Zaanannim or Zaanaim, *the unloading of Tents*, from the strange sight of the encampment of nomads in tents amidst the regular cities and villages of the mountains." "Even to the present day the Bedouins more or less friendly disposed wander about in the north of Palestine, in the plain of Jezreel, on Gilboa, and on Tabor." See Lange's *Commentary*. "The reconnaissance survey along the watershed from Hûnin led across a succession of mountain peaks, forming the great western vale of the Jordan. The highlands—we are in the tribe of Naphtali—form a series of valleys with which the country is intersected, the ridges between them being described as somewhat of the character of open glades, gently sloping towards the sea. The hills are well wooded, though the oaks are being thinned out to supply the Damascus market with charcoal. At the last peak the hill slopes to the southward, overlooking a little plain, one mile wide and two long, lying sheltered among the surrounding hills. This is the plain of Zaanaim." *Our Work in Palestine*, pp. 174, 175.

Adami, Nekeb, Jabneel, Lakum, are all unknown.

and the outgoings thereof] The boundary is traced from the south-west towards the north-east to the sources of the Jordan, above the Lake of Galilee.

34. *and then the coast turneth*] From the Jordan on the east, the southern border of Naphtali turned westward to Aznoth-tabor, not identified, but probably a border town on the line which separated this tribe from Issachar, and "struck," or coincided with, Zebulun on the south and Asher on the west. The site of *Hukkok* is unknown.

Hukkok, and reacheth to Zebulun on the south side, and reacheth to Asher on the west side, and to Judah upon Jordan *toward* the sunrising. And the fenced cities *are* 35 Ziddim, Zer, and Hammath, Rakkath, and Chinnereth, and Adamah, and Ramah, and Hazor, and Kedesh, and 36 37

Judah upon Jordan] So our Version renders it, following the Vulgate, *Et in Juda ad Jordanem:* Others, following the Masoretic punctuation, would put a colon at Judah, so that it would run, "and Judah; the Jordan was toward the sunrising" i. e. the eastern boundary of the tribe. The word *Judah* here has been explained by the fact that the sixty cities, *Havoth-jair* (Num. xxxii. 41), which were on the eastern side of Jordan opposite to Naphtali, were reckoned as belonging to Judah, because Jair their founder was descended on the father's side from Judah through Hezron. Comp. 1 Chron. ii. 21—24. Others would identify it with a village.*el-Jehudijeh*, marked on Dr Smith's map, north of *Tibrin*, but this is not satisfactory.
35. *And the fenced cities*] Note the expression and the number of them in this locality. "It was no doubt good policy to protect the northern frontier by a belt of fortresses, as the south was protected by the fenced cities of Judah." *The Speaker's Commentary* in loc. *Ziddim* and *Zer* are unknown.
Hammath] Afterwards a Levitical city, ch. xxi. 32, called Hammon in 1 Chron. vi. 76. The name comes from a root signifying "to be warm," and hints at the hot springs which existed here. "At the southern extremity of the strip of level ground, on which the ancient city of Tiberias stood, are some warm fountains, which have a temperature of 144 Fahr. with an extremely salt and bitter taste, and a strong smell of sulphur. These fountains are mentioned by Pliny, 'Ab Occidente Tiberiade *aquis calidis* salubri,' and frequently by Josephus, under the name *Ammaus*='Warm Baths.' This is probably a Greek form of the Hebrew *Hammath*, a town of Naphtali." Porter's *Handbook*, II. p. 423.
Rakkath] (= "*bank*," "*shore*") is by the Rabbins identified with Tiberias. For *Chinnereth* see above, note on ch. xi. 2.
36. *Adamah*] is unknown, as also *Ramah*, which must not be mistaken for the Ramah of ver. 29.
Hazor] See above, xi. 1, 6—10. Dr Robinson would identify it with *Tel Khuraibeh*, Captain Wilson and Anderson with *Tel Hara*. "Here were found the remains of an ancient fortress, a city with its walls and towers still to be traced, and on the eastern slope, the usual concomitants of old ruins, broken glass and pottery." Here, they both agree, was the long-lost Hazor, which "lay over" the lake Hûleh. "The position," says Captain Wilson, "is one of great strength and overhangs the lake. Every argument which Robinson adduces in favour of *Tel Khuraibeh* applies with much greater force to these ruins." Dr Porter, however, refuses to accept either theory, arguing that as the strength of Jabin lay in *chariots*, "we must look

38 Edrei, and En-hazor, and Iron, and Migdal-el, Horem, and Beth-anath, and Beth-shemesh; nineteen cities with their 39 villages. This *is* the inheritance of the tribe of the children of Naphtali according to their families, the cities and their villages.

for Hazor on the lower slopes of the mountains, so as to be easily accessible for chariots." *Our Work in Palestine*, p. 177.

37. *Kedesh*] or *Kedesh Naphtali* (="*the Holy Place of Naphtali*"), see above, ch. xii. 22, originally, as we have seen, was a royal, and probably a sacred city of the Canaanites. It was conquered by Joshua (ch. xii. 22), and made subsequently "a city of refuge." Here (*a*) Barak was born; here (*b*) he was when Deborah summoned him to fight the battle of his country; hither (*c*) the prophetess came with him; and hence (*d*) having rallied the warriors of Zebulun and Naphtali he marched with 10000 men to Tabor (Judg. iv. 1—10).

Edrei, and En-hazor] are unknown. This Edrei must not be confounded with the well-known Edrei in Bashan.

38. *Iron*] has not been identified. *Migdal-el* has been by some supposed to be the Magdala of Matt. xv. 39, the place of which is now occupied by a miserable collection of hovels known as *el-Mejdel*, on the western side of the Lake of Gennesareth, and at the S.E. corner of the plain. Neither *Horem*, *Beth-anath*, nor *Beth-shemesh* has at present been identified.

39. *This is the inheritance*] The territory appropriated to Naphtali was thus enclosed on three sides by that of other tribes. (*a*) On the *west* was Asher, (*b*) on the *south* Zebulun, (*c*) and on the *east* Manasseh beyond the Jordan. Cut off from the great plain of Esdraelon by the mass of the mountains of Nazareth, it had communication on the east with the fertile district of the Sea of Galilee, and the splendidly watered country of the springs of the Jordan. The dying Jacob had compared Naphtali to a "*spreading terebinth*" (Gen. xlix. 21, mistranslated "a hind let loose") of the uplands of Lebanon, shooting forth *goodly boughs;* and the great Lawgiver had described him as *satisfied with favour, and full with the blessing of the Lord* (Deut. xxxiii. 23), but the grand opportunities so graciously given were not turned to the best account. The capabilities of its plains, of the thoroughfare and traffic of the Sea of Galilee (Gen. xlix. 13), were not developed by the tribe. One hero—and one only—was produced by it, Barak of Kedesh-Naphtali, who dwelt in the mountain district (Judg. iv. 6). See above, verse 37. But after this exploit, Naphtali, like Asher, resigned itself to intercourse with the heathen, "and learned their works" (Ps. cvi. 35). See Smith's *Dict. of the Bible;* Ritter's *Geog. of Palestine*, IV. p. 338; Stanley's *Sinai and Palestine*, p. 363. "With the exception of the transient splendour of the days of Barak and of Gideon, the four northern tribes hardly affect the general fortunes of the nation. It is not till the Jewish is on the point of breaking into the Christian Church that these northern tribes acquire a new interest.

40—48. *The Inheritance of the Tribe of Dan.*

And the seventh lot came out for the tribe of the children 40 of Dan according to their families. And the coast of their 41 inheritance was Zorah, and Eshtaol, and Ir-shemesh, and 42 Shaalabbin, and Aijalon, and Jethlah, and Elon, and Thim- 43 nathah, and Ekron, and Eltekeh, and Gibbethon, and 44 Baalath, and Jehud, and Bene-berak, and Gath-rimmon, and 45/46

'Galilee' then, by reason of its previous isolation, springs into overwhelming importance. 'The land of Zebulun, the land of Naphtali, by the way of the sea, beyond Jordan, Galilee of the Gentiles; the people which sat in darkness saw great light, and to those who sat in the region and shadow of death light is sprung up' (Isai. ix. 1, 2; Matt. iv. 15, 16)." Stanley's *Lectures*, I. 231.

40—48. THE INHERITANCE OF THE TRIBE OF DAN.

40. *the seventh lot*] came out to the smallest of all the tribes, that of Dan, descended from the fifth son of Jacob. The position of the tribe during the march through the wilderness had been n the north side of the Tabernacle, the hindmost of the long procession between Naphtali and Asher. At the census in the desert it was the most numerous of all the tribes with the exception of Judah, containing 62,700 men able to bear arms.

41. *And the coast*] allotted to the tribe, in spite of the numbers just mentioned, was the smallest of all. Compressed into the narrow space between the north-western hills of Judah and the Mediterranean, it was surrounded by the three most powerful tribes of the whole confederacy, Ephraim and Benjamin on the north and east, Judah on the south and south-east.

was Zorah] Observe that the boundaries of this tribe are not defined. They naturally follow from those of Judah, Ephraim, and Benjamin.

Zorah, and Eshtaol] See above, ch. xv. 33. For *Ir-shemesh = Beth-shemesh =* the modern *'Ain-Shems*, see above, ch. xv. 10.

42. *Shaalabbin]* = "*the place of foxes;*" comp. the story of Samson, Judg. xv. 4. It appears in 1 Kings iv. 9 as the home of one of David's " mighty men." For *Ajalon* see above, ch. x. 12; *Jethlah* has not been identified.

43. *Elon*] The site of this place is still undiscovered. For *Thimnathah* see above, ch. xv. 10; for *Ekron*, xiii. 3.

44. *Eltekeh, and Gibbethon*] occur as Levitical cities in ch. xxi. 23. The sites are not identified; *Baalath* may be *Deir Balût*. It was fortified by Solomon (1 Kings ix. 18), and is placed by Josephus near Gezer. See Jos. *Ant.* VIII. 6. 1.

45. *Jehud*] may, it is thought, be still traced in the village of *El-Yehudiyeh* in the district of Lydda. Robinson's *Bib. Res.* III. 45. *Bene-berak* has not been identified; *Gath-rimmon* we find (ch. xxi. 24) given to the Levites, but the site is unknown.

Me-jarkon, and Rakkon, with the border before Japho.
47 And the coast of the children of Dan went out *too little* for
them: therefore the children of Dan went up to fight against
Leshem, and took it, and smote it with the edge of the

> 46. *Me-jarkon, and Rakkon*] still remain to be discovered.
> *with the border before Japho*] i.e. with the whole district extending to the suburbs opposite to Japho.
> *Japho*] (= "*beauty*") is the Hebrew form of the more familiar Joppa (2 Chron. ii. 16; Ez. iii. 7). It was situated on the south-west coast of Palestine, and having a harbour attached to it was afterwards the port of Jerusalem. It was the spot (*a*) whither the cedar and pinewood were floated from Phœnicia by Hiram, king of Tyre, for Solomon's temple (2 Chron. ii. 16); (*b*) whither similar materials were conveyed by the permission of Cyrus for the rebuilding of the second temple under Zerubbabel (Ez. iii. 7); (*c*) where Jonah took ship to flee "from the presence of the Lord" (Jon. i. 3); (*d*) where Jonathan Maccabæus met Ptolemy (1 Mac. xi. 6); (*e*) where St Peter had the vision on the housetop of Simon the tanner (Acts x. 9—18). On the east the town is surrounded by a wide circle of gardens and groves of noble trees. "The figs and oranges of Joppa are noted for their size and flavour. The water-melons, which thrive on the sandy soil around, are in great repute, and are carried in great numbers to Alexandria and Cairo. Through all Syria, too, they have a reputation...... The horticulturist Bové, who visited the place in 1832, observed three kinds of figs, apricots, almonds, pomegranates, peaches, oranges, pears, and apples, plums, bananas and grapes, while the sugar-cane grows to the height of five or six feet." Ritter, *Geog. Pal.* IV. 259. In A.D. 1188 Saladin destroyed its fortifications, to be rebuilt by Richard of England, who was here confined by sickness. In 1253 it was occupied by St Louis, and afterwards fell into the hands first of the Sultans of Egypt and then of the Turks.
> 47. *went out too little for them*] The words "too little" are inserted in our Version. They are not found in the original Hebrew, which literally means, **the border of the children of Dan went out from them**, i.e. **the border of the children of Dan was extended**. "Squeezed into the narrow strip between the mountains and the sea, its energies were great beyond its numbers." Stanley's *Sin. and Pal.*, p. 395; *Lectures*, p. 268.
> *went up to fight*] " Stieded vp, and fouȝten," Wyclif. Hard pressed by the Amorites, whom they were unable to expel from the plain (Judg. i. 34), and by the Philistines, they longed for an addition to their territory, they sent out five spies from two towns in the low country, who tracked the Jordan to its source beyond the waters of Merom, and came to an eminence on which rose the town of
> *Leshem*] or *Laish*, far up in northern Palestine, the modern *Tell el-Kâdy* near *Bâniâs*. It was a colony from Sidon, and its inhabitants, separated from their mother city by the huge mass of Lebanon and half of Anti-Lebanon, "*dwelt quiet and secure*" (Judg. xviii. 7), in the

sword, and possessed it, and dwelt therein, and called Leshem, Dan, after the name of Dan their father. This *is* 43 the inheritance of the tribe of the children of Dan according to their families, these cities with their villages.

enjoyment of the warm climate and exquisite scenery, and tilling the fertile soil, irrigated by many streams. The spies marked the spot, and on their return bade their brethren arise, and take possession of *a place where there is no want of any thing that is in the earth* (Judg. xviii. 10), and the soil of which " even now produces large crops of wheat, barley, maize, sesame, rice, and other plants with very little labour...... while horses, cattle, and sheep fatten on the rich pastures, and large herds of black buffaloes luxuriate in the streams and deep mire of the marshes." See Thomson's *Land and the Book*, p. 214; Robinson, *Bib. Res*. III. 396.

therefore the children of Dan went up to fight] On receiving the news six hundred Danites from Zorah and Eshtaol girded on their weapons of war (Judg. xviii. 11), and pushed their way to the sources of the Jordan, and finding the town of Laish just as the spies had described it, far from its mother city, dwelling quiet and secure, they burst upon it, scaled its walls (Judg. xviii. 27), and

took it] and set it on fire, massacring the inhabitants. Then they rebuilt the town, and dwelt therein, and

called Leshem, Dan, after the name of Dan their father] The name Tell el-Kâdi=" *the mound of the Judge*," still preserves the ancient Dan="*judge.*" See Tristram's *Land of Israel*, p. 580.

48. *This is the inheritance of the tribe...of Dan*] In length it extends but 14 miles from Joppa to Ekron, but it was one of the most fertile tracts in the land, the cornfield and garden of southern Palestine. The dying Jacob had said of the tribe (Gen. xlix. 16):

> "Dan shall *judge* his people,
> As one of the tribes of Israel.
> Dan shall be a *serpent by the way*,
> An *adder* in the path,
> That *biteth the horse heels*,
> So that his rider shall fall backward;"

and, as it has been observed, " the privilege of Dan was, that he was to lie in wait for the invader from the south or from the north." "*A serpent*," an indigenous, home-born "*adder*," to bite the heels of the invading stranger's horse; "*a lion's whelp*" (Deut. xxxiii. 22), small and fierce, to "*leap from the heights of Bashan*," on the armies of Damascus or Nineveh. "*For thy salvation, O Lord, have I waited*" seems to have been his war cry, as if of a warrior in the constant attitude of expectation. Once only in the history of the tribe, so far as we know, was this expectation fully realised—in the life of Samson. Stanley's *Lectures*, I. p. 269.

49—51. *The Inheritance assigned to Joshua.*

49 When they had made an end of dividing the land for inheritance by their coasts, the children of Israel gave an
50 inheritance to Joshua the son of Nun among them: according to the word of the LORD they gave him the city which he asked, *even* Timnath-serah in mount Ephraim: and he
51 built the city, and dwelt therein. These *are* the inheritances, which Eleazar the priest, and Joshua the son of Nun, and the heads of the fathers of the tribes of the children of Israel, divided for an inheritance by lot in Shiloh before the LORD, *at* the door of the tabernacle of the congregation. So they made an end of dividing the country.

49—51. THE INHERITANCE ASSIGNED TO JOSHUA.

49. *When they had made an end*] After all the tribes had been provided for, a modest inheritance was assigned to their noble-hearted leader, who with unselfish generosity was contented with far less than many others would have claimed under similar circumstances.

among them] The portion assigned was among the mountains of his native tribe of Ephraim.

50. *according to the word of the Lord*] We do not find any Divine injunction in the Pentateuch to the effect that Joshua was to receive a special portion in the Land of Canaan. But as Caleb had received a definite promise of the same kind, which is not to be found in its literal form in the Pentateuch, we may conclude that a like promise had been been made to Joshua.

even Timnath-serah] In Judg. ii. 9 the name of the city given to the Israelitish leader is altered to *Timnath-heres*="*portion of the sun.*" In the same place it is defined as having been situated "*in the mount of Ephraim, on the north side of the hill Gaash.*" The word Timnath, or Timnah, means "allotted portion," and was given to several places. It is now generally identified with *Tibnah*, between *Jifna* and *el-Mejdel*, and was first discovered by Dr Eli Smith in 1843, where he found the ruins of a considerable town. Opposite the town was a much higher hill, in the north side of which were several excavated sepulchres. "Of all sites I have seen," says Lieut. Conder, "none is so striking as that of Joshua's home, surrounded as it is with deep valleys and wild rugged hills." Paula is described by St Jerome as "satis mirata quod distributor possessionum sibi aspera et montana delegisset" (Epist. CVIII., *Epitaph. Paulæ*).

and he built the city] or perhaps rather, **fortified** it. The site may have been previously unoccupied, and named Timnath-serah = "*remaining portion,*" by Joshua himself.

1—6. *The Divine Command respecting the Cities of Refuge.*

The LORD also spake unto Joshua, saying, Speak to the 20 children of Israel, saying, Appoint out for you cities of refuge, 2 whereof I spake unto you by the hand of Moses: that the 3 slayer that killeth *any* person unawares *and* unwittingly may flee thither: and they shall be your refuge from the avenger

CH. XX. 1—6. THE DIVINE COMMAND RESPECTING THE CITIES OF REFUGE.

1. *The Lord also spake unto Joshua*] As soon as the Tribes had received the portion of their inheritance, the Lord directed that Joshua should carry out the injunctions which Moses had left respecting the Cities of Refuge for the accidental homicide.

2. *cities of refuge*] "The cityes of fugityues," Wyclif. Prior to the Mosaic age, it was required of the nearest of kin, as a matter of duty, to avenge the death of a slain relative. He was called the *Goel* or *Avenger*, and together with his office inherited the property of the deceased. Sometimes a whole family took upon them this duty (2 Sam. xiv. 7). Among the Arab tribes of the present day, "any bloodshed whatever, whether wilful or accidental, laid the homicide open to the *duteous* revenge of the relatives and family of the slain person, who again in their turn were then similarly watched and hunted by the opposite party, until a family war of extermination had legally settled itself from generation to generation, without the least prospect of a peaceful termi-nation." It was the aim of the Mosaic Law, without altogether abolishing this long-established custom, to mitigate its evils as far as possible.

whereof I spake unto you] The general directions on this subject will be found in (*a*) Exod. xxi. 13; (*b*) Num. xxxv. 9 ff.; (*c*) Deut. xix. 2. The reference to them here is one of the numerous instances in which the book of Joshua presupposes the existence of the Pentateuch.

3. *That the slayer that killeth any person unawares*] In accordance with these regulations a wide distinction was made between the man who committed wilful murder, and one who slew another by mistake, in ignorance, and unintentionally. (*a*) In the former case the guilty criminal met with no compassion from the Mosaic Code. He was regarded as accursed. The horns of the altar were to be no refuge for him. He was to be dragged from them by force to suffer his doom, nor could rank or wealth exempt him from it (Num. xxxv. 31, 32). (*b*) In the latter case, where life had been taken unawares, a more merciful system of legislation intervened. In contradistinction to the customs of the Greeks and Romans and even of the Middle Ages, which made places of sanctuary available to *criminals of every kind*, the Jewish Lawgiver reserved them for unintentional acts of murder, and for these alone. The distinguishing marks of such acts are clearly laid down in Num. xxxv. 25—34; Deut. xix. 4—6.

from the avenger of blood] "that he moue ascaap the wrath of the

of blood. And when he that doth flee unto one of those cities shall stand *at* the entering of the gate of the city, and shall declare his cause in the ears of the elders of that city, they shall take him into the city unto them, and give him a place, 5 that he may dwell among them. And if the avenger of blood pursue after him, then they shall not deliver the slayer up into his hand; because he smote his neighbour unwit-
6 tingly, and hated him not beforetime. And he shall dwell in that city, until he stand before the congregation for judgment, *and* until the death of the high priest that shall be in those days: then shall the slayer return, and come unto his

neiȝboure, that is wreker of the blood," Wyclif. The involuntary shedder of blood was permitted to take flight to a city of refuge.

4. *shall stand at the entering of the gate of the city*] not i. e. outside the gate of the city, but in the forum, or public place of judgment. Comp. Ruth iv. 1, 2.

in the ears of the elders of that city] Before the fugitive could avail himself of the shelter conceded by the laws, he was to undergo a solemn trial, and make it appear to the satisfaction of the magistrates of the place ("the aldren of the citie," Wyclif), where the homicide was committed, that it was purely accidental.

and give him a place] If he succeeded in so doing, the elders were to "give him a place," i. e. receive him into the protection of the city, and permit him to reside there.

5. *And if the avenger of blood pursue*] "And when the blood wreker him pursue," Wyclif. The steps are now prescribed which were to be taken, in the event of the Avenger of Blood pursuing the homicide. He was not to be delivered up into his hands, but kept securely.

6. *until the death of the high priest*] "To the tyme that the great priest dye," Wyclif. The protection granted was provisional, until the manslayer and the pursuer could be duly heard by the assembly of the elders of the city where the occurrence took place, and the guilt or innocence of the former established. In the latter case the homicide was safely lodged in the City of Refuge until the death of the anointed High priest (Num. xxxv. 25).

then shall the slayer return] The death of the ruling High priest, "the head of the theocracy and representative of the whole people," was regarded as of such importance that any other death was, so to speak, forgotten in consequence, and an amnesty ensued during which the manslayer was at liberty to return to his home. Thus as on the one hand by disallowing compensation by money in the case of wilful murder, the Jewish Law shewed a just regard for human life, and put the poor on the same footing as the rich, so on the other "the asylum afforded by Moses displayed the same benign regard for human life in respect of the homicide himself. Had no obstacle been put in the way of the *Goel*, instant death would have awaited any one who had the

own city, and unto his own house, unto the city from whence he fled.

7—9. *The Selection of the Cities of Refuge.*

And they appointed Kedesh in Galilee in mount Naph- 7 tali, and Shechem in mount Ephraim, and Kirjath-arba,

misfortune to occasion the death of another. By his wise arrangements, however, Moses interposed a seasonable delay, and enabled the manslayer to appeal to the laws and justice of his country. Momentary wrath could hardly execute its fell purposes, and a suitable refuge was provided for the guiltless and unfortunate." Kitto's *Biblical Cyclopædia*, I. p. 527.

7—9. THE SELECTION OF THE CITIES OF REFUGE.

7. *And they appointed*] Rather, they **sanctified, set apart for a sacred purpose**. The Cities of Refuge were intended to preserve the People and the Land of Jehovah from blood-guiltiness. Hence the appointment to so high a purpose carried with it also the idea of solemn consecration. "They seuerden," Wyclif translates it in the first edition, "thei ordeyneden" in the later edition. The cities selected were three on either side of the Jordan, almost equally remote from each other,

  (*a*) *On the West.*   (*b*) *On the East.*
  1. *Kedesh*, in Naphtali.   1. *Golan*, in Bashan.
  2. *Shechem*, in Mount Ephraim. 2. *Ramoth-Gilead*, in Gad.
  3. *Hebron*, in Judah.   3. *Bezer*, in Reuben.

It requires only to look at the map to see how wisely these spots were marked out, so as to make a "City of Refuge" easy of access from all parts of the land. They were chosen, it will be observed, out of the priestly and Levitical cities, as likely to be inhabited by the most intelligent part of the community. According to Maimonides, all the fortyeight Levitical cities (enumerated in the next Chapter) had the privilege of asylum, but these six cities were required to receive and lodge the homicide gratuitously.

Kedesh] was the most *northerly* city on the West. See above, xii. 22.

in Galilee] In that part of the province afterwards called "Galilee." This name which in the Roman age was applied to a large province, seems to have been originally confined to a little "*circuit*" or "*region*" —*Galil, Galilah, Galilæa*—round Kedesh-Naphtali, in which were situated the twenty towns given by Solomon to Hiram, king of Tyre, as payment for the transportation of timber from Lebanon to Jerusalem (1 Kings ix. 11).

Shechem] was the central city on the west of the Jordan; see above, ch. viii. 30; and ch. xvii. 7; *in Mount Ephraim.* See above, ch. xvii. 15.

8 which *is* Hebron, in the mountain of Judah. And on the *other* side Jordan *by* Jericho eastward, they assigned Bezer in the wilderness upon the plain out of the tribe of Reuben, and Ramoth in Gilead out of the tribe of Gad, and Golan in 9 Bashan out of the tribe of Manasseh. These were the cities appointed for all the children of Israel, and for the stranger that sojourneth among them, that whosoever killeth *any*

Kirjath-arba, which is Hebron] The most southerly of the selected cities on the west; see above, ch. x. 3, xiv. 15.
in the mountain of Judah] On this mountain-district, see above, ch. xi; 21.
8. *Bezer*] was the most southerly of the cities chosen on the east of the Jordan. It was in the same latitude as Jericho.
in the wilderness upon the plain] On or near the upland "downs" of Reuben, probably not far from Heshbon. With the other two cities on the east of Jordan Bezer had been selected by Moses for this purpose at the time of the conquest of Gilead and Bashan (Deut. iv. 43).
Ramoth in Gilead] is called *Ramath-mizpeh* in ch. xiii. 26. This town (=*the heights of Gilead*) was one of the great fortresses on the east of Jordan, and commanded the region of Argob and the towns of Jair (see above, ch. xiii. 26). It is probable also it was the spot where Jacob made his covenant with Laban (Gen. xxxi. 43—53). For subsequent notices of it see (*a*) 1 Kings iv. 13; (*b*) 1 Kings xv. 17—22; (*c*) 2 Kings ix. 14.
Golan in Bashan] was the most northerly city chosen on the east of the Jordan (Deut. iv. 43). Its very site is now unknown, though once a place of great power and influence, which gave its name to a province, *Gaulanitis*, east of Galilee, = the modern *Jaulân*. The district was once densely populated, but is now almost completely deserted.
9. *These were the cities appointed*] "Civitates constitutæ," Vulgate. "The citees ordeyned," Wyclif.
for the stranger that sojourneth] "And to comlyngis that dwellen among hem;" Wyclif. Observe that the Mosaic Law applied its merciful provisions not only to the members of the Elect Nation, as though they were a sacred "caste," but to the "stranger" also that sojourned among them. The existence of such a class of "naturalized foreigners" in Israel is easily accounted for:—
(*a*) The "*mixed multitude*" that came out of Egypt (Exod. xii. 38) formed one element;
(*b*) *The remains of the Canaanites*—never wholly extirpated—formed a second;
(*c*) *Captives taken in war* formed a third;
(*d*) *Fugitives, hired servants, merchants* formed a fourth. The census of these in Solomon's time gave a return of 153,600 males (2 Chron. ii. 17), which was nearly equal to about a tenth of the whole population.

person at unawares might flee thither, and not die by the hand of the avenger of blood, until he stood before the congregation.

1—3. *The Demand of the Levites.*

Then came near the heads of the fathers of the Levites 21 unto Eleazar the priest, and unto Joshua the son of Nun,

that whosoever killeth any person] Jewish commentators tell us how in later times, in order that the asylum offered to the involuntary homicide might be more secure, (*a*) the roads leading to the Cities of Refuge were always kept in thorough repair, and required to be at least 32 cubits broad; (*b*) all obstructions were removed that might stay the flier's foot or hinder his speed; (*c*) no hillock was left, no river was allowed over which there was not a bridge; (*d*) at every turning there were posts erected bearing the words "*Refuge*," "*Refuge*," to guide the unhappy man in his flight; (*e*) when once settled in such a city the manslayer had a convenient habitation assigned to him, and the citizens were to teach him some trade in order that he might support himself.—See Kitto's *Biblical Cyclopædia*, I. p. 527.

CH. XXI. 1—3. THE DEMAND OF THE LEVITES.

1. *Then came near the heads of the fathers of the Levites*] "The princes of the meynees of Leuy," Wyclif. All the descendants of Jacob had now been provided for save the sons of Levi. The dying patriarch had spoken solemnly and sadly of this tribe, as also of that named after his second son (Gen. xlix. 5—7),

" Simeon and Levi are brethren;
Instruments of cruelty are in their habitations......
I will *divide them in Jacob*,
And *scatter them in Israel*."

Like other prophecies and promises of Scripture, his words were destined to be moulded and modified by subsequent events. How they were fulfilled in the history of Simeon we have already seen. But though they were still more literally fulfilled in the case of the children of Levi, "the curse was with them turned into a blessing." Their zeal and fidelity were put to the proof and not found wanting on the occasion of the terrible apostasy at Horeb (Exod. xxxii. 25—29), and although they were still destined to be "divided in Jacob," it was as the successors of the earlier priesthood of the first-born and representatives of the holiness of the people. "As the Tabernacle was the outward and visible sign of the presence among the people of their invisible King, so the Levites were to be, among the other tribes of Israel, as the royal body-guard that waited exclusively on Him" (Num. i. 47—54, iii. 5—13).

unto Eleazar the priest] The duties they had already discharged during the wanderings in the wilderness could not fail to be much

and unto the heads of the fathers of the tribes of the children
2 of Israel; and they spake unto them at Shiloh in the land of
Canaan, saying, The LORD commanded by the hand of
Moses to give us cities to dwell in, with the suburbs thereof
3 for our cattle. And the children of Israel gave unto the
Levites out of their inheritance, at the commandment of the
LORD, these cities and their suburbs.

4—8. General Description of the Levitical Cities.

4 And the lot came out for the families of the Kohathites: and the children of Aaron the priest, *which were* of the Levites, had by lot out of the tribe of Judah, and out of the tribe of Simeon, and out of the tribe of

modified by the settlement in the Promised Land and the establishment of the Tabernacle in a fixed locality. They themselves now needed a fixed abode, and the heads of the tribe, therefore, approached the High Priest and the distributors of the land, and requested that adequate provision might be made for their requirements.

2. *The Lord commanded*] They reminded them of the command of Jehovah respecting themselves, which is found in Num. xxxv., and where directions had been given that 48 cities (Num. xxxv. 6, 7), with outlying suburbs of meadow-land for the pasturage of their flocks and herds, should be assigned them.

3. *And the children of Israel gave*] The successor of Moses did not fail to carry out faithfully the Divine Command, and preparations were made for assigning to them certain cities for their possession.

out of their inheritance] "Distinctness and diffusion" were the great points to be attained in their case, and therefore out of the inheritance of their brethren provision was made for them in such a way that, as during the wanderings they had guarded the Tabernacle of Jehovah, so now they should be "scattered" as widely as possible in Israel, to bear witness that the people still owed allegiance to Him.

4—8. GENERAL DESCRIPTION OF THE LEVITICAL CITIES.

4. *the lot came out*] As in the case of the inheritance of the other tribes, so in the apportioning of their cities to the Levites, recourse was had to the sacred lot. "It had probably been decided beforehand what cities each tribe was to give up, and therefore it only now remained for the lot to determine to which branch of the Levites each city should be given."

the families of the Kohathites] The Levites were divided into three families, (*a*) *the Gershonites*, (*b*) *the Kohathites*, (*c*) *the Merarites*, so named after the three sons of Levi (Gen. xlvi. 11). The family-tree stood as follows:—

Benjamin, thirteen cities. And the rest of the children of 5 Kohath had by lot out of the families of the tribe of Ephraim, and out of the tribe of Dan, and out of the half tribe of Manasseh, ten cities. And the children of Gershon 6 *had* by lot out of the families of the tribe of Issachar, and out of the tribe of Asher, and out of the tribe of Naphtali, and out of the half tribe of Manasseh in Bashan, thirteen cities. The children of Merari by their families *had* out of 7

Levi.

1. Gershon.   2. Kohath.   3. Merari.

1. Amram.   2. Izhar.   3. Hebron.   4. Uzziel.

1. Aaron.   2. Moses.

The Kohathites held the first rank, as being the family to which Aaron belonged, and while the priesthood was confined to the house of Aaron, the posterity of Moses were reckoned as Levites, on an equality with the rest of the descendants of Levi (Num. iii.; 1 Chron. vi. 48, 49). It had been the duty of the Kohathites, during the wanderings, on the removal of the Tabernacle, to bear all the sacred vessels, including the Ark itself, the table of shewbread, the seven-branched candlestick, the altars of incense and of burnt-offering (Num. iii. 31, iv. 6, 9, 15; Deut. xxxi. 25).

and the children of Aaron the priest] As the first lot was drawn by the Kohathites, so again the first of theirs fell to the Aaronites or priests.

out of the tribe of Judah] To the priests of the line of Aaron thirteen cities were assigned out of the tribes of Judah, Simeon, and Benjamin.

5. *And the rest of the children of Kohath*] i.e. those who sprang from Moses, Izhar, Hebron, and Uzziel, and formed the non-priestly portion, shared ten cities in the land of Ephraim, Dan, and half Manasseh west of the Jordan.

6. *And the children of Gershon*] The eldest of the three sons of Levi during the march through the wilderness had been stationed behind the Tabernacle, on the west side (Num. iii. 23). It had been their duty to take charge of the tapestry of the Tabernacle, all its curtains, hangings, and coverings, the pillars of the hangings, and the implements used in connection therewith (Num. iii. 21—26, iv. 22—28).

had by lot] Thirteen cities out of the tribes of Issachar, Asher, Naphtali, and the half-tribe of Manasseh east of the Jordan.

7. *The children of Merari*] The descendants of the third son of Levi, had been stationed during the encampment to the north of the Tabernacle, being placed together with the Gershonites "under the

the tribe of Reuben, and out of the tribe of Gad, and out 8 of the tribe of Zebulun, twelve cities. And the children of Israel gave by lot unto the Levites these cities with their suburbs, as the LORD commanded by the hand of Moses.

9—19. *The Cities of the Descendants of Aaron.*

9 And they gave out of the tribe of the children of Judah, and out of the tribe of the children of Simeon, these cities 10 which are *here* mentioned by name, which the children of Aaron, *being* of the families of the Kohathites, *who were* of the 11 children of Levi, had: for theirs was the first lot. And they gave them the city of Arbah the father of Anak, which *city is* Hebron, in the hill *country* of Judah, with the suburbs 12 thereof round about it. But the fields of the city, and the villages thereof, gave they to Caleb the son of Jephunneh 13 for his possession. Thus they gave to the children of Aaron the priest Hebron with her suburbs, *to be* a city of

hand" of Ithamar "the son of Aaron." They had been entrusted with the heavier portions of the Tabernacle furniture, such as the boards, pillars, and bars, and therefore had been permitted together with the Gershonites to use the oxen and waggons contributed by the congregation, while the Kohathites were only supposed to remove the sacred vessels on their shoulders (Num. vii. 1—9).

had out of the tribe of Reuben] They received twelve cities from the tribes of Reuben, Gad, and Zebulun.

9—19. THE CITIES OF THE DESCENDANTS OF AARON.

9. *And they gave*] We have now first a list of the cities *of the priests* of the line of Aaron.

out of the tribe of the children of Judah] The list now given divides itself into two parts:
 (*a*) The nine cities which the sons of Aaron received in the country of Simeon and Judah (verses 9—16);
 (*b*) The four cities which they received in the country of Benjamin (verses 17—19).
11. *the city of Arbah*] See above, xv. 13.
which city is Hebron] See above, xv. 13.
12. *But the fields of the city*] of Hebron and its villages, i.e. the arable land had been already assigned to Caleb (see above ch. xiv. 13). Whence we may conclude "that the Levites only received as many houses in the cities assigned them, as their numerical strength required, and that it was these which remained in their hands as an inalienable possession." See Keil's *Commentary*.

refuge for the slayer; and Libnah with her suburbs, and 14 Jattir with her suburbs, and Eshtemoa with her suburbs, and 15 Holon with her suburbs, and Debir with her suburbs, and 16 Ain with her suburbs, and Juttah with her suburbs, *and* Beth-shemesh with her suburbs; nine cities out of those two tribes. And out of the tribe of Benjamin, Gibeon with her 17 suburbs, Geba with her suburbs, Anathoth with her suburbs, 18 and Almon with her suburbs; four cities. All the cities of 19 the children of Aaron, the priests, *were* thirteen cities with their suburbs.

20—26. *Cities of the rest of the Kohathites.*

And the families of the children of Kohath, the Levites 20 which remained of the children of Kohath, even they had the cities of their lot out of the tribe of Ephraim. For they 21 gave them Shechem with her suburbs in mount Ephraim, *to be* a city of refuge for the slayer; and Gezer with her suburbs, and Kibzaim with her suburbs, and Beth-horon with her 22 suburbs; four cities. And out of the tribe of Dan, Eltekeh 23

13. *Libnah*] See above ch. x. 29; *Jattir*, see xv. 48; *Eshtemoa*, see xv. 50.
15. *Holon*] See ch. xv. 51; 1 Chron. vi. 58.
Debir] See ch. xv. 15, 49.
16. *Ain*, see xv. 32, xix. 7; *Juttah*, xv. 55; *Beth-shemesh*, xv. 10.
17. *Gibeon*] See ch. ix. 3; *Geba*, xviii. 24.
18. *Anathoth*] lay on or near the great road from the north to Jerusalem. Its modern name is *Anâta*, on a broad ridge 1¼ hours N.N.E. of the Holy City. (*a*) Hither Abiathar was banished by Solomon, after the failure of his attempt to raise Adonijah to the throne (1 Kings ii. 26); (*b*) here Jeremiah the prophet was born (Jer. i. 1, xi. 21—23, xxix. 27, xxxii. 7, 8, 9).
Almon] or *Alemeth*, according to the parallel list in 1 Chron. vi. 60; now '*Almît* or *Almuta*, about a mile N.E. of *Anathoth*.

20—26. CITIES OF THE REST OF THE KOHATHITES.

20. *And the families of the children of Kohath*] i.e. those who were not of the priestly order, received
(*a*) Four cities in *Ephraim*,
(*b*) Four in *Dan*,
(*c*) Two in *Western Manasseh*.
21. *Shechem*] See above xvii. 7, xx. 7; *Gezer*, see x. 33.
22. *Kibzaim* = probably to *Jokmeam* (1 Chron. vi. 68); *Beth-horon*, see ch. x. 10.
23. *Eltekeh*] See ch. xix. 44; *Gibbethon*, ch. xix. 44.

24 with her suburbs, Gibbethon with her suburbs, Aijalon with her suburbs, Gath-rimmon with her suburbs; four cities. 25 And out of the half tribe of Manasseh, Tanach with her suburbs, and Gath-rimmon with her suburbs; two cities. 26 All the cities *were* ten with their suburbs for the families of the children of Kohath that remained.

27—33. *The Cities of the Gershonites.*

27 And unto the children of Gershon, of the families of the Levites, out of the *other* half tribe of Manasseh *they gave* Golan in Bashan with her suburbs, *to be* a city of refuge for the slayer; and Beeshterah with her suburbs; two cities. 28 And out of the tribe of Issachar, Kishon with her suburbs, 29 Dabareh with her suburbs, Jarmuth with her suburbs, En- 30 gannim with her suburbs; four cities. And out of the tribe of Asher, Mishal with her suburbs, Abdon with her suburbs, 31 Helkath with her suburbs, and Rehob with her suburbs; 32 four cities. And out of the tribe of Naphtali, Kedesh in Galilee with her suburbs, *to be* a city of refuge for the slayer; and Hammoth-dor with her suburbs, and Kartan with her 33 suburbs; three cities. All the cities of the Gershonites according to their families *were* thirteen cities with their suburbs.

24. *Aijalon*] See x. 12; *Gath-rimmon*, see xix. 45.
25. *Tanach*] See ch. xii. 21; *Gath-rimmon*, or *Bileam* (1 Chron. vi. 70)=*Ibleam*, see above, ch. xvii. 11.

27—33. THE CITIES OF THE GERSHONITES.

27. *And unto the children of Gershon*] were assigned thirteen cities,
(*a*) Two in *Eastern Manasseh*,
(*b*) Four in *Issachar*,
(*c*) Four in *Asher*,
(*d*) Three in *Naphtali*.
Golan in Bashan] See ch. xx. 8; '*Beesh-terah* or *Beeshterah*, without any division of the syllables. The name is a contraction of *Beth-Ashterah*=*the house of Ashterah*, or *Ashtaroth*, a city of Og; see ch. xii. 4, and 1 Chron. vi. 71.
28. *Kishon*]=the Kishion of ch. xix. 20; *Dabareh*, see xix. 12.
29. *Jarmuth*] Called *Remeth* in Josh. xix. 21; *Ramoth* in 1 Chron. vi. 73; *En-gannim*, see xix. 21.
30. *Mishal*] See ch. xix. 26 (Heb.); *Abdon*=Hebron, xix. 28.
31. *Helkath*] ch. xix. 25; comp. 1 Chron. vi. 75; *Rehob*, xix. 28.
32. *Kedesh in Galilee*] See ch. xix. 37; *Hammoth-dor*, xix. 35; *Kartan*=*Rakkath*, ch. xix. 35, and written Kirjathaim, 1 Chron. vi. 76.

vv. 34—41.] JOSHUA, XXI. 189

34—42. *The Cities of the Merarites.*

And unto the families of the children of Merari, the rest of 34 the Levites, out of the tribe of Zebulun, Jokneam with her suburbs, and Kartah with her suburbs, Dimnah with her sub- 35 urbs, Nahalal with her suburbs; four cities. And out of the 36 tribe of Reuben, Bezer with her suburbs, and Jahazah with her suburbs, Kedemoth with her suburbs, and Mephaath with 37 her suburbs; four cities. And out of the tribe of Gad, Ramoth 38 in Gilead with her suburbs, *to be* a city of refuge for the slayer; and Mahanaim with her suburbs, Heshbon with her suburbs, 39 Jazer with her suburbs; four cities in all. So all the cities 40 for the children of Merari by their families, which were remaining of the families of the Levites, were *by* their lot twelve cities. All the cities of the Levites within the pos- 41

34—42. THE CITIES OF THE MERARITES.

34. *And unto the families of the children of Merari*] were assigned twelve cities, viz.,
  (*a*) Four in *Zebulun*,
  (*b*) Four in *Reuben*,
  (*c*) Four in *Gad*.
Jokneam] See xix. 11; *Kartah* and *Dimnah* unknown.
35. *Nahalal*] See ch. xix. 15 (Heb.).
36. *Bezer*] See ch. xx. 8; *Jahazah*, ch. xiii. 18 (Heb.).
37. *Kedemoth*] xiii. 18; *Mephaath*, see ch. xiii. 18.
38. *Ramoth in Gilead*] See ch. xx. 8; *Mahanaim*, ch. xiii. 26.
39. *Heshbon*] ch. xiii. 17; *Jazer*, see ch. xiii. 25.
41. *All the cities of the Levites...were forty and eight cities*] As will be clear from the following table :—

		TRIBES.	CITIES.
i. **Kohathites**	(*a*) *Priests*	Judah and Simeon	= 9
		Benjamin	= 4
	(*b*) *Not priests*	Ephraim	= 4
		Dan	= 4
		Half Manasseh (West)	= 2
ii. **Gershonites**............		Half Manasseh (East)	= 2
		Issachar	= 4
		Asher	= 4
		Naphtali	= 3
iii. **Merarites**		Zebulun	= 4
		Reuben	= 4
		Gad	= 4

48

session of the children of Israel *were* forty and eight cities
42 with their suburbs. These cities were every one with their
suburbs round about them : thus *were* all these cities.

43—46. *Conclusion.*

43 And the LORD gave unto Israel all the land which he
sware to give unto their fathers; and they possessed it, and
44 dwelt therein. And the LORD gave them rest round about,
according to all that he sware unto their fathers : and there
stood not a man of all their enemies before them; the LORD
45 delivered all their enemies into their hand. There failed

43—46. CONCLUSION.

43. *And*] These verses conclude the history of the division of the land, and connect the two halves of the Book (*a*) chapter i.—xii.; (*b*) chapter xiii.—xxi.

the Lord gave unto Israel] By the distribution of the land amongst the tribes, the promise which Joshua had received after the death of Moses (Josh. i. 2) had been fulfilled, as also that which centuries before he had made to Abraham the ancestor of the Elect Nation (see Gen. xii. 7, xv. 18).

and they possessed it, and dwelt therein] Compare the same expression in ch. xix. 47.

44. *And the Lord gave them rest*] Moreover He gave them rest round about, in accordance with His promise to their forefathers. Comp. (*a*) Exod. xxxiii. 14, "And He said, My presence shall go with thee, and *I will give thee rest.*" (*b*) Deut. iii. 20, "Until the Lord *have given rest* unto your brethren." (*c*) Deut. xxv. 19, "When the Lord thy God hath *given thee rest* from all thine enemies round about, in the land which the Lord thy God giveth thee for an inheritance."

there stood not a man] "Noone of the Enemyes is hardi to withstoond hem," Wyclif. For even though the Canaanites were not all exterminated, yet those who remained did not venture upon an attack on the Israelites so long as they remained loyal and steadfast to their invisible King, and as long as Joshua and his contemporaries lived. "It was no part of the Divine purpose that the native population should be annihilated suddenly (Exod. xxiii. 29; Deut. vii. 22); but they were delivered into the hand of Israel, and their complete dispossession could have been effected at any time by the Divine aid which was never wanting when sought."

the Lord delivered all their enemies] See above ch. ii. 24. Hence, though Israel after the death of Joshua became slothful in the work, and never obtained complete possession of the land, never, e.g. conquered Tyre and Sidon, still this was no breach of the Divine promise, for its *complete* fulfilment depended upon Israel's fidelity.

not ought of any good thing which the LORD had spoken unto the house of Israel; all came to pass.

1—8. *Joshua's Farewell Address to the two Tribes and a Half.*

Then Joshua called the Reubenites, and the Gadites, 22 and the half tribe of Manasseh, and said unto them, Ye 2 have kept all that Moses the servant of the LORD commanded you, and have obeyed my voice in all that I commanded you: ye have not left your brethren these many 3 days unto this day, but have kept the charge of the commandment of the LORD your God. And now the LORD 4 your God hath given rest unto your brethren, as he promised them: therefore now return ye, and get ye unto your tents, *and* unto the land of your possession, which Moses the ser-

45. *There failed not*] Comp. ch. xxiii. 14, 15. None of the gracious promises of God to Israel remained unfulfilled.

any good thing] Or, **aught of all the good word**=the sum of the reiterated assurances which God had made to the nation. Of these the possession of the land of Canaan was regarded as the essence and central point, because this possession was to be for Israel the foundation of all further blessings, the pledge of the continued fulfilment of the rest of the promises of God.—See Keil's *Commentary.*

CH. XXII. 1—8. JOSHUA'S FAREWELL ADDRESS TO THE TWO TRIBES AND A HALF.

1. *Then Joshua*] The author of the section from chapters xiii.—xxi. having given his account, marked with truth and accuracy, of the division of the land, the appointment of the Cities of Refuge and the Levitical cities, describes in the three following chapters, which close the book, (*a*) the release of the two tribes and a half to their homes beyond the Jordan; (*b*) their return, and erection of an altar on the Jordan; (*c*) the embassy from Israel on account of this altar; (*d*) the apology of the eastern tribes and return of the embassy; (*e*) Joshua's last discourses to the people; (*f*) his death; and (*g*) the death of Eleazar.

called the Reubenites] This took place not immediately after the close of the war, but after the completion of the division of the land and the appointment of the Levitical cities, in which the Trans-Jordanic tribes had as much interest as the other tribes.

2. *all that Moses*] See (*a*) Num. xxxii. 20—22; (*b*) Deut. iii. 18—20; (*c*) Josh. i. 12—17.

3. *the charge of the commandment*] They had kept their obligations to Moses, to Joshua, and to Jehovah.

4. *hath given rest*] Comp. ch. xxi. 44, xxiii. 1.
which Moses] See ch. xiii. 8.

5 vant of the LORD gave you on the *other* side Jordan. But take diligent heed to do the commandment and the law, which Moses the servant of the LORD charged you, to love the LORD your God, and to walk in all his ways, and to keep his commandments, and to cleave unto him, and to 6 serve him with all your heart and with all your soul. So Joshua blessed them, and sent them away: and they went 7 unto their tents. Now to the *one* half of the tribe of Manasseh Moses had given *possession* in Bashan: but unto the *other* half thereof gave Joshua among their brethren on *this* side Jordan westward. And when Joshua sent them away also 8 unto their tents, then he blessed them, and he spake unto them, saying, Return with much riches unto your tents, and with very much cattle, with silver, and with gold, and with brass, and with iron, and with very much raiment: divide the spoil of your enemies with your brethren.

9, 10. *Return of the Tribes. Erection of an Altar on the Jordan.*

9 And the children of Reuben and the children of Gad and the half tribe of Manasseh returned, and departed from the children of Israel out of Shiloh, which *is* in the land of Canaan, to go unto the country of Gilead, to the land of their

5. *But take diligent heed*] "Se onli that ȝe kepen attentifly." Wyclif. In their natural isolation in their eastern homes from their brethren of the west, it was above all things necessary that they should remember Him from whom their success and prosperity had proceeded. Comp. the counsels of Moses, Deut. vi. 6, 17, xi. 22.

6. *So Joshua blessed them*] Comp. (*a*) the blessing of the workers of the Tabernacle (Exod. xxxix. 43), and (*b*) the blessing of Caleb by Joshua (Josh. xiv. 13).

7. *Now to the one half*] The repetition here of what has been already described more fully (Josh. xvii. 5, &c.), may seem to us superfluous. But "it agrees with the fulness, abundant in repetitions, of the ancient Hebrew style of narrative." Keil. "A modern author will refer his readers to what he has stated elsewhere. The Jewish historian scarcely ever quotes or reminds, but repeats so much as may be necessary to make his account of the transaction in hand fully intelligible by itself." The Speaker's *Commentary, in loc.*

8. *with your brethren*] i.e. with the members of the tribes who had remained on the east side of the Jordan, to whom, according to Num. xxxi. 27, one half belonged.

possession, whereof they were possessed, according to the word of the LORD by the hand of Moses. And when they came unto the borders of Jordan, that *are* in the land of Canaan, the children of Reuben and the children of Gad and the half tribe of Manasseh built there an altar by Jordan, a great altar to see to. ·

9, 10. RETURN OF THE TRIBES. ERECTION OF AN ALTAR ON THE JORDAN.

9. *out of Shiloh*] where the division of the land had been carried out. See Josh. xviii. 1.

which is in the land of Canaan] Only the country west of the Jordan is regarded as the *Land of Canaan*. That on the east of the river is simply called here *Gilead* (comp. Num. xxxii. 1, 28, 29), although it embraced Gilead and Bashan, the kingdoms of Sihon and Og.

10. *unto the borders of Jordan*] More literally, **the circles of the Jordan**. Comp. Josh. xiii. 2, "the borders (or *circles*) of the Philistines;" Joel iii. 4, "all the coasts (or *circles*) or Palestine;" Matt. iii. 5; "the region *round about* Jordan." The region indicated is a portion of what is now called the *Ghor* of the Jordan, the low tract or plain along the river, through which it flows. Wyclif renders it, "whanne thei weren comen to the mynde hyllis of Jordan."

that are in the land of Canaan] That is on the west side of "the Ghor." They desired to anticipate any assertion that the Jordan constituted in itself a barrier between them and their western brethren and the Sanctuary of God at Shiloh.

a great altar to see to] i. e. **an altar great to behold**; so high and wide that it would be seen from a great distance. "An auter of mychilnes with out mesure," Wyclif. The site of this interesting memorial has been lately discovered by the officers of the Survey of Palestine. It is an almost inaccessible mountain, except from the north, where the ascent is called *Tal'at abn 'Ayd* = "the going up to Ed." It projects like a white bastion towards the river, some twenty miles north of Jericho, and close to the line of march from Shiloh to Gilead, and on its summit are the remains of a huge monument of masonry, bearing traces of fire on its upper surface. It is mentioned in the Jewish Talmud under the name of *Surtabeh*, and is said to have been a beacon station.

Mentioned only once in the Bible, this altar, erected by the two and a half tribes on their return from Western Palestine as a "witness" that they too were co-heirs with their brethren on the other side of the river, had dropped entirely out of all hope of recovery. The place has now been found by Lieut. Conder, its name still existing, on the high peak known as Kurn Surtabeh, in the valley of the Jordan. Independently of the special interest attaching to the spot, this recovery illustrates remarkably the vitality of the old Biblical names. (*Quarterly Statement*, 1874, p. 241.)

to see to] = to behold. "Faire to *see to*, goodlie to behold." AJ

11—20. *Embassy from Israel to the Two and a Half Tribes.*

11 And the children of Israel heard say, Behold, the children of Reuben and the children of Gad and the half tribe of Manasseh have built an altar over against the land of Canaan, in the borders of Jordan, at the passage of the chil-
12 dren of Israel. And when the children of Israel heard *of it*, the whole congregation of the children of Israel gathered themselves together *at* Shiloh, to go up to war against them.
13 And the children of Israel sent unto the children of Reuben,

aspectum præclarus. Baret, *Alvearie*, s. v: "If such rank corne be once cut down with the syth...certain it is that the grain in the ear will be longer to *see to*, howbeit void and without any floure within it." Holland's *Pliny*, XVIII. 17; *Bible Word-Book*, p. 425;

"Care and utmost shifts,
How to secure the lady from surprisal,
Brought to my mind a certain shepherd lad
Of small regard to *see to*." Milton's *Comus*, 618.

11—20. EMBASSY FROM ISRAEL TO THE TWO AND A HALF TRIBES.

11. *heard*] News of the step taken by the trans-Jordanic tribes so suddenly and without any consultation, reached the ears of their brethren, and gave rise to "great searchings of heart."
in the borders] i.e. *the circles of Jordan*, as in verse 10.
at the passage of the children of Israel] More literally, **by the side of the sons of Israel**. Comp. Exod. xxv. 37, xxxii. 15.
12. *gathered themselves together*] The act of their trans-Jordanic brethren, done without any authority of the High Priest, appeared at first sight to be a direct infringement of the express commands against another altar and other worship (Lev. xvii. 8, 9; Deut. xii. 5—7, xiii. 12—18). It was open to the suspicion that they meant, if not to adopt another worship, at least to set up another and an independent establishment for worship, which, besides the obvious tendency to idolatry, could not fail in the event to destroy the connection by which the tribes were linked together. "The obligation of all the Israelites to resort three times in the year for worship to the sole altar of the people, was admirably suited to retain them as one people by continually keeping before their minds their common origin and common obligations; but if a separate establishment were allowed to exist there could be no difficulty in divining that they would cease to put themselves to the trouble of visiting the parent establishment in Canaan, and would, in no long time, come to regard themselves, with a country so congenial to their pastoral character and a geographical separation so complete, as a distinct people."

and to the children of Gad, and to the half tribe of Manasseh, into the land of Gilead, Phinehas the son of Eleazar the priest, and with him ten princes, of each chief house a prince 14 throughout all the tribes of Israel; and each one *was* a head of the house of their fathers among the thousands of Israel. And they came unto the children of Reuben, and to the 15 children of Gad, and to the half tribe of Manasseh, unto the land of Gilead, and they spake with them, saying, Thus 16 saith the whole congregation of the LORD, What trespass *is* this that ye have committed against the God of Israel, to turn away *this* day from following the LORD, in that ye have builded you an altar, that ye might rebel *this* day against

13. *And the children of Israel sent*] The holy jealousy which inspired them did not induce them to proceed hastily, or without proper enquiry. They resolved to send a deputation to ascertain the meaning of what had been done.

Phinehas] In Hebrew *Pinchas*, in the Apocryphal Books *Phinees*, was the son of Eleazar and grandson of Aaron (Exod. vi. 25). While yet a youth he had been memorable for his zeal and energy at the critical moment of the sin of Peor at Shittim, and appeased the Divine wrath and put a stop to the plague which was destroying the nation (Num. xxv. 7). For this he received the special approbation of Jehovah, and the promise that the priesthood should remain in his family for ever (Num. xxv. 10—13). This seems to have raised him to a very high position in the nation, and he figures rather than his father as the leading member of the hierarchy;—(*a*) In the conflict with Midian (Num. xxxi. 6), (*b*) in this dispute with the Reubenites, (*c*) in the war with the Benjamites (Judg. xx. 28) he is the chief oracle and adviser. The memory of the zealous priest was very dear to the Jews. He is specially commemorated in one of the Psalms (cvi. 30, 31), and the priests who returned from the captivity are enrolled in the official lists as the sons of Phinehas (Ezra viii. 2; 1 Esdr. v. 5). In his Egyptian name he bore the last trace of the sojourn of the nation in "the land of Ham." His tomb, a place of great resort to Jews and Samaritans, is shewn at *Awertah*, 4 miles south-east of *Nablus*.

14. *ten princes*] Representing the nine and a half tribes west of the Jordan.

head of the house] Each of them was **prince of a fathers' house among the thousands of Israel.** Comp. Judg. vi. 15; 1 Sam. x. 19, 21. "They were thus persons of great weight of character and approved discretion, entitled by their position to demand an explanation, and less likely than younger men to have their judgments warped or compromised by the hasty impulses of passion."

16. *that ye might rebel*] See Num. xiv. 9; Lev. xvii. 8, 9; Deut. xii. 13, 14.

17 the LORD? *Is* the iniquity of Peor *too* little for us, from which we are not cleansed until this day, although there was 18 a plague in the congregation of the LORD, but that ye must turn away *this* day from following the LORD? and it will be, *seeing* ye rebel to day against the LORD, that to morrow he 19 will be wroth with the whole congregation of Israel. Notwithstanding, if the land of your possession *be* unclean, *then* pass ye over unto the land of the possession of the LORD, wherein the LORD's tabernacle dwelleth, and take possession among us: but rebel not against the LORD, nor rebel against us, in building you an altar beside the altar of the LORD 20 our God. Did not Achan the son of Zerah commit a trespass in the accursed thing, and wrath fell on all the congregation of Israel? and that man perished not alone in his iniquity.

21—31. *Defence of the Two Tribes and a Half.*

21 Then the children of Reuben and the children of Gad and the half tribe of Manasseh answered, and said unto the 22 heads of the thousands of Israel, The LORD God of gods,

17. *the iniquity of Peor*] i.e. of Baal Peor. In four passages Peor occurs as a contraction for Baal Peor, (*a*) Num. xxv. 18, twice; (*b*) xxxi. 16; and (*c*) in this place. He makes allusion to the apostasy in the staying of which he himself had borne so memorable a part, and many have suspected that there were still some amongst them who were hankering after the licentious orgies of Baal worship. We shall find Joshua himself alluding to the same propensity (Josh. xxiv. 14—23).

although there was a plague] Of which upwards of 24,000 of the people died.

19. *if the land of your possession be unclean*] i.e. without an altar to the Lord, and in the midst of many heathen dwelling amongst them.

the land of the possession of the Lord] the land of your possession. Observe the antithesis.

20. *Did not Achan*] Phinehas finally reminds the tribe of the recent crime of Achan (Josh. vii. 1 ff.) which had involved in its consequences not only the man himself, but his children, and the entire people (Josh. vii. 1—5).

21—31. DEFENCE OF THE TWO TRIBES AND A HALF.

21. *Then the children of Reuben*] The two tribes and a half proceed to defend themselves and to shew that their object was in all respects the very reverse of that imputed to them.

22. *The Lord God of gods*] Rather, **The Lord, the God of gods**; or, the three names may be taken separately, cf. Ps. l. 1. They commence

the LORD God of gods, he knoweth, and Israel he shall know; if *it be* in rebellion, or if in transgression against the LORD, (save us not this day,) that we have built us an altar 23 to turn from following the LORD; or if to offer thereon burnt offering or meat offering, or if to offer peace offerings thereon, let the LORD himself require *it;* and if we have not 24 *rather* done it for fear of *this* thing, saying, In time to come your children might speak unto our children, saying, What have you to do with the LORD God of Israel? For the LORD 25 hath made Jordan a border between us and you, ye children of Reuben and children of Gad; ye have no part in the LORD: so shall your children make our children cease from fearing the LORD: therefore we said, Let us now prepare to 26

in the most solemn manner by invoking God Himself to witness as to the innocence of their intentions. The form in which they do this is the most emphatic that language can express. There are three principal names of God in Hebrew,—El, Elohim, Jehovah. Here all the three are used together and repeated twice to mark the earnestness of their protestation. "El, Elohim, Jehovah—El, Elohim, Jehovah." "The moost strong Lord God of Israel," Wyclif. He knoweth. The verse is "invested with a mournful interest, for it is that on which Welsh, the minister of the army of the Covenanters, preached before the battle of Bothwell Bridge." Stanley's *Lectures*, I. 221.

if it be] The particle rendered "if" is here used as the formula of an oath. The apodosis follows at the close of ver. 23, "*let the Lord Himself require it.*"

save us not this day] "If bi inwit of trespassynge this auter we han maad vp, keep he vs not, but punyshe now," Wyclif. This is an imprecation addressed immediately to God. "A parenthetic clause in which the excited feeling passionately invoking evil upon itself passes into the appeal to the Most High." Comp. Deut. x. 17; Job x. 7, xxiii. 10. The words are almost equivalent to our form "So help me God."

23. *require it*] Comp. Deut. xviii. 19, "And it shall come to pass, that whosoever will not hearken unto my words which he shall speak in my name, I will *require it of him;*" 1 Sam. xx. 16, "So Jonathan made a covenant with the house of David, saying, Let the Lord even *require it* at the hand of David's enemies."

24. *and if we have not*] More literally, **and if not rather from anxiety, for a reason we have done this thing.** The word rendered "fear" is translated "care" in Ezek. iv. 16; "carefulness" Ezek. xii. 18, 19.

25. *ye children of Reuben and children of Gad*] The half tribe is omitted here, and again in verses 33, 34. Perhaps for the sake of brevity.

26. *Let us now prepare to build*] "Exstruamus nobis altare," Vulgate. "Make we out to vs an auter," Wyclif.

build us an altar, not for burnt offering, nor for sacrifice:
27 but *that* it *may be* a witness between us, and you, and our generations after us, that *we* might do the service of the LORD before him with our burnt offerings, and with our sacrifices, and with our peace offerings; that your children may not say to our children in time to come, Ye have no
28 part in the LORD. Therefore said we, that it shall be, when they should *so* say to us or to our generations in time to come, that we may say *again*, Behold the pattern of the altar of the LORD, which our fathers made, not for burnt offerings, nor for sacrifices; but it *is* a witness between us
29 and you. God forbid that we should rebel against the LORD, and turn *this* day from following the LORD, to build an altar for burnt offerings, for meat offerings, or for sacrifices, besides the altar of the LORD our God that *is* before his tabernacle.
30 And when Phinehas the priest, and the princes of the congregation and heads of the thousands of Israel which *were* with him, heard the words that the children of Reuben and the children of Gad and the children of Manasseh
31 spake, it pleased them. And Phinehas the son of Eleazar

27. *be a witness*] Instead of meaning a separation, they had set up their altar as a monument to future ages of the connection between the tribes divided by the river, so that if, at any time to come, their descendants should attempt to cast off the connection and assert their own independence, or if the Israelites should hereafter attempt to disown their union, and declare that the people beyond the river "had no part in the Lord," this monument might be pointed to in evidence of the fact. Observe the calmness maintained by the accused tribes. There is no syllable of reproach or recrimination in their vindication of themselves.

28. *Behold the pattern*] Some have imagined that the altar set up had an actual resemblance to the altar of burnt-offering at the Tabernacle. But this could hardly be. There may have been some general resemblance in their structure, which was of earth heaped up and huge stones.

it is a witness between us and you] Comp. Josh. iv. 6, 7 ; and Gen. xxxi. 48.

29. *God forbid*] Literally, **Far be it from us.** LXX. μὴ γένοιτο. Wyclif translates it, "God shilde fro vs this hidous gilt." The speakers express in the strongest manner their abhorrence of the idea of forsaking Jehovah.

30. *it pleased them*] Or, **it was good in their eyes.** Comp. Gen.

the priest said unto the children of Reuben, and to the children of Gad, and to the children of Manasseh, *This* day we perceive that the LORD *is* among us, because ye have not committed this trespass against the LORD: now ye have delivered the children of Israel out of the hand of the LORD.

32—34. *Return of the Embassy.*

And Phinehas the son of Eleazar the priest, and the princes, 32 returned from the children of Reuben, and from the children of Gad, out of the land of Gilead, unto the land of Canaan, to the children of Israel, and brought them word again. And the thing pleased the children of Israel; and the chil- 33 dren of Israel blessed God, and did not intend to go up against them in battle, to destroy the land wherein the children of Reuben and Gad dwelt. And the children of 34 Reuben and the children of Gad called the altar *Ed:* for it *shall be* a witness between us that the LORD *is* God.

xxxiv. 18, "And their words *pleased* Hamor, and Shechem Hamor's son;" xli. 37, "And the thing was *good in the eyes of* Pharaoh;" xlv. 16, "And it *pleased* Pharaoh well, and his servants" (where see Margin); and see 2 Sam. iii. 36; 1 Kings iii. 10.

31. *is among us*] Phinehas recognises the presence of God in the congregation, because His Providence had restrained their brethren from even the semblance of idolatry.

out of the hand of the Lord] As otherwise a punishment like that in Num. xxv. 9 might have again fallen on the whole people.

32—34. RETURN OF THE EMBASSY.

33. *blessed God*] Compare 1 Chron. xxix. 20, "And David said to all the congregation, Now *bless* the Lord your God. And all the congregation *blessed* the Lord God of their fathers;" Neh. viii. 6, "And Ezra *blessed* the Lord, the great God;" Dan. ii. 19, "Then Daniel *blessed* the God of heaven;" Luke ii. 28, "Then took he Him up in his arms, and *blessed* God, and said."

did not intend] i.e. did not carry out their intention of going up to war against them, as they first thought of doing when "they gathered themselves together at Shiloh;" see above *v.* 12.

34. *called the altar Ed*] The word *Ed* is not found after altar in the Hebrew, nor is it represented in the LXX. or Vulgate, nor are the words in the next clause, "shall be," in the original. The words indicate the title which was placed upon the altar, "a witness between us that the Lord is God." Wyclif renders the verse, "And the sones of Ruben and the sones of Gad clepen the auter, that thei hadden maad, *Oure Witnessynge, that the Lord he be God.*"

1—16. *Joshua's first Farewell Addrsss.*

23 And it came to pass a long time after that the LORD had given rest unto Israel from all their enemies round about, 2 that Joshua waxed old *and* stricken in age. And Joshua called for all Israel, *and* for their elders, and for their heads, and for their judges, and for their officers, and said unto 3 them, I am old *and* stricken in age: and ye have seen all that the LORD your God hath done unto all these nations because of you; for the LORD your God *is* he that hath 4 fought for you. Behold, I have divided unto you *by lot* these nations that remain, to be an inheritance for your tribes, from Jordan, with all the nations that I have cut off, 5 even *unto* the great sea westward. And the LORD your God, he shall expel them from before you, and drive them from out of your sight; and ye shall possess their land, as the 6 LORD your God hath promised unto you. Be ye therefore very courageous to keep and to do all that is written in the book of the law of Moses, that *ye* turn not aside therefrom 7 *to* the right hand or *to* the left; that *ye* come not among these nations, these that remain amongst you; neither make

CH. XXIII. 1—16. JOSHUA'S FIRST FAREWELL ADDRESS.

1. *had given rest*] Comp. Josh. xxi. 43, 44, xxii. 3, 4.
waxed old] Comp. Josh. xiii. 1, "Now Joshua was old and stricken in years."
stricken in age] Heb. *come into days;* "of ful eld age," Wyclif.
2. *called for all Israel*] Where we are not told. But perhaps at Timnath-serah (Josh. xix. 50), or possibly at Shiloh. On the occasion of his second farewell discourse the tribes were convened at Shechem (Josh. xxiv. 1).
and for their elders] The word *"and"* is not found in the Hebrew. If any word is to be supplied, it should be "even" or "namely". The terms *elders, heads, judges and officers* are explanatory.
I am old] He begins by reminding them of his own advance in years.
3. *the Lord your God is he*] See Exod. xiv. 14. Of his own merits and exploits the modest hero makes no mention.
4. *these nations that remain*] Joshua reminds them that not only the nations who had been actually conquered, but the remnants still unsubdued, were delivered into their power.
6. *Be ye therefore very courageous*] Joshua exhorts them to bravery and constancy in the same terms as he had been exhorted himself. See above, i. 7.
7. *That ye come not among these nations*] He especially warns them

mention of the name of their gods, nor cause to swear *by them*, neither serve them, nor bow yourselves unto them. But cleave unto the LORD your God, as ye have done unto 8 this day. For the LORD hath driven out from before you 9 great nations and strong : but *as for* you, no man hath *been able to* stand before you unto this day. One man of you 10 shall chase a thousand: for the LORD your God, he *it is* that fighteth for you, as he hath promised you. Take good heed 11 therefore unto yourselves, that ye love the LORD your God. Else if ye do in any wise go back, and cleave unto 12 the remnant of these nations, *even* these that remain among you, and shall make marriages with them, and go in unto them, and they to you : know for a certainty that the LORD 13 your God will no more drive out *any of* these nations from before you; but they shall be snares and traps unto you, and scourges in your sides, and thorns in your eyes, until ye

against all intercourse with the heathen nations, and, above all, against any participation in their idolatries.

make mention of the name of their gods] "To make mention of the names of the gods (Exod. xxiii. 13), to swear by them, to serve them with offerings, and to bow down to them, i.e. call upon them in prayer, represent the four expressions of divine worship." See Deut. vi. 13, x. 20.

9. *For the Lord*] He again reminds them of the true Source of their strength, and to Whom they were indebted for their late victories.

10. *One man of you*] Comp. Lev. xxvi. 8; Judg. iii. 31, xv. 15; 2 Sam. xxiii. 8.

12. *if ye do*] "If ye do in any wise turn back, and cleave to the remnant of these nations, these that remain with you, and make marriages with them, and ye come among them, and they among you, know for a certainty that the protection of the Almighty will fail you, and His arm will no more give you success against them."

13. *snares*] The word thus rendered denotes (i) a net, trap-net, especially of a fowler; (ii) a snare such as seizes and holds beasts or men by the feet. Comp. Job xviii. 9, "the gin shall take him by the heel;" Jer. xviii. 22, "they have...hid *snares* for my feet." The form of this trap-net appears from the passages Amos iii. 5, and Ps. lxix. 22. It was in two parts, which, when set, were spread out upon the ground and slightly fastened with a stick, so that as soon as a bird or beast touched the stick, the parts flew up and enclosed the bird in the net, or caught the foot of the animal.

thorns in your eyes] The warnings of Joshua are severer even than those of Moses (Num. xxxiii. 55), "nowe thanne wite 3e that the Lord 3oure God do hem not awey before 3oure face, but to 3ow thei shulen be into a diche, and greene, and hurtynge of 3oure side and a *staak in 3oure eyen*, to the tyme that he doo 3ou a wey," Wyclif.

perish from off this good land which the LORD your God
14 hath given you. And behold, *this* day I am going the way
of all the earth: and ye know in all your hearts and in all
souls, that not one thing hath failed of all the good things
which the LORD your God spake concerning you; all are
come to pass unto you, *and* not one thing hath failed
15 thereof. Therefore it shall come to pass, *that* as all good
things are come upon you, which the LORD your God
promised you; so shall the LORD bring upon you all evil
things, until he have destroyed you from off this good land
16 which the LORD your God hath given you. When ye have
transgressed the covenant of the LORD your God, which he
commanded you, and have gone and served other gods, and
bowed yourselves to them; then shall the anger of the LORD
be kindled against you, and ye shall perish quickly from off
the good land which he hath given unto you.

1—15. *The Second Parting Address.*

24 And Joshua gathered all the tribes of Israel to Shechem,

14. *I am going the way of all the earth*] i.e. on the way to death, which a man goes and returns not; the way which all the earth, the whole world, must take, "into the land of darkness and the shadow of death." Comp. Job x. 21; and 1 Kings ii. 2, where the words are used by David in his last address to Solomon.

15. *it shall come to pass*] He reiterates his solemn warning against backsliding, and recalls to their minds the promises and threats contained in the last address of Moses to the people.

all evil things] "whateuer thing of yuelis he manaasside;" Wyclif. Comp. Lev. xxvi. 14—39; Deut. xxviii. 15—68, xxix. 14—28, xxx. 1—15. The sublimity of the denunciations of the Hebrew lawgiver contained in these passages "surpasses anything in the oratory or the poetry of the whole world. Nature is exhausted in furnishing terrific images; nothing, excepting the real horrors of the Jewish history—the miseries of their sieges, the cruelty, the contempt, the oppressions, the persecutions, which, for ages, this scattered and despised and detested nation have endured—can approach the tremendous maledictions which warned them against the violation of their Law." Milman's *History of the Jews*, I. 211.

16. *ye shall perish*] The latter part of this 16th verse occurs word for word in Deut. xi. 17.

CH. XXIV. 1—15. THE SECOND PARTING ADDRESS.

1. *And Joshua gathered all the tribes of Israel*] that they might listen to his last charge, and be bound by his parting words to an ever-

JOSHUA, XXIV.

and called for the elders of Israel, and for their heads, and for their judges, and for their officers; and they presented themselves before God. And Joshua said unto all the people, 2 Thus saith the LORD God of Israel, Your fathers dwelt on the *other* side of the flood in old time, *even* Terah, the father

lasting covenant of faithfulness to the God who had done such great things for them. The former charge had been made to the rulers only and the chiefs, this was addressed to the whole nation. Not that the whole nation was present, but that all the tribes sent representatives to the great and solemn gathering.

to Shechem] The LXX. here has Shiloh, but all other versions and the MSS. read *Shechem*. No spot could have been more appropriate:—

(*a*) Here Abraham, "the solitary, childless patriarch, who had listened to the voice that spake at Ur of the Chaldees," received the first recorded promise of the goodly land (Gen. xii. 6, 7), and here he built his first altar to the Lord;

(*b*) Here Jacob had settled after his long sojourn in Mesopotamia, and purified his household from the remains of idolatry by burying their Teraphim under an oak (Gen. xxxiii. 18—20, xxxv. 2, 4);

(*c*) Here the bones of Joseph were laid (Josh. xxiv. 32; Acts vii. 16);

(*d*) Here, from the heights of Ebal and Gerizim, the blessings and curses of the Law had been solemnly enunciated, and the nation had already bound itself by a covenant to Jehovah (Josh. viii. 30—35).

and they presented themselves before God] We saw in Josh. viii. 31 that the Hebrew Leader raised an altar on Mount 'Ebal "of whole stones," where sacrifices were offered before the building of the Tabernacle. Shechem was thus truly a "sanctuary of the Lord" (Josh. xxiv. 26), and those now assembled there were gathered "before God;" comp. Job i. 6, ii. 1, or, as it is in the Hebrew, with the article, "the God," the only true and living *Elohim*. "How grand a gathering it was! There stood the victor in a hundred battles, now 'old and stricken in age;' for it was already 'a long time after that the Lord had given rest unto Israel from all their enemies.' Before him was gathered all Israel, 'their elders, their heads, their judges, and their officers,' and he opened that mouth from which such words of might, and trust, and prayer had issued in the days of their troubles, and he spake to them what all felt to be his last counsels and commandments." Bishop Wilberforce's *Heroes of Hebrew History*, p. 132.

2. *Thus saith the Lord God of Israel*] The title is significant. It recurs in verse 23. Joshua recalls to the minds of the people the mercies of God as displayed in five great events:—

(i) The Call of Abraham;
(ii) The Deliverance from Egypt;
(iii) The Defeat of the Amorites on the east of the Jordan, and the frustration of the machinations of Balaam;
(iv) The Passage of the Jordan and Capture of Jericho;
(v) The Victories over all the nations of Canaan.

on the other side of the flood] Or better, **on the other side of the**

of Abraham, and the father of Nachor: and they served
3 other gods. And I took your father Abraham from the
other side of the flood, and led him throughout all the land
of Canaan, and multiplied his seed, and gave him Isaac.
4 And I gave unto Isaac Jacob and Esau: and I gave unto

river, i.e. the Euphrates, in Ur of the Chaldees, and then in Haran (Gen. xi. 28, 31). "Biȝond the flood," Wyclif.

Terah] The ancestor, through Abram, Nahor, and Haran, of the great families of the Ishmaelites, Israelites, Midianites, Moabites, and Ammonites (Gen. xi. 24—32). With his son Abram, his daughter-in-law Sarai, and his grandson Lot, he went in a north-westerly direction from Ur "into the land of Canaan; and they came unto Haran, and dwelt there" (Gen. xi. 31), and at Haran he died at the age of 205 years (Gen. xi. 32).

and they served other gods] The objects of nature, especially the heavenly bodies, were in those far-back times invested with a "glory" and a "freshness" which has long since "passed away" from the earth. They seemed to be instinct with a divinity which exercised an almost irresistible fascination over their first beholders. The sight of the "sun when it shined, and of the moon walking in brightness," was a temptation as potent to them as to us it is inconceivable. "Their heart was secretly enticed, and their mouth kissed their hand" (Job xxxi. 26, 27). There was also another form of idolatry, though less universal in its influence. "There were giants on the earth in those days;" giants, if not actually, yet by their colossal strength and awful majesty; the Pharaohs and Nimrods, whose form we still trace on the ornaments of Egypt and Assyria in their gigantic proportions, the mighty hunters, the royal priests, the deified men. From the control of these powers, before which all meaner men bowed down, from the long ancestral prepossessions of 'country and kindred and father's house,' the first worshippers of One who was above all alike, had painfully to disentangle themselves." Stanley's *Jewish Church*, I. 15, 16. Of the worship of "images," or "Teraphim," we have traces in Gen. xxxi. 19, 30, 34. Tradition asserts that Terah was a maker of idols, and that Abraham was persecuted in Ur of the Chaldees for refusing to take part in idolatries.

3. *And I took*] Joshua says nothing more of the life of Abraham than that Jehovah caused him to wander through the Land of Canaan, and finally gave him a son Isaac.

and gave him Isaac] Which means "*Laughter*," as one "born out of due time," when Hope might have ceased to hope, and all fulfilment of the Promise seemed impossible. It was either at Gerar or Beersheba that Sarah gave birth to him (Gen. xxi. 2).

4. *And I gave unto Isaac Jacob*] After he too and Rebekah had been childless upwards of nineteen years.

Jacob]=*he that holds by the heel*, or *supplanter* (Gen. xxv. 26).

Esau]=*hairy, rough;* whose robust frame and rough aspect were the type of a wild and daring nature.

Esau mount Seir, to possess it; but Jacob and his children went down *into* Egypt. I sent Moses also and Aaron, and I 5 plagued Egypt, according to *that* which I did amongst them: and afterward I brought you out. And I brought your 6 fathers out of Egypt: and you came unto the sea; and the Egyptians pursued after your fathers with chariots and horsemen *unto* the Red sea. And when they cried unto the 7 LORD, he put darkness between you and the Egyptians, and

mount Seir] = "*rough*," or "*rugged*," extended along the east side of the valley of Arabah, from the Dead Sea to the Elamitic Gulf. The name may either have been derived from Seir the Horite, who appears to have been the chief of the aboriginal inhabitants (Gen. xxxvi. 20), or, what is perhaps more probable, from the rough aspect of the whole country. These Horites, the excavators of those singular rock-dwellings found in such numbers in the ravines and cliffs around Petra, were dispossessed by the descendants of Esau (Deut. ii. 12, 22), they were divided into tribes under a sheikh, or "duke" (Gen. xxxvi. 20—30).

but Jacob] who alone was to have Canaan for himself and his posterity, "went down into Egypt," as is related in Gen. xlv. 1—28, xlvi. 6; Acts vii. 15.

5. *I sent Moses also and Aaron*] Comp. Exod. iii. 10. This is the second proof of the Divine favour, *the deliverance of Israel out of Egypt*. The chief incidents of this great event are succinctly alluded to; (1) the mission of Moses and Aaron; (2) the infliction of the plagues upon Egypt; (3) the destruction of the Egyptians in the Red Sea.

I plagued Egypt] See Exod. vii.—xii. "Y smoot Egipt with many signes and wondris," Wyclif. (1) The turning the water into blood; (2) frogs; (3) lice, or gnats; (4) flies; (5) murrain; (6) boils and blains; (7) thunder, lightning, and hail; (8) locusts; (9) darkness; (10) slaying of the firstborn.

6. *And I brought your fathers*] Comp. Exod. xii. 37—42; 51.

and the Egyptians pursued after your fathers] Astonished that they had not made good their flight into Asia, and deeming them entangled in the land and shut in by the wilderness, the Egyptian monarch directed all his forces, his horses and his chariots, to give chase to the fugitives (Exod. xiv. 9).

7. *when they cried unto the Lord*] The Israelites were encamped on the western shore of the Red Sea, when suddenly a cry of alarm ran through the vast multitude. Over the ridges of the desert hills were seen the well-known horses, the terrible chariots of the Egyptian host; "Pharaoh pursued after the children of Israel, and they were sore afraid."

he put darkness] "He settide derknessis bitwix 30u and Egipcians," Wyclif. A grand, poetical description. In the midst of the terror and perplexity of the Israelites the Angel of God, who went before them in the pillar of cloud and fire, stationed himself behind them so as to deepen the gloom in which the Egyptians were advancing, and afford

brought the sea upon them, and covered them; and your eyes have seen what I have done in Egypt: and ye dwelt in 8 the wilderness a long season. And I brought you into the land of the Amorites, which dwelt on the *other* side Jordan; and they fought with you : and I gave them into your hand, that ye might possess their land; and I destroyed them from

light and encouragement to the Israelites. Comp. Exod. xiv. 20; Ps. lxxviii. 12—14.

and brought the sea upon them] Determined to prevent the escape of their prey, the Egyptians had rushed on amidst the pitchy darkness that surrounded them into the pass between the walls of water standing up on either side of the Chosen People, but the hand of Moses was uplifted, and straightway the waters began to break and give way, and the sea to return in his strength. The engulphing waves closed over them; all efforts to escape were fruitless; horse and chariot and horseman "sank like lead in the mighty waters" (Exod. xv. 10).

and covered them] "And hilide hem," Wyclif. A good illustration of the meaning of the A. S. hélen=to *cover, conceal*, whence the word *Hell, the covered place, the invisible underworld*.

your eyes have seen] The trembling panic-stricken host stood still and saw "the salvation of the Lord" (Exod. xiv. 13), and the great work which He did upon the Egyptians (Exod. xiv. 31).

a long season] Even forty years, a year for each day the spies had been engaged in searching out the land" (Num. xiv. 33, 34), during which time every one of the generation from twenty years old and upwards died, and their carcases lay bleaching in the wilderness (1 Cor. x. 5; Heb. iii. 17).

8. *And I brought you*] The *third* proof of God's favour is here indicated; (*a*) *the victory of the nation over the Amorites*, and (*b*) *the frustrating of Balaam's purposed curse*.

the land of the Amorites] For the meaning of this name see above, ch. iii. 10. Tempted by the rich pasture lands east of the Jordan, a colony of the Amorites appears to have crossed it, and having driven the Moabites with great slaughter and the loss of many captives from the country south of the Jabbok (Num. xxi. 26—29), they made the wide chasm of the Arnon the boundary of their territory. The Amorite chief Sihon made Heshbon his capital; while Og, of the giant race of the Rephaim, entrenched himself in the wonderful district called *Argob*, or "the stony." See above, ch. xii. 4.

and they fought with you] having refused the request of the Israelitish leader for a peaceful passage through their territory (Num. xxi. 33).

I destroyed them from before you] Sihon himself, his sons, and all his people, were smitten with the sword, his walled towns were captured, and his numerous flocks and herds taken (Num. xxi. 27—30), while Og was utterly routed, and his threescore cities fenced with high walls, gates and bars, besides unwalled towns a great many, fell into the hands of the Israelites (Num. xxi. 33—35). Long afterwards the subjugation of

before you. Then Balak the son of Zippor, king of Moab, 9
arose and warred against Israel, and sent and called Balaam
the son of Beor to curse you: but I would not hearken unto 10
Balaam; therefore he blessed you still: so I delivered you
out of his hand. And ye went over Jordan, and came unto 11
Jericho: and the men of Jericho fought against you, the
Amorites, and the Perizzites, and the Canaanites, and the
Hittites, and the Girgashites, the Hivites, and the Jebusites;
and I delivered them into your hand. And I sent the 12

these *great kings, famous kings, mighty kings*, was deemed worthy of being ranked with the deliverance from Egypt. See Ps. cxxxv. 10—12, cxxxvi. 15—21.

9. *Then Balak the son of Zippor*] He is also mentioned in Judg. xi. 25; Mic. vi. 5; Rev. ii. 14. The Israelites were at this time encamped in the plains of Shittim, "the *meadow of the Acacias*."

and warred against Israel] In conjunction with the Midianites (Num. xxii. 1 *ss*).

sent and called Balaam] (Num. xxii. 5) from Pethor, far away from the encampment of the Israelites, beyond the Euphrates, among the mountains of the east, whence his fame had spread, across the Assyrian desert, to the shores of the Dead Sea. "As warrior chief (by that combination of soldier and prophet already seen in Moses himself) he ranked with the five kings of Midian" (Num. xxxi. 8).

to curse you] For he was regarded throughout the whole East as a Prophet, whose blessing or whose curse was irresistible. Balak, who lacked the courage to meet the Israelites in arms, thought to lay upon them the powerful ban of the mighty seer. "Even at the present day the pagan Orientals, in their wars, have always their magicians with them to curse their enemies, and to mutter incantations for their ruin. In our own war with the Burmese, the generals of the natives had several magicians with them, who were much engaged in cursing our troops." Kitto's *Bible Illustr.* II. 214.

10. *I would not hearken unto Balaam*] See Deut. xxiii. 5. Twice, across the whole length of the Assyrian desert, the messengers of Balak, with the Oriental bribes of divination in their hands, were sent to conjure forth the prophet from his distant home. Three times the altars were built and the victims slain, but each time the seer found himself unable to comply with the wishes of the king; he could not curse him whom God had not cursed, or defy him whom Jehovah had not defied.

11. *And ye went over Jordan*] The fourth proof of the Divine favour: (*a*) *the Passage of the Jordan*, and (*b*) *capture of Jericho*; and the fifth (*c*) *the victory over the Canaanites*.

the men of Jericho] i.e. the citizens of Jericho. Comp. Judg. ix. 2, 3, "the *men* of Shechem;" Judg. xx. 5, "the *men* of Gibeah;" 2 Sam. xxi. 12, "the *men* of Jabesh-gilead."

the Amorites] On this enumeration of the nations, see above, ch. iii. 10.

hornet before you, which drave them out from before you, *even* the two kings of the Amorites; *but* not with thy sword, 13 nor with thy bow. And I have given you a land for which ye did not labour, and cities which ye built not, and ye dwell in them; of the vineyards and oliveyards which ye 14 planted not do ye eat. Now therefore fear the LORD, and serve him in sincerity and in truth : and put away the gods which your fathers served on the *other* side of the flood, and

12. *And I sent the hornet before you*] "Misique ante vos *crabrones*" Vulg.: "And I sent before ȝou hors fleeȝis," Wyclif, or "flies with venemouse tongis." In Exod. xxiii. 28, we find it predicted "And I will send *hornets* before thee, which shall drive out the Hivite, the Canaanite, and the Hittite, from before thee;" and in Deut. vii. 20, "Moreover the Lord thy God will send *the hornet* among them, until they that are left, and hide themselves from thee, be destroyed." Elsewhere the bees appear as an image of terrible foes. Comp. Deut. i. 44, "And the Amorites, which dwelt in that mountain, came out against you, and chased you, *as bees do*, and destroyed you in Seir, even unto Hormah." Ps. cxviii. 12, "They compassed me about *like bees*." Not only were bees exceedingly numerous in Palestine, but hornets in particular infested some parts of the country. Some would understand the word here in its literal sense, but it more probably expresses under a vivid image the consternation, with which Jehovah would inspire the enemies of the Israelites. Comp. Deut. ii. 25; Josh. ii. 11.

not with thy sword] Compare the same thought in Psalm xliv. 3.

13. *cities which ye built not*] All this happened as Jehovah had promised, Deut. vi. 10.

14. *Now therefore fear the Lord*] Comp. Job xxviii. 28, "Behold, *the fear* of the Lord, that is wisdom; and to depart from evil is understanding;" Ps. ii. 11, "Serve the Lord with fear, and rejoice with trembling;" Prov. i. 7, "*The fear of the Lord* is the beginning of knowledge."

in sincerity and in truth] "with perfite herte and most trewe," Wyclif. The Greek word here rendered "sincerity" in the LXX. occurs also in 1 Cor. v. 8, "let us keep the feast...with the unleavened bread of *sincerity* and truth;" 2 Cor. i. 12, "For our rejoicing is this, the testimony of our conscience, that in simplicity and godly *sincerity*...we have had our conversation in the world;" 2 Cor. ii. 17, "but as of *sincerity*, but as of God, in the sight of God speak we in Christ." The Latin word from which our "sincerity" comes, denotes "honey without wax," unmixed purity. The Greek word is considered by some to be founded on the idea of something held up in the rays of the sun, and proved to be without speck or flaw.

put away the gods which your fathers served] Two epochs of ancestral idolatry are here alluded to; (*a*) on the other side of the flood, i. e. the Euphrates, in Mesopotamia; and (*b*) in Egypt. Some have supposed that the expression alludes to idolatry "in the heart," but this is unin Egypt; and serve ye the LORD. And if it seem evil unto 15 you to serve the LORD, choose you *this* day whom you will serve; whether the gods which your fathers served that *were* on the *other* side of the flood, or the gods of the Amorites, in whose land ye dwell: but as for me and my house, we will serve the LORD.

16—24. Reply of the People to Joshua's Address.

And the people answered and said, God forbid that we 16 should forsake the LORD, to serve other gods; for the LORD 17

tenable. (i) In Lev. xvii. 7 we read, "they (the people) shall *no more offer their sacrifices unto devils*, after whom they have gone a whoring." (ii) Again in Amos v. 25, 26, quoted by St Stephen in his address before the Sanhedrim (Acts vii. 42, 43), "Have ye offered (= did ye offer) unto Me sacrifices and offerings in the wilderness forty years, O house of Israel? But ye *have borne the tabernacle of your Moloch and Chiun your images, the star of your god, which ye made to yourselves.*" (iii) Once more, in Ezek. xx. 6, 7, 8 we read, "In the day that I lifted up my hand unto them, to bring them forth of the land of Egypt...then said I unto them, Cast ye away every man the abominations of his eyes, and defile not yourselves with the idols of Egypt...but they rebelled against Me, and would not hearken unto Me; they did *not every man cast away the abominations of their eyes, neither did they forsake the idols of Egypt.*" Joshua's words plainly imply his sad conviction that there were still idolaters amongst them in secret, as there were in the days of Jacob before him, Gen. xxxv. 2, and of Samuel after him, 1 Sam. vii. 3, seq.

15. *choose you this day*] Like Elijah afterwards on Carmel (1 Kings xviii. 21), the Hebrew leader challenges the people with the utmost freedom to decide once for all that day whom they would serve. He gives them their choice between the old worship of Penates or household gods practised by their fathers, and the Baal-worship of the Amorites, if they would not serve Jehovah, Who had brought them out of Egypt.

as for me and my house] Whatever may be the decision of the people, Joshua tells them what he and his family are resolved to do. "*I and my house will serve Jehovah.*" Compare the words of the Lord respecting Abraham, "I know him, that he will command his children and his household after him, and they shall keep the way of the Lord, to do justice and judgment," Gen. xviii. 19.

16—24. REPLY OF THE PEOPLE TO JOSHUA'S ADDRESS.

16. *And the people answered and said*] Struck by the solemn earnestness of the address of their leader, the entire people, with one voice, responded to his call by loud and hearty declarations of their determined faithfulness to their covenant with Jehovah.

our God, he *it is* that brought us up and our fathers out of the land of Egypt, from the house of bondage, and which did those great signs in our sight, and preserved us in all the way wherein we went, and among all the people through 18 whom we passed: and the LORD drave out from before us all the people, even the Amorites which dwelt in the land: *therefore* will we also serve the LORD; for he *is* our God. 19 And Joshua said unto the people, Ye cannot serve the LORD: for he *is* a holy God; he *is* a jealous God; he will 20 not forgive your transgressions nor your sins. If ye forsake

17. *for the Lord our God, he it is*] The people ground their promises of fidelity for the future on the dealings of God with them in the past, (i) their deliverance from Egypt; (ii) the great signs wrought in that land; (iii) their preservation in the wilderness; (iv) the expulsion of the Amorites.

19. *Ye cannot serve the Lord*] Joshua checks their hasty impulsiveness and confident protestation of fidelity, by reminding them of the difficulty involved in serving Jehovah aright; and he specially would have them dwell on (i) His holiness, and (ii) His jealousy. His words remind us of our Lord's warnings in the Sermon on the Mount, "*No man can serve two masters: for either he will hate the one, and love the other; or else he will hold to the one, and despise the other. Ye cannot serve God and mammon*" (Matt. vi. 24).

he is a holy God] Comp. Lev. xix. 2; 1 Sam. vi. 20; Ps. xcix. 5, 9; Isai. v. 16. Holiness is the principle that guards the eternal distinction between Creator and creature, between God and man; it preserves the Divine dignity and *majesty* from being infringed by the Divine love; it eternally excludes everything evil and impure from the Divine nature. Comp. Isai. vi. 3, "*Holy, Holy, Holy*, is the Lord of Hosts." See Martensen's *Christian Dogmatics*, pp. 99, 100. The plural *Elohim*, here used, "directs attention to the infinite riches and infinite fulness contained in the one Divine Being, and therefore to the fact that, if we were to believe in innumerable gods, and endow them with perfection, they would still all be contained in the one *Elohim*." Hengstenberg.

he is a jealous God] "Deus enim sanctus et *fortis æmulator est*," Vulgate. "A strong feruent loouyere," Wyclif. Numerous passages in the Prophets bring out the idea of God as One, Who requires of His people, whom He has married, the unbroken fidelity of marriage, and punishes most inflexibly any attachment to another god, any departure from Him, whilst He continues His blessings upon love and fidelity even to distant generations. Comp. Jer. ii. 2; Ezek. xvi. 8, 22, 60, xxiii. 3, 8, 19; Hos. ii. 16. "The Divine zeal is just the energy of Divine holiness. His jealousy turns especially against (1) idolatry, and (2) all sin, by which His holy Name is desecrated." Oehler's *Theology of the Old Testament*, I. 166, 167.

he will not forgive] Compare the words of God to Moses respect-the LORD, and serve strange gods, then he will turn and do you hurt, and consume you, after that he hath done you good. And the people said unto Joshua, Nay; but we will 21 serve the LORD. And Joshua said unto the people, Ye *are* 22 witnesses against yourselves that ye have chosen you the LORD, to serve him. And they said, *We are* witnesses. Now therefore put away, *said he*, the strange gods which *are* 23 among you, and incline your heart unto the LORD God of Israel. And the people said unto Joshua, The LORD our 24 God will we serve, and his voice will we obey.

25—28. *Solemn Renewal of the Covenant.*

So Joshua made a covenant with the people that day, 25

ing the Angel of the Covenant, "Beware of him, and obey his voice, provoke him not; for *he will not pardon your transgressions:* for My Name is in him," Exod. xxiii. 21; and comp. Num. xiv. 35; Deut. xviii. 19; Jer. v. 7. Forgiveness is conditional on repentance and amendment of life.

20. *then he will turn*] He will turn round; He will alter His attitude towards you. "Convertet se et affliget vos atque subvertet," Vulgate. "The Lord schal turne hym silf, and schal turment jou," Wyclif. Comp. Josh. xxiii. 15; Isai. lxiii. 10.

after that he hath done you good] i. e. without any regard to the fact that He hath done you good, and poured His benefits upon you.

21. *Nay; but we will*] The people repeat their protestations of fidelity to Jehovah, and vow to serve Him with sincerity.

22. *Ye are witnesses against yourselves*] Clearly and unmistakeably the people had declared that they had chosen the service of Jehovah. By so doing, in the event of their falling away, they would condemn themselves by their own evidence, and would be obliged to admit that Jehovah had a right to punish them for their unfaithfulness.

We are witnesses] Literally, **Witnesses are we against ourselves.**

23. *Now therefore put away*] "Now thanne, he said, do 3e awey alien goddis fro the middil of 3ou," Wyclif. He again reverts to their secret practice of idolatry. Comp. Gen. xxxv. 2; 1 Sam. vii. 3.

24. *And the people said*] For the third time (comp. verses 16 and 21) the representatives of the nation avow that they will serve Jehovah and hearken only to His voice.

25—28. SOLEMN RENEWAL OF THE COVENANT.

25. *So Joshua made a covenant*] "Percussit ergo Josue in die illo fœdus," Vulgate. "Thanne Josue smoot a boond of pees," Wyclif. A covenant had been concluded by God on Sinai with Israel (Exod. xix. 20) and solemnly ratified with

(*a*) burnt-offerings and peace-offerings at the foot of the mount;
(*b*) the reading of every word of the Law in the ears of the people;

and set them a statute and an ordinance in Shechem.
26 And Joshua wrote these words in the book of the law of
God, and took a great stone, and set it up there under an
27 oak, that *was* by the sanctuary of the LORD. And Joshua

(c) the sprinkling of one half of the blood of the victims on the altars and the roll containing the covenant conditions, and the other half on the people (Exod. xxiv. 3—8; Heb. ix. 19, 20).
This covenant Moses had renewed in "the field" of Moab (Deut. xxix. 1), with
(a) a transcription of the blessings and curses of the Law;
(b) a solemn delivery of it to the priests, to be placed beside the Ark in the Holy of Holies, and to be read, in the hearing of all the people, once every seven years, at the Feast of Tabernacles (Deut. xxxi. 9—11, 25, 26).
Joshua, who had been present at the ratification of both the previous covenants, renews it now, and doubtless with august ceremonial.

and set them a statute] "And settide forth to ȝe puple comaundementis and domes in Sichen," Wyclif. Comp. Exod. xv. 25. He determined and established "what in matters of religion should be with Israel law and right."

26. *And Joshua wrote*] As Moses at Sinai wrote all the words that Jehovah had spoken in a book, probably a papyrus-roll (Exod. xxiv. 4), so Joshua now inscribed "minutes" of the transactions connected with this renewal of the covenant at Shechem.

in the book of the law of God] This protocol he placed inside the roll of the Law of Moses.

and took a great stone] Like
(a) The stone which Jacob set up at Bethel (Gen. xxviii. 18);
(b) The pillar of stones which the same patriarch set up on his return from Padan-aram (Gen. xxxi. 44—46);
(c) The twelve pillars which Moses set up at Sinai (Exod. xxiv. 4);
(d) The twelve stones set up to mark the passage of the Jordan (Josh. iv. 3).

under an oak] Or rather, **under the oak which was in the sanctuary of Jehovah.** See above, ch. xxiv. 1. "This spot, called in Gen. xii. 6 and Gen. xxxv. 4, '*Allon-Moreh*,' 'the oak of Moreh' or of Shechem, is called by the Samaritans *Ahron-Moreh*, 'the Ark of Moreh,' from a supposition that in a vault underneath is buried the Ark. The Mussulmans call it '*Rigad el Amad*,' 'the place of the Pillar,' or '*Sheykh-el-Amad*,' 'the Saint of *the Pillar*.'" Stanley's *Lectures*, I. 280, n. Possibly beside the old consecrated oak of Abraham and Jacob their altar was still remaining, and it is to be remembered that Joshua himself had built an altar on Mount Ebal, and therefore close to Shechem (Josh. viii. 30). Thus many reasons conspired to give a sacred character to "the border of the sanctuary," the mountain "*which the right hand of the Lord had purchased*" (Ps. lxxviii. 54) at Shechem.

said unto all the people, Behold, this stone shall be a witness unto us; for it hath heard all the words of the LORD which he spake unto us: it shall be therefore a witness unto you, lest ye deny your God.

So Joshua let the people depart, every man unto his inheritance. 28

29—33. *Death of Joshua and Eleazar.*

And it came to pass after these things, that Joshua 29

27. *this stone shall be a witness*] So in Gen. xxxi. 48, 52, Laban says to Jacob, "This heap *is a witness* between me and thee this day;" and in Deut. xxxi. 19, 21, 26, Moses says, "Write ye this song for you......that *this song may be a witness* for me against the children of Israel."

for it hath heard] By a poetical *prosopopœia* Joshua describes the stone as *hearing* the words of God, since it had been set up for the purpose of reminding the people of the promise which they had made unto the Lord, and, in case they should be unfaithful, of bearing witness against them.

lest ye deny your God] "Ne forte postea negare velitis et mentiri Domino Deo vestro," Vulgate. "Lest perauenture ȝe wolden denye aftirward, and lye to ȝoure Lord God," Wyclif. Comp. Josh. vii. 11 (Heb.); Job xxxi. 28; Prov. xxx. 9; Lev. xix. 11, 12.

28. *let the people depart*] On the breaking up of this august assembly every man returned to the lot of his inheritance in the newly acquired and goodly Land of Promise. For the section to verse 31 comp. Judg. ii. 6—10. "Nothing can be conceived more impressive or more sublime than the circumstances of this last public interview of the aged Leader with the people whom he had put in possession of the goodly land of Canaan, and who had so often followed him in his victorious path. In the midst of the elders, the chiefs, and magistrates of Israel; surrounded by a respectful people, formerly bondsmen of Pharaoh, but now in possession of a rich and beautiful country, and the sole survivors of an untoward generation, their illustrious and venerable commander—the oldest man in all their nation—spoke to them as to his sons. And of what did he speak? He was a soldier, and his career had been essentially military; but he spoke to them, not of conquest— the sound of the trumpet and the gleam of the sword cannot be recognised in his address—but of the holiness and the obedience which become the people chosen of God. It is such a discourse as a patriarch might have given upon his deathbed, or a prophet might have uttered from the valley of vision."—Kitto's *Bible Illustrations*, II. 314.

29—33. DEATH OF JOSHUA AND ELEAZAR.

29. *And it came to pass*] With the close of Joshua's parting address comes the close also of his own life. The historian proceeds to bring the book to a conclusion, and tells us of (i) the death of Joshua; (ii) the

the son of Nun, the servant of the LORD, died, *being* an
30 hundred and ten years old. And they buried him in the
border of his inheritance in Timnath-serah, which *is* in
mount Ephraim, on the north side of the hill of Gaash.
31 And Israel served the LORD all the days of Joshua, and all
the days of the elders that overlived Joshua, and which had
known all the works of the LORD, that he had done for
Israel.

conduct of the people after his death; (iii) the burial of the remains of
Joseph, which had been brought out of Egypt; (iv) the death of
Eleazar the high-priest.

Joshua...the servant of the Lord, died] His work was now over.
His work of war, and his work of peace. His age when he died was
precisely that which Joseph reached (Gen. l. 26), a hundred and ten
years.

30. *And they buried him in the border of his inheritance in Timnath-
serah*] For the probable site of this spot, see above, Josh. xix. 50. A
photograph brought out by the "Palestine Exploration Committee"
gives a representation of the tomb of Joshua. "It is certainly the most
striking monument in the country," says Lieut. Conder, "and strongly
recommends itself to the mind as an authentic site." The tomb is a
square chamber, with five excavations in three of its sides, the central
one forming a passage leading into a second chamber beyond. A great
number of lamp-niches cover the walls of the porch—upwards of 200—
arranged in vertical rows. A single cavity with a niche for a lamp may
be identified, it is thought, with the resting-place of the warrior-chief of
Israel.

the hill of Gaash] This mountain is also mentioned in Judg. ii. 9;
2 Sam. xxiii. 30; 1 Chron. xi. 32. The Alexandrine and Arabic versions
have appended to verse 30 the traditionary legend that the knives of
stone, with which Joshua performed the rite of circumcision at Gilgal,
were buried with him.

31. *And Israel served the Lord*] The remarks here made as to the
conduct of the nation after the death of Joshua are quite in keeping with
the design of the book. They afford "evidence of the fruit, which
resulted from Joshua's faithful activity for the Lord in Israel." "As
on the dark sky when some flashing meteor has swept across it with a
path of fire, there remains still after the glory has departed a lingering
line of light, so was it with this mighty man, glorious in life, and leaving
even after he was gone, the record of his abundant faithfulness still to
hold for a season heavenward the too wandering eyes of Israel."—Bp
Wilberforce's *Heroes of Hebrew History*, p. 154.

that overlived Joshua] Heb. **that prolonged their days after Joshua.**
Comp. Judg. ii. 7, margin.

all the works of the Lord] in the delivery of the nation from Egyptian
bondage, their guidance through the desert, and their settlement in the
Promised Land.

And the bones of Joseph, which the children of Israel 32 brought up out of Egypt, buried they in Shechem, in a parcel of ground which Jacob bought of the sons of Hamor the father of Shechem for an hundred pieces of silver: and it became the inheritance of the children of Joseph. And 33 Eleazar the son of Aaron died; and they buried him in a hill that pertained to Phinehas his son, which was given him in mount Ephraim.

32. *And the bones of Joseph*] For the careful instructions of this patriarch respecting his remains, see Gen. l. 24, 25; and for their careful removal from Egypt by Moses, see Exod. xiii. 19.

brought up out of Egypt] The body of the patriarch was embalmed, and placed in an Egyptian coffin. The sacred burden had been borne by the two tribes of the house of Joseph all through the wanderings of the wilderness, and was now reverently laid

in a parcel of ground] which Jacob had bought for a hundred pieces of silver, of the sons of Hamor (Gen. xxxiii. 19), and given "to the favourite son of his favourite Rachel."

an hundred pieces of silver] or *lambs*, "for an hundrid yonge scheep," Wyclif. See Gen. xxxiii. 19, margin; but comp. Acts vii. 16.

and it became] i.e. the plot of ground, as well as Shechem.

33. *Eleazar the son of Aaron*] It seems probable that Eleazar had died during the lifetime of Joshua. He was the third son of Aaron, by Elisheba, daughter of Amminadab. After the death of Nadab and Abihu without children (Lev. x. 1, 2; Num. iii. 4), Eleazar was appointed chief over the principal Levites. He comes before us

(*a*) Ministering with his brother Ithamar during their father's lifetime.

(*b*) Invested on Mount Hor, as the successor of Aaron, with the sacred garments (Num. xx. 28).

(*c*) Superintending the census of the people (Num. xxvi. 3, 4).

(*d*) Taking part in the distribution of the Land after the conquest (Josh. xiv. 1).

and they buried him in a hill] "Et sepelierunt eum in Gabaath-Phinees filii ejus," Vulgate, which Wyclif curiously mistranslates "and Phynees and his sones birieden him in Gabaa."

in a hill] The word here employed for "hill" is "Gibeah," which gives its name to several towns and places in Palestine, which would doubtless be generally on or near a hill. This place was Gibeah-Phinehas, the city of his son, which had been given to the latter on Mount Ephraim. Robinson identifies it with the *Gaba* of Eusebius and Jerome, and the modern *Chirbet Jibia*, 5 miles north of Guphna, towards *Nablûs* or Shechem. "His tomb is still shewn in a little close overshadowed by venerable terebinths, at *Awertah*, a few miles S.E. of Nablûs." Stanley's *Lectures*, I. 281, n.

INDEX I.

Aaron, descendants of, provision for, 186, 187
Abel-Shittim. *See* Shittim
Abib. *See* Nisan
Abraham, history of, 204; tradition concerning, 204; purchase of Machpelah, 33
Accursed thing, why so called, 59, 63, 66
Achan, sin of, 63; discovery of, 67, 68; punishment of, 69, 196
Achar, name for Achan, 63
Achor, valley of. *See* Valley
Achsah, daughter of Caleb, 134; her request, 135. *See* Othniel
Achshaph, city of, 97; king of, slain, 97, 110
Achzib, position of, 170; modern name of, 170
Acoustic properties of valley between Ebal and Gerizim, 76
Adam, city of, 46; situation of, 46; modern name, 46. *See* Zaretan
Adonizedek, significance of name, 83; one of the kings of South Canaan, 83; defeated and slain by Joshua, 92
Adullam, cave of, 110; city of, 110; king of, slain, 110
Adummim, meaning of, 130; position of, 130
Ai, situation of, 63, 64; mentioned in Genesis, 63; importance of its position, 64; final capture, 73. *See* Tel
Ain, meaning of, 163; words combined with, 163
Ajalon, valley of. *See* Valley
Allon to Zaanannim, 172. *See* Zaanannim
Altar, "of Blessing and of Cursing," 74, 75; its site called "Sanctuary of the Lord," 203; "on the Jordan," 193; description of, 193; title on, 199 (*see* Ed); recent discovery of site, 193
Ammonites, special directions concerning, 120
Amorites, meaning of, 44; position of, 44, 98; origin of, 44; migrations of, 44; victory of, over Moabites, 44, 206; subjugation of, 206; confederate kings called, 85
Anab, city of Judah, 104
Anak, three sons of, 134
Anakims, origin of, 84; distribution of, 104; various names of, 104; coalesce with Philistines, 105; destruction of, 105

Anathoth, city of, 187
Aphek, or Aphekah, royal city of Canaanites, 110, 140; given to Judah, 141; a city in the extreme north of Asher, 114, 170; its classical and modern names, 114, 170
April, month of, 45
Arabah. *See* Plains, South
Arad, position of, 110
Arba, father of Anak, 84; called Arbah, 186
Archi, 143
Argob, position of, 122, 206; description of, 122
Ark of covenant, names of, 42; description of, 42, 43; carried over Jordan, 46; round Jericho, 56
Arnon, river, position, 44; meaning of, 106; course of, 106
Aroer, of Reuben, 107; built on an island, 107, 115, 117; of Gad, 120
Ashdod, town of Judah, 105, 140; the Azotus of the N.T., 105; Scripture references to, 105
Ashdod-pisgah, 96, 107, 118
Asher, tribe, territory of, 169—171; character of, 171; extent of, 171; prophecy concerning, 171; subsequent history, 171
Asher, city of, town in W. Manasseh, 148
Ashkelon, position and importance of, 113; scripture events connected with, 113; prophecies concerning, 113; connection with Crusaders, 113
Ashtaroth, residence and capital of Og, 80, 108, 116, 122; why so called, 122; modern name of, 108, 188
Authorship of Joshua, changes, 191
Avenger of blood, or Goel, 179—181
Avim, the, or Avites, 113; their origin, position, and migrations, 113
Azekah, position of, 86; references to, 86

Baalah, original name of Kirjath-jearim, 81, 132. *See* Kirjath-jearim
Baalah, mount, 133
Baal-gad, position of, 102, 114; other names of, called Cæsarea Philippi in N. T., 102; great beauty of neighbourhood, 103

INDEX I.

Baal-hermon, border of Hivites' territory, 44
Baal-perazim, name explained, 132; position and history, 131, 132
Babylonish garment, 68; a product of the Babylonish looms, 68
Balaam, killed among the Dukes of Sihon, 118; reference to his history by Joshua, 55, 207; similar magicians in Eastern armies, 207. *See* Undesigned Coincidences
Balak, king of Moab, 207
Bamoth-baal, meaning of, 117; situation of, 117
Banias. *See* Jordan, sources of
Barada, river of Damascus, 32
Barley harvest. *See* Harvests
Bashan, pasture-downs and cattle of, 34; bulls of, 34; extent of, 39, 40
Beer, or Bor, meaning of, 163
Beeroth, city of Benjamin, 81, 160; situation of, 77, 81
Beersheba, city of, double meaning of name, 137; wells of, 137, 138
Benjamin, tribe, territory of, 158, 159; smallness of, 161; cities of, 160, 161
Benjamites, character and history of, 161
Beth-arabah, 129, 141, 161
Beth-aven, position of, 63, 64; play on the word in Hosea, 64
Beth-baal-meon, meaning of, 117; position, 117
Beth-dagon, city of Judah, 139; city of Asher, 169
Bethel, or Luz. *See* Luz
Beth-hogla, position and description of, 129, 159
Beth-horon, battle of, 85—90; referred to by Isaiah, 6; meaning of word, 86; the upper and the lower, 143, 144, 158, 159
Beth-jeshimoth = " House of the wastes," 107
Bethlehem, a town in Zebulun, 166
Bethlehem Ephratah, a town in Judah, 166
Beth-marcaboth = " House of Chariots," 162; significance of name, 162
Beth-nimrah, 121
Beth-peor, 118
Beth-shean, or Beth-shan, position and description of, 149; subsequent history, 149
Beth-shemesh = " House of the Sun," position, 132; events connected with, 133; remains of, 133; a town in Issachar, 167
Beth-tappuah = " House of Apples," 140
Beth-zur, city of, 141
Bezer in Reuben, 181; a city of refuge, 181, 182
Blessings and curses of the Law, read in the Valley between Ebal and Gerizim, 76
Blood-guiltiness, 41
Blunt's Undesigned Coincidences, referred to on Flax Harvest and Passover, 46; capture of Lachish, 93; death of Balaam, 119
Bohan, stone of, 130, 159
Book of the Law, importance of, 33; Covenant written in, 212
Boundaries of Land of Promise, 32

Cabul, city and district of, 170
Caleb, his family and ancestors, 125; first mention of, 125; connection with Joshua, 125; speech of, to Joshua, 125—127; Joshua's prayer for, 127; his possession. *See* Hebron
Camp, at Gilgal, strength of, 49, 50; became permanent, 53
Campaigns of Joshua, length of, 103, 104
Canaan, Father of the Amorites, 44
Canaan, Central, conquest of, 83—92
Eastern, partition of, 111—123
Northern, conquest of, 97—102
Southern, conquest of, 92—97
Canaanites, meaning of word, 44, 98; position of, 44, 98; sometimes same as Hittites, 33; extermination commanded, 15, 102
Captain of the Lord's host, appearance of to Joshua, 54, 55; meaning and significance of, 55; his interview with Joshua resumed, 56
Carmel, Mount = "the Park," 111; why so called, 111; Scripture notices of, 111; flank of, inhabited by Perizzites, 44; a city of Judah, 141
Cattle, sometimes preserved in capture of cities, 60, 70, 101
Caves, frequent in Palestine, 40, 41; Scripture mention of, 90, 113, 114
Chariots of iron, 100, 152
Chephirah, 77; situation of, 81; identification of, 81
Chesalon, 132
Chesulloth, 167
Chinnereth, city of Naphtali, 98, 173
Chinneroth, sea of, 107, 121; names of, in the New Testament, 107
Circumcision, discontinued in wilderness, 51; renewed by Joshua, 19, 20, 51; to whom the rite was then administered, 51
Cities, Levitical, description of, 184—186; of the descendants of Aaron, 186, 187; of the Kohathites, 187, 188; of the Gershonites, 188; of the Merarites, 189
Cities, of Gilead, 120;—of Judah, fourfold division of, 136; (*a*) of the South, 137, 138; (*b*) in the Lowland, 138—140: (*c*) in the mountains, 140, 141; (*d*) in the wilderness, 141, 142;—of Palestine, 102
Cities of Refuge, 179—183; names of, 181; numbers of, 181; laws concerning, 180; Jewish traditions about, 183
Coasts, meaning and peculiar use of, 117
Coffin, the Egyptian, of Joseph, 77, 215; deposited at Shechem, 77, 215

INDEX I.

Congregation, or Church, 154
Countries, three, meaning of, 150
Courtesy, Eastern, observed towards women, 38
Covenant of Sinai, how made by Moses, 211, 212; solemnly renewed by Joshua, after taking of Ai, 74—77; and again before his death, 211—213
Crocodiles in the Holy Land, 169; Crocodile brook, 169
Cubits, 2000, Sabbath-day's journey, 43, 46
Curse pronounced on city of Jericho, 59; on builder of Jericho, 62; classical instances of curses pronounced on other cities, 59, 62, 63
Curses of the Law, the, 76; read in ears of the people, 76

Dabbasheth = Camel's hump, 164
Dan, city of, 176, 177. *See* Laish
Dan, tribe of, 175; territory of, 175—177; extent of, 177; Jacob's prophecy concerning, 177
Darkness, suddenness after sunset in the East, 38
Day, miraculously prolonged, 89
Dead Sea, Southern portion or tongue of, 129; West of, occupied by Amorites, 44; called Sea of the Plain, 46
Debir, (*a*) a town of Judah, ancient names of, 95, 134; position of, 95; taken by Joshua, 95; and by Othniel, 134
(*b*) Another town of Judah, 130
(*c*) Another town of Gad, 120, 121
(*d*) One of the five kings hanged by Joshua, 92
Dibon, Dibon-gad, or Dimon, 115; position of, 115; scene of the discovery of the Moabite stone, 116
Dor, city of, 98; position, 98; district of, various names of, 98, 149; history of, 98
Dukes of Sihon = vassals, 118; their history, 118
Dust on head, symbol of mourning, 65; Scripture and classical references to, 65

Eastern Palestine, conquered kings of, 106—109
Eating together, a symbol of friendship among Orientals, 80
Ebal, mount, 74, 75; situation of, 74, 75; events connected with, 76; valley between it and Gerizim, 76; the recital of the blessings and cursings there, 76; altar built on, 75, 203, 212
Ed, the altar, explanation of name, 199
Edersheim's Israel in Canaan, his remark on, the stoning of Achan, 69; sun standing still, 89; an undesigned evidence of antiquity of Book of Joshua, 105; sons of Joseph, 154
Edrei, meaning of, 108; battle of, 108;

peculiarities of situation, 108; one of the capitals of Og, 122
Eglon, position of, 84, 139; modern name, 84; taken by Joshua, 94; king of, slain by him, 94, 109
Egypt, the Brook of, 113, 129
Ekron, city of Beelzebub, 113, 133; one of five Philistine towns, 113
Eleazar, the priest, presides over the division of the land, 123; events of his life, 215; death of, 215; tomb of, 215; its modern name, 215
Embassy, of Gibeonites to Joshua, 77; of Israelites to the two tribes and a half, 194
Emims, 104
Endor, position of, 149; incidents connected with subsequently, 149
Engannim, meaning of, 167; village and fountain of, 167; Scripture incident connected with, 167
Engedi = "spring of the gazelle," 142; events connected with, 90, 142
Enrogel, supposed position of, 130; Biblical mention of it elsewhere, 130
En-shemesh, waters of, 130; present name of, 130
Ephraim and Manasseh, comparative numbers of, 150; boundaries of, 148; blessings of Jacob on, 151
Ephraim, mountain of, position, 151; description of, 151, 153; referred to in Scripture, 151
Ephraim, tribe of, 144; position, 144; "separate" cities of, 145, 148; territory of, 144, 145
Esdraelon, plain of, 152; anciently inhabited by the Canaanites proper, 44; called "Plain of Jezreel," 152; events of which it was the scene, 152; suitable for "chariot-cavalry," 152
Eshkalonites, the, people of Ashkelon, 113. *See* Ashkelon
Espy, meaning and uses of word, 125, 126
Euphrates river, origin and meaning of the word, 33; E. boundary of Land of Promise, 32; called "the flood," 33, 208
Ewald's History of Israel, remarks on extermination of Canaanites, 17; extent of the country beyond Jordan, 116; long independence of the Geshurites and Maachathites, 116; the half tribe of Manasseh, 122
Exodus, the, season of, 45; description of, 205, 206
Explanation of the two tribes and a half, of their "great altar," 196—199

Farewell, Joshua's, to the two and a half tribes, 191, 192
Farewell address, Joshua's first, to all Israel, 200, 202; his second, 25, 202—209
Father of Gilead, peculiar meaning of, 146

INDEX I.

Feet upon necks of captives, 91; meaning of symbol, 91; Scripture references to it in Old and New Testament, 91

Fenced cities, nature of fortifications of in Palestine, 90, 91; value of, 49, 50, 173

Five lords, cities of Philistines governed by, 113

Flax, stalks of, on Rahab's roof, 39; importance of crops of it in Palestine, 39; allusions to this by Hosea, 39; flax harvest, *see* Blunt's Undesigned Coincidences

Flood, other side of, meaning of expression, 203, 204

Forests of Israel, ancient, 151, 153

Fuller, his reference to windings of the Jordan, 32, 129

Gaash, hill of, 214

Gad, tribe of, 121; possessions of, 34, 120, 121; warlike character of, 121; subsequent history of, 121, 122; remarkable men of, 121, 122

Gal = cairn, 74

Galilee, position, 181; meaning of, 181; towns of, 181

Gate, shutting of, necessary precaution in the East, 38

Gath, position of, 105; importance of position, 105; one of five royal cities, 105

Gath-hepher, 165

Gaulanitis, tract of, 182

Gaza, situation of, 96; antiquity, 96; great strength, 96; never subdued by Israelites, 96, 105, 113, 140

Geba = hill, 161

Gebal, maritime town, 114; different names of its inhabitants, 114; same as Byblus, 114; its celebrity, 114

Geder, probable position of, 109; king of, slain, 109

Gehenna = Ge-Hinnom, 131

Gennesareth, Lake of, 107; East of, inhabited by Girgashites, 44

Gerizim, Mount, 75; situation of, 75; valley between it and Ebal, 76; covenant renewed there, 76; acoustic properties of the valley of, 76

Gershonites, descendants of eldest son of Levi, duties of, 185; cities of, 188; position in march through the wilderness, 185

Geshurites, "of Bashan," 108; their situation, 108; independence of, 116; "of the Desert," 112

Gezer, position of, 93, 94, 144; recent remarkable identification of, 94, 109; its connection with Pharaoh and Solomon, 94

Ghôr of the Jordan, 46, 50, 193

Gibeah = hill, 160; name of several towns, 160; "of Saul," 161

Gibeah-haaraloth, meaning of, 51

Gibeon, one of four towns of the Hivites, 77; peculiar government of, 78; meaning of name, 78, 161; position of, 78, 83, 96; modern name, 78; sun stands still over, 88

Gibeonites, stratagem by which they impose on Joshua, 78, 79; massacre of by Saul, 41; their fidelity to Israel, 83

Giblites, the land of, 114. *See* Gebal. Translated "stone-squarers," 114

Gilead, inheritance of Manasseh, 120, 146; meaning of word, 146; different applications of name, 107, 146, 193; extent and size of, 146

Gilead, grandson of Manasseh, 147

Gilgal, fortified by Joshua, 49; its site, 50, 53; its modern name, 53; other mention of, 50; meaning of word, 53; history under Saul and Samuel, 53; other towns of same name, 79, 111, 130, 159

Giloh, city of Judah, 140

Girgashites, family of the Hivites, 44; omitted in all enumerations of the "Seven Nations" except one, 44; supposed position of, 44

Gittites, the, 113; meaning of word, 113. *See* Gath

Golan in Bashan, 182; a city of refuge, 181

Goshen, town and district in S. Judah, 96, 102

Hai, name in Genesis for Ai. *See* Ai

Hailstones, fall of, from heaven, at battle of Beth-horon, 86; other instances, 86, 87

Halak, meaning of, 102; situation of, 102

Hamath, northern boundary point of Palestine under Solomon, 11, 12, 114; importance of its position, 114; called "Hamath the Great," 114

Hammath, or Hammon, 173; hot springs of, 173

Hanging, a punishment, 18, 74, 92; only till eventide, 74, 92

Hannathon, meaning of, 165; position, 165

Haran, Terah died at, 204

Harden the heart, God said to, 103; meaning of this, 103; Scripture instances of, 103

Harith, the Wady of, 71, 143

Harlot. *See* Rahab

Harvests in Palestine, times of, 45, 46

Havoth-Jair, sixty cities captured by Jair, 122; position, 122; to whom given, 122

Hazar-susah, meaning and significance of, 162

Hazor, meaning of, 97; position, 97, 173, 174; subsequent mention of, 97; taken and burned by Joshua, 101. *See* Jabin

Heap of stones, two words used for, 74; memorial of punishment, 69; raised on graves, 69, 74. *See* Tel

INDEX I.

Hebron, in Judah, original name of, 84, 127; great antiquity of, 84; situation of, 84; taken by Joshua, 94; its great elevation, 126, 127; given by Joshua to Caleb, 127, 133; its name twice changed, 104, 127; ceded by Caleb to the Levites, 186; a city of refuge, 181; town of same name in Asher, 170, 188

Heeren's Asiatic Nations, remarks in on Babylonian looms, 68

Hell, meaning and derivation of word, 206

Hengstenberg on word Elohim, 210

Hepher, father of Zelophehad, 147; city of, 110; king of, slain, 110

Hermon, anciently possessed by the Hivites, 44; meaning of word, 106; why so called, 106

Heshbon, capital of the Amorites, 106; position of, 106; ruins of, 107

Heth, or Cheth, father of the Hittites, 33, 44

Hewers of wood, 82; called Nethinim, 82; duties of, 82; Scripture references to, 82

Hiel, the builder of Jericho, 62

Hills of Judah, country of, 95, 136

Hinnom, nothing known of him, 131; valley of, described, 131; events connected with, 131

Hittites, origin of, 33, 44; first mention of, 33, 44; relation to other nations of Canaan, 44; sometimes used for Canaanites, 33. *See* Kirjath-arba

Hivites, omitted in first enumeration of the "Seven Nations," 44; and in report of the spies, 44; when first mentioned, 44; character of, 44; geographical position, 44, 98

Hoham, one of the five confederate kings, 84, 92; meaning of name, 84

Holy Place, first so called in the Promised Land, 48

Homicide, laws regarding, 179

Horam, king of Gezer, 93; slain by Joshua, 94

Horites, aboriginal inhabitants of Seir, 205; dispossessed by Edomites, 205; how governed, 205

Hormah, situation of, 109; king of, slain, 109; defeat of Israelites at, 109; called Zephath, 109, 138, 162

Hornets, reference to, 208

Horses, first use of, in Canaanite warfare, 91

Hough, meaning of, 99, 100; reason of the command to, 101

House, Rahab's, preserved from falling, 61

Houses, sometimes built on walls in old towns, 40

Jaazer, city of Gad, position of, 120; taken by Israel from Amorites, 120

Jabbok, meaning of, 107; a boundary of the Amorites, 44

Jabin, official title of kings of Hazor, 97; title explained, 97; joins northern confederacy against Joshua, 97; slain by him, 101, 110

Jabneel, name of two towns (*a*) in boundary of Judah, 133; (*b*) in boundary of Naphtali, 172

Jacob and Esau, meaning of names explained, 204

Jahaza, scene of victory over Sihon, 117; different names for, 117; given to Reuben, 117

Jair, son of Manasseh, 122, 146; conqueror of the Argob, 122, 146

Japhia (*a*)="glancing," a town of Zebulun, 165; position and neighbourhood of, 165; its history under the Romans, 165; (*b*) king of Lachish, 84; joins southern league against Joshua, 84; slain by him, 92, 109

Japho (="beauty") or Joppa, 176; events in Scripture connected with, 176; gardens and groves of, 176; its connection with the Crusaders, 176

Jarmuth, town of Judah, position and importance of, 84, 139; modern name of, 84, 139

Jasher, Book of, 89; quotations from, 86—89; composition of, 89; meaning of word, 89

Ibleam, town of W. Manasseh, 149, 188; event connected with, 149

Idolatry, incurable proneness of the nation to, in Mesopotamia, Egypt and Palestine, 10, 208, 209; various kinds of, in the ancient world, 10, 204, 209

Jealous, meaning and force of the word, 210

Jearim, mount (or "Hor-jearim")= "mountain of forests," 132; name given to border town of Chesalon, 132

Jebus, meaning of word, 131; strong fortress occupied by the Jebusites, 44; one of the names of Jerusalem, 44, 131; called sometimes Jebusi, 83, 159, 161

Jebusites, always placed last among the "Seven Nations," 44; the old inhabitants of Jebus, or Jerusalem, 44, 98, 161; their "Lower City" taken by the Israelites, 142

Jephunneh, father of Caleb, 125; doubt as to his nationality, 125

Jericho, meaning of word, 36; position, 36; importance to Israelites of its early capture, 36, 37; its wealth, 37; strength of fortifications, 36; its siege, 56, 58; capture and destruction, 57—61; given to the Benjamites, 62, 160; incidents in our Lord's life connected with it, 62. *See* also "Jordan by Jericho," "Water of Jericho," and "Curse."

Jerusalem, anciently possessed by the Jebusites, 44; and called Jebus, 83;

meaning of word, 83; five different names by which called, 83; its latitude and longitude, 83; its great elevation, 83; and military strength, 83, 84; given to Benjamin, 161

Jeshurun, meaning of, 89; name of the Jewish nation, 89

Jezreel, 166; meaning of, 167; position, 167; events connected with, 167; modern name of, 167

Jobab, king of Madon, 97; joins northern confederacy against Joshua, 97; slain by him, 101, 110

Jokneam of Carmel, 111; city of Zebulun, 111, 164; given to Levites, 189; river before, *see* Kishon

Jordan, river, meaning of word, 31; its sources, 31; its windings, 32; its course, 32; its threefold bank, 42; periodical inundation of, 45; passage of by Israelites, 45, 46; typical significance of passage, 24, 26, 47; four descriptions of the passage, 49

Jordan, borders, or circles, of, 193; Ghôr of, 193; "Judah upon," 173; Plain of, terrace on, 48

Jordan by Jericho, meaning of explained, 123, 143, 182

Joseph, bones of, buried in Shechem, 77, 215

Joseph, house of, inheritance, 143, 144; size of his territory, 144

Joseph, sons of, 124; their complaint to Joshua, 150; subsequent discontent, 153

Josephus, his remarks on

Age of Joshua when he assumed the command, 13

Alleged cruelties against Canaanites, 15

Site of Gilgal, 53

Sun standing still, 89

Hailstorm at Battle of Beth-horon, 86, 87, 89

Situations of Chesulloth, 166, 167; Baalath, 175

Joshua, book of, why so called, 5; its authority confirmed by allusions in (*a*) *the Psalms*, 5; (*b*) *the Prophets*, 6; (*c*) *the New Testament*, 6; enquiry as to its authorship, 6; the object for which it was written, 8; its style, 8; analysis of its contents, 8

Joshua, his original name, 9; meaning of, 9; change of, 9; triple division of his life, 9;

(*a*) *In Egypt*, 9; idolatry there practised, 10; bondage of the Israelites, 10;

(*b*) *In the Sinaitic Desert*, 10; battle of Rephidim, 10; the giving of the Law, 10; the noise of war in the camp, 11; the prophesying of Eldad and Medad, 11; the mission of the spies, 11; the murmuring of the people, 12; the sentence, 12; events witnessed by Joshua during the wanderings, 12;

(*c*) *His career in Canaan*, 13; capture of Jericho, 13; campaign against the southern kings, 13; campaign against the northern kings, 13; division of the land, 13; retirement to Timnath-serah, 14; his last charge, 14; his death, 14; his character, 15

Joshua, as a type of Christ, 22; suggested by Holy Scripture, 22; exhibited in (*a*) the name common to both, 23; and its purport, 23; in (*b*) the idea of a conqueror exhibited by both, 23; in (*c*) community of suffering with the people rescued, 23; in (*d*) succession to Moses and the Law, 24; in (*e*) the incidents at the Jordan, 24; in (*f*) the closing scenes of the life of the leader of Israel and the Ascension of our Lord and His session at the right hand of God, 25

Joshua, the work of, 15; extermination of the Canaanites, 15; enjoined by Moses, 15; necessitated by their moral degeneracy, 16; not inflicted summarily, 17; but after (*a*) repeated warnings, 17; and (*b*) repeated postponements, 17; when inflicted, accompanied by (*a*) the most unique arrangements, 18; (*b*) unheard-of restrictions on all natural impulses to plunder and lust, 18, 19; (*c*) every possible provision for enforcing the lesson that it was the Divine Judgment they were inflicting on idolatry and sin, 18

Isaac, meaning of name, 204; birthplace of, 204

Issachar, territory of, 166—168; prophecies of, characteristics of, 168; richness and desolation of inheritance, 168

Jubilee, trumpets of, 56

Judah, tribe of, boundaries and territory of, 128—133; length and breadth of, 136; fourfold division of, 136; cities of, grouped and enumerated, 136

Juttah, a city of Judah, 141, 187; connection of, with David, 141

Kadesh-barnea, position, 96; events connected with, 96; most important encampment next to Sinai, 125

Kanah = "brook of reeds," 145, 148

Kedesh in Naphtali, = "the Holy Place of Naphtali," 174; a city of refuge, 181; called Kedesh in Galilee, 181; king of, slain by Joshua, 110, 111; a town of Issachar, 111, 167, 188

Kedemoth, city of Reuben, 117, 189

Keil's Commentary, references to his remarks on

Authorship of Book of Joshua, 7; design of the writer, 8; milk and honey of Holy Land, 52; defenders of the

INDEX I.

camp at Gilgal, 52; blessings and cursings of the law, 76; victuals of Gibeonites tasted by Israelites, 80; mountain of Halak, 102; dukes of Sihon, 118; Eleazar, 123; Jephunneh, 125; Hebron, 127; Dead Sea, 128; Caleb's daughter, 134; discrepancy in numbers of cities of Judah, 138; daughters of Zelophehad, 147; time of setting up Tabernacle, 156; cities of the Levites, 186; Joshua's farewell, 191; Hebrew style of narrative, 192; Gaash, 214

Keilah, in Judah, position, 139; events connected with it in the life of David, 139

Kenaz, difficulty as to his relationship to Othniel, 134; probably a family name, 125

Kenezite, doubt as to meaning, 125

Kings, name of independent chieftains in Palestine, 63; catalogue and numbers of conquered kings in E. and W. Palestine, 106—111; confederacy of five against Gibeon, 83, 84; their flight and execution, 89—92; conquest of, in S. Palestine, 92—95; confederacy of, in N. Canaan, 97

Kirjathaim, or Kiriathaim, 117; name on Moabite stone, 117

Kirjath-arba, meaning and origin of name, 84; name of Hebron, 84, 134, 186; chief city of the Anakims, 84, 134; Hittites dwelt near in time of Abraham, 44

Kirjath-baal, name of Kirjath-jearim, 141, 159

Kirjathiarius, name of Kirjath-jearim, 81

Kirjath-jearim, one of the four cities of the Gibeonites, 77, 132; meaning of, 81, 132; situation of, 81; allotted to Judah, 81, 132, 159; Ark remained at, 81, 132; once one of the special seats of Baal-worship, 81

Kirjath-sannah = "town of palms," name of Debir, 95, 134, 140

Kirjath-sepher = "City of Books," name of Debir, 95; taken by Othniel, 134

Kishon, or, river before Jokneam, 164; meaning of, 164; reference to, 164

Kitto's Bible Illustrations, on
Courtesy observed towards Rahab, 38; Babylonish garment, 68; old sacks of the Gibeonites, 78; clouted shoes, 79; mouldy bread, 79; hailstones of the East, 87

Kitto's Biblical Cyclopædia, on Mosaic laws about homicide, 180, 181, 183; magicians in Eastern armies, 207; Joshua's last farewell, 213

Knives, sharp = "of flint," 51; used by Joshua, 51; by Zipporah, 51; mentioned by Herodotus, 51; tradition about, 214

Kohathites, descendants of second son of Levi, 184; position and duties during the wanderings, 185; priesthood confined to one section of them, 185; cities assigned
(*a*) to the Kohathite Priests, 186, 187
(*b*) to the Kohathite Levites, 187, 188

Lachish, doubtful position of, 84; subsequent references to, 84; taken on "second day," 93; undesigned coincidence in connection with this, 93

Laish, or Leshem, original name of city of Dan, 176; situation of, 176; origin of, 176; scenery around, 177; taken and burned by children of Dan, 177

Land flowing with milk and honey, why expression is descriptive of Palestine, 52; passages where it occurs, 52

Land of Canaan = country W. of Jordan, 193

Law, copy of, various interpretations of meaning of, 75; inscribed on great stones, 74, 75

Law, historical events of, duty of parents to explain fully to children, 50

League, any, with Canaanites forbidden, 81; with the Gibeonites, made by Joshua, 81; broken by Saul, 81, 82; faithfully observed by Gibeonites, 83

Leagues, of the kings against Joshua. *See* Kings

Lebanon, meaning of word, 32; N. boundary of Holy Land, 32

Lenormant's Manual of Oriental History, on strategy of Israelites under Joshua, 37

Level, high, of parts of Palestine, 161

Levi and the Priesthood, genealogical table of, 185

Levites, no inheritance for, 116, 124; reasons for this, 116, 123, 124, 184; provision for, 116, 124; variously described, 157; Jacob's prophecy concerning, how fulfilled, 183; demand made by them to Joshua, 183, 184; their special functions, 183, 184

Libnah, meaning of, 93; situation, 93, 130; taken by Joshua, 93; king of, slain, 110

Lighted off, meaning, and other uses of, 135

Line, scarlet, meaning of, 41; how made, 41

Living God, force of expression, 44

Locusts, illustration of, 57

Lord, 39; Lord God of gods, 196, 197; Lord God of Israel, 203; significance of each of these titles respectively

Lots, various uses of, 66, 123; custom of great antiquity, 66, 123, 124; mentioned by Homer, 66; used by the Romans, 66, 123; sometimes dice thrown, 67; sometimes tesseræ flung into a vessel, 67;

INDEX I. 223

mentioned by Herodotus, 123; where casting of, by Joshua commenced, 125 Lowlanders. *See* Canaanites

Luz (or Bethel), an ancient Canaanite city, 64; mentioned in time of Abraham, 64; of Jacob, 64, 110; called Bethel by Jacob, 64; doubtful whether "city" of Luz and "Holy place" called Bethel are the same, 64, 143; two different interpretations, 143; Mr Grove's opinion, 143; name "Bethel" not finally appropriated till after the conquest by Joshua, 64; events which rendered place famous, 110; king of, sends help to Ai, 72; slain by Joshua, 110

Maachathites, the, 108; position of, 108; long independence of, 116
Maaleh-acrabbim, meaning of, 128; position of, 129
Macgregor's Rob Roy on the Jordan, quoted, on the windings of the Jordan, 32; Lake Merom, 99; Crocodiles in the Holy Land, 169
Machir, eldest son of Manasseh, 122, 146; power of his descendants, 122, 146; position and nature of territory assigned them, 122, 146; his descendants settled on E. of Jordan, 146
Machpelah, bought from the Hittites by Abraham, 33
Madon, city in N. Canaan, joins league against Joshua, 97; king of, slain by him at waters of Merom, 110
Mahanaim = "two hosts," 120; events connected with, 121
Makkedah, doubtful position of, 86; Canaanites pursued thither by Joshua, 86; concealment of kings in a cave at, 89, 90; their execution, 92; king of, slain by Joshua, 110
Manasseh, son of Joseph, meaning and reason of name, 146; rapid increase in the number of the tribe, 150
Manasseh, half tribe of, 34, 122; possessions on East of Jordan, 34, 120, 122, 123; increase of their numbers, 123
Manasseh, Western, "ten portions" of, 147; boundaries of, 148—150; warlike character of tribe, 121, 122; cities of, in other tribes, 148, 149
Manna, cessation of, 54; Old and New Testament references to it, 54
Maon, city of Judah, 141; events in life of David connected with it, 141; modern name, 104
Mareshah, city of Judah, 139
Mearah, meaning of, 113; situation, 114
Medeba, plain of, when first mentioned, 115; position of, 115
Mediterranean, or Great Sea, W. boundary of Holy Land, 32
Megiddo, commanding position of, 111;

scene of important events, 111; king of, slain by Joshua, 110; defeat of, 150
Mensuration, art of, Israelites familiar with, 157; commission for, appointed by Joshua, 156; way it was carried out, 156
Mephaath, town of Reuben, 117
Merarites, descendants of third son of Levi, 185; position and duties of, during the wanderings, 185, 186; cities assigned them, 189
Merom, Lake, position, 99; modern name, 99; description of, 99. *See* Jordan, sources of
Merom, Waters of, battle at, 99, 100
Midbah. *See* Wilderness
Midianites, princes of, 118; elders of, 119; undesigned coincidence connected with, 119
Migdal-el, thought to be the Magdala of N. T., 174
Milman's History of the Jews, references to their national judgments, 202
Minister, title of Joshua, 31; force of, 31
Mishor, meaning of, 34, 115
Mizpeh = Belle Vue, 161; land of, possessed by Hivites, 44; name of several places in Palestine, 98, 99; of Moab, 99; "of Judah," 139; "of Benjamin," 160; "of Gad," or Gilead, 120. *See* Ramoth-Mizpeh
Mizraim, son of Ham, 113; his descendants, 113
Mizrephoth-maim, 100; meaning of, 100, 101; possibly same as Zarephath, 115
Moabite Stone, where discovered, 116; the four names found on, 117
Moon, standing still of. *See* Sun
Morad, 65
Morrow after Passover, peculiar meaning of, 54
Moses, the servant of the Lord, 31; burial of, at Beth-Peor, 31; oath of, unrecorded in Pentateuch, 126; his grant of land to Eastern Tribes, 115—123; and to daughters of Zelophehad, 147; directions left by him about Levitical cities, 184; his posterity reckoned among the Levites, 185
Mouldy, Hebrew word for, 79; elsewhere translated "cracknels," 79
Mountain, the, place of shelter for spies, description and position of, 40, 41; "of Hebron," 126, 127; of the valley, 117, 118
Mountains, the, of Judah, 104; of Israel, 104, 105; evidence of antiquity of book of Joshua in connection with, 104, 105
Mountaineers. *See* Amorites
Murder, wilful, Mosaic laws respecting, 179; contrasted with Greek and Roman laws, 179

Napheth, or elevated tracts, 98

INDEX I.

Naphtali, territory of tribe, 171—174; numbers of, 172; boundaries, 172, 174; prophecy concerning, mistranslated, 174; subsequent history of tribe, 174, 175
Nations, seven heathen, of Canaan, various enumerations of, 44
Nations of Gilgal, meaning of term, 111; king of, slain, 111
Negeb = "Land of the South," 95, 96, 102, 136. *See* South
Nephtoah, fountain of, 132, 159
Nether, explanation of, 136
Nethinim, meaning of, 82; duties of, 82; Scripture references to, 82
Neviim Rishonim = "earlier prophets," 5; portion of Jewish Canon, 5; books comprised in it, 5
Nisan, 10th day of, day of crossing the Jordan, 45, 49; meaning and significance of this date, 34, 43; 7th, 8th and 5th days referred to, 34
North Palestine, confederacy and subjugation of, 97—102
Now, meaning and force of, at the opening of book of Joshua, 31
Nun, father of Joshua, 9; his descent from Ephraim, 9

Oak, the, of Shechem, or of Moreh, 79, 212; of Mamre, 54
Oath, exacted from Rahab by spies, 40, 41; full meaning of, 40
Oehler's Theology of Old Testament, on stone inscriptions and hieroglyphics, 75; jealousy of God, 210
Officers, different meanings of word in the original, 34, 42; other instances of, 34, 42
Og, king of Bashan, his territory, 34, 107, 108, 116; conquered by the Israelites, 206, 207
Old corn, peculiar meaning of, 53
Old Testament, Jewish division of, 5 (note)
Ophrah in Benjamin, 160
Othniel, doubt as to his relationship to Caleb, 134; takes Kirjath-sepher, 134; marries Caleb's daughter, 135

Palestine, retrospect of conquest of, 102; seven-fold division of, 102
Palestine Exploration Fund, discoveries and reports of, on
   Ancient site and name of Gezer, 94
   Cave of Adullam, 110; country of Naphtali, 172
   Site of Altar on the Jordan, 193
   Joshua's tomb, 214
Palestine, Southern, conquest of, 92—97; fourfold division of, 95, 96; survey of campaigns in, 95, 96
Parched corn, meaning of, 54
Passover, celebration of, at the Jordan, 19, 20, 53

Passover cakes, 54
Pearson on the Creed, references to, 9, 23, 24, 26
Peor, contraction of Baal-peor, 196
Perizzites, one of the "seven nations," 44; meaning of word, 44; supposed locality of, 44
Philistines, when first mentioned, 112; origin of, 104, 113; position, 112; power of, 112, 113; how reckoned as Canaanites, 113; subsequently coalesce with the Anakims, 105
Philistines, the, Galilee of, 112
Phinehas, son of Eleazar, meaning of name, 195; accompanies delegates from Israelites to the Eastern Tribes, 195; memorable events of his life, 195; his tomb still shewn, 195
Pillar of Cloud, Ark takes place of, 43
Piram, king of Jarmuth, 84; hanged by Joshua, 91, 109
Plain, the, = the Arabah, 102, 107; "on the East," 106; of Jezreel or Esdraelon, 152; of the Philistines, 96
Plains, the, of Jericho, or Arboth-Jericho, 50; of Moab, 123; South of Chinneroth, meaning of, 97, 98
Plaster, writing on, 75; its durability, 75
Porter's Handbook, references to, on Edrei, 108; Salcah, 108; city of Asher, 148; Japhia, ascent to, 165; richness and desolation of inheritance of Issachar, 168, 169; inheritance of tribe of Asher, 171; fountains of Hammath, 173; position of Hazor, 174
Prayer of Joshua, before Ai, 65, 66; in battle of Beth-horon, 88; for Caleb, 127
Prince of the Lord's host. *See* Captain
Processions, village bridal, 135
Promised Land, boundaries of. *See* Boundaries
Pusey's Commentary on Daniel referred to, 171; on Obadiah, 164

Quarantania, name of supposed scene of our Lord's 40 days' fast, 41
Quarterly Statement. *See* Palestine Exploration Fund

Rabbah, capital of the Ammonites, 120
Rahab, courtesan and lodging-house keeper of Jericho, 37; her occupations, 37; her courage and faith in hiding the spies, 38, 39; her rescue from the sack of the city, 61; her marriage with Salmon, 61; the ancestress of Jesse, 61; and of the Messiah, 37, 61; her faith commended by St Paul and St James, 37
Rakkath, town in Naphtali, 173; meaning of, 173; situation, 173
Ramah, of Benjamin, 160; of Asher, 170; of Naphtali, 173

INDEX I.

Ramath = "a height," like Ramah and Ramoth, 161
Ramath, "of the South," 163
Ramath-mizpeh, early sanctuary in time of Jacob, 120; its modern name, 120. *See* Ramoth-gilead
Ramoth-gilead = "the heights of Gilead," 120, 182; city of refuge, 181; called Ramath-mizpeh, 120; its other names, 120; memorable events connected with, 120, 182
Remmon-methoar, explanation of, 165
Rending the clothes, 65; by Reuben, 65; by Jacob, 65; by Joseph's brethren, 65; by Joshua, 65
Reproach of Egypt, double meaning of, 52
Rereward = "rearguard," 58; Scripture allusions to, 58
Rest, meaning of word, 35; other uses of it, 105, 127, 190
Reuben, tribe of, territory of, 34, 116—119; prophecy of Jacob concerning, 119; subsequent history, 120; obscurity of, 120
Rhinokolura, the river of Egypt, 112
Ritter's Geography of Palestine, remarks from, on windings of the Jordan, 32; position of Jerusalem, 84; plain of Esdraelon, 152; inheritance of Asher, 171; of Naphtali, 174; trees and gardens of Joppa, 176
Robinson's Bible Researches, referred to, on troops employed against Ai, 70; site of Chephirah, 81; position of Jerusalem, 84; Beth-horon, 159; site of Ramah, 170; Hazor, 173; neighbourhood of Laish, 177
Roofs, Eastern, flat, useful for various purposes, 39; battlements required, 39; Roman and Italian, 39
Rosenmüller, quotations from, 80, 156
Rye, and flax, harvest. *See* Harvests

Sabbath day's journey. *See* Cubits
Salcah, position and description of, 108; prophecies fulfilled in, 108
Salmon, marries Rahab, 61
Salt, City of, 142; Covenant of, 80; Valley of, 142
Sanctify yourselves, meaning of command to, 43
Scarlet thread. *See* Line
Sea of the Plain = Dead Sea, or Salt Sea, 46, 107
Seir, Edomite mountain range of, 205; meaning of word, 205; origin of name, 205; situation of, 205; given to Esau, 205. *See* Horites. Another range in boundary of Judah, 132; why so called, 132
Seven, significance of number, among the Hebrews, 57; among different nations, 57. *See* "Week," and "Swear"
Shaalabbin = "the place of foxes," 175

JOSHUA

Shakespeare, quotations from, 56, 58, 64, 79, 87, 100, 126, 136
Shebarim = the mines, 64
Shechem. city in Mount Ephraim, 75, 181; situation, 75, 148, 181; central city on West of Jordan, 181; one of the cities of refuge, 181; events, and sacred associations connected with, 76, 203, 212
Shechem, a son of Manasseh, 147
Shephêlah, the, meaning of, 77, 96; situation of, 96, 112, 136
Shihor-libnath, or Crocodile Brook, 169
Shiloh, meaning of word, 158; erection of Tabernacle at, 153—158; remarks on selection of site, 155, 158; description of, 155
Shimron, city of, 97; its full name, 97; position, 97; king of, defeated and slain by Joshua, 97, 101, 110
Shimron-meron. *See* Shimron
Shittim, or Abel Shittim, encampment of Israelites at, 36; meaning of word, 36, 207; scripture references to, 36; situation and description of, 36; spies sent from, to view Jericho, 36; breaking up of the encampment there, 42
Shoe, unloosing, a mark of reverence, 55
Shoes, material of in East, 78
Shunem, town of Issachar, 166; position of, 167; scripture incidents connected with, 167
Sibmah, town of Reuben, 117; position of, 117; prophecies concerning, 117
Sihon, king of the Amorites, or of Heshbon, his territory described, 34, 106; occupied by Reuben, 34; conquest of, referred to, 106, 206, 207. *See* Dukes
Sihor, the river of Egypt, 112, 113
Simeon, tribe of, territory of, 161—164; within that of Judah, 162; villages of, 163; prophecy of Jacob concerning, 163; not mentioned in prophecy of Moses, 163; obscurity of the tribe, their character and history, 163, 164; prophecy of Obadiah fulfilled in, 164
Sincerity, meaning and use of word, 208
Sion = "the elevated," name of Hermon, 106
Slack, derivation and meaning of, 85
Smith's Biblical Dictionary, articles referred to, on knives of flint, 51; seven, number, 57; caves, 90; fenced cities, 91; Ashkelon, 113; Manasseh, 123; Wilderness, 137; Land of Gilead, 146; Tabernacle, 156; Cabul, 170; Naphtali, 174
Snares, different kinds described, 201
Solaria. *See* Roofs
South, country of the, described, 95, 96, 136; = Teman, 113; Land of the South, 163; "they of the South," 164
Speaker's Commentary referred to on wedge of gold, 68; fenced cities of Naphtali, 173; Joshua's farewell, 192

15

INDEX I.

Spear, Joshua's, 72; various kinds of, 72
Spies, sent to view Jericho, 36—38; and Ai, 64
Springs, country of the, described, 96, 107; of water, meaning of, 135; Upper and Nether, given to Caleb's daughter, 135; meaning and position of them, 136
Stanley's (Dean) Lectures on Jewish Church, on character of Joshua, 14; his name, 22; bulls of Bashan, 34; drying of the Jordan bed, 47; Jewish fortified cities, 50; Battle at Waters of Merom, 99; Machir, 122; request of Caleb's daughter, 136; sacred lots, 158; Land of Naphtali, 175; inheritance of Dan, 177; ancient idolatries, 204; oak of Shechem, 212; tomb of Eleazar, 215
Stanley's Sinai and Palestine, referred to on windings of Jordan, 32; position of Jericho, 36; scene of our Lord's Temptation, 40, 41; ravines near Ai, 71; slow pace of Eastern armies, 81; position of Jerusalem, 83, 84; Battle of Bethhoron, 85; Second Part of Book of Joshua, 112; history and character of Reubenites, 120; Benjamites, 161; Simeonites, 162, 163; Mountain of Hebron, 127; gift of Hebron to Caleb, 127; Maaleh-akrabbim, 129; Adummim, 130; Engedi, history and description of, 142; defeats of Gilboa and Megiddo, 150; selection of Shiloh as site for Tabernacle, 155; tribes of Issachar, 168, Asher, 171, Naphtali, 174
Stone, Moabite, 116, 117; of Bohan, 130, 159; of Shechem, 212, 213
Stone-squarers. *See* Giblites
Stones, bevelled, of the Temple, 114
Stones, great, set up as memorials or witnesses of past events, 47, 48, 50, 69, 74, 212, 213; set up by Jacob, 47, 212; by Moses, 212; by Samuel, 47; by Joshua in Gilgal, 48, 50, 212; in the bed of the Jordan, 48; in the Valley of Achor, 69; on Mount Ebal, 74, 75; before the cave at Makkedah, 92; under the Oak of Shechem, 212, 213; sometimes became causes of idolatry, 50
Stoning, a punishment for blasphemy and idolatry, 69
Stood still, meaning of as applied to the sun, 88; as applied to cities, 101
Straitly shut up, meaning of, 55, 56
Stranger that sojourneth = naturalized foreigners, 182; variously accounted for, 182
Subdue, meaning of, 156
Suburbs, of cities, explained, 124
Succoth = Booths, 121; where situated, 121; events famous for, 121
Sun and moon, standing still of, 88; an answer to Joshua's prayer of faith, 87, 88; story taken from Book of Jasher, 89; referred to by Isaiah, and Habakkuk, 6; manner of the protraction of light not told, 88; Edersheim's translation, 89; account of Josephus, 89
Surtabeh, Talmudic name of great altar, 193
Swear, = "to do seven times," 57

Taanach, one of six separate cities given to W. Manasseh, 148; position and celebrity of, 110, 111; king of, slain by Joshua, 110; tributary, but not conquered, city, 149, 150; name still retained, 111; given to the Levites, 188
Tabernacle, set up at Gilgal, 48; at Shiloh, 153—158; at Nob, 156; at Gibeon, 156; lots cast by Eleazar and Joshua at door of, 178; called "The Tabernacle of the Congregation," 154, 155; or "Tabernacle," or "Tent," "of meeting," 155, 157; meaning of, 155
Tabor, mountain and town of Zebulun, 167. See also 164
Tappuah in Judah, position of, 110; modern name, 110; king of, slain, 110; meaning of name, 140
Tel = heap, 73; Palestine a land of *Tels*, 73; Ai made a *Tel* for ever, 73, 74
Teman, = the South, 113
Temptation, our Lord's, supposed scene of, 41
Terah, father of Abraham, 203; his descendants, 204; idolatry of, 204; tradition about, 204
Terebinth, of Mamre, 54; spreading, 174
This day, unto, force and frequency of expression in Book of Joshua, 48; places where it occurs, 48; proofs in these historical allusions that the Book, as we have it, was compiled after the death of Joshua, 7, § 7
Thomson's Land and the Book, references to windings of Jordan, 32; ravines near Ai, 70; old writings on stones, 75; Valley of Gerizim, 77; Well of Enrogel, 130, 131; Bethshean, 149; Endor, 149; crocodiles in Palestine, 169; capture of Laish, 177
Timnah, or Timnath, or Thimnathah, a town of Dan, 132, 133, 175; another town of Judah, 141
Timnath-serah, or Timnath-heres, the city and home of Joshua, 178, 200; meaning of, 178; position and beauty of, 178; description by Lieut. Conder, 214; Joshua buried there, 214
Tirzah, a suburb of Samaria, 111; situation of, 111; Scripture mention of, 111; beauty of, 111; king of, slain by

Joshua, 111; one of the five daughters of Zelophehad, 147
Token, or sign, true, meaning of, 40
Treasury of the Lord, certain spoils in war reserved for, 60
Trespass, committed a, significant meaning of, 63
Tribes, Two and a Half, Joshua's exhortations to, 34, 35; possessions of, 34, 106—109, 115—123; boundaries of, 115, 116; number of fighting men in, 35. *See* Altar and Embassy
Tristram's Land of Israel, descriptions of, Plains of Shittim, 36; overflowings of Jordan, 45; Valley of Gerizim, 76; Wilderness of Judæa, 142; Plain of Esdraelon, 152; situation and ruins of Shiloh, 155; city of Dan, 177
Tristram's Land of Moab, descriptions of, River Arnon, 106; ruins of Heshbon, 107; Kirjathaim, 117; Zareth-shahar, 117, 118; shore of Dead Sea, 128; Engedi, 142
Trumpets of rams' horns, description of, 56; elsewhere referred to, 57
Truthfulness, low standard of, in ancient times, 38
Tyre, city of, in Asher, 170; conquest of not attempted by Israelites, 170, 190

Upper and Nether Springs. *See* Springs
Urim and Thummim, neglect of by Joshua, 80, 81

Vale, country of the, described, 96
Valley, "The," division of Palestine, 102; of Achor, 69; of Ajalon, 88; of Elah, 139; of Gerizim, 74, 75, 76; of the Giants, or Valley of Rephaim, 131, 132, 152 (*see* Baal-Perazim); of Hinnom, 131; of Jiphthah-el, 165; of Jezreel, 152; of the Jordan, 42, 121; of Israel, 102; of Mizpeh, 101; of Nazareth, 165; of the Orontes, 12, 114; of Salt, 142
Van de Velde, his narrative referred to, 46, 130, 149
Vaughan's Heroes of Faith, Faith of Rahab, 38; of the army encompassing Jericho, 56, 60
Vehicles, not used in Palestine at the present day, 152
Victuals, meaning of word, 34; of the Gibeonites partaken of, by the Israelites, 180
View = to review, 64
Villages = farm premises, 119; where built, 152

Walls of Jericho, fall of, attributed to faith of the army, 60, 61, 62, 63
Water of Jericho, the, meaning of, 143
Wedge of gold, a, meaning of, 68

Week of seven days, among what nations in use, 57
Western Palestine, conquered kings of, 109—111
Wheat harvest. *See* Harvests
White Mountain, the. *See* Lebanon
Whole stones, altar of, on Mt Ebal, 74, 75; meaning of, 75; always required, 75
Wilberforce's Heroes of Hebrew History, on character of Joshua, 11; wars of Joshua, 22; gospel in Joshua, 25; the Lord's appearance to Joshua, 55; Joshua's farewell, 203; Joshua's career, 214
Wilderness, or Midbah, or Arabah, 137; position of, 137, 143; of Judæa described, 142; upon the Plain, 182
Window, escape of spies from, 40; similar instance in New Testament, 40
Wine-bottles of Gibeonites, 78; allusion to such in New Testament, 78
Wist, derivation and meaning of, 38
Wordsworth's (Bishop) Commentary, on Curse pronounced on Jericho, 62; confession of Achan, 67, 69; apparent discrepancy in numbers of troops at Ai, 70
Worship, Divine, four elements of, 201
Wyclif's translation, quotations from, *passim*

Xaloth, town of, 167

Zaanaim, Plain of, 172; description of, 172
Zaanannim, Allon to, =Oak by Zaanannim, 172; meaning of, 172; references to, 172
Zabdi, or Zimri, grandfather of Achan, 63
Zaretan, or Zarthan, 46; situation of, 46; Adam, that is beside, meaning of, 46; modern name, 46
Zareth-shahar = "splendour of the dawn," 117; position of, 117; description of, 118
Zarhites, the, house of, 67
Zebulun, territory of, 164—166; numbers of, 164; subsequent history and character of tribe, 166
Zelah, burial-place of Saul, 161
Zelophebad, second son of Hepher, 147; request of daughters of, to Joshua, 147; their inheritance, 147
Zephath, or Hormah, 109
Zidon, the great metropolis of Phœnicia, 100, 170; included in Asher, but not conquered by him, 170, 190
Ziklag, position, 162; meaning of, 138; events connected with, 138, 162
Zin, desert of, 129; spot in desert of, 129
Ziph, city of Judah, 141; events connected with, 141; another town of Judah, 137
Zoreah, city of, 138
Zuzims, or Zamzummims, 104

INDEX II.

(Words and Phrases explained.)

About a whole day, 89
Accursed, 59, 63
Allon to Zaanannim, 172
Altar Ed, 199
Ambush, 70
Anathema, 59, 66
Any good thing, 191
Appointed cities, 181, 182
Asked not counsel, 80, 81
At the passage, 194
Babylonish garment, 68
Before the Lord, 68
Blessed or blessing, 127, 135, 192, 199
Blood, bloodguilty, 41
Book of the Law, 33, 212
Buildeth Jericho, 62
Cast lots, 67
Cherem, 62, 66, 67
Circles, 112, 193
City in the midst of the river, 117
Clouted, 78
Coast, 117
Committed a trespass, 63
Compass, 129
Compassed, 132, 159, 165
Congregation, 154
Copy of the Law, 75
Counted to the Canaanite, 113
Deo dati, or donati, 82
Devoted, 40, 59, 62
Discomfited, 85, 86
Dukes, 118
Entering of the gate, 180
Espy, 125, 126
Father of Gilead, 146
Fear of, 197
Fenced cities, 90
Fetched a compass, 129
Folly, 67
From Adam, 46
Frontier fortress, 50
Gal, 74
Galilee, 181
Galilee of the Philistines, 112, 193
Gehenna, 131
God forbid, 198
Going down, 65
Hell, 206
Hewers of wood, 82
Hill, 215
Hills, 77, 95
Hough, 99, 100, 101
Intend, 199
Jealous, 210
Jordan by Jericho, 143
Kings, 37, 63

Land of Canaan, 193
Lighted off, 135
Lord God of gods, 196
Lot, fall of, 67, 147
Mæniana, 39
Midst of Jordan, 48
Moe, 86, 87
Morrow after Passover, 54
Morrow after Sabbath, 54
Mouldy, 79
Napheth, 98
Negeb, 95
Nether, 136
Nethinim, 82
Neviim Rishonim, 5
Numbered, 71
Officers, 34, 42
Old, 53, 70, 78
Parched corn, 54
Pleased, 198, 199
Quarantania, 41
Reproach of Egypt, 52
Rereward, 56, 58
Rested, 105, 127
Sabbath day's journey, 43
Sanctify, 43, 66
Second, 51, 93
Sharp knives, 51
Sincerity, 208
See to, 193, 194
Separate cities, 145
Slack, 85, 156
Snares, 201
Solaria, 39
South, 135
Springs, 95, 135
Stood still, 88, 101
Straitly, 55, 56
Stranger that sojourneth, 182
Subdue, 156
Suburbs, 124
Swear, 57
Tel, 73, 74
Three countries, 150
Time appointed, 72
Token, 40
Took of, 80
Trespass, 63
Use of the bow, 89
Utterly destroyed, 40, 60
Victuals, 34
View, 64
Villages, 119, 152
Wedge, 68
Wine bottles, 78
Wist, 38, 72

CAMBRIDGE: PRINTED BY C. J. CLAY, M.A. AT THE UNIVERSITY PRESS.

THE CAMBRIDGE BIBLE FOR SCHOOLS

Opinions of the Press.

"We were quite prepared to find in Canon Farrar's St Luke a masterpiece of Biblical criticism and comment, and we are not disappointed by our examination of the volume before us. It reflects very faithfully the learning and critical insight of the Canon's greatest works, his 'Life of Christ' and his 'Life of St Paul,' but differs widely from both in the terseness and condensation of its style. What Canon Farrar has evidently aimed at is to place before students as much information as possible within the limits of the smallest possible space, and in this aim he has hit the mark to perfection. The introduction deals with the Gospels generally, and with St Luke's in particular. It gives an excellent biographical sketch of St Luke, points out the evidences for the authenticity of St Luke's Gospel, gives in detail the characteristics of the Gospel, furnishes an analysis of its contents, states the chief ancient manuscripts of the Gospels, and presents us with a brief account of the Herods as mentioned in the Gospels and the Acts. The special characteristics of the work are these:—(1) All important mistranslations of the Authorised Version are corrected; (2) the apparent inconsistencies with the other Gospels are harmonised; (3) as a rule, Scripture is made to interpret Scripture; (4) the results of the highest and most recent textual criticism and of fresh scholarship, as well as of historical research, are extensively utilised to clear up obscurities and to illustrate the mind and meaning of the Evangelist; (5) illustrations of the text—either in its language or its sentiment—are frequently drawn from literary sources, ancient and modern. We must further draw attention to the valuable appendix, which, amongst other mooted points, discusses the double genealogies of Christ and the difficult question was 'the Last Supper an actual Passover?' It is only fair to say that as a series the 'Cambridge Bible for Schools' has no equal in point of excellence and usefulness, and that Canon Farrar's work is quite the best of the series."—*The Examiner.*

"In many of our Grammar Schools and High Schools, at least the elder lads are now 'examined' in some portion of Holy Scripture, and have to 'get it up' as they would a book of Virgil or of Homer. In a large proportion of these schools the Scripture Examination is conducted by members of the Cambridge University. The examiners have found, as was natural, that, while on every other subject handbooks of the most accessible and serviceable kind abound, there is an absolute dearth of similar manuals on the several books of Scripture. Now the lads in our schools, and even the junior students of our colleges, can hardly be expected to keep a long array of commentaries on their shelves, or to be able to use them to much purpose even if they have access to them. Hence the Syndics of the University Press have decided to produce a series of the Scripture manuals of which there is just now so great a need, and have selected Canon Perowne as general editor of the series. No better selection could have been made. The name of Dr Perowne is a guarantee for good and scholarly work; while his intimate acquaintance with the Biblical scholars of every Church and school of thought will enable him to secure the co-operation of the men best fitted to assist him.

"The first volume of the series now lies before me—a small octavo of two hundred pages. Paper and type are as good as can be desired. And into this small volume Dr Maclear, besides a clear and able Introduction to the Gospel, and the text of St Mark, has compressed many hundreds of valuable and helpful notes. In short, he has given us a capital manual of the kind required—containing all that is needed to illustrate the text, i.e. all that can be drawn from the history, geography, customs, and manners of the time. Of course it is part of a *School Bible*, and does not trace the sequence of thought in the Gospel, or emphasize the truths taught in it; still less does it deduce and discuss doctrines. But as a handbook, giving in a clear and succinct form the information which a lad requires in order to stand an examination in the Gospel, it is admirable... I can very heartily commend it, not only to the senior boys and girls in our High Schools, but also to Sunday-school teachers, who may get from it the very kind of knowledge they often find it hardest to get."—*Expositor.*

"The scheme is well started in the little book before us. Dr Maclear has formed a sound conception of the kind of book needed for school purposes, and has made his contribution thoroughly serviceable. ...With the help of a book like this, an intelligent teacher may make 'Divinity' as interesting a lesson as any in the school course. The notes are of a kind that will be, for the most part, intelligible to boys of the lower forms of our public schools; but they may be read with greater profit by the fifth and sixth, in conjunction with the original text."—*The Academy.*

"St Mark is edited by Dr Maclear, Head Master of King's College School. It is a very business-like little book. The text is given in paragraphs, and each paragraph has a title, which reappears as a division of the notes. The introduction, which occupies twenty pages, is clear and good, and concludes with an analysis of the book. There are maps and an index. The notes are pointed and instructive, and constantly give words and phrases from Wicliff's version, and quotations from classical and modern authors, which add greatly to the interest of the work and to its usefulness for schools. There is a good list of writers who have undertaken other parts of this edition of the Bible, including the editor and his distinguished brothers, Professor Plumptre, Canon Farrar, Dr Moulton, and Mr Sanday."—*Contemporary Review.*

"*The Gospel according to S. Mark*, with Notes and Introduction, by Rev. G. F. Maclear, D.D. (Cambridge University Press), is a publication which will be of the highest value for all teaching purposes; it is beautifully executed in all respects, and deserves a high recommendation."—*Literary Churchman.*

"*The Gospel according to St Mark*, with Notes by the Rev. G. F. Maclear, D.D., is the first of a series of Text-books upon the Bible, divided into handy portions, suitable for school use. The whole of the

OPINIONS OF THE PRESS. 3

Bible will be in due course annotated and published in separate parts, at a moderate price, by the Syndicate of the Cambridge University Press. If the succeeding books of the series shall be as well edited as the one now before us, we may confidently predict a large sale for them.... Dr Maclear's introductory chapters and analysis of the Gospel of St Mark are excellent....Of course the notes betoken an accurate and scholarly acquaintance with the Greek text. This manual will be found most useful to schoolmasters and Sunday-school teachers; to them the cheapness of this book (only half-a-crown) will be an additional recommendation."—*John Bull.*

"We welcome with enthusiasm this first fruit of the banding together of eminent divinity students of our Universities under the editorship of Dr Perowne, and are not sorry that it represents the labours of so experienced a scholar and teacher as Dr Maclear, upon the Gospel of St Mark. We gather from it an earnest of the handy and compact arrangement to be looked for in the contents of the volumes to follow, the ordering of the requisite introductory matter, the conciseness yet sufficiency of the notes to the text, the fullness of the *general* index, and the discreet choice of that of special words and phrases."—*English Churchman.*

"*The Gospel according to St Matthew*, by the Rev. A. Carr. This valuable series of school books is under the editorship of Professor Perowne, and is doing a great and thorough educational work in our schools. The volume before us condenses in the smallest possible space the best results of the best commentators on St Matthew's Gospel. The introduction is able, scholarly, and eminently practical, as it bears on the authorship and contents of the Gospel, and the original form in which it is supposed to have been written. It is well illustrated by two excellent maps of the Holy Land and of the Sea of Galilee."—*English Churchman.*

"*The Book of Joshua.* Edited by G. F. Maclear, D.D. We have the first instalment of what we have long desiderated, a School Commentary on the books of Scripture. If we may judge of the work contemplated by the sample before us it has our heartiest commendation. With Dr J. J. S. Perowne for General Editor and an eminent list of well-known Biblical scholars as contributors, we have the highest guarantee that the work will be completed in a scholarly, useful, and reliable form. The introductory chapter of the present volume on the life, character, and work of Joshua is ably and attractively written.... The 'notes' will be found brief, terse, pointed, and suggestive. The historical illustrations are apposite and felicitous. The maps and geographical explanations are accurate and valuable. The book ought to be in the hands of every teacher, and even clergymen will find it a valuable accession to their list of commentaries. We await the issue of the remaining volumes with interest."—*Weekly Review.*

"A very important work in the nature of a Scriptural text-book for the use of students has been undertaken by the Syndics of the Cambridge University Press—namely, the separate issue of the several books of the Bible, each edited and annotated by some Biblical scholar of high reputation....The value of the work as an aid to Biblical study, not merely in schools but among people of all classes who are desirous to have intelligent knowledge of the Scriptures, cannot easily be overestimated."—*The Scotsman.*

"Among the Commentaries which are in course of publication, the *Cambridge Bible for Schools* (Cambridge University Press) deserves mention. It is issued in conveniently-sized volumes, each containing a Book of the Old or New Testament. We have just received two of these volumes—one, on *The Book of Joshua*, prepared by Dr Maclear, of the King's College School; the other, by Professor Plumptre, on *The Epistle of St James*. That they are designed for the use of schools sufficiently indicates the scope of the annotations which accompany the text of each of these books. That on the Book of Joshua is enriched with notices of the most recent discoveries in Biblical archæology and geography. The illustrations, however, are not confined to such notices, but embrace a wider exegesis. It has, moreover, two maps and a very good index of the contents of the annotations. The volume on the Epistle of St James is, independently of a sufficient commentary, enriched with a useful introduction, in which the authorship of the Epistle and the time when written are discussed with the fulness which we had a right to expect from Dr Plumptre. The series will be valuable to schools; but it will by no means exhaust its usefulness there. More advanced readers of Holy Scripture than are to be found in our public schools will derive assistance from these handy volumes, which, when completed—if completed as those already published give us reason to expect—will be a welcome addition to our commentaries on Holy Scripture."—*John Bull.*

"*St Matthew*, edited by A. Carr, M.A. *The Book of Joshua*, edited by G. F. Maclear, D.D. *The General Epistle of St James*, edited by E. H. Plumptre, D.D. (Cambridge University Press). These volumes are constructed upon the same plan, and exhibit the same features as that on 'St Mark's Gospel,' of which we gave a full account on its issue. The introductions and notes are scholarly, and generally such as young readers need and can appreciate. The maps in both Joshua and Matthew are very good, and all matters of editing are faultless. Professor Plumptre's notes on 'The Epistle of St James' are models of terse, exact, and elegant renderings of the original, which is too often obscured in the authorised version."—*Nonconformist.*

"The issue of the Bible in sections, although not an entirely novel plan, is now, we believe, adopted for the first time with a special view to school use, each book in this series being intended as a separate text-book, complete in itself, with its introduction, notes, and maps. The system which has always been adopted with the best results in regard to secular school-books can scarcely fail to be equally valuable when applied to the sacred volume, and, as the names of the editors will show, the most eminent scholars and divines of the day are being employed upon the work. The text adopted in the edition is that of Scrivener's Cambridge Paragraph Bible, the notes in every case being printed under the text. When completed, the Bible will form a most valuable work for reference as well as for its more immediate purpose."
—*Publishers' Circular.*

"*The General Epistle of St James*, with Notes and Introduction. By Professor Plumptre, D.D. (University Press, Cambridge). This is only a part of the Cambridge Bible for Schools, and may be bought for a few pence. Nevertheless it is, so far as I know, by far the best exposition of the Epistle of St James in the English language. Not

OPINIONS OF THE PRESS.

Schoolboys or Students going in for an examination alone, but Ministers and Preachers of the Word, may get more real help from it than from the most costly and elaborate commentaries."—*Expositor.*

"With Mr Carr's well-edited apparatus to St Matthew's Gospel, where the text is that of Dr Scrivener's Cambridge Paragraph Bible, we are sure the young student will need nothing but a good Greek text.... We should doubt whether any volume of like dimensions could be found so sufficient for the needs of a student of the first Gospel, from whatever point of view he may approach it."—*Saturday Review.*

"THE CAMBRIDGE BIBLE FOR SCHOOLS: St Matthew, Joshua, Jonah, Corinthians, and James. We have on a former occasion drawn the attention of our readers to the first volume of this excellent series— St Mark. The volumes indicated above have now been published, and fully maintain the high standard won by the first. They furnish valuable and precise information in a most convenient form, and will be highly esteemed by students preparing for examinations, and also by Sunday-school teachers and others. They are particularly valuable in furnishing information concerning history, geography, manners and customs, in illustration of the sacred text."—*The Baptist.*

"THE CAMBRIDGE BIBLE FOR SCHOOLS:—*The First Epistle to the Corinthians.* Edited by Professor Lias. *Jonah.* Edited by Archdeacon Perowne. (Cambridge University Press.) Every fresh instalment of this annotated edition of the Bible for schools confirms the favourable opinion we formed of its value from the examination of its first number. The origin and plan of the Epistle are discussed with its character and genuineness. The analysis of its contents is very full and clear, and will be found of great service to the teachers of the more advanced classes in Sunday-schools and to the leaders of Bible-classes. The notes at the foot of the text are brief, but suggestive. We should recommend the committee of the City Missions, and all who have charge of rural evangelization societies, to put this book into the hands of their agents....The moral teaching of the book is so valuable, and the light it sheds upon the growth of religion amongst the Jews so interesting, that these elements ought to receive the largest share of an editor's attention."—*The Nonconformist.*

"Dr Maclear's commentary for Schools on *The Book of Joshua* is, as may be anticipated from him, clear and compendious. The historical books of the Old Testament are especially adapted for such an exegesis, elucidating many minute points, which might escape the observation of a less careful student. Another volume of the same series, *The Gospel of St Matthew,* with Mr Carr's annotations, deserves equally high praise. The commentary is terse and scholarly, without losing its interest for ordinary readers. The maps, the index, and the tabulated information in the Appendix all enhance the usefulness of this handy little volume. The name of the editor, Dr Plumptre, is in itself enough to recommend the edition of *The General Epistle of St James,* in the same series. More copious than the companion volumes, it contains some lengthy notes in the form of an excursus—*e.g.* on the personal relation of St Paul and St James the Less."—*Guardian.*

"The last part, the Book of Jonah, is from the hand of (The Ven. T. T.) Perowne, Archdeacon of Norwich. The little work is well done, written in a graceful, lucid, and cheerful style, which will be attractive to young readers. The notes contain information and reflection in a very just proportion, the great preponderance being given to information."—*The British and Foreign Evangelical Review.*

"*The Acts of the Apostles.*—Edited by J. Rawson Lumby, D.D., Norrisian Professor of Divinity.—We said before, in noticing former volumes, not only the schoolboy or girl, or the student preparing for examination, but the general reader and devout Christian will find these handy books most edifying. The editors have drawn from history, geography, and the manners and customs of the East, everything that will illustrate the text and make it clear to the dullest comprehension."
—*Cambridge Chronicle.*

"We believe we have already spoken of previous volumes in terms of praise. Indeed, it would be difficult to speak too highly of the volumes before us, especially that edited by Professor Lumby. They carry on the same 'lines' as their predecessors, and are eminently adapted for the needs of those schools where it is the custom to set a portion of Scripture to be got up just like a book of Virgil or Homer. The notes are foot-notes, and explain with clearness and brevity all the points of interest, geographical, topographical, and archæological, touched upon in the text."—*Educational Times.*

"*The Book of Joshua.* By the Rev. G. F. Maclear, D.D. *Jonah.* By the Ven. T. T. Perowne, B.D. *The Gospel according to St Matthew.* By the Rev. A. Carr, M.A. *The Gospel according to St Mark.* By the Rev. G. F. Maclear, D.D. *The Acts of the Apostles* (i—xiv). By J. Rawson Lumby, D.D. We cannot have a healthier intellectual exercise than an impartial examination of the structure and contents of Scripture, and there are no books more likely to aid such an examination than the Manuals issued by the Syndics of the University Press. Works of more solid worth-have not been published. The text adopted throughout is that of Scrivener's Cambridge Paragraph Bible. Each part contains a careful and scholarly introduction on the authorship, the date, the sources, &c., of the book. The notes are terse and suggestive, giving in few words the gist of elaborate researches. They abound in fine textual criticism, no less than in valuable doctrinal and ethical comments. Dr Maclear is thoroughly at home in such an historical book as *Joshua.* He draws illustrations from all quarters, especially from old English literature, and writes in a style of great elegance. The volume on *Jonah* is a literary gem, both on apologetic and hermeneutical grounds. In Mr Carr's *Matthew* there is, in addition to keen verbal criticism and archæological research, a determined effort to trace the course of thought in the inspired text, to point out the *nexus* between the various sections and verses of the Gospel. Mr Carr has all the qualifications which vigorous and refined scholarship can give, and possesses what is of far higher value, clear spiritual insight. Mr Lumby's manner of work is known to most of our readers from his papers in the *Expositor.* His notes on the *Acts* will certainly enhance his reputation, and form a valuable commentary on one of the most important books of the New Testament....All these books are, in fact, a valuable addition to our Biblical expositions, original contributions to a subject of transcendant importance; and while they cannot fail to be valued by those for whom they are expressly designed, we have a shrewd suspicion that they will be still more highly appreciated by minds of a riper order. The maps which most of the manuals contain are beautifully executed, and will be a great aid to the intelligent study of the Scriptures. Canon Perowne, to whom the general editorship of the series has been entrusted, may be congratulated on the success which the scheme has so far achieved. 'The Cambridge Bible for Schools' is one of the most popular and useful literary enterprises of the nineteenth century."—*Baptist Magazine.*

"THE CAMBRIDGE BIBLE FOR SCHOOLS—*The Second Epistle to the Corinthians.* By Professor LIAS. *The General Epistles of St Peter and St Jude.* By E. H. PLUMPTRE, D.D. We welcome these additions to the valuable series of the Cambridge Bible. We have nothing to add to the commendation which we have from the first publication given to this edition of the Bible. It is enough to say that Professor Lias has completed his work on the two Epistles to the Corinthians in the same admirable manner as at first. Dr Plumptre has also completed the Catholic Epistles."—*Nonconformist.*

"(1) *The Acts of the Apostles.* By J. RAWSON LUMBY, D.D. (2) *The Second Epistle of the Corinthians,* edited by Professor LIAS. The introduction is pithy, and contains a mass of carefully-selected information on the authorship of the Acts, its designs, and its sources. ......The Second Epistle of the Corinthians is a manual beyond all praise, for the excellence of its pithy and pointed annotations, its analysis of the contents, and the fulness and value of its introduction." —*Examiner.*

"*The Cambridge Bible for Schools.*—The Cambridge University Press has not made of late years a more valuable contribution to the literature of the age than this series of books of the Bible, which has been prepared specially for schools....We have been most careful to examine *St Matthew,* edited by Rev. A. Carr, M.A., as our thoughts are directed in the line of the International Lessons for the first six months of the next year, and we are very pleased to direct our readers' attention to a work which is calculated to be so helpful to them. The introductory portion is very able, so full of interesting matter, and yet so concisely put. This quality of conciseness characterises the notes throughout, and as they appear on the same page as the letter press to which they relate, facility of reference is thus obtained."—*The Sunday School Chronicle.*

"THE CAMBRIDGE BIBLE FOR SCHOOLS.—The 2nd Epistle to the Corinthians, with Notes, Map, and Introduction. By the Rev. J. J. Lias, M.A. We have here a noteworthy sample of the thoroughness of the editing of the various books of the English Bible under the superintendence of Dean Perowne, and a trustworthy earnest of his choice of the best coadjutors for each particular volume. The Rev. Professor Lias, M.A., is not unknown as a profound Biblical scholar; but, if he were, his arrangement and discrimination of materials, his shrewd weighing of arguments where there is crux for commentators, the general soberness and serviceableness of his notes would recommend him to those who require a scholarly editor for even the Bible in English. These are and ought to be many, and it is no small boon to them that the Syndics of the Cambridge Pitt Press are alive to their need and desire. We have examined the notes, and can only say that their soundness and orthodoxy are such as to give a comfortable assurance that Cambridge and Lampeter undergraduates are fortunate in being guided by such sound and sage divines as Professor Lias."—*The English Churchman and Clerical Journal.*

"*The Cambridge Bible for Schools.*—Romans: Edited by Handley C. G. Moule, M.A. In this work, small as it looks, the Biblical student has a biography of St Paul; an analysis of his famous epistle; parallels between the writings to the Romans and Galatians; a sketch of the argument; and a most elaborate mass of notes, with alphabetical index, reflecting to one glance the industry and erudition of the annotator. Dean Perowne, who undertakes the editorship of this series, confesses that whilst reviewing the notes and checking any omissions, he has left each contributor to the unfettered exercise of his own judgment, and to each commentary its own individual character. Of the enormous expenditure of research, and thought, and learning, we should fail to convey an adequate idea if we attempted it. It would be a mistake to suppose that this work is fitted only for scholars. If not indispensable to every reader of the Scriptures it offers at least to all a great help, and it has been so well digested and arranged that it may be used as an index and work of reference, or as a treatise."—*The Sherborne, Dorchester, and Taunton Journal.*

"*The Cambridge Bible for Schools.—The Epistle to the Romans.* By H. C. G. Moule, M.A. This admirable school series continues its work. Mr Moule treats in this new volume of one of the profoundest of the New Testament Books. His work is scholarly, clear, full, and devout, and we are thankful that such volumes find their way into our schools....... The volumes, taken as a whole, are admirable."— *The Freeman.*

"The Rev. H. C. G. Moule, M.A., has made a valuable addition to THE CAMBRIDGE BIBLE FOR SCHOOLS in his brief commentary on the EPISTLE TO THE ROMANS. The "Notes" are very good, and lean, as the notes of a School Bible should, to the most commonly accepted and orthodox view of the inspired author's meaning; while the Introduction, and especially the Sketch of the Life of St Paul, is a model of condensation. It is as lively and pleasant to read as if two or three facts had not been crowded into well-nigh every sentence." —*Expositor.*

"It is seldom we have met with a work so remarkable for the compression and condensation of all that is valuable in the smallest possible space as in the volume before us. Within its limited pages we have 'a sketch of the Life of St Paul,' which really amounts to a full and excellent biography; we have further a critical account of the date of the Epistle to the Romans, of its language, and of its genuineness. The notes are numerous, full of matter, to the point, and leave no real difficulty or obscurity unexplained."—*The Examiner.*

"To the mature reader, the book may be most confidently recommended. He will have his reserve about the theology, but he will find it an admirably careful and complete commentary, avoiding no difficulties, tracing out distinctly the sequences of thought, and expressing in perspicuous language what St Paul meant, or, at least, what a learned and intelligent critic believed him to have meant."—*The Spectator.*

UNIVERSITY PRESS, CAMBRIDGE.
April, 1880.

PUBLICATIONS OF

The Cambridge University Press.

THE HOLY SCRIPTURES, &c.

The Cambridge Paragraph Bible of the Authorized English Version, with the Text revised by a Collation of its Early and other Principal Editions, the Use of the Italic Type made uniform, the Marginal References remodelled, and a Critical Introduction prefixed, by the Rev. F. H. SCRIVENER, M.A., LL.D., one of the Revisers of the Authorized Version. Crown Quarto, cloth gilt, 21*s.*

THE STUDENT'S EDITION of the above, on *good writing paper*, with one column of print and wide margin to each page for MS. notes. Two Vols. Crown Quarto, cloth, gilt, 31*s.* 6*d.*

The Lectionary Bible, with Apocrypha, divided into Sections adapted to the Calendar and Tables of Lessons of 1871. Crown Octavo, cloth, 3*s.* 6*d.*

Breviarium ad usum insignis Ecclesiae Sarum. Fasciculus II. In quo continentur PSALTERIUM, cum ordinario Officii totius hebdomadae juxta Horas Canonicas, et proprio Completorii, LITANIA, COMMUNE SANCTORUM, ORDINARIUM MISSAE CUM CANONE ET XIII MISSIS, &c. &c. juxta Editionem maximam pro CLAUDIO CHEVALLON et FRANCISCO REGNAULT A. D. MDXXXI. in Alma Parisiorum Academia impressam: labore ac studio FRANCISCI PROCTER, A.M., et CHRISTOPHORI WORDSWORTH, A.M. Demy 8vo., cloth, 12*s.*

The Pointed Prayer Book, being the Book of Common Prayer with the Psalter or Psalms of David, pointed as they are to be sung or said in Churches. Embossed cloth, Royal 24mo, 2*s.*
The same in square 32mo, cloth, 6*d.*

The Cambridge Psalter, for the use of Choirs and Organists. Specially adapted for Congregations in which the "Cambridge Pointed Prayer Book" is used. Demy 8vo. cloth, 3*s.* 6*d.* Cloth limp cut flush, 2*s.* 6*d.*

The Paragraph Psalter, arranged for the use of Choirs by BROOKE FOSS WESTCOTT, D.D., Canon of Peterborough, and Regius Professor of Divinity, Cambridge. Fcp. 4to. 5*s.*

Greek and English Testament, in parallel columns on the same page. Edited by J. SCHOLEFIELD, M.A. late Regius Professor of Greek in the University. *New Edition, with the marginal references as arranged and revised by* DR SCRIVENER. Cloth, red edges. 7*s.* 6*d.*

London: Cambridge Warehouse, 17 *Paternoster Row.*

3000
12/4/80

PUBLICATIONS OF

Greek and English Testament. THE STUDENT'S EDITION
of the above on *large writing paper*. 4to. cloth.   12*s*.

Greek Testament, ex editione Stephani tertia, 1550. Small
Octavo.   3*s*. 6*d*.

The Gospel according to St Matthew in Anglo-Saxon and
Northumbrian Versions, synoptically arranged: with Collations of
the best Manuscripts.   By J. M. KEMBLE, M.A. and Archdeacon
HARDWICK.   Demy Quarto.   10*s*.

The Gospel according to St Mark in Anglo-Saxon and
Northumbrian Versions, synoptically arranged, with Collations
exhibiting all the Readings of all the MSS.   Edited by the Rev.
Professor SKEAT, M.A.   Demy Quarto.   10*s*.

The Gospel according to St Luke, uniform with the preceding, edited by the Rev. Professor SKEAT.   Demy Quarto.   10*s*.

The Gospel according to St John, uniform with the preceding, edited by the Rev. Professor SKEAT.   Demy Quarto.   10*s*.

The Missing Fragment of the Latin Translation of the
Fourth Book of Ezra, discovered, and edited with an Introduction
and Notes, and a facsimile of the MS., by R. L. BENSLY, M.A.,
Fellow of Gonville and Caius College.   Cloth, 10*s*.

THEOLOGY—(ANCIENT).

Sayings of the Jewish Fathers, comprising Pirqe Aboth
and Pereq R. Meir in Hebrew and English, with Critical and
Illustrative Notes; and specimen pages of the Cambridge University
Manuscript of the Mishnah 'Jerushalmith'.   By C. TAYLOR,
M.A., Fellow and Divinity Lecturer of St John's College.   Demy
Octavo.   10*s*.

Theodore of Mopsuestia's Commentary on the Minor Epistles
of S. Paul.   The Latin Version with the Greek Fragments,
edited from the MSS. with Notes and an Introduction, by H. B.
SWETE, B.D., Rector of Ashdon, Essex, and late Fellow of
Gonville and Caius College, Cambridge.   In two Volumes.
Vol. I., containing the Introduction, and the Commentary upon
'Galatians—Colossians.   Demy Octavo.   12*s*.

Sancti Irenæi Episcopi Lugdunensis libros quinque adversus
Hæreses, versione Latina cum Codicibus Claromontano ac Arundeliano denuo collata, præmissa de placitis Gnosticorum prolusione, fragmenta necnon Græce, Syriace, Armeniace, commentatione perpetua et indicibus variis edidit W. WIGAN HARVEY,
S.T.B. Collegii Regalis olim Socius.   2 Vols.   Demy Octavo.   18*s*.

THE CAMBRIDGE UNIVERSITY PRESS. 3

M. Minucii Felicis Octavius. The text newly revised from the original MS. with an English Commentary, Analysis, Introduction, and Copious Indices. Edited by H. A. HOLDEN, LL.D. Head Master of Ipswich School, late Fellow of Trinity College, Cambridge. Crown Octavo. 7s. 6d.

Theophili Episcopi Antiochensis Libri Tres ad Autolycum. Edidit, Prolegomenis Versione Notulis Indicibus instruxit GULIELMUS GILSON HUMPHRY, S.T.B. Post Octavo. 5s.

Theophylacti in Evangelium S. Matthæi Commentarius. Edited by W. G. HUMPHRY, B.D. Demy Octavo. 7s. 6d.

Tertullianus de Corona Militis, de Spectaculis, de Idololatria, with Analysis and English Notes, by GEORGE CURREY, D.D. Master of the Charter House. Crown Octavo. 5s.

THEOLOGY—(ENGLISH).

Works of Isaac Barrow, compared with the original MSS., enlarged with Materials hitherto unpublished. A new Edition, by A. NAPIER, M.A. of Trinity College, Vicar of Holkham, Norfolk. Nine Vols. Demy Octavo. £3. 3s.

Treatise of the Pope's Supremacy, and a Discourse concerning the Unity of the Church, by ISAAC BARROW. Demy Octavo. 7s. 6d.

Pearson's Exposition of the Creed, edited by TEMPLE CHEVALLIER, B.D., late Professor of Mathematics in the University of Durham, and Fellow and Tutor of St Catharine's College, Cambridge. Second Edition. Demy Octavo. 7s. 6d.

An Analysis of the Exposition of the Creed, written by the Right Rev. Father in God, JOHN PEARSON, D.D., late Lord Bishop of Chester. Compiled for the use of the Students of Bishop's College, Calcutta, by W. H. MILL, D.D. late Regius Professor of Hebrew in the University of Cambridge. Demy Octavo, cloth. 5s.

Wheatly on the Common Prayer, edited by G. E. CORRIE, D.D. Master of Jesus College, Examining Chaplain to the late Lord Bishop of Ely. Demy Octavo. 7s. 6d.

London: Cambridge Warehouse, 17 *Paternoster Row.*

The Homilies, with Various Readings, and the Quotations from the Fathers given at length in the Original Languages. Edited by G. E. CORRIE, D.D. Master of Jesus College. Demy Octavo. 7s. 6d.

Two Forms of Prayer of the time of Queen Elizabeth. Now First Reprinted. Demy Octavo. 6d.

Select Discourses, by JOHN SMITH, late Fellow of Queens' College, Cambridge. Edited by H. G. WILLIAMS, B.D. late Professor of Arabic. Royal Octavo. 7s. 6d.

Cæsar Morgan's Investigation of the Trinity of Plato, and of Philo Judæus, and of the effects which an attachment to their writings had upon the principles and reasonings of the Fathers of the Christian Church. Revised by H. A. HOLDEN, LL.D. Head Master of Ipswich School, late Fellow of Trinity College, Cambridge. Crown Octavo. 4s.

De Obligatione Conscientiæ Prælectiones decem Oxonii in Schola Theologica habitæ a ROBERTO SANDERSON, SS. Theologiæ ibidem Professore Regio. With English Notes, including an abridged Translation, by W. WHEWELL, D.D. late Master of Trinity College. Demy Octavo. 7s. 6d.

Archbishop Usher's Answer to a Jesuit, with other Tracts on Popery. Edited by J. SCHOLEFIELD, M.A. late Regius Professor of Greek in the University. Demy Octavo. 7s. 6d.

Wilson's Illustration of the Method of explaining the New Testament, by the early opinions of Jews and Christians concerning Christ. Edited by T. TURTON, D.D. late Lord Bishop of Ely. Demy Octavo. 5s.

Lectures on Divinity delivered in the University of Cambridge. By JOHN HEY, D.D. Third Edition, by T. TURTON, D.D. late Lord Bishop of Ely. 2 vols. Demy Octavo. 15s.

GREEK AND LATIN CLASSICS, &c.

(*See also* pp. 12, 13.)

The Agamemnon of Aeschylus. With a translation in English Rhythm, and Notes Critical and Explanatory. By BENJAMIN HALL KENNEDY, D.D., Regius Professor of Greek. Crown 8vo. 6s.

The Theætetus of Plato by the same Editor. [*In the Press.*

London: Cambridge Warehouse, 17 Paternoster Row.

P. Vergili Maronis Opera, cum Prolegomenis et Commentario Critico pro Syndicis Preli Academici edidit BENJAMIN HALL KENNEDY, S.T.P., Graecae Linguae Professor Regius. Cloth, extra fcp. 8vo, red edges, price 5s.

Select Private Orations of Demosthenes with Introductions and English Notes, by F. A. PALEY, M.A., Editor of Aeschylus, etc. and J. E. SANDYS, M.A., Fellow and Tutor of St John's College, and Public Orator in the University of Cambridge.
Part I. containing Contra Phormionem, Lacritum, Pantaenetum, Boeotum de Nomine, Boeotum de Dote, Dionysodorum. Crown Octavo, cloth. 6s.
Part II. containing Pro Phormione, Contra Stephanum I. II.; Nicostratum, Cononem, Calliclem. Crown Octavo, cloth. 7s. 6d.

The Bacchae of Euripides, with Introduction, Critical Notes, and Archæological Illustrations, by J. E. SANDYS, M.A., Fellow and Tutor of St John's College, and Public Orator. [*Nearly ready*.

M. T. Ciceronis de Natura Deorum Libri Tres, with Introduction and Commentary by JOSEPH B. MAYOR, M.A., Professor of Classical Literature at King's College, London, together with a new collation of several of the English MSS. by J. H. SWAINSON, M.A., formerly Fellow of Trinity College, Cambridge. [*Nearly ready.*

M. T. Ciceronis de Officiis Libri Tres with Marginal Analysis, an English Commentary, and Indices. Third Edition, revised, with numerous additions, by H. A. HOLDEN, LL.D., Head Master of Ipswich School. Crown Octavo, cloth. 9s.

M. T. Ciceronis pro Cn. Plancio oratio by the same Editor.
[*In the Press.*

Plato's Phædo, literally translated, by the late E. M. COPE, Fellow of Trinity College, Cambridge. Demy Octavo. 5s.

Aristotle. The Rhetoric. With a Commentary by the late E. M. COPE, Fellow of Trinity College, Cambridge, revised and edited by J. E. SANDYS, M.A., Fellow and Tutor of St John's College, and Public Orator. 3 Vols. Demy 8vo. £1 11s. 6d.

ΠΕΡΙ ΔΙΚΑΙΟΣΥΝΗΣ. The Fifth Book of the Nicomachean Ethics of Aristotle. Edited by HENRY JACKSON, M.A., Fellow of Trinity College, Cambridge. Demy 8vo, cloth. 6s.

Pindar. Olympian and Pythian Odes. With Notes Explanatory and Critical, Introductions and Introductory Essays. Edited by C. A. M. FENNELL, M.A., late Fellow of Jesus College. Crown 8vo. cloth. 9s.

The Isthmian and Nemean Odes by the same Editor.
[*Preparing.*

London: Cambridge Warehouse, 17 Paternoster Row.

SANSKRIT AND ARABIC.

Nalopakhyanam, or, The Tale of Nala; containing the Sanskrit Text in Roman Characters, followed by a Vocabulary and a sketch of Sanskrit Grammar. By the Rev. THOMAS JARRETT, M.A., Regius Professor of Hebrew. Demy Octavo. 10s.

The Poems of Beha ed din Zoheir of Egypt. With a Metrical Translation, Notes and Introduction, by E. H. PALMER, M.A., Lord Almoner's Professor of Arabic in the University of Cambridge. 3 vols. Crown Quarto. Vol. II. The ENGLISH TRANSLATION. Paper cover, 10s. 6d. Cloth extra, 15s. [Vol. I. The ARABIC TEXT is already published.]

MATHEMATICS, PHYSICAL SCIENCE, &c.

A Treatise on Natural Philosophy. Volume I. Part I. By Sir W. THOMSON, LL.D., D.C.L., F.R.S., Professor of Natural Philosophy in the University of Glasgow, and P. G. TAIT, M.A., Professor of Natural Philosophy in the University of Edinburgh. Demy 8vo. cloth, 16s.

Elements of Natural Philosophy. By Professors Sir W. THOMSON and P. G. TAIT. Part I. *Second Edition.* 8vo. cloth, 9s.

An Elementary Treatise on Quaternions. By P. G. TAIT, M.A., Professor of Natural Philosophy in the University of Edinburgh. *Second Edition.* Demy 8vo. 14s.

A Treatise on the Theory of Determinants and their Applications in Analysis and Geometry. By ROBERT FORSYTH SCOTT, M.A., of Lincoln's Inn; Fellow of St John's College, Cambridge. Demy 8vo. 12s.

Counterpoint. A practical course of study. By Professor G. A. MACFARREN, Mus. Doc. Second Edition, revised. Demy 4to. cloth. 7s. 6d.

The Analytical Theory of Heat. By JOSEPH FOURIER. Translated, with Notes, by A. FREEMAN, M.A., Fellow of St John's College, Cambridge. Demy 8vo. 16s.

Mathematical and Physical Papers. By GEORGE GABRIEL STOKES, M.A., D.C.L., LL.D., F.R.S., Fellow of Pembroke College and Lucasian Professor of Mathematics. Reprinted from the Original Journals and Transactions, with additional Notes by the Author. Vol. I. [*Nearly ready.*

London: Cambridge Warehouse, 17 Paternoster Row.

THE CAMBRIDGE UNIVERSITY PRESS. 7

The Electrical Researches of the Honourable Henry Cavendish, F.R.S. Written between 1771 and 1781, Edited from the original manuscripts in the possession of the Duke of Devonshire, K.G., by J. CLERK MAXWELL, F.R.S. Demy 8vo. cloth, 18s.

Hydrodynamics, a Treatise on the Mathematical Theory of Fluid Motion, by HORACE LAMB, M.A., formerly Fellow of Trinity College, Cambridge; Professor of Mathematics in the University of Adelaide. Demy 8vo. cloth, 12s.

The Mathematical Works of Isaac Barrow, D.D. Edited by W. WHEWELL, D.D. Demy Octavo. 7s. 6d.

Illustrations of Comparative Anatomy, Vertebrate and Invertebrate, for the Use of Students in the Museum of Zoology and Comparative Anatomy. Second Edition. Demy 8vo. cloth, 2s. 6d.

A Catalogue of Australian Fossils (including Tasmania and the Island of Timor), by R. ETHERIDGE, Jun., F.G.S., Acting Palæontologist, H.M. Geol. Survey of Scotland. Demy 8vo. 10s. 6d.

A Synopsis of the Classification of the British Palæozoic Rocks, by the Rev. ADAM SEDGWICK, M.A., F.R.S., with a systematic description of the British Palæozoic Fossils in the Geological Museum of the University of Cambridge, by FREDERICK M^CCOY, F.G.S. One vol., Royal Quarto, cloth, Plates, £1. 1s.

A Catalogue of the Collection of Cambrian and Silurian Fossils contained in the Geological Museum of the University of Cambridge, by J. W. SALTER, F.G.S. With a Preface by the Rev. ADAM SEDGWICK, F.R.S. With a Portrait of PROFESSOR SEDGWICK. Royal Quarto, cloth, 7s. 6d.

Catalogue of Osteological Specimens contained in the Anatomical Museum of the University of Cambridge. Demy 8vo. 2s. 6d.

Astronomical Observations made at the Observatory of Cambridge by the Rev. JAMES CHALLIS, M.A., F.R.S., F.R.A.S., Plumian Professor of Astronomy from 1846 to 1860.

Astronomical Observations from 1861 to 1865. Vol. XXI. Royal Quarto, cloth, 15s.

LAW.

A Selection of the State Trials. By J. W. WILLIS-BUND, M.A., LL.B., Barrister-at-Law, Professor of Constitutional Law and History, University College, London. Vol. I. Trials for Treason (1327—1660). Crown 8vo., cloth. 18s. Vol. II. [*In the Press.*

London: Cambridge Warehouse, 17 *Paternoster Row.*

The Fragments of the Perpetual Edict of Salvius Julianus, Collected, Arranged, and Annotated by BRYAN WALKER, MA., LL.D., Law Lecturer of St John's College, and late Fellow of Corpus Christi College, Cambridge. Crown 8vo., cloth. *Price 6s.*

The Commentaries of Gaius and Rules of Ulpian. (*New Edition.*) Translated and Annotated, by J. T. ABDY, LL.D., late Regius Professor of Laws, and BRYAN WALKER, M.A., LL.D., Law Lecturer of St John's College. Crown Octavo, 16s.

The Institutes of Justinian, translated with Notes by J. T. ABDY, LL.D., and BRYAN WALKER, M.A., LLD., St John's College, Cambridge. Crown Octavo, 16s.

Selected Titles from the Digest, annotated by BRYAN WALKER, M.A., LL.D. Part I. Mandati vel Contra. Digest xvii. 1. Crown Octavo, 5s.

Part II. De Adquirendo rerum dominio, and De Adquirenda vel amittenda Possessione, Digest XLI. 1 and 2. Crown 8vo. 6s.

Grotius de Jure Belli et Pacis, with the Notes of Barbeyrac and others; accompanied by an abridged Translation of the Text, by W. WHEWELL, D.D. late Master of Trinity College. 3 Vols. Demy Octavo, 12s. The translation separate, 6s.

HISTORICAL WORKS.

Life and Times of Stein, or Germany and Prussia in the Napoleonic Age, by J. R. SEELEY, M.A., Regius Professor of Modern History in the University of Cambridge. With Portraits and Maps. 3 vols. Demy 8vo. 48s.

Scholae Academicae: some Account of the Studies at the English Universities in the Eighteenth Century. By CHRISTOPHER WORDSWORTH, M.A., Fellow of Peterhouse; Author of "Social Life at the English Universities in the Eighteenth Century." Demy Octavo, cloth, 15s.

History of Nepāl, translated from the Original by MUNSHI SHEW SHUNKER SINGH and Pandit SHRĪ GUNĀNAND; edited with an Introductory Sketch of the Country and People by Dr D. WRIGHT, late Residency Surgeon at Kāthmāndū, and with numerous Illustrations and portraits of Sir JUNG BAHĀDUR, the King of Nepāl, and other natives. Super-Royal Octavo, 21s.

The University of Cambridge from the Earliest Times to the Royal Injunctions of 1535. By JAMES BASS MULLINGER, M.A. Demy 8vo. cloth (734 pp.), 12s.

London: Cambridge Warehouse, 17 *Paternoster Row.*

THE CAMBRIDGE UNIVERSITY PRESS.

History of the College of St John the Evangelist, by THOMAS BAKER, B.D., Ejected Fellow. Edited by JOHN E. B. MAYOR, M.A., Fellow of St John's. Two Vols. Demy 8vo. 24s.

The Architectural History of the University and Colleges of Cambridge, by the late Professor WILLIS, M.A. With numerous Maps, Plans, and Illustrations. Continued to the present time, and edited by JOHN WILLIS CLARK, M.A., formerly Fellow of Trinity College, Cambridge. [*In the Press.*

CATALOGUES.

Catalogue of the Hebrew Manuscripts preserved in the University Library, Cambridge. By Dr S. M. SCHILLER-SZINESSY. Volume I. containing Section I. *The Holy Scriptures;* Section II. *Commentaries on the Bible.* Demy 8vo. 9s.

A Catalogue of the Manuscripts preserved in the Library of the University of Cambridge. Demy 8vo. 5 Vols. 10s. each.

Index to the Catalogue. Demy 8vo. 10s.

A Catalogue of Adversaria and printed books containing MS. notes, preserved in the Library of the University of Cambridge. 3s. 6d.

The Illuminated Manuscripts in the Library of the Fitzwilliam Museum, Cambridge, Catalogued with Descriptions, and an Introduction, by WILLIAM GEORGE SEARLE, M.A., late Fellow of Queens' College, and Vicar of Hockington, Cambridgeshire. 7s. 6d.

A Chronological List of the Graces, Documents, and other Papers in the University Registry which concern the University Library. Demy 8vo. 2s. 6d.

Catalogus Bibliothecæ Burckhardtianæ. Demy Quarto. 5s.

MISCELLANEOUS.

Statuta Academiæ Cantabrigiensis. Demy 8vo. 2s.

Ordinationes Academiæ Cantabrigiensis. New Edition. Demy 8vo., cloth. 3s. 6d.

Trusts, Statutes and Directions affecting (1) The Professorships of the University. (2) The Scholarships and Prizes. (3) Other Gifts and Endowments. Demy 8vo. 5s.

A Compendium of University Regulations, for the use of persons in Statu Pupillari. Demy 8vo. 6d.

London: Cambridge Warehouse, 17 Paternoster Row.

The Cambridge Bible for Schools.

GENERAL EDITOR: J. J. S. PEROWNE, D.D., DEAN OF PETERBOROUGH.

THE want of an Annotated Edition of the BIBLE, in handy portions, suitable for school use, has long been felt.

In order to provide Text-books for School and Examination purposes, the CAMBRIDGE UNIVERSITY PRESS has arranged to publish the several books of the BIBLE in separate portions, at a moderate price, with introductions and explanatory notes.

Some of the books have already been undertaken by the following gentlemen:

Rev. A. CARR, M.A., *late Fellow of Oriel College, Oxford.*
Rev. T. K. CHEYNE, M.A., *Fellow of Balliol College, Oxford.*
Rev. S. COX, *Nottingham.*
Rev. A. B. DAVIDSON, D.D., *Prof. of Hebrew, Free Church Coll. Edinb.*
Rev. F. W. FARRAR, D.D., *Canon of Westminster.*
Rev. A. E. HUMPHREYS, M.A., *Fellow of Trinity College, Cambridge.*
Rev. A. F. KIRKPATRICK, M.A., *Fellow and Lecturer of Trinity College.*
Rev. J. J. LIAS, M.A., *Professor at St David's College, Lampeter.*
Rev. J. R. LUMBY, D.D., *Norrisian Professor of Divinity.*
Rev. G. F. MACLEAR, D.D., *Head Master of King's Coll. School, London.*
Rev. H. C. G. MOULE, M.A., *Fellow of Trinity College, Cambridge.*
Rev. W. F. MOULTON, D.D., *Head Master of the Leys School, Cambridge.*
Rev. E. H. PEROWNE, D.D., *Master of Corpus Christi College, Cambridge, Examining Chaplain to the Bishop of St Asaph.*
The Ven. T. T. PEROWNE, B.D., *Archdeacon of Norwich.*
Rev. A. PLUMMER, M.A., *Master of University College, Durham.*
Rev. E. H. PLUMPTRE, D.D., *Professor of Biblical Exegesis, King's College, London.*
Rev. W. SANDAY, D.D., *Principal of Bishop Hatfield Hall, Durham.*
Rev. W. SIMCOX, M.A., *Rector of Weyhill, Hants.*
Rev. ROBERTSON SMITH, M.A., *Professor of Hebrew, Aberdeen.*
Rev. A. W. STREANE, M.A., *Fellow of Corpus Christi College.*
Rev. H. W. WATKINS, M.A., *Warden of St Augustine's Coll. Canterbury.*
Rev. G. H. WHITAKER, M.A., *Fellow of St John's College, Cambridge; Honorary Chancellor of Truro Cathedral.*
Rev. C. WORDSWORTH, M.A., *Rector of Glaston, Rutland.*

London: Cambridge Warehouse, 17 *Paternoster Row.*

Now Ready.

THE BOOK OF JOSHUA. By the Rev. G. F. MACLEAR, D.D. With Two Maps. Cloth. 2s. 6d.

THE BOOK OF JONAH. By Archdeacon PEROWNE. With Two Maps. Cloth. 1s. 6d.

THE GOSPEL ACCORDING TO ST MATTHEW. By the Rev. A. CARR, M.A. With Two Maps. Cloth. 2s. 6d.

THE GOSPEL ACCORDING TO ST MARK. By the Rev. G. F. MACLEAR, D.D. With Two Maps. Cloth. 2s. 6d.

THE GOSPEL ACCORDING TO ST LUKE. By the Rev. F. W. FARRAR, D.D. With Four Maps. Cloth. 4s. 6d.

THE ACTS OF THE APOSTLES. Part I., Chaps. I.—XIV. By the Rev. Professor LUMBY, D.D. Cloth. 2s. 6d.

THE EPISTLE TO THE ROMANS. By the Rev. H. C. G. MOULE, M.A. Cloth. 3s. 6d.

THE FIRST EPISTLE TO THE CORINTHIANS. By the Rev. Prof. LIAS, M.A. With a Plan and Map. Cloth. 2s.

THE SECOND EPISTLE TO THE CORINTHIANS. By the Rev. Prof. LIAS, M.A. With a Plan and Map. Cloth. 2s.

THE GENERAL EPISTLE OF ST JAMES. By the Rev. E. H. PLUMPTRE, D.D. Cloth. 1s. 6d.

THE EPISTLES OF ST PETER AND ST JUDE. By the Rev. E. H. PLUMPTRE, D.D. Cloth. 2s. 6d.

Preparing.

THE GOSPEL ACCORDING TO ST JOHN. By the Rev. W. SANDAY, D.D., and the Rev. A. PLUMMER, M.A.

THE BOOK OF JEREMIAH. By the Rev. A. W. STREANE, M.A. [*Nearly ready.*

THE FIRST BOOK OF SAMUEL. By the Rev. A. F. KIRKPATRICK, M.A.

THE BOOKS OF HAGGAI AND ZECHARIAH. By Archdeacon PEROWNE.

In Preparation.

THE CAMBRIDGE GREEK TESTAMENT
FOR SCHOOLS AND COLLEGES,

with a Revised Text, based on the most recent critical authorities, and English Notes, prepared under the direction of the General Editor,

THE VERY REVEREND J. J. S. PEROWNE, D.D.,
DEAN OF PETERBOROUGH.

The books will be published separately, as in the Cambridge Bible for Schools.

London: Cambridge Warehouse, 17 Paternoster Row.

THE PITT PRESS SERIES.

ADAPTED TO THE USE OF STUDENTS PREPARING
FOR THE
UNIVERSITY LOCAL EXAMINATIONS,
AND THE HIGHER CLASSES OF SCHOOLS.

I. GREEK.

Luciani Somnium Charon Piscator et De Luctu. (*New Edition with Appendix.*) With English Notes, by W. E. HEITLAND, M.A., Fellow of St John's College, Cambridge. *Price 3s. 6d.*

The Anabasis of Xenophon, Book VI. With a Map and English Notes by ALFRED PRETOR, M.A., Fellow of St Catharine's College, Editor of Sophocles (Trachiniæ) and Persius. *Price 2s. 6d.*

―――― **Books I. III. IV. and V.** By the same Editor. *Price 2s. each.* **Book II.** *Price 2s. 6d.*

Agesilaus of Xenophon. The Text revised with Critical and Explanatory Notes, Introduction, Analysis, and Indices. By H. HAILSTONE, M.A., late Scholar of Peterhouse, Cambridge, Editor of Xenophon's Hellenics, etc. *Price 2s. 6d.*

Aristophanes—Ranae. With English Notes and Introduction by W. C. GREEN, M.A., Assistant Master at Rugby School. Cloth. *3s. 6d.*

Aristophanes—Aves. By the same Editor. *New Edition.* Cloth. *3s. 6d.*

Euripides. Hercules Furens. With Introduction, Notes and Analysis. By J. T. HUTCHINSON, B.A., Christ's College, and A. GRAY, B.A., Fellow of Jesus College, Cambridge. *Price 2s.*

II. LATIN.

M. T. Ciceronis de Amicitia. Edited by J. S. REID, M.L., Fellow of Gonville and Caius College, Cambridge. *Price 3s.*

M. T. Ciceronis de Senectute. Edited by J. S. REID, M.L., *Price 3s. 6d.*

P. Vergili Maronis Aeneidos Liber VII. Edited with Notes by A. SIDGWICK, M.A., Tutor of Corpus Christi College, Oxford. *Price 1s. 6d.*

―――― **Books VI. VIII. X. XI. XII.** By the same Editor. *Price 1s. 6d. each.*

―――― **Books VII. VIII.** bound in one volume. *Price 3s.*

―――― **Books X. XI. XII.** bound in one volume. *Price 3s. 6d.*

London: Cambridge Warehouse, 17 Paternoster Row.

PITT PRESS SERIES (*continued*).

Quintus Curtius. A Portion of the History (Alexander in India). By W. E. HEITLAND, M.A., Fellow and Lecturer of St John's College, Cambridge, and T. E. RAVEN, B.A., Assistant Master in Sherborne School. With Two Maps. *Price* 3*s.* 6*d.*

Gai Iuli Caesaris de Bello Gallico Comment. I. II. With Maps and Notes by A. G. PESKETT, M.A. Fellow of Magdalene College, Cambridge. *Price* 2*s.* 6*d.*

Gai Iuli Caesaris de Bello Gallico Comment. IV., V., and Com. VII. By the same Editor. *Price* 2*s.* each.

P. Ovidii Nasonis Fastorum Liber VI. With Notes by A. SIDGWICK, M.A. Tutor of Corpus Christi College, Oxford. *Price* 1*s.* 6*d.*

M. T. Ciceronis Oratio pro Archia Poeta. By J. S. REID, M.L., Fellow of Gonville and Caius College, Cambridge. *Price* 1*s.* 6*d.*

M. T. Ciceronis pro L. Cornelio Balbo Oratio. By J. S. REID, M.L., Fellow of Gonville and Caius College. *Price* 1*s.* 6*d.*

Beda's Ecclesiastical History, Books III., IV., printed from the MS. in the Cambridge University Library. Edited, with a life, Notes, Glossary, Onomasticon, and Index, by J. E. B. MAYOR, M.A., Professor of Latin, and J. R. LUMBY, D.D., Norrisian Professor of Divinity. *Price* 7*s.* 6*d.*

M. T. Ciceronis in Q. Caecilium Divinatio et in C. Verrem Actio. With Notes by W. E. HEITLAND, M.A., and H. COWIE, M.A., Fellows of St John's Coll., Cambridge. *Price* 3*s.*

M. T. Ciceronis in Gaium Verrem Actio Prima. With Notes by H. COWIE, M.A., Fellow of St John's Coll. *Price* 1*s.* 6*d.*

M. T. Ciceronis Oratio pro L. Murena, with English Introduction and Notes. By W. E. HEITLAND, M.A., Fellow of St John's College, Cambridge. Second Edition. *Price* 3*s.*

M. T. Ciceronis Oratio pro Tito Annio Milone, with English Notes, &c., by the Rev. JOHN SMYTH PURTON, B.D., late Tutor of St Catharine's College. *Price* 2*s.* 6*d.*

M. Annaei Lucani Pharsaliae Liber Primus, with English Introduction and Notes by W. E. HEITLAND, M.A., and C. E. HASKINS, M.A., Fellows of St John's Coll., Cambridge. 1*s.* 6*d.*

London: Cambridge Warehouse, 17 Paternoster Row.

PITT PRESS SERIES (*continued*).
III. FRENCH.

Histoire du Siècle de Louis XIV. par Voltaire. Chaps. I.—XIII. Edited with Notes Philological and Historical, Biographical and Geographical Indices, etc. by GUSTAVE MASSON, B.A. Univ. Gallic., Assistant Master of Harrow School, and G. W. PROTHERO, M.A., Fellow and Lecturer of King's College, Cambridge, Examiner for the Historical Tripos. *Price* 2s. 6d.

——— **Part II. Chaps. XIV.—XXIV.** By the same Editors. With Three Maps. *Price* 2s. 6d.

Le Verre D'Eau. A Comedy, by SCRIBE. With a Biographical Memoir, and Grammatical, Literary and Historical Notes, by C. COLBECK, M.A., late Fellow of Trinity College, Cambridge; Assistant Master at Harrow School. *Price* 2s.

M. Daru, par M. C. A. SAINTE-BEUVE (Causeries du Lundi, Vol. IX.). With Biographical Sketch of the Author, and Notes Philological and Historical. By GUSTAVE MASSON, B.A. Univ. Gallic., Assistant Master and Librarian, Harrow School. *Price* 2s.

La Suite du Menteur. A Comedy by P. CORNEILLE. With Notes Philological and Historical by the same. *Price* 2s.

La Jeune Sibérienne. Le Lépreux de la Cité D'Aoste. Tales by COUNT XAVIER DE MAISTRE. With Biographical Notices, Critical Appreciations, and Notes, by the same. *Price* 2s.

Le Directoire. (Considérations sur la Révolution Française. Troisième et quatrième parties.) Par MADAME LA BARONNE DE STAËL-HOLSTEIN. With Notes by the same. *Price* 2s.

Fredégonde et Brunehaut. A Tragedy in Five Acts, by N. LEMERCIER. With Notes by the same. *Price* 2s.

Dix Années d'Exil. Livre II. Chapitres 1—8. Par MADAME LA BARONNE DE STAËL-HOLSTEIN. With Notes Historical and Philological. By the same. *Price* 2s.

Le Vieux Célibataire. A Comedy, by COLLIN D'HARLEVILLE. With Notes, by the same. *Price* 2s.

La Métromanie, A Comedy, by PIRON, with Notes, by the same. *Price* 2s.

Lascaris, ou Les Grecs du XVE Siècle, Nouvelle Historique, par A. F. VILLEMAIN, with a Selection of Poems on Greece, and Notes, by the same. *Price* 2s.

London: Cambridge Warehouse, 17 *Paternoster Row.*

PITT PRESS SERIES (*continued*).

IV. GERMAN.

Hauff, Das Wirthshaus im Spessart. By A. SCHLOTTMANN, Ph.D., Assistant Master at Uppingham School. *Price* 3s. 6d.

Der Oberhof. A Tale of Westphalian Life, by KARL IMMERMANN. With a Life of Immermann and English Notes, by WILHELM WAGNER, Ph.D., Professor at the Johanneum, Hamburg. *Price* 3s.

A Book of German Dactylic Poetry. Arranged and Annotated by WILHELM WAGNER, Ph.D., Professor at the Johanneum, Hamburg. *Price* 3s.

Der erste Kreuzzug (1095—1099) nach FRIEDRICH VON RAUMER. THE FIRST CRUSADE. Arranged and Annotated by WILHELM WAGNER, Ph.D., Professor at the Johanneum, Hamburg. *Price* 2s.

A Book of Ballads on German History. Arranged and Annotated by WILHELM WAGNER, PH.D., Professor at the Johanneum, Hamburg. *Price* 2s.

Der Staat Friedrichs des Grossen. By G. FREYTAG. With Notes. By WILHELM WAGNER, PH.D. Professor at the Johanneum, Hamburg. *Price* 2s.

Goethe's Knabenjahre. (1749—1759.) Goethe's Boyhood: being the First Three Books of his Autobiography. Arranged and Annotated by the same Editor. *Price* 2s.

Goethe's Hermann and Dorothea. With an Introduction and Notes. By the same Editor. *Price* 3s.

Das Jahr 1813 (THE YEAR 1813), by F. KOHLRAUSCH. With English Notes by the same Editor. *Price* 2s.

V. ENGLISH.

The Two Noble Kinsmen, edited with Introduction and Notes by the Rev. Professor SKEAT, M.A., formerly Fellow of Christ's College, Cambridge. Cloth, extra fcap. 8vo. *Price* 3s. 6d.

Bacon's History of the Reign of King Henry VII. With Notes by the Rev. Professor LUMBY, D.D., Fellow of St Catharine's College, Cambridge. Cloth, extra fcap. 8vo. *Price* 3s.

Sir Thomas More's Utopia. With Notes by the Rev. Professor LUMBY, D.D. *Price* 3s. 6d.

Locke on Education. With Introduction and Notes by the Rev. R. H. QUICK, M.A. *Price* 3s. 6d.

Other Volumes are in preparation.

London: Cambridge Warehouse, 17 Paternoster Row.

UNIVERSITY OF CAMBRIDGE LOCAL EXAMINATIONS.

EXAMINATION PAPERS,
for various years, with the *Regulations for the Examination*.
Demy Octavo. 2s. each, or by Post 2s. 2d.
(*The Regulations for the Examination in 1880 are now ready*.)

CLASS LISTS FOR VARIOUS YEARS.
6d. each, by Post 7d. For 1878, Boys 1s. Girls 6d.

ANNUAL REPORTS OF THE SYNDICATE,
With Supplementary Tables showing the success and failure of the Candidates.
2s. each, by Post 2s. 2d.

HIGHER LOCAL EXAMINATIONS.
EXAMINATION PAPERS FOR 1879,
to which are added the Regulations for 1880.
Demy Octavo. 2s. each, by Post 2s. 2d.

REPORTS OF THE SYNDICATE.
Demy Octavo. 1s., by Post 1s. 1d.

CAMBRIDGE UNIVERSITY REPORTER.
Published by Authority.
Containing all the Official Notices of the University, Reports of Discussions in the Schools, and Proceedings of the Cambridge Philosophical, Antiquarian, and Philological Societies. 3d. weekly.

CAMBRIDGE UNIVERSITY EXAMINATION PAPERS.
These Papers are published in occasional numbers every Term, and in volumes for the Academical year.

VOL. V. Parts 41 to 55. PAPERS for the Year 1875—6, 12s. *cloth.*
VOL. VI. ,, 56 to 69. ,, ,, 1876—7, 12s. *cloth.*
VOL. VII. ,, 70 to 86. ,, ,, 1877—8, 12s. *cloth.*
VOL. VIII. ,, 87 to 104. ,, ,, 1878—9, 12s. *cloth.*

London:
CAMBRIDGE WAREHOUSE, 17 PATERNOSTER ROW.
Cambridge: DEIGHTON, BELL AND CO.
Leipzig: F. A. BROCKHAUS.

CAMBRIDGE: PRINTED BY C. J. CLAY, M.A. AT THE UNIVERSITY PRESS.

www.ingramcontent.com/pod-product-compliance
Lightning Source LLC
Chambersburg PA
CBHW021401230426
43666CB00006B/606